Shall We Play the Festschrift Game?

Diana Santos · Krister Lindén · Wanjiku Ng'ang'a
Editors

Shall We Play the Festschrift Game?

Essays on the Occasion of Lauri Carlson's 60th Birthday

Springer

Editors
Diana Santos
Department of Literature, Area Studies
and European Languages
University of Oslo
Oslo, Norway

Wanjiku Ng'ang'a
School of Computing & Informatics
University of Nairobi
Nairobi, Kenya

Krister Lindén
Department of Modern Languages
University of Helsinki
Helsinki, Finland

ISBN 978-3-642-30772-0 ISBN 978-3-642-30773-7 (eBook)
DOI 10.1007/978-3-642-30773-7
Springer Heidelberg New York Dordrecht London

Library of Congress Control Number: 2012946035

Printed on acid-free paper

Springer is part of Springer Science+Business Media (www.springer.com)

Playing the Festschrift Game

1 Presentation

There are not many people who can be said to have influenced and impressed researchers in so many disparate areas and language-geographic fields as Lauri Carlson, as is evidenced in the present Festschrift.

Lauri's insight and acute linguistic sensitivity and linguistic rationality have spawned findings and research work in many areas, from non-standard etymology to hard-core formal linguistics, not forgetting computational areas such as parsing, terminological databases, and, last but not least, machine translation.

In addition to his renowned and widely acknowledged insights on tense and aspect, and their relationship with nominal quantification, and his ground-breaking work in dialogue using game-theoretic machinery, Lauri has in the last fifteen years as Professor of Language Theory and Translation Technology contributed immensely to areas such as translation, terminology and general applications of computational linguistics.

The three editors of the present volume have successfully performed doctoral studies under Lauri's supervision, and wish with this volume to pay tribute to his supervision and to his influence in matters associated with research, and scientific, linguistic and philosophical inquiry, as well as to his humanity and friendship as a definitely non-bossy supervisor.

Diana still recalls with gratitude the short periods either in Helsinki or in Lisbon, where discussions on tense and aspect matters took place:

> The pertinence of Lauri's questions, questioning what at the time seemed unquestionable matters to me. The need to try to explain seemingly evident things in my understanding of my own native language was a sobering and extremely useful exercise. His genuine interest in language in general, and languages in particular, was also contagious, and the turning point in my PhD study and possibly my whole research career—came about by Lauri buying a cheap edition of Steinbeck's *The Pearl* and its translation into Portuguese, and challenging me to prove that my translation rules were backed by real-world evidence. Naturally, as soon as we started looking at the texts themselves, a whole new world opened. Parallel corpora studies can now be said to constitute a well-established and productive field. Lauri does not even claim to have played a serious part in it. But he will clearly remain for me one of its founders, or rather one of its most important sources of inspiration.

After his graduation, Krister was involved in an English-to-Finnish Machine Translation project under the supervision of Lauri Carlson, who later also became the primary supervisor of his thesis:

> His vast knowledge of both applied and formal linguistics combined with his down-to-earth remarks paved my way to linguistics. Later, Lauri again proved his worth in gold when he, with a few keystrokes, fleshed out a definition of synonymy and how to implement it in practice for our joint project on creating a Finnish wordnet, which is now the second largest wordnet in the world after the famous Princeton WordNet.

Given her non-linguistic background at the start of her PhD study, Wanjiku is hugely appreciative of Lauri's mentorship and patience that saw her acquire the requisite linguistic knowledge, that enabled her to work with Swahili:

> Working with a then resource-scarce language required clever combination of resources and methods, and Lauri was very supportive of my lines of inquiry, a testament to his liberal thinking and open-mindedness, and I remember our meetings fondly. Our varied discussions on language, culture and religion helped me understand and appreciate the intricacies of language and the strengths and limitations of machine learning approaches to language processing. In addition, I benefited immensely from exposure to some of his networks—collaborative linkages which were crucial for my research, and others which persisted after my doctoral studies and which continue to shape my career to date.

2 Book Contents

Here, we provide a brief overview of the book's contents by describing, for each paper, the pertinent research questions and the points of contact with the other texts. This brief overview serves to harmonise the various contributions, and should in no way diminish the need to read each chapter individually.

The general nature of linguistic inquiry and how methods and empirical data should be tackled is the subject of Fred Karlsson's contribution, *Is There a Crisis in Generative Linguistics?*, an answer to a paper by Lauri on a similar subject. A quite original and interesting related subject is the way etymology is construed in different traditions, with David Nash's thought-provoking piece on language history in Australia, *"It's Etymology Captain, But Not As We Know It": 'Pump' in North Australia.*

Translation in History by Nicholas Ostler takes us on the challenging endeavor of making sense of translation diachronically and provides a new dimension to an ever-present activity in our times. Andrew Chesterman's chapter, *Catford Revisited*, provides a new view on Catford, an early theorist of translation who deserves to be rediscovered and reappraised, in his view. Diana Santos's contribution, *The Next Step for the Translation Network* delineates a computational program for studying human translations based on large corpora, as a direct follower to the proposal sketched in her dissertation.

An intriguing investigation on the concept of core vocabulary is provided by Lars Borin's *Core Vocabulary: A Useful But Mystical Concept in Some Kinds of Linguistics*, which provides thought-provoking material on some basic concepts in need of rethinking. On a practical note, Krister Lindén, Jyrki Niemi and Mirka Hyvärinen provide an interesting evaluation of the Finnish wordnet and its coverage of the Finnish core vocabulary in *Extending and Updating the Finnish Wordnet.* As mentioned, Lauri Carlson was instrumental when creating the initial version of the Finnish wordnet. An exciting related subject, in a different frame of mind, is Janet Pierrehumbert's work on *Burstiness of Verbs and Derived Nouns*, which merges formal semantics and statistical insights to Lauri's probably dearest subject of all, discourse.

Creating cutting-edge linguistic-computational resources, both for Finnish and for other languages, is the subject of *Outsourcing Parsebanking: The FinnTreeBank Project* by Atro Voutilainen, Tanja Purtonen and Kristiina Muhonen, where the authors suggest and demonstrate a novel way for developing large treebanks. In order to assist the treebanking effort, Anssi Yli-Jyrä's article *On Dependency Analysis via Contractions and Weighted FSTs* deals with an improved parsing technique for dependency parsers, presenting a system which is a radical improvement on his dissertation work, of which Lauri was one of the supervisors.

New analyses of linguistic phenomena round up this widely varied book: Patrick McConvell and Jane Simpson discuss some intriguing features of case marking in *Fictive Motion Down Under: The Locative-Allative Case Alternation in Some Australian Indigenous Languages*, describing several forms to mark the different location of events and of participants, and proposing a grammaticalisation path, while also comparing with parallel phenomena in Finnic. Aet Lees studies the expression of obligation and need in this last language family using Bible translations, in her chapter *Necessive Expressions in Finnic Bible Translations*, which handles the subject diachronically.

Wanjiku N'gang'a's *Building Swahili Resource Grammars for the Grammatical Framework*, in addition to the theoretical part of resource grammar writing, reports on an aid for visually-impaired mobile phone users that has been developed using the Grammatical Framework. Her work builds on the Grammatical Framework of Aarne Ranta, whose chapter *On the Syntax and Translation of Finnish Discourse Clitics* not only discusses Finnish discourse clitics but also describes a Finnish–English machine translation system that handles this interesting issue in Finnish grammar. In fact, it should be mentioned that this last chapter achieves the highest number of connections to Lauri's main interests: discourse, translation, formal analysis, and computation.

3 Contributions

In addition to the authors, a number of people have also contributed to this book in various capacities. Maria Vilkuna and Antti Arppe helped in reviewing the contributions. Jyrki Niemi undertook the job of converting all the non-LaTeX contributions to LaTeX and unifying the ones provided in LaTeX. Finally, we are grateful to Seija Carlson for her help and for keeping it all a secret!

We would also like to acknowledge Lauri's friends and colleagues who would have wanted to write a chapter but did not manage to do so—either because we were unable to contact them and they consequently were unaware of this noble initiative, or due to pressing time constraints.

We are also grateful to all the authors, who willingly participated in the cross-review process, providing valuable feedback which has undoubtedly resulted in the high quality and readability of this book. We as editors are therefore extremely grateful for this added value.

Acknowledgements Diana Santos acknowledges the support of the University of Oslo in preparing this volume, and Krister Lindén would like to thank the FIN-CLARIN infrastructure project at the University of Helsinki.

Oslo
Helsinki
Nairobi

Diana Santos
Krister Lindén
Wanjiku Ng'ang'a

Contents

Contributors

Lars Borin Språkbanken, Department of Swedish, University of Gothenburg, Gothenburg, Sweden

Andrew Chesterman Translation Studies, Department of Modern Languages, University of Helsinki, Helsinki, Finland

Mirka Hyvärinen Department of Modern Languages, University of Helsinki, Helsinki, Finland

Fred Karlsson General Linguistics, Department of Modern Languages, University of Helsinki, Helsinki, Finland

Aet Lees Department of Linguistics, University of Sydney, Sydney, Australia

Krister Lindén Department of Modern Languages, University of Helsinki, Helsinki, Finland

Patrick McConvell School of Language Studies, Australian National University, Canberra, Australia

Kristiina Muhonen Department of Modern Languages, University of Helsinki, Helsinki, Finland

David Nash School of Language Studies, The Australian National University, Canberra, Australia

Wanjiku Ng'ang'a School of Computing and Informatics, University of Nairobi, Nairobi, Kenya

Jyrki Niemi Department of Modern Languages, University of Helsinki, Helsinki, Finland

Nicholas Ostler Foundation for Endangered Languages, Bath, England, UK; School of Oriental and African Studies, London, England, UK

Janet B. Pierrehumbert Department of Linguistics, and Northwestern Institute on Complex Systems, Northwestern University, Evanston, IL, USA

Tanja Purtonen Department of Modern Languages, University of Helsinki, Helsinki, Finland

Aarne Ranta University of Gothenburg, Gothenburg, Sweden

Diana Santos University of Oslo, Oslo, Norway

Jane Simpson School of Language Studies, Australian National University, Canberra, Australia

Atro Voutilainen Department of Modern Languages, University of Helsinki, Helsinki, Finland

Anssi Yli-Jyrä Department of Modern Languages, University of Helsinki, Helsinki, Finland

Is There a Crisis in Generative Linguistics?

Fred Karlsson

Abstract Several recent critiques have claimed that the empirical foundations of generative linguistics are weak due to the reliance on informally gathered grammaticality judgments drawn from the intuitions of the researcher. Phillips (In: Japanese/Korean linguistics, vol. 17, 2009) argued i.a. that, in order for there to be a theoretical crisis, two criteria should be fulfilled, namely (i) intuitive judgments have led to generalizations that are widely accepted yet bogus, and (ii) misleading judgments form the basis of important theoretical claims or debates. Furthermore Phillips claimed that (i, ii) have not been fulfilled. I argue that (i, ii) have in fact been satisfied because Chomsky's (Q. Prog. Rep.—Mass. Inst. Technol., Res. Lab. Electron. 41:64–65, 1956; Syntactic structures. Mouton, The Hague, 1957) intuition-based claim that English is not a finite-state language is demonstrably false.

In his article "Should we impeach armchair linguists?", Phillips (2009) asked whether there is a crisis in generative linguistics. Several recent critiques had claimed that the empirical foundations of generative linguistics are weak due to the reliance on informally gathered grammaticality judgments drawn from the intuitions of the researcher. Here is Phillips' answer:

> The claim is not just that one finds questionable examples in linguistics papers, but that lax data-collection standards have led to the growth of theories that are based upon bogus data. If these charges stick, then we face a genuine crisis. In order for there to be a crisis, however, it would need to be the case that (i) Intuitive judgments have led to generalizations that are widely accepted yet bogus. (ii) Misleading judgments form the basis of important theoretical claims or debates. (iii) Carefully controlled judgment studies would solve these problems. Although I sympathize with the complaint that one can find many cases of poor data collection in the linguistics literature, I am not sure that any of (i)–(iii) is correct. A surprising number of the critiques that I have read present no evidence of the supposed damage that informal intuitions have caused, and among those that do provide specific examples it is rare to find clear evidence of the lasting impact of questionable judgments. (Phillips 2009: 3)

Phillips thus held that criteria (i, ii) have not been satisfied. As for (iii), he argued that experimental data from large-scale rating studies and acceptability tests

F. Karlsson (✉)
General Linguistics, Department of Modern Languages, University of Helsinki, Helsinki, Finland
e-mail: fred.karlsson@helsinki.fi

D. Santos et al. (eds.), *Shall We Play the Festschrift Game?*,
DOI 10.1007/978-3-642-30773-7_1,

"are likely to be less of a panacea than we are sometimes led to believe" even if he acknowledged the value of experimentation as a supplementary data-gathering method, alongside introspection.

My thesis here is that (i) and (ii) are in fact satisfied. My test-case will be one of the fundamental claims of generative grammar, articulated by Chomsky (1956: 65), that English is not a finite-state language, plus one of its corollaries. Here is Chomsky's whole argument which I shall call *English-not-FSL*:

> Turning now to the English language, we find that there are infinite sets of sentences with just the mirror-image properties of [the artificial language] L_1. For example, let $S_1, S_2, S_3, \ldots$, be declarative sentences. Then the following are all English sentences:
>
> (1) (i) If S_1, then S_2.
> (ii) Either S_3, or S_4.
> (iii) The man who said that S_5, is arriving today.
>
> These sentences have dependencies between "if" and "then", "either" and "or", "man" and "is". But we can choose S_1, S_3, and S_5 in (1) as (1i), (1ii), or (1iii) themselves. Proceeding to construct sentences in this way, we arrive at sentences with dependency sets of more than any fixed number of terms, just as in the case of L_1. English is therefore not a finite-state language. (Chomsky 1956: 65)

From this an important corollary can be deduced: syntactic recursion, especially nested recursion (center-embedding) is unlimited. This I call *Unlimited-center-embedding*. Both English-not-FSL and Unlimited-center-embedding have played an enormous role in the theoretical genesis of generative grammar. Note that the truth of Unlimited-center-embedding is the one and only criterion deciding whether natural language syntax is finite-state or context-free, i.e. whether English-not-FSL is true. If Unlimited-center-embedding is false, English-not-FSL too is false and natural language syntax is (in principle) of finite-state character.

It would be easy to list hundreds of scholarly articles, text books and overviews from linguistics and neighboring disciplines where English-not-FSL and Unlimited-center-embedding are taken to be truths established by the early Chomsky. Here are some representative examples from theoretical, mathematical, computational and psycholinguistics:

> First we will observe that English has characteristics that put it outside the class of regular languages. Then we will consider a simple theory of syntax that is essentially like the theory of finite automata or finite state grammars, and conclude that the theory is inadequate (Chomsky 1956, 1957). (Bach 1974: 187)

> The demonstration that English is not a finite automaton language was one of the first results to be achieved in the nascent field of mathematical linguistics (Chomsky 1956, 1957, Chap. 3). ... This illustrates one sort of practical result that can sometimes be obtained from the study of formal languages. (Partee et al. 1993: 478–479)

> Chomsky (1957) showed that natural language cannot be characterised by a finite-state device. In particular, it cannot produce arbitrarily long sequences of multiple center-embedded structures. (Harley 1995: 152)

> Every computational linguistics graduate student knows, from the first textbook that introduces the Chomsky hierarchy, that English has constructs, such as center embedding, that cannot be described by any finite-state grammar. (Hobbs et al. 1997: 383)

> The fact that a sentence with, say, ten dependent clauses is unlikely to be spoken and would be impossible to understand at first hearing does not detract from Chomsky's argument that a recursive (i.e. infinitely repeatable) rule of embedding must, in principle, be allowed for in English grammar. Clearly, it would be arbitrary to say that embeddings can only be carried out three times or that sentences can only be of a certain length. (Greene 1972: 26)

Chomsky obviously intuited his examples (1i–iii) as well as his subsequent claims about sentences of unlimited embedding complexity; at least he did not report that his analysis was based either on observation of language use (i.e. corpus work) or on experimentation. Surely English-not-FSL and Unlimited-center-embedding are widely accepted generalizations in the sense of Phillips' criterion (i), and also important theoretical claims as meant by his criterion (ii). Many (all?) generative linguists still subscribe to Unlimited-center-embedding and English-not-FSL in the spirit just quoted, despite counterarguments of critics like Levelt (1974) and Manaster Ramer (1983). For example, the hypothesis by Hauser et al. (2002), that the faculty of language in the narrow sense (FLN) only includes recursion, is an extended variant of Unlimited-center-embedding.

The crucial question is whether Unlimited-center-embedding is true. Using the third possible data-gathering method, extensive corpus study of i.a. English, Finnish, German, Latin and Swedish, I demonstrated in Karlsson (2007), first (a) that multiple center-embedding of clauses is practically non-existing in spoken language; (b) that the limit of multiple center-embedding in written language is three, but such constructions are extremely rare and mostly more than 100 years old, making double center-embedding the only reasonably productive type of center-embedding; and (c) of the extant double center-embeddings (more than 100 authentic instances), contrary to the hypothesis of Miller and Chomsky (1963), the most common type of multiple center-embedding is *self-embedding* with two relative clauses; this is the only type of central self-embedding that occurs.

My interpretation of these empirical data is that they falsify the hypothesis of Unlimited-center-embedding and considerably downplay the general significance of recursion, especially its theoretically most important manifestation as nesting (i.e. center-embedding); of course, left- and right-branching recursion is equal to iteration. Consequently, English-not-FSL too is false, English (and other languages) are regular languages. Upholding the idea of Unlimited-center-embedding at competence level, and relegating the restrictions on center-embedding to the domain of performance, begs the question and makes the hypothesis of Unlimited-center-embedding immune to criticism.

Finally, let us reiterate Phillips' two first criteria:

> In order for there to be a crisis, however, it would need to be the case that (i) Intuitive judgments have led to generalizations that are widely accepted yet bogus. (ii) Misleading judgments form the basis of important theoretical claims or debates.

Both (i) and (ii) are demonstrably at hand—and, ergo, so is the crisis. Of course, it is quite another matter whether the community of practitioners of generative linguistics is willing to admit this state of affairs. When I submitted the above comments for consideration to be published in the journal *Linguistic Inquiry* in June 2010, the editors needed only three days to refuse my offering with the main argument that there was nothing new in my analysis because Karlsson (2007) already had presented the relevant empirical data. I consider this a classical instance of gate-keeping: research paradigms (in their Kuhnian 'senile phase' of development) are not to be disturbed by outsiders.

Now that I have the privilege of publishing these remarks in Lauri Carlson's Festschrift, I want, by way of conclusion, to briefly address an issue he brought up in his contribution (Carlson 2006) to my Festschrift. Lauri launched the highly interesting idea that spoken language syntax is closer to written language syntax than many linguists claim these days, namely given that spoken language is analyzed with due consideration being paid to the immediate discourse context (which e.g. helps to fill in ellipses). This idea I find intriguing and hopefully it will be fleshed out some day.

There is just one detail I want to take issue with. Lauri claimed (Carlson 2006: 128) that one "... expect[s] to find in real speech artful periods like" (here cited in the original form from Albert Engström's journal *Strix*, 1902):

> *Om dig, Eriksson, om hvilken jag ej kunnat tänka mig något dylikt, har jag, då du, då jag till följd av iråkad snuva, nös, skrattade, ändrat uppfattning.*
> 'Of you, Eriksson, whom I would not have thought capable of it, I have, now that you, when I had to sneeze due to a head cold, burst into a laugh, changed my opinion.'

My rejoinder here is that such a sentence is, in fact, extremely unlikely to occur even in writing because it displays a type of multiple center-embedding that has (so far) not been attested in any type of authentic language use, that is self-embedding of two adverbial clauses of the same type (two *då* 'when' clauses). The primary purpose of Engström's journal *Strix* was to excel in enlightened humor. So here we are not dealing with ordinary spoken language but rather with a deliberate norm breach of a soft constraint in written language (the ban on certain types of self-embedding) and it is this breach which generates the humorous effect.

References

Bach, Emmon. 1974. *Syntactic theory*. New York: Holt, Rinehart and Winston.

Carlson, Lauri. 2006. Parsing spoken dialogue. In *A man of measure: Festschrift in honour of Fred Karlsson. on his 60th birthday*, eds. Mickael Suominen, Antti Arppe, Anu Airola, Orvokki Heinämäki, Matti Miestamo, Urho Määttä, Jussi Niemi, Kari K. Pitkänen, and Kaius Sinnemäki. Vol. 19 of *SKY journal of linguistics*, 128–137. Turku: The Linguistic Association of Finland. http://www.linguistics.fi/julkaisut/sky2006special.shtml (special supplement).

Chomsky, Noam. 1956. On the limits of finite-state description. *Quarterly Progress Report—Massachusetts Institute of Technology, Research Laboratory of Electronics* 41: 64–65.

Chomsky, Noam. 1957. *Syntactic structures*. The Hague: Mouton.

Greene, Judith. 1972. *Psycholinguistics*. Harmondsworth: Penguin.

Harley, Trevor. 1995. *The psychology of language. From data to theory*. Hove: Erlbaum.

Hauser, Marc D., Noam Chomsky, and W. Tecumseh Fitch. 2002. The faculty of language: what is it, who has it, and how did it evolve? *Science* 298: 1569–1579.

Hobbs, Jerry R., Douglas Appelt, John Bear, David Israel, Megumi Kameyama, Mark Stickel, and Tyson Mabry. 1997. FASTUS: A cascaded finite-state transducer for extracting information from natural-language text. In *Finite-state language processing*, eds. Emmanuel Roche and Yves Schabes, 383–406. Cambridge: The MIT Press.

Karlsson, Fred. 2007. Constraints on multiple center-embedding of clauses. *Journal of Linguistics* 43: 365–392.

Levelt, Willem J.M. 1974. *Formal grammars in linguistics and psycholinguistics. Vol. II: Applications in linguistic theory*. The Hague: Mouton.

Manaster Ramer, Alexis. 1983. Soft formal underbelly of theoretical syntax. In *Papers from the 19th regional meeting*, 256–262. Chicago: Chicago Linguistic Society.

Miller, George A., and Noam Chomsky. 1963. Finitary models of language users. In *Handbook of mathematical psychology, II*. eds. R. Duncan Luce, Robert R. Bush, and Eugene Galanter. New York: Wiley.

Partee, Barbara H., Alice ter Meulen, and Robert E. Wall. 1993. *Mathematical methods in linguistics*. Dordrecht: Kluwer.

Phillips, Colin. 2009. Should we impeach armchair linguists. In *Japanese/Korean linguistics*, eds. Shoichi Iwasaki, Hajime Hoji, Patriciam M. Clancy, and Sung-Ock Sohn, Vol. 17. Stanford: CSLI.

“It’s Etymology Captain, but Not as We Know It”: *Pump* in North Australia

David Nash

Abstract We consider the words originating from the English word ‘bamboo’ borrowed into the indigenous languages of northern Australian and denoting the didjeridu (drone pipe) or other aerophones. The word ‘bamboo’ must have been first acquired by speakers of Australian Aboriginal languages in the 19th century, and in north Australia where the large stem plant is endemic, namely in the region of Darwin. The available data is organised in support of an hypothesised spread whereby the word was applied to the aerophone made from bamboo, and then to similar aerophones made of other wood. In this sense, ‘bamboo’ (as *pampu*) spread inland southwards, and eastwards to western Cape York Peninsula. In western Cape York Peninsula the word lost the final vowel, and in this form was borrowed southwards and applied to the particular aerophone the ‘emu caller’, used to attract the emu (a large flightless game bird). A comparable distribution is collated for an indigenous word denoting aerophones: *kurlumpu(rr)* and corresponding forms in various north Australian languages. The study demonstrates how some etymological headway can be made on loanwords in languages with only a recent documentary record.

1 Introduction

The etymology of a particular word traces combinations of inheritance and borrowing, describing shifts in form and meaning along the way. When borrowing is involved, the path can be quite idiosyncratic, and uncovering it requires a deduction

It is a pleasure to associate this paperlet with Lauri Carlson. We knew each other as fellow graduate students in linguistics at MIT, and also shared a group apartment. Lauri would occasionally put to us his roommates (mostly native speakers of English of various kinds) that a (to us implausible) pair of English words would prove to be etymologically related, and invariably on us reaching for dictionaries he would turn out to be right. An earlier version appeared as blog posts (Nash 2011a, 2011b). I am grateful to the editors for providing this opportunity, and for their forebearance.

D. Nash (✉)
School of Language Studies, The Australian National University, Canberra, Australia
e-mail: david.nash@anu.edu.au

D. Santos et al. (eds.), *Shall We Play the Festschrift Game?*,
DOI 10.1007/978-3-642-30773-7_2, © Springer-Verlag Berlin Heidelberg 2012

beyond the Comparative Method. See for instance Trask (1996: 351–353) for an appraisal of the kind of study involved.

When the documentary record for the languages involved is only recent, as for Australian languages, the task is perforce more inferential. But if we confine ourselves to the historical period, that is, since written records began around two centuries ago, then etymologies in Australia can be pursued, using at least some shreds of evidence of a kind not available for the prehistoric period. In this note, I exemplify this first by studying a word of regional Aboriginal English, and then by looking at a cognate set in Australian languages with the same range of meanings. Along the way we see the hazards of translation on the colonial frontier, even with respect to 'concrete' artefacts.

2 'Pump' in North Queensland

The published grammar of the Kalkatungu language of western Queensland has this entry in the 'Weapons, tools, etc.' section of the glossary:

> 'pump' (decoy device for attracting birds) **kuḷumpu**[1] (Blake 1979: 179)

This entry is fairly opaque to speakers of Australian English. What kind of decoy, the reader wonders, would be named with the English word for a fluid propulsion device (let alone a kind of footwear!).

The author (BB) elaborated[2] that he based the entry on a sound recording of an interview with Mrs Lardie Moonlight (LM) conducted by his colleague Gavan Breen (GB), who has kindly provided me with his careful transcript of the relevant excerpt, and later played me the sound recording.

> GB (<BB[3]): You plant so the emu won't see you.
> LM: Yes, dig a hole and put the little bough around it, sit in it with a pump, call him // *yu:ridja(y) yini* / *wùdingálkuwa* // *wudingalkuwa* /// he sitting down there in the hole for that emu to come; he blowing that pump, pumping his *kúrumbu* // *kúrlúmbuyan i.ni*
> GB: What was the pump like? How did they make it?
> LM: Out of the little oller [sc. hollow] tree, they knock the hollow tree down and they put a haxe [sc. axe] round it, you know, make it small, they blow it then.
> GB: Oh, yes, it makes a noise and the emu comes up to see what the noise is.
> LM: Oh yeah, they make a lovely noise too.
> (Breen Field Tape 283, AIATSIS AV tape A2459b, 24 May 1972, Boulia, Queensland)

The morphological analysis of the Kalkatungu is:[4]

---

[1] ḷ represents l-with-dot-under, the apico-domal lateral. Blake (1979: 4) noted that 'All the informants spoke English in most situations, some of them using a fair admixture of Pidgin features.'

[2] Blake and I exchanged a number of email messages on this in April–May 2011.

[3] Breen was working through a set of elicitation sentences that Blake had drawn up.

[4] Here I revert to the spellings of Blake (1979), cast in a practical orthography whereby e.g. *rl* is the apico-domal lateral; and ignoring the phonetic length marking of the first vowel in *i.ni*.

yurru	tjaa	ini	utingarr-ku-a,	kurlumpu-yan	ini
man	this	sit/remain	emu-dative-ligature	pump-having	sit/remain

'This man is sitting with the pump (waiting) for the emu.'

The 19th century ethnographer Roth (1897: 97) was familiar with that district, and described how men imitated the 'call' of an emu using 'a hollow log some 2½ feet to 3 feet long ...', adding that 'These "call-tubes" are met with throughout North-West-Central Queensland'. Anell's (1960: 19) map shows reports of 'emu-callers' from seven locations from the south Gulf country in Queensland across to Charters Towers (and another two locations in northern NSW). The emu-caller has been likened to a cut-off didjeridu, and indeed there is a market nowadays for ones of recent manufacture, witness a Google search on the term.

So that explains what the thing is: the Kalkatungu were indeed describing a traditional device of theirs. But what of the glossing word 'pump'?

The English word *pump* is hard to relate here semantically. But as well as the emu-caller there is one other tubular aerophone long used and made by Aboriginal people in northern Australia: the didjeridu. And in western Cape York Peninsula (CYP) it is called *pamp*, phonetically matching the English word spelled *pump*. The key is this entry in Alpher's (1991) *Yir-Yoront lexicon*:

> **PAMP** *(N) Etymology: < English* **bamboo**, *probably via one or more other Aboriginal languages.*
> DIDGERIDOO. **Olo pamp palarrng**. He's blowing a didgeridoo. *Note: A recent cultural introduction to the area and not played at Kowanyama.*
> **YO-PAMP** *(N) SCI: plant.*
> CASTOR BEAN, PALMA CHRISTI, RICINUS COMMUNIS. *Note: Not a bamboo. L.E.*[5] *'kerosene bush'.*

A quite similar word is recorded in Kuuk Thaayorre, the neighbouring language to the north:

> yuk **pamp** –a nn **bamboo** flute pipe (Foote and Hall 1992–1995: 101; nn abbreviates noun)

The slight differences in meaning and form are instructive. First, the denotation is a smaller aerophone, one traditionally used in the Torres Strait islands, made from a slender species of bamboo native to the Cape York region. The bamboo flute or pan-pipe apparently spread south prehistorically along western Cape York Peninsula, as the Wik languages have their own terms for it (Peter Sutton, p.c.). Also the 'Bone or reed (blown like pan-pipe)' was reported further south, from the southeast Gulf of Carpentaria, by the 19th century ethnographer W. E. Roth (Roth 1902 per Moyle 1967 map), so it could well be that slender bamboo substituted for other materials in the pan-pipe. In any case, it seems that when the English word *bamboo* arrived in

[5]Local English. How and when the *pamp* word came to also denote the introduced castor bean plant calls for integration into my account. Edwards and Black (1998) list the same word *yok pamp* 'castor bean (*Ricinus communis*)' in Kokoberrin, a neighbouring language to the south; no word is listed denoting an aerophone or bamboo. The castor bean plant and bamboo have in common that they have hollow jointed stems (as drawn to my attention by David Wilkins, p.c.) and they are fast growing, suckering, colony forming plants.

the region, it was applied in some places at least also to the pan-pipe. This may well have been prior to and thus independent of the arrival of the didjeridu in western Cape York Peninsula (CYP).

As to the form of the Kuuk Thaayorre word, Barry Alpher (p.c.) noted that loss of an earlier final V2 (i.e. the vowel at the end of a disyllabic word) is common to all these western CYP languages, and points out that the oblique form in Kuuk Thaayorre is *pampa*, with echo-vowel *a* instead of *u*; this implies that Kuuk Thaayorre heard *pamp* (rather than *pampu*) when the word was borrowed into that language. I join Alpher (p.c.) in proposing that when *bamboo* from frontier English or creole was first borrowed into a western CYP language, *pampu* was truncated to *pamp* by loan adaptation (Alpher and Nash 1999: 14–15), and the truncated form was borrowed further into Kuuk Thaayorre.

But what of Yir-Yoront *pamp*, which we are told does not comprise bamboo. Well, a possible explanation is that it came as the name of the didjeridu, when this instrument arrived, ultimately from Arnhem Land. I haven't seen an account of how this happened, but a parallel arrival in the southern Gulf has been explained this way:

> The didgeridoo first entered Mornington Island in the 1930s as a result of visits to other Aboriginal settlements by the mission boat the *Morning Star*. This vessel was crewed by local tribesmen and paid occasional visits to Arnhem Land's Yirrkala mission. Items of material culture, including the didgeridoo, were brought back to Mornington Island from these visits. (iDIDJ Australia 2004)[6]

This same mission vessel's circuit also included Aurukun settlement, where lived speakers of many of the Wik languages north of Kuuk Thaayorre, but the Wik Mungkan dictionary (Kilham et al. 1986) does not record any *pamp* or didjeridu word.

In any case, in the Northern Territory the didjeridu has long been called *pampu* in Aboriginal English (with stress on the first syllable) and the word is fairly widespread especially in the northern half of the NT, and in the languages of people who adopted the didjeridu in historical times. Arthur's (1996) *Aboriginal English* has an entry for it, labelled '[northern Aust.]' and noting 'Also bamboo pipe'.[7]

The ethnomusicologist Moyle (1981: 322) remarked thirty years ago:

> The fact that bamboo didjeridus were quite common among northerly groups in the Northern Territory during the last century is confirmed by the word 'bamboo' which is still used in

[6]The "interactive map shows the major areas in the 'Top End' of Australia where the didgeridoo is traditionally found", in Exhibition of Didgeridoos. Memmott (1980: 271–272) recorded the word *pampu* 'didjeridu' in oral history recalling new artefacts that came to Mornington Island with the *Morning Star* in the 1920s–30s.

[7]Somewhat surprisingly Arthur's (1996) earliest citation is as late as 1969; along with a 1957 reference to *bamboo puller* 'a didgeridoo player'. These are antedated by Worms (1953: 278): "the Arnhem Land tribes also have a 'bamboo', a sort of crude trumpet made from a narrow branch of a tree". Balfour's (1901) title applied the expression "bambu trumpets" in 1901. It might be thought that as *bambu* is a Malay word it could have been borrowed through Makassarese (Mkr) contact rather than through English; however Walker and Zorc (1981: 118) list only *bamutuka* 'pipe' < Mkr *pammudúkaŋ* 'bamboo opium pipe' root word Mkr *uduʔ*, Malay *udut* 'to suck-at, smoke'.

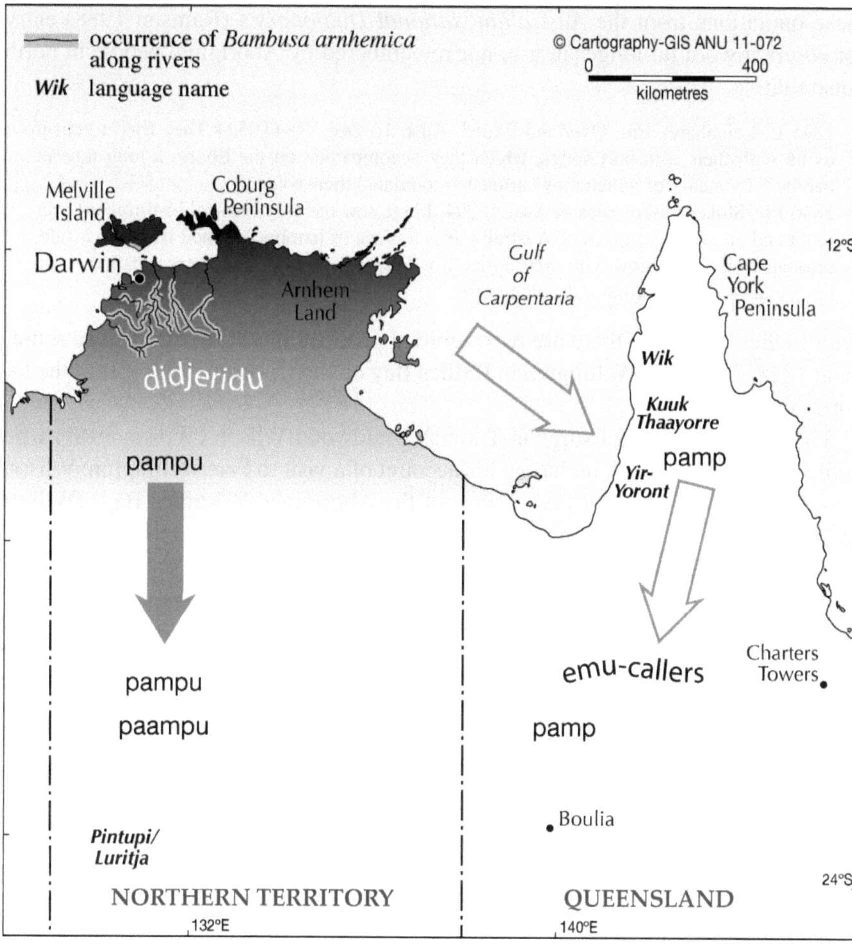

Fig. 1 Northern Australia, showing hypothesised spread of the *bamboo* word, open arrows indicate spread is inferred. Shading shows 19th century range of the didjeridu. Based on Anell (1960), Moyle (1981), and *Bambusa* range from Franklin (2008)

> the lingua franca by some Aborigines when referring to the instrument, though 'didjeridu' may be gaining ground.
> The suggestion here is that the first didjeridus were of bamboo; and that because of the availability of bamboo in the north-western region of the Northern Territory, the first didjeridu players may well have belonged to that region.

Bambusa arnhemica is the only one of the three endemic species of bamboo in Australia which is suitable for making a didjeridu. Botanists including Franklin (2008) have shown that the species is confined to Western Arnhem Land and the Daly River districts, as shown by the river lines on the map in Fig. 1.

The earliest records of the didjeridu are from this part of northern Australia, and these were made from bamboo, as noted by the earliest observers. Consider first these quotations from the *Australian National Dictionary*'s (Ramson 1988) entry for *eboro*, a word no longer in use, nor remembered by Aboriginal people in north Australia:

> 1845 L. Leichhardt Jrnl. Overland Exped. Aust. 16 Dec. (1847) 534 They tried to cheer us up with their corrobori songs, which they accompanied on the Eboro, a long tube of bamboo, by means of which they variously modulated their voices.
> 1846 J.L. Stokes Discoveries in Aust. I. 394, I here saw the only musical instrument I ever remarked among the natives of Australia. It is a piece of bamboo thinned from the inside, through which they blow with their noses. It is from two to three feet long, is called ebroo [sic], and produces a kind of droning noise.

Prior to these writings, there are two recorded observations at the short-lived settlement 1828–29 at Fort Wellington in Raffles Bay on the Cobourg Peninsula at the far north of Australia.

The first was by naval surgeon Thomas Braidwood Wilson (Wilson 1967) who published in 1835 a book including his account of a visit to Fort Wellington. Wilson provided an illustration entitled 'Dance of the Aborigines of Raffles Bay' (Wilson 1835: 88) and described the dance 'to the music, produced by one of their part from a long hollow tube' (Wilson 1835: 87), which Kim Akerman (an expert on Australian material culture) believes is 'the earliest depiction of the didjeridu or eboro in use'.[8] Akerman (p.c.) continued:

> I think it is a bamboo one for two reasons:
>
> 1. The diameter—which is much more in proportion to the early bamboo didjeridus that I have seen, when compared with wooden ones; and
> 2. The lightness of the material is demonstrated by the fact that it is being held in one hand off the ground.
>
> These points do not prove it is bamboo but I think greatly raises the possibility.

Wilson's (1835: 319) vocabulary from Raffles Bay includes

> Ebero ... *Their musical instrument*

which is the earliest known record of this term, predating the 1845 use by Leichhardt as quoted above from the *eboro* entry in the *Australian National Dictionary* (Ramson 1988). Note that the word has apparently dropped out of use on the Cobourg Peninsula (Bruce Birch, p.c.).

The second observation is by Captain Collet Barker (Bach 1966) who was Commandant of Fort Wellington. In his journal Barker described what we recognise as the didjeridu:

> Mago had brought a kind of musical instrument, a large hollow cane about 3 feet long bent at one end. From [this] he produced two or three low & tolerably clear & loud notes, answering to the tune of didoggerry whoan, & he accompanied Alobo with this while he sang his treble. (Mulvaney and Green 1992: 113)

[8]There is a rock art image of a human figure playing a didjeridu in Kakadu National Park (Chaloupka 1993) which may well predate Wilson's drawing.

Barker's word 'cane' here would not apply to a hollow limb from a tree. Note by the way his expression *didoggerry whoan*: this prefigures the word *didjeridu* for which the *Australian National Dictionary*'s (Ramson 1988) earliest citation is as late as 1919.

So, while the didjeridu has long been made from a variety of timbers, the association of the didjeridu and the bamboo plant is well established and derives from the northwestern part of the Northern Territory. The early settlements in that region (Raffles Bay, Port Essington,[9] and then Darwin) are the plausible site of adoption of the term *pampu* among Aboriginal people, and we can infer that they learnt the word *pampu* from the early contacts with English speakers, and applied it to the didjeridu. The *pampu* word spread both to people who already had the didjeridu (and their own term for it), such as to the east in Arnhem Land, and also with the didjeridu itself to other people to the south who had no previous term of their own. I have indicated the southerly spread with the solid arrow on the accompanying map; as far south as for instance *paampu* "didgeridoo; from English 'bamboo'; not used in Central Australia" in the *Pintupi/Luritja dictionary* (Hansen and Hansen 1992). The route along the Overland Telegraph Line south from Darwin has long been a conduit for the spread of innovations, and presumably was involved in particular in how Eylmann (1908: 376, Table XXIV Fig. 5) in 1897 happened to observe a bamboo 'trumpet' among the Warumungu of the central Northern Territory.

Another factor which might have had an influence is folk-etymology, with two aspects: (1) the English word *pump* could cover the repetitive exertion producing pulses of air, a kind of pumping; and, for the emu-caller, (2) onomatopoeia: the word *pamp* mimics the sound of the hand-struck emu-caller.

In sum, it seems that people familiar with the emu-caller adopted the 'bamboo' word for that somewhat similar aerophone. We can deduce that it reached the Kalkatungu via western Cape York Peninsula,[10] because they adopted the truncated form *pamp* (while their language usually preserves the final vowel of a loan word). I have indicated this hypothesis by the hollow arrows on the above map.

There is another link between the two aerophones:

> A suggestion that the 'emu decoy', reported in several parts of Australia, may have been a precursor of the didjeridu in some areas is to be found in an extract from Roth (1902).[11] (Moyle 1981: 327)

So, curiously, by spreading from the didjeridu to the emu-caller, the word may have reversed the course of an earlier adaptation deriving the didjeridu from the emu-caller.

---

[9]Balfour (1901: 33) includes a photograph of 'three bambu trumpets ... from the Alligator tribe, Port Essington' in the Pitt Rivers Museum, Oxford. See items 1900.55.273 and 274 and 1900.71.12 in the databases at http://www.prm.ox.ac.uk.

[10]There is evidence for a parallel trade link: Sharp (1952) noted that stingray barbs from the Yir-Yoront area were exchanged for ground stone axe heads sourced a long way south, subsequently matched with quarries in Kalkatungu country (Davidson et al. 2005: 108).

[11]Roth's (1902: 23–24) report was from further east, from north-east Queensland.

3 *Kurlumpu*

The Kalkatungu word *kuḷumpu*, where I began, also looks to have an intriguing etymology. Being a word indigenous to Australia however its story can only be prehistoric inference. Table 1 contains the apparently cognate words I have found, cast in the source spelling or the current orthography. (Note that in the relevant Australian languages there is a single series of stop consonants, variously but not distinctively spelled with the voiced or voiceless symbols.) The words are presented in a geographic order northwest to southeast, which is also from the longer more complex form to the shorter forms.

The apparent cognates in Table 1 span a major linguistic divide in Australia, that between the Pama-Nyungan (PNy) family across most of the continent, and the disparate languages of other families across northern Australia. Given the time depth of the separation of these families and the scarcity of inherited shared vocabulary, we can presume that the cognate set in Table 1 involves borrowing, fitting with the relatively recent diffusion of the denoted artefacts, especially the didjeridu. The linguistic evidence tugs in two ways as to the direction of the diffusion: the non-Pama-Nyungan languages show more variation (initial *k* possibly lenited to *w* in Alawa; final *ng* separable in Miriwoong), whereas the *rr* segment is attested only in a Pama-Nyungan language (Warlpiri, and likely cognate with the final *t* in Mudburra). Drawing on extra-linguistic evidence, it might be thought that the word spread south (from non Pama-Nyungan languages) along with the didjeridu; but it is also possible that the word denoted a pre-existing aerophone in Pama-Nyungan languages, and was later applied to the didjeridu.

There is another apparent cognate set spanning some non-Pama-Nyungan languages of north Australia, which can be matched to the above in the first two syllables, shown in Table 2.

The words in Table 2 matching in just the first two syllables are yet to be demonstrated to be related. Similarly, for guidance of future research I mention as intriguing potential cognates some other words in Pama-Nyungan languages which are quite similar in form, but with a rather different meaning:

1. Wulguru *kulumpuru* 'tree with honey in it' (Donohue 2007: 41) (per Claire Bowern, p.c.; Price 1885: 30: *Cooloomboro* 'Tree "Sugar Bag" In which the natives find the Honey'); the meaning connection would be through 'hollow tree'. The Wulguru language was spoken about 1,000 km to the east on the Queensland coast around Townsville; the *r* is Donohue's reconstitution which matches an apical flap or retroflex glide.
2. Warumungu *kulumpurr* ~ *kulumpul* 'hard, loud', an eastern neighbour of Warlpiri
3. Warlmanpa *kurlumpurrnga* '(upper) arm', another eastern neighbour of Warlpiri; compare also Warlmanpa's non-Pama-Nyungan neighbour Jingulu *gurlumbu* 'thigh bone' (Chadwick 1975: 123). The speculative meaning connection could be through the match in size and shape between an arm and the Warlpiri trumpet.

Table 1 Apparently cognate words for *kuḷumpu*

Language	Dictionary entry	Source
Miriwoong	*gooloomboong* 'didjeridu'; final *-ng* marks a nominal, and masculine on an adjective; added to introduced nouns e.g. *babaloong* 'buffalo', *wadameleng* 'water melon'; also coverb as in *gooloomboob ganiya* 'he played the didjeridu'	Kofod (1978: 76n; p.c.)
Gajirrabeng (Gajirrawoong)	*gooloomboong* 'didjeridoo' 'frequently used by Miriwung speakers and yet occasionally they reflect that [these] are really Gadjerong'	Kofod (1978: 76n)
Gija	*gooloomboo-ny* 'didjeridu'	Frances Kofod (p.c.)
Alawa	*wurlumbu n. bambu, dijaridu;* didjeridu, bamboo. Once wulumbu. Prob. also applies to any instrument played similarly (e.g. brass instrument); • *Wurlumbu didung-jilanna.* Deibin pulum bambu, they were playing didjeridu	Sharpe (2001)
Jingulu	kūlum-būpi 'trumpet'	Gillen (1901) (Chingilli)
Ngarnka	urlūng-būngma 'trumpet'	Gillen (1901) (Gnanji)
Wambaya	kulūmbū 'trumpet'	Gillen (1901) (Umbaia)
Gurindji (PNy)	*kulumpung* 'didjeridu'	Patrick McConvell (p.c.)
Mudburra (PNy)	*kulumput* 'pampu'	Peter Sutton (p.c., recorded in ceremonial context in 1983)
Warlpiri (PNy)	*kurlumpurrngu* 'trumpet, didjeridu, guitar'	Swartz (1997), Patrick (2011)
Unknown Queensland Gulf language (PNy)	*colombo*, associated with 'a hardwood drone pipe collected from the Gulf of Carpentaria'[a]	item A2928 in the SA Museum; documented at AA298 to have arrived in 1897 from Philip Sydney Watson who had Gregory Downs station (in the southern Gulf) (Philip Jones, p.c.)
Kalkatungu (PNy)	*kuḷumpu* 'emu-caller'	Blake (1979: 179)

[a]Edge-Partington (1898: 136, Fig. 3) (referred to by Balfour 1901: 33) drew this with caption 'Musical instrument of hard wood hollowed by termites. "Blown like a bullock horn." Native name *oolomba*. Gulf of Carpentaria. Adelaide Museum.' The item has an inscription, applied in the SA Museum, probably in 1911–12, which clearly reads *colombo* (Philip Jones, p.c.)

Table 2 Other apparently cognate words for *kuḻumpu*, matching in the first two syllables

Language	Dictionary entry	Source
Alawa[a]	*gulurrun* ~ *gulurun* 'didjeridu', L gulurrung, golorrong	Sharpe (2001)
Yanyuwa	*ma-kulurru (noun)* **1**. musical instrument **2**. didgeridoo. Made from a hollow length of wood, not traditional to the Yanyuwa	Bradley and Kirton (1992: 195) = p. 202 of PDF
	ma- is the Class 5 prefix, with manufactured items	Bradley and Kirton (1992: 58–59) = pp. 66–67 of PDF
Gun-nartpa	*ngorla* 'didjeridu', *-ngorla* 'hollow' (*gun-ngorla* 'hollow tree', *an-ngorla* 'hollow metal pipe')	Margaret Carew (p.c.), Glasgow (1994)
Jingulu	*gulugugbi* 'didjeridu' *gurlumbi* 'thigh bone'	Chadwick (1975: 123)
Yir-Yoront	*ko+rlonhl* ~ *ko+rronyl* ~ *ko+ronyl* '1. syrinx shell; 2. shell trumpet'	Alpher (1991: 188)

[a]A similar term has somehow found its way into Kunwinjku but in a ceremonial context which is not in the public domain

4 Conclusion

Discovering the etymology of particular words (as form-meaning pairs) is difficult enough in language families with a documented history, but some headway can be made also with languages with only a recent documentary record, as I have shown for a couple of terms for various aerophones in northern Australian languages: *pampu* from English *bamboo*, and *kulumpu(rr)* of uncertain origin.

Acknowledgements I am grateful to Kim Akerman, Barry Alpher, Barry Blake, Gavan Breen, Yukihiro Doi 土井幸宏, Murray Garde, Philip Jones, Grace Koch, Harold Koch, Frances Kofod, Patrick McConvell and Peter Sutton for assistance, and to Aet Lees and Fred Karlsson for helpful review comments. I have benefited from the Pama-Nyungan etymological database funded by NSF grant 844550 'Pama-Nyungan and Australian Prehistory' awarded to Claire Bowern. Thanks also to ANU Cartography for preparing the map, and to Nic Peterson for the question which started me on this.

References

Alpher, Barry. 1991. *Yir-Yoront lexicon: sketch and dictionary of an Australian language*. Vol. 6 of *Trends in linguistics, documentation*. Berlin: Mouton de Gruyter.

Alpher, Barry, and David Nash. 1999. Lexical replacement and cognate equilibrium in Australia. *Australian Journal of Linguistics* 19: 5–56.

Anell, Bengt. 1960. *Hunting and trapping methods in Australia and Oceania*. Vol. 18 of *Studia ethnographica upsaliensia*. Uppsala.

Arthur, Jay M. 1996. *Aboriginal English: A cultural study*. London: Oxford University Press.

Bach, J. 1966. Barker, Collet (1784–1831). *Australian Dictionary of Biography* 1: 57. http://www.adb.online.anu.edu.au/biogs/A010054b.htm.

Balfour, Henry. 1901. Three bambu trumpets from Northern Territory, South Australia. *Man* 1: 33–34. http://www.jstor.org/stable/2840669

Blake, Barry J. 1979. *A Kalkatungu grammar*. Vol. 57 of *Pacific linguistics*. Canberra: Dept. of Linguistics, Research School of Pacific Studies, Australian National University.

Bradley, John, Jean Kirton, and Yanyuwa Community. 1992. Yanyuwa Wuka: language from Yanyuwa country, a Yanyuwa dictionary and cultural resource. http://espace.library.uq.edu.au/view/UQ:11306.

Chadwick, Neil. 1975. *A descriptive study of the Djingili language*. Canberra: Australian Institute of Aboriginal Studies.

Chaloupka, George. 1993. *Journey in time: The world's longest continuing art tradition: the 50,000-year story of the Australian Aboriginal rock art of Arnhem Land*. Chatswood: Reed.

Davidson, Iain, Nick Cook, Matthew Fischer, Malcolm Ridges, June Ross, and Stephen Sutton. 2005. Archaeology in another country: exchange and symbols in north west central Queensland. In *Many exchanges: archaeology, history, community and the work of Isabel McBryde*, eds. Ingereth Macfarlane, Mary-Jane Mountain, and Robert Paton. Vol. 11 of *Aboriginal history monographs*, 101–128. Canberra: Aboriginal History Inc.

Donohue, Mark. 2007. *Wulguru: a salvage study of a North-Eastern Australian language from Townsville*. Vol. 463 of *Languages of the world. Materials*. München: Lincom.

Edge-Partington, James. 1898. *An album of the weapons, tools, ornaments, articles of dress of the natives of the Pacific islands: Drawn and described from examples in public & private collections in England*. Vol. III. Issued for private circulation by James Edge-Partington & Charles Heape.

Edwards, Shaun Kalk, and Paul Black. 1998. The Kokoberrin and their languages. Unpublished manuscript, Cairns and Darwin. AIATSIS Library MS 4584.

Eylmann, Erhard. 1908. *Die Eingeborenen der Kolonie Sudaustralien*. Berlin: Reimer Dietrich. http://www.archive.org/details/dieeingeborenen00eylmgoog.

Foote, Tom, and Allen Hall. 1992–1995. *Kuuk Thaayorre dictionary. Thaayorre/English*. Brisbane: Jollen Press.

Franklin, Donald C. 2008. Taxonomic interpretations of Australian native bamboos (*Poaceae: Bambuseae*) and their biogeographic implications. *Telopea* 12: 179–191. http://www.rbgsyd.nsw.gov.au/_data/assets/pdf_file/0019/95401/Tel122179Fra.pdf.

Gillen, Francis James. 1901. Comparative table of languages. In *MSS 09 G47 in manuscripts & archival collections*, Vol. 5, 834–841. The University of Adelaide Library. http://www.adelaide.edu.au/library/special/mss/gillen/.

Glasgow, Kathleen. 1994. *Burarra–Gun-nartpa dictionary: with English finder list*. Darwin: Summer Institute of Linguistics, Australian Aborigines and Islanders Branch. http://ausil.org.au/Resources/DigitalResources/Dictionaries/tabid/1118/Default.aspx.

Hansen, Ken C., and Lesley E. Hansen. 1992. *Pintupi/Luritja dictionary*. Alice Springs: Institute for Aboriginal Development.

iDIDJ Australia. 2004. Mornington Island didgeridoos. http://www.ididj.com.au/exhibitions/morningtonIsland.html.

Kilham, Christine, Jeanie Adams, Jack Bell, and Garry Namponan. 1986. *Dictionary and sourcebook of the Wik-Mungkan language*. Berrimah: Summer Institute of Linguistics, Australian Aborigines Branch.

Kofod, Frances. 1978. The Miriwung language (East Kimberley): A phonological and morphological study. M.A. thesis, University of New England, Armidale, NSW.

Memmott, Paul. 1980. Lardil properties of place: An ethnological study in man-environment relations. Doctoral diss., School of Geography, Planning and Architecture, The University of Queensland. http://espace.library.uq.edu.au/view/UQ:192103.

Moyle, Alice M. 1967. *Songs from the Northern Territory*. Canberra: Australian Institute of Aboriginal Studies.

Moyle, Alice M. 1981. The Australian didjeridu: A late musical intrusion. *World Archaeology* 12: 321–331.

Mulvaney, D.J., and Neville Green. 1992. *Commandant of solitude: the journals of Captain Collet Barker 1828–1831*. Melbourne: Melbourne University Press at the Miegunyah Press.

Nash, David. 2011a. Emu-callers, the didjeridu, and bamboo. http://www.paradisec.org.au/blog/2011/04/emu-callers-the-didjeridu-and-bamboo/, posted on Endangered Languages & Cultures on 23 April 2011, 10:19 pm.

Nash, David. 2011b. Trumpeting revival at Lajamanu. http://www.paradisec.org.au/blog/2011/05/trumpeting-revival-at-lajamanu/, posted on Endangered Languages & Cultures on 2 May 2011, 12:17 pm.

Patrick, Jasmine. 2011. Kurlumpurrungu. http://ntmojos.indigenous.gov.au/index.php/videos/kurlumpurrungu/, video and transcript, published online at NT Mobile Journalists (NT MO-JOs) on 1 April 2011, 10 am.

Price, Charles. 1885. Language of Townsville area (Coonambella). 94-page mansucript photocopy, AIATSIS Library MS 330.

Ramson, W.S., ed. 1988. *The Australian national dictionary: a dictionary of Australianisms on historical principles. (AND)*. Melbourne: Oxford University Press. http://www.oup.com.au/and/.

Roth, Walter Edmund. 1897. *Ethnological studies among the north-west-central Queensland aborigines*. Brisbane: Government Printer.

Roth, Walter Edmund. 1902. *Games, sports and amusements. North Queensland ethnography: Bulletin 4*. Brisbane: Government Printer.

Sharp, Lauriston. 1952. Steel axes for stone-age Australians. *Human Organization* 11: 17–22.

Sharpe, Margaret C. 2001. *Alawa nanggaya nindanya yalanu rugalarra = Alawa–Kriol–English dictionary*. Prospect: Caitlin Press.

Swartz, Stephen. 1997. *Warlpiri yimi kuja karlipa wangka*. Berrimah: Summer Institute of Linguistics, Australian Aborigines and Islanders Branch, Warlpiri Translation Project. http://203.122.249.186/Lexicons/Warlpiri/lexicon/main.htm.

Trask, R.L. 1996. *Historical linguistics*. London: Arnold.

Walker, Alan, and R. David Zorc. 1981. Austronesian loanwords in Yolngu-Matha of northeast Arnhem Land. *Aboriginal History* 5: 109–134.

Wilson, Gwendoline. 1967. Wilson, Thomas Braidwood (1792–1843). *Australian Dictionary of Biography* 2: 612. http://www.adb.online.anu.edu.au/biogs/A020555b.htm.

Wilson, T.B. 1835. *Narrative of a voyage round the world*. London: Sherwood, Gilbert & Piper. http://hdl.handle.net/2027/nyp.33433000403760.

Worms, E.A. 1953. Australian ghost drums, trumpets and poles. *Anthropos* 48: 278–281. http://www.jstor.org/stable/40451198.

Translation in History

Nicholas Ostler

Abstract Ancient civilizations' lack of interest in others' languages largely entailed use of single metropolitan languages as a lingua franca. Encoding translations might be employed to broadcast a message beyond the lingua franca's range. Decoding translations, on the other hand, were more significant, in giving access to bodies of foreign learning: three significant such programmes were those into Chinese, Arabic and Latin. There was also a widespread thrust for various vernacular translations at the time of the European Reformation. Such programmes have often been motivated implicitly by a need to stamp texts of foreign origin with local authority. After the conquest of Mexico which followed close on the invention of vernacular grammar, encoding translations of scripture for proselytism were supplemented with theoretically-based processes of language learning. Translation, overall, has been an alternative strategy to using a lingua franca, for overcoming language barriers, and one that may connote more respect for individual languages.

Multilinguality is older than recorded human history, but interest in it—or in other people's languages—is much more recent. It is a commonplace of discussions of the foreign-language competence of some of the oldest known ancient civilizations (notably Egypt, China, Greece) that there was little knowledge, or even informed speculation, about neighbours' languages. (For Egypt, see Goedicke (1960, 1966); for China, Behr (2004); for Greece, Harrison (1998).)

In Iran, and subsequently in the whole domain of the Persian empire, which was well enough organized to maintain an extent from India to Sudan for over two centuries (550–333 BC), literacy was curiously regarded not as a high skill in itself, but rather as a communications service which should be provided (by foreign experts) for the convenience of Persian rulers. As a result, two literate foreign languages (first, Elamite, close to home in south-western Iran, and latterly Aramaic, which had become the convenient lingua franca of the Assyrian-Babylonian domains, and

N. Ostler (✉)
Foundation for Endangered Languages, Bath, England, UK

N. Ostler
School of Oriental and African Studies, London, England, UK

D. Santos et al. (eds.), *Shall We Play the Festschrift Game?*,
DOI 10.1007/978-3-642-30773-7_3,

then the interlingua of the whole empire), were long viewed just as written media supported by scribes. Texts were typically composed in translation—from dictation by some important personages—and also read out not literally, but in translation by other scribes, into whatever language the recipient was using. This was known in middle Persian as the process of *uzvarišn* 'understanding'. It was a kind of translation, but more like a common code, with oral access to it in Persian and other useful spoken languages of the empire (Polotsky 1971; Greenfield 1985; Ostler 2010: 75).

Ancient empires usually addressed the problem of crossing language barriers only tacitly, by ignoring it: in effect, each promoted one language (usually their own metropolitan speech and script) as a lingua franca, which foreigners might need to learn if they wanted access to the empire's world, which for their purposes (at the very extremes of then feasible logistics) was the whole world.[1] They might offer some translation of imperial propaganda into subject languages that happened to be literate: indeed, an irony of multilingual inscriptions (such as Augustus' political testament of 14 AD in Ankara (*monumentum Ancyranum*), Ptolemy's Rosetta Stone of 196 BC in Egypt, Darius's Behistun inscription ca 500 BC in Persia and Aśoka's rock inscriptions ca 260 BC in India) is that they show that the populations addressed were monolingual in different languages: they needed to be addressed in something besides the empire's single chosen language. But they also show that the imperial authorities recognized significant subject populations with literate languages of their own.

These were *encoding* translations: propagating a known message to foreigners. *Decoding* translations, by contrast, which betoken an interest in understanding what foreigners have to say, have been much rarer: they show that a significant class of insiders were aware that they had something to learn. This motive is not so rare for interpreting activity, which is conducted orally. Interpreters may—as scouts or spies—be providing foreign intelligence, or—as merchants—simply finding out what is available abroad, and on what terms. But decoding translations, when they are undertaken by translators, may be of fundamental significance for the future of the culture which undertakes them.

An early example looms at the western end of the Greek-speaking world, in Rome's domains. Rome's power had encroached seriously on the eastern Mediterranean (and hence Greek kingdoms) in the early second century BC. A surprising result of this aggression was a new Roman enthusiasm—which would last for a good six centuries—for the Greek cultural identity, including serious competence in the Greek language, both spoken and written. Roman Hellenism was impressively thoroughgoing, and it included the project, carried out by several Roman scholars, most influentially Cicero in the first century BC, and Boethius in the fifth-sixth AD, of translating all major monuments of Greek learning into Latin. 500 years later, this would become the foundation of western European education.[2]

[1]Compare Roman empire's *pax totius orbis* "settlement of the whole world", *imperium sine fine* or "power without limit" with Indian *diganta rājya* or "power to the horizons". See Pollock (2000: 239) and Ostler (2007: 300–301).

[2]*Graecia capta ferum victorem cepit et artes induit agresti Latio*, as Horace puts it in his *Epistles*, ii.1, 156–157, written two centuries later: "Captive Greece captured her wild conqueror, and

Such cultural translations were always undertaken by highly learned scholars or pilgrim monks, since it requires major intellectual endeavour to become capable of understanding foreign recited or written texts, especially in eras before there was any general understanding of grammatical analysis or availability of dictionaries. In fact, it was at first necessary to use teams of scribes and interpreters in the translation process, since no one individual had all the skills required for a polished translation.

The most magnificent examples of these large-scale decoding undertakings are the millennium-long programme (first to tenth centuries AD) to translate Buddhist scriptures from Indian languages into the languages of the Silk Road and ultimately Chinese and Tibetan; the Muslim Abbasid caliphate's movement, centred on Baghdad, to translate Greek science (much of it sourced through Syriac and Persian) into Arabic (in the ninth to twelfth centuries AD); and the subsequent quest by western European scholars (in the twelfth and thirteenth centuries AD) to convert Arabic and Greek texts into Latin, mainly in medicine, mathematics and philosophy (Fuchs 1930; Gutas 1998: 136–150; d'Alverny 1982).

Comparable, but more widely distributed, was the vast encoding effort to translate Manichaean scriptures. These had originated in Mani's third-century Syriac (Aramaic), but in the next four centuries were made available in at least ten other languages, as far as Latin in the west, and Chinese in the east (Lieu 1998).

The Manichaean faith's active multilingualism is quite distinctive, since most proselytizing sects at the time tended to stick with particular languages for their communities, providing a sort of religious lingua franca which converts would acquire: most of the mystery cults of the Roman empire (e.g. of Isis, Christ, Sabazios or Mithras) used Greek; and among the many cults of India, Buddhists used Gandhari in the north, Pali in the south, both Aryan dialects distinct from the supposedly 'perfect' Sanskrit, which was often associated with Hindu worship led by Brahmans.

However, when Roman Christianity was taken as the official religion of Constantine's empire, Latin soon supplanted Greek, first through translations of its sacred texts (epistles, Gospels and then the rest of the Bible), then through adoption for its administration, and finally by translating the Church's liturgy (Ostler 2007: 111–115). This was one of many translation movements which had political, if not nationalist, overtones, a fact demonstrated by the limits of its authority: despite their association with the highest level of political authority, Latin scriptures or liturgy were never accepted in the Greek-using eastern Mediterranean. One can compare the nation-building motive of King Alfred's support of Anglo-Saxon translations from Latin in ninth-century Wessex (Montgomery 2000), or indeed all the multifarious translations of the Bible which were undertaken in reformed Protestant Europe from the fifteenth to the nineteenth centuries. Beyond the decoding motive (not crucial, since there were plenty of Latin-trained clergy around to explain the text) there was also a pronounced need to naturalize the roots of authority in this cardinal text of Christianity. Just as the Church of Rome had wanted to demonstrate its independence of Hebrew and Greek holy writ, so the emerging nations of Europe needed

clothed rustic Latium in the arts". See Ostler (2007), Chap. 5, and Chap. 13, for the much later effects.

to show that their religion too was autonomous, and available to all directly in their mother-tongue.

At a supranational level, something of the same motive can be seen in the activities of Europe's translating scholars of the twelfth century, who worked from Arabic and Greek. This was the time of the Crusades, and there was no sympathy, let alone deference, for the Muslim and Orthodox worlds, where these languages were current. The sources the scholars used evidently contained knowledge hitherto unknown to them, but once translated this became an asset of the Latin-using world, available to be integrated into the world-view of Catholic Christendom, without further reference to its political and spiritual rivals to the south and east.

These twelfth-century translators were like the first-millennium translators of Buddhist texts in that they needed to use teams centred on bilingual interpreters. However, three centuries later, when the Reformation was causing a festival of Bible translation across Europe, the situation was very different. Translation had effectively been theorized, if not yet mechanized. Since the era of Antonio de Nebrija's grammar and dictionary of Spanish in the late fifteenth century, it had become clear that every language, ancient or modern, living or dead, could be given a grammar, with explicit rules. The implementation of this has been called by Sylvain Auroux the *grammatisation* of Europe, and it was fundamental step in conceiving languages as distinct entities which could represent their respective nations. Furthermore, those literate in one language could be made literate in another by learning its rules, and the meanings of its words as recorded in a bilingual dictionary (Auroux 1994; Ostler 2007: 256–259). This mechanized approach to language learning was something new.

It led, almost immediately, to a change in practice in the production of translations. Nebrija had presented his grammar to Queen Isabel in 1492, with the eerie prediction that the Spanish empire and language would conquer new realms as yet unknown. Just thirty years later, when these realms had duly been discovered, Spanish monks began to work with the languages of the Americas. The traditional practice would have been to wait, and at last to find naturally-raised bilinguals; but now for the first time, the monks did linguistic fieldwork and compiled their own grammars and dictionaries of the American languages. Then they wrote their own (encoding) translations of Christian liturgies directly in languages that they had just, artificially, learnt. General linguistics was now being applied to decode unknown languages, and then re-applied to encode Christian literature back into them. The American languages, thereby, had literacy thrust upon them, by courtesy of the Spanish (Ostler 2007; 263–264; for the onset of bilingual dictionaries, see Boisson et al. 1991, and specifically in Europe, 284–285).

The subsequent history of language discovery and recording by various European colonial powers round the world is widespread and intricate, but essentially worked out the conceptual scheme invented by Nebrija and his monastic followers. Worldwide, any arbitrary language could be decoded, reduced to writing, and analysed into a grammar and a bilingual dictionary. Together with these analytic devices would come a set of Christian texts encoded into the language for the benefit of native speakers and foreign learners alike. That was in the heyday of missionary linguistics. This new literature, replete with foreign thoughts and perhaps mistranslations too, might then have an unintended transformative effect on the language itself.[3] Nowadays, such new grammars and dictionaries are more often accompanied by a corpus of native, or at least elicited and interpreted, texts in the language (recorded and transcribed, but decoded with an interlinear translation). Translation remains pervasive in our knowledge of alien languages, but delivered more systematically than when it was provided intuitively by bilinguals.

The babel of multilinguality in the world has always erected language barriers which have limited human contact and co-operation. And when communication is required beyond the neighbourhood group—as in widespread empires, markets or religions—the numbers of bilingual people that arise naturally have been too few to solve the problem. Rather, the problem has historically been overcome in two ways. One is the establishment of a lingua franca, a common language accessible to many. The other is to combine literacy and bilingualism to give translation, which extracts knowledge from one language and formulates it in another.

A lingua franca, since it may be the only developed language in its environment, can easily flourish alone (say, as the metropolitan language of an empire), without spreading any knowledge of—or respect for—other languages. Influential lingua-francas have tended rather to spread a sense of linguistic complacency, even intolerance of diversity.

By contrast, the use of translation, since it presupposes (or—in the case of missionary linguistics—can create) literacy in both languages, naturally connotes, and tends to create a sense of potential equality between languages.[4] This gives the hope that the vast expansion of translations (along with language literacy) in the modern world is some sort of ethical advance.

References

d'Alverny, Marie-Thérèse. 1982. Translations and translators. In *Renaissance and renewal in the twelfth century*, eds. Robert L. Benson and Giles Constable, 421–462. Cambridge: Harvard University Press.

Auroux, Sylvain. 1994. *La révolution technologique de la grammatisation*. Liège: Mardaga.

[3]David Nash comments: The 'back translation' of scripture rendered in Australian languages shows that these translations may have been mystifying to native converts; even the Aranda New Testament (1956), a translation revised by T.G.H. Strehlow who had learnt the language (now spelt 'Arrernte') from childhood, is said to have many calques, only understandable if one already knows the source; Strehlow's translation practice is discussed in Hill (2002).

[4]This conclusion may seem perverse, by its contrast with some modern studies of imperialism, e.g. Cheyfitz (1991). It is notable, however, that this work, which inveighs against the iniquities of 'translation' within the imperial enterprise, does not quote a single phrase from an indigenous language, even translated into English, and hence does not talk about real translation at all. It is about unacceptable attitudes, rather than decipherable messages; about denial of 'language', in some literary sense, rather than intercomprehension of actual languages.

Behr, Wolfgang. 2004. 'To translate' is 'to exchange' 譯者言易也—linguistic diversity and the terms for translation in ancient China. In *Mapping meanings: the field of new learning in late Qing China*, eds. Michael Lackner and Natascha Vittinghoff, 173–209. Leiden/Boston: Brill.
Boisson, Claude, Pablo Kirtchuk, and Henri Béjoint. 1991. Aux origines de la lexicographie: les premiers dictionnaires monolingues et bilingues. *International Journal of Lexicography* 4: 261–315.
Cheyfitz, Eric. 1991. *The poetics of imperialism. Translation and colonization from The Tempest to Tarzan*. London: Oxford University Press.
Fuchs, Walter. 1930. Zur technischen Organisation der Übersetzungen buddhistischer Schriften ins Chinesische. *Asia Major* 6: 84–103.
Goedicke, Hans. 1960. The title  in the Old Kingdom. *Journal of Egyptian Archaeology* 46: 60–64.
Goedicke, Hans. 1966. An additional note on ꜥꜣ 'foreigner'. *Journal of Egyptian Archaeology* 52: 172–174.
Greenfield, J.C. 1985. Aramaic in the Achaemenian empire. In *The Cambridge history of Iran*, ed. Ilya Gershevitch, Vol. 2 of *Median and Achaemenian periods*, 698–713. Cambridge: Cambridge University Press. Chap. 15.
Gutas, Dimitri. 1998. *Greek thought, Arabic culture*. New York: Routledge.
Harrison, Thomas. 1998. Herodotus' conception of foreign languages. In *Histos* 2. http://www.dur.ac.uk/Classics/histos/1998/harrison.html.
Hill, Barry. 2002. Night work for Luther. In *Broken song: T.G.H. Strehlow and aboriginal possession*. Knopf. Chap. 3.
Lieu, Samuel N.C. 1998. *Manichaeism in Central Asia and China*. Leiden: Brill.
Montgomery, Scott L. 2000. *Science in translation*. Chicago: University of Chicago.
Ostler, Nicholas. 2007. *Ad infinitum: A biography of Latin*. London: Harper Press.
Ostler, Nicholas. 2010. *The last lingua franca: English until the return of Babel*. London: Penguin.
Pollock, Sheldon. 2000. Cosmopolitan and vernacular in history. *Public Culture* 12: 591–625.
Polotsky, Hans Jacob. 1971. Aramäisch prš und das "Huzvaresch". In *Collected papers*, ed. E.Y. Kutscher, 631–643. Jerusalem: Magnes Press.

Catford Revisited

Andrew Chesterman

Abstract The article casts a critical retrospective glance over J.C. Catford's influential contribution to Translation Studies. Some of the strengths and weaknesses of tying a translation theory to a linguistic theory are discussed, together with the problems of building a deductive theory relying mainly on invented examples. Catford's evident interest in machine translation is noted, and also his incorporation of pragmatic aspects such as relevance. The distinction drawn between equivalence and correspondence is theoretically important, and his analysis of translation shifts has been highly influential on later work. His definition of translation as textual replacement rather then meaning transfer, and his language-bound concept of meaning itself, have been much debated.

J.C. Catford has had a bad press in Translation Studies. However, Lauri Carlson once told me he thought Catford was unduly neglected by contemporary translation scholars—hence my choice of topic for this volume.

Catford's (1965) classic *A Linguistic Theory of Translation* was published nearly half a century ago. Its sub-heading is "An Essay in Applied Linguistics", and it was based on a series of lectures at the Edinburgh University School of Applied Linguistics. Translation was only one of Catford's interests: he was also a phonetician and a general linguist. In standard introductions or surveys of Translation Studies, the book is indeed classified as a *linguistic* theory, and the implication is usually that it somehow belongs to ancient history, long before such major developments as Skopos Theory or the Cultural Turn. In a survey of linguistic approaches to translation, Fawcett (1997: 56) dismisses Catford's contribution as "disappointing". Munday (2001) outlines Catford's classification of shifts, but does not seem too impressed. Snell-Hornby (2006), in her own history of Translation Studies, gives Catford no more than a single sentence, which surprisingly appears to take him as a representative of generative grammar. A *Meta* review nearly twenty years after the book's publication is also disappointed in the book's lack of relevance to the normal practice of translation, and regards it as being of "historical academic interest only" (Henry 1984: 56).

A. Chesterman (✉)
Translation Studies, Department of Modern Languages, University of Helsinki, Helsinki, Finland

D. Santos et al. (eds.), *Shall We Play the Festschrift Game?*,
DOI 10.1007/978-3-642-30773-7_4, © Springer-Verlag Berlin Heidelberg 2012

Are these dismissive reactions justified? Perhaps we can now see more in Catford than meets the eye? What kind of conversation might one have with him today, in the light of how translation theory has developed over the past decades?

1 The Nature of the Theory

Catford establishes his theory of translation within a specific general theory of linguistics: an early version of Halliday's systemic grammar (set out e.g. in Halliday 1961), itself much influenced by Firth. Halliday's framework is taken mostly as given, with only a few minor modifications. The advantage of this is that Catford's translation theory is firmly anchored in a more general theoretical context, and is largely consistent. Catford assumes that a theory of translation has to do with a kind of relation between *languages*, and is consequently a branch of Comparative Linguistics. This warns us that much of his theory may turn out to be more relevant to Contrastive Analysis than to translation in the normal sense of the word. Relations between languages, however, are said to be not always symmetrical (20): this is of course true of translation, but would not apply to non-directional (e.g. semantically based) Contrastive Analysis. We should recall, too, the linguistic context of the 1960s, and the attempts at that time to be more "objective" about language and meaning.

Logically enough, the presentation starts with a definition of translation, and then outlines a typology. Catford's definition, which has become famous, is: "Translation [is] the replacement of textual material in one language (SL) by equivalent textual material in another language (TL)" (20). At this point, he picks out two of this definition's central terms for comment: 'textual material' and 'equivalent'. (Curiously, he does not take up the term 'replacement' here, which will be crucial to him.) Defending his use of 'textual material' (rather than 'text'), he says that this term "underlines the fact that in normal terms it is not the entirety of a SL text which is translated, that is, replaced by TL *equivalents*" (20, emphasis original). This is because normally there is no replacement of SL graphology by equivalent TL graphology.

This argument, which surfaces at several points, raises a problem. It is only because the underlying linguistic theory sets up graphological (and phonological) levels alongside those of grammar and lexis, that Catford has to say that normally "it is not the entirety of a SL text which is translated". This claim is not justified by reasons internal to translation practice, and thus seems to introduce unnecessary distance between the theory and its object. Catford's point here also illustrates his top-down method of arguing, deductive rather than inductive. This is shown most strikingly in his initial typology of translation, which immediately follows his definition.

On the one hand, one would like to applaud Catford for setting up a typology that is explicitly justified by the underlying theory with its categories of levels and ranks. On the other hand his proposed typology seem curiously artificial when set against translation practice, as critics have pointed out. His main categories are: full vs partial, and total vs restricted. The first distinction relates to the extent of the translation: for Catford a 'text' can be anything from a morpheme to a complete library, apparently (21); so you can either translate all or some of a text, perhaps leaving some items untranslated. The second distinction relates to the linguistic levels involved. 'Total' translation means replacing all the levels (grammar, lexis, phonology, graphology); but replacements of these latter two levels are not "equivalent". Restricted translation then relates to only one level, for example phonological translation. Further distinctions concern translation at different ranks (clause, group etc.).

As far as I know, the concepts and terms of this typology have not been adopted in later work in the field of Translation Studies. They have not been seen to be pragmatically useful, and in this respect Catford's theory has failed to "catch on". Scholars may also have been less than convinced by Catford's assumption that there is an important distinction to be made between (a) replacing SL textual material with *equivalent* TL material, and (b) replacing it with *non-equivalent* material. The first is the definition of translation itself, and the second is part of the definition of "total" translation (since the replacing graphology and phonology are not normally "equivalent"). It appears from this typology that Catford's translation theory sets out to be so general that the normal everyday world of actual translation is only represented in one small corner of the object to be described. "Total translation" is "what is most usually meant by 'translation'" (22), but it is given rather less space in Catford's presentation than his other types and subtypes. "Lexical" and "grammatical translation" would nowadays be treated as kinds of code-switching.

2 Equivalence and Correspondence

In distinguishing between empirically observed textual equivalence and formal correspondence, Catford makes an important point that has been reflected in much later work. A textual equivalent, he says (27), is "any TL text or portion of text which is observed on a particular occasion [...] to be the equivalent of a given SL text or portion of text". This formulation may remind later scholars of Toury's (1995) argument that a translation is any TL text that is accepted as conforming to TL norms about what a translation is supposed to be. Toury's argument has been criticized as circular, but his point was that any definition of translation is culture-bound. For Catford, what is or is not equivalent is bound to the view of an observer. This observer is a "competent bilingual or translator" (27). So a text is equivalent if a competent translator says it is: this is precisely the argument proposed by Pym (2004) several decades years later. Equivalence is *produced* by translators, and then implicitly claimed by them, a claim that is (or is not) then accepted by the client and later readers. Catford appears to regard this claim as being dependent on the subjective opinion of a competent translator, rather than on the shared opinion of a community, or on norms; and this ultimately makes his approach more subjective than he may have realized. A single translator appears to be enough. Commutation can also be used to establish what is equivalent: change something in the source, and see what changes in the translation as a result. (Recall Toury's "replacing" and "replaced" segments!) But these changes are also made by the competent bilingual translators, of course (among whom the scholar may include himself, as Catford implicitly does with the examples he cites).

There are, of course, problems here. One is Catford's apparent assumption that these competent translators will agree on what is or is not equivalent, together with the implied assumption that there is, in a given context, just one equivalent. As we know, such agreement is a matter of degree; this means that judgements about equivalence must also be matters of degree, depending on who is judging, on the context, the purpose of the assessment, and so on. Catford appears here to be relying on something like Chomsky's infamous community of homogeneous native speakers. An associated problem is how to decide who is, or is not, a competent bilingual or translator in the first place, as if this were a clear-cut category.—All in all, it seems that Catford is pitching his argument more at an abstract, philosophical level than an empirical one here.

Statements about specific textual equivalents can be formulated in terms of unconditioned, and then conditioned, equivalence probabilities, which in turn lead to the possibility of translation rules or "algorithms" (31). In this way, Catford looks explicitly in the direction of machine translation.

The importance given to formal correspondence underlines the relevance of Catford's theory for Contrastive Analysis. Formal correspondence can only be relative, to be sure. However, it also relies on textual equivalence, since otherwise there would appear to be no motivation to want to state a formal correspondence between two text segments in the first place (32), unless the research context is one of language typology. There thus remains a tension in Catford's theory between a translational view (based on equivalence) and a contrastive view. The contrastive view is reinforced by the focus on relations between *languages* (or *systems*, such as those of prepositions or articles). Catford is indeed concerned with langue rather than parole, but this tension is also visible in the way he occasionally frames his analysis in terms of utterances (e.g. 37, 39) and even speech acts (e.g. 52). (Austin's (1962) *How to Do Things with Words* had appeared a few years earlier.)

In hindsight, one can see that Catford's formal correspondence, when applied to texts rather than languages, lives on in Translation Studies as a version of Nida's formal equivalence. It also provides a theoretical justification for what is perhaps the most frequently cited part of Catford's approach, his analysis of translation shifts, defined as "departures from formal correspondence" (73). But there is very little in Catford that would match the notion of dynamic equivalence. There is a chapter on language varieties in translation, which makes use of early Hallidayan categories of register etc. However, explicit mentions of the notion of function are rare, although context, situation and culture are recognized to be important.

3 Assumptions About Meaning

Catford's assumption that meaning is language-specific, and thus cannot be "transferred" from one language to another, derives from his adoption of Firth's anti-mentalist theory of language and meaning (see e.g. Firth 1957). Meaning is understood as "the total network of relations entered into by any linguistic form" (35), a view that is simply taken for granted, not argued for. No account of taken of any alternative view, for instance of the notion that meanings are universal and objectively "there", or that meanings are not language-specific but speaker- and/or hearer-specific, or situation-specific. Or that some meanings might be more language-specific than others (although this is perhaps implied by some of the points made later about translatability).

This assumption means that Catford must disregard not only the widespread folk understanding that translators "transfer meaning", but also the very etymology of the word "translation" itself, and that of its many cognates in other languages. However, it is easy for him to show that perfectly acceptable translations do not necessarily have absolutely the *same* meaning. (An alternative approach would have been to argue that meaning is transferred, but not entirely—that translation is largely a matter of metonymy, not metaphor, as argued later e.g. by Tymoczko (1999: 54–55, 279).) But Catford is tied to his parent theory, chooses not to challenge it and accepts the consequences. One consequence is that a new concept and term—transference—must be introduced to account for cases that we might now call the strategy of translating by using a loanword (as when an English translation of a Finnish text contains the word 'sauna'). True, the English item probably does not carry quite the same contextual meaning as the Finnish, so Catford can maintain his claim that meaning is not transferred. But against this one could argue, from the viewpoint of a different theory of meaning, that *some* meaning has been transferred. Meaning, for Catford, often seems to be a black-and-white affair.

In translation, says Catford, conditions of translation equivalence are met if the target text expresses the *relevant* features of "situational substance" that are expressed by the source. This condition of relevance comes as a vital additional requirement to his first statement, which only stipulates that the two texts must share "(at least some of) the same features of [situational] substance" (50). This inclusion of the relevance requirement is the closest Catford gets to bringing in any pragmatic dimension into his theory. "Sameness of situation" is of course problematic, and is accordingly relativized (52).

At this point we see again a disadvantage of being chained to a cover-theory. Catford proceeds to argue that, because of the status of different "substances" (phonic, graphic, situational) in the theory, and because of the way he has defined translation equivalence, there can therefore be no "translation" for instance between the phonic and the graphic, because they are different substances. So he is forced to say that when an oral utterance is replaced by a written one, say in a subtitle, it is not the case that a phonological item has been "translated" by a graphological one. The "translation" comes about only because both items are exponents of a grammatical category that in turn has a contextual meaning that relates to a shared feature of situation-substance. The conclusion follows from the premises, but is so counter-intuitive that one wonders why the premises are not questioned. One could surely do with Occam's Razor here.

In defence of Catford's reliance on a general theory of grammar, it could be argued that he is aiming more to increase the coverage of this theory itself, by showing its relevance to translation, than to develop a specific theory of translation. But I think this argument would still be susceptible to the problems touched on above, which raise doubts about the applicability of the general theory to empirical human translation.

The final chapter on the limits of translatability returns to the notion of relevance. Translatability is, of course, a cline, and the position of a given translation task on this cline will depend primarily on the extent to which linguistically relevant features of the source text are bound to the source language itself, and to which extent these features are functionally relevant, as in the case of puns. This is linguistic untranslatability. Cultural translatability, on the other hand (e.g. the strange notion of a sauna in English), is less "absolute". If one tried to translate 'sauna' into English e.g. as 'bathroom', this would give rise to curious collocations of bathrooms and birch twigs etc., which leads Catford to conclude that perhaps cultural untranslatabilites are ultimately reducible to collocational ones, and collocations are part of linguistics, so all can be covered by a grand linguistic theory. And this in turn would be good news for machine translation...

4 Use of Examples

In hindsight, one of the strangest aspects of Catford's book is his use of examples. They are taken from a wide range of languages, but almost every example is invented and given outside any context. So we have for instance "The/A woman came out of the house" in English and Russian, to show different ways of expressing definiteness—Russian uses word order (28); terms for different sibling relations in English and Burushaski (40); or an Anglo-Yiddish joke (for which he thanks his wife) to illustrate the importance of the Yiddish rise-fall tone ^, which I cite in full (54).

Judge: Did you steal a horse?
Interpreter: Hot ir gestolen a pferd?
Accused: Ikh hob gestolen a ^pferd?
Judge: What did he say?
Interpreter: He said 'I stole a horse'.

There are two exceptions. On pages 30 and 33 mention is made of a French short story and its translation, which are used as a source of data on the frequencies of different translations of French *dans* and other prepositions. This is a literary text, about 12,000 words long. No source is given. And on page 102 we are surprised to find mention of a "genuine" translation from French, one sentence long, and again from a literary work. Literary works might be assumed to have an obvious, albeit vague skopos (purpose); but none of the other examples in the book are contextualized in any way. In a book purporting to be a theory of translation, this is curious. The only translator assumed to be responsible for the other examples is Catford himself, as a linguist with a good knowledge of at least French, and evidently a scholar's familiarity with aspects of some less-known languages.

I mention this not in criticism of the theoretical ideas themselves (some of which can be criticized on other grounds, as I have indicated), but because of how this use of empirical data relates to Catford's own assumptions about what a theory is. In the Preface, he writes: "The present volume [is primarily concerned] with the analysis of what translation *is*. It proposes general categories to which we can assign our observations of particular instances of translation, and it shows how these categories relate to one another" (vii, emphasis original). That is, the aim is a descriptive theory, consisting of general categories that are related in ways that are motivated by the theory. The categories are thus theory-driven, they are ready boxes into which our various empirical observations can be placed; but they do not derive initially from the empirical observations themselves. Re-reading the book, the categories occasionally remind me of a Procrustean bed, to the dimensions of which all data must be persuaded to fit. If one then mostly invents one's own data, this task is easier. The examples selected become illustrations of the possibility of a given category, but no more than that. They do not substantiate claims that a given category is well-motivated, or prototypical, or notably more significant than some other category.

5 What Do We Conclude?

One of the striking features of Catford's theory is its degree of consistency, despite the occasional tension between translational and contrastive approaches. Given a particular underlying linguistic theory, the translation theory is logically derived from it, step by step. I was reminded of the similarly top-down approach taken by Skopos Theory (e.g. in Reiß and Vermeer 1984), starting with a series of axioms and deriving more detailed statements from them, although Skopos Theory wavers between descriptive and prescriptive attitudes. Catford is more consistent, keeping to a descriptive line throughout. He has a liking for taxonomies, and is prepared to follow the logic of his categorizations even if they lead him some distance from the primary contours of the actual object of research. Catford is indeed outlining a general theory of translation, one that will cover all types of translation; but throughout the book there is an emphasis on subtypes such as graphological and phonological translations and transliterations which are certainly not central to ordinary practice, and have been virtually neglected by subsequent work in the field.

There is no attempt to be prescriptive. But there is no attempt at explanation, either, which makes the theory somewhat superficial. No extra-theoretical motivation of categories is given, for instance. No testable generalizations are proposed, no hypotheses generated.

The reliance on a particular linguistic theory, and moreover on a particular (early) stage of that theory, is problematic. As the linguistic theory develops, the translation theory becomes dated. In Halliday's later versions of systemic grammar, for instance, the lexical and grammatical levels merge into lexicogrammar (see e.g. Halliday 1985 and later works), but this is obviously not reflected in changes in Catford's translation theory. Other ways of analysing language varieties are similarly left out of consideration, as are later developments that give more weight to pragmatic considerations (such as communicative functions). In this latter respect too, Catford's theory is a child of the 1960s. More generally, we see the risk of setting up any translation theory that is not independent and autonomous, based on its own concepts and terms. (There are of course valid reasons for seeking to embed a theory of translation in a more general theory of language, or of communication, as suggested also by Gutt (1990). But that would be a separate topic of discussion.)

In hindsight, again, it seems clear that Catford had one eye on developments in machine translation and the future of computers. His notion of conditioned translation rules have the general form "X is translated as Y, under conditions ABC, with probability P" (my summary of Catford's argument on pp. 30–31). Early machine translation programs operated on just such rules. Translation scholars today may also be reminded of the form of Toury's (1995) "laws" of translation (not concerning the translation of given source-text items, but aiming to capture more general characteristics of the translation process). Toury's laws of interference and increased standardization are similarly conditioned, and similarly probabilistic.

Catford's final comment on cultural untranslatability—that if this can ultimately be described in terms of *linguistic* untranslatability, this would give translation theory more power and also broaden the horizon of machine translation—might even be seen as one of the seeds of the contemporary attempts to set up a semantic web.

His legacy surely includes other seeds too, and not only the shifts idea. Despite his 1960s linguistic framework, he does see the importance of relevance, situation and context; the distinction between formal correspondence and textual equivalence is fundamental (although not exclusive to him), as is the contextualizing of the notion of equivalence itself. While his non-use of empirical translation data leaves him open to criticism, the theory he presents has a high degree of internal consistency, which is both a strength and a limitation. We are reminded how difficult it is to build a theory that is not only internally consistent but also open to refinement (or indeed rejection) as it is tested against evidence; one that allows the generation of new ideas and hypotheses; and one that seeks not just to describe but also to explain.

In my view, then, Catford is still an important source of ideas and insights, and well worth re-reading, albeit with a critical eye. I certainly count him among those who have influenced my own thinking about translation.

References

Austin, J.L. 1962. *How to do things with words*. Oxford: Clarendon Press.
Catford, J.C. 1965. *A linguistic theory of translation*. Oxford: Oxford University Press.

Fawcett, Peter. 1997. *Translation and language*. Manchester: St. Jerome.
Firth, J.R. 1957. *Papers in linguistics 1934–1951*. London: Oxford University Press.
Gutt, Ernst-August. 1990. A theoretical account of translation—without a translation theory. *Target* 2: 135–164.
Halliday, M.A.K. 1961. Categories of the theory of grammar. *Word* 17: 241–292.
Halliday, M.A.K. 1985. *An introduction to functional grammar*. London: Arnold.
Henry, Ronald. 1984. Points of inquiry into total translation. A review of J.C. Catford's *A Linguistic Theory of Translation*. *Meta* 29: 152–158.
Munday, Jeremy. 2001. *Introducing translation studies*. London: Routledge.
Pym, Anthony. 2004. *The moving text*. Amsterdam: Benjamins.
Reiß, Katharina, and Hans J. Vermeer. 1984. *Grundlegung einer Allgemeinen Translationstheorie*. Tübingen: Niemeyer.
Snell-Hornby, Mary. 2006. *The turns of translation studies*. Amsterdam: Benjamins.
Toury, Gideon. 1995. *Descriptive translation studies and beyond*. Amsterdam: Benjamins.
Tymoczko, Maria. 1999. *Translation in a postcolonial context*. Manchester: St. Jerome.

The Next Step for the Translation Network

Diana Santos

Abstract This paper offers a new introduction to the translation network model, a tool conceived to describe human translation in a linguistically adequate way in the field of tense and aspect. After describing the main tenets of the model and discussing its original properties in the light of translation studies, I acknowledge its lack of empirical validation so far. Therefore I turn to a quantitative presentation of the large amounts of syntactically annotated Portuguese corpora publically available at Linguateca in terms of tense and aspect operators, discussing their content and some annotation options (from the underlying PALAVRAS parser developed by Eckhard Bick). A research program for a corpus-based description of Portuguese tense and aspect phenomena is then put forward, with illustration of several different statistical techniques to explore the material, motivating it as the next step to validate the concrete English–Portuguese and Portuguese–English translation networks suggested in my doctoral dissertation of 1996.

1 Presentation

This chapter is a step in transforming the concept of the translation network (TN), the main contribution of my PhD thesis supervised and inspired by Lauri Carlson, into an empirically verifiable tool for the modelling and study of translation of tense and aspect.

After briefly reviewing the main tenets of the model, already described elsewhere (Santos 1996a, 2000) and abundantly illustrated with examples, see for instance Santos (2012), this text will discuss, and try to partially answer, how the automatic analysis of large amounts of text can provide algorithms to populate the monolingual (Portuguese) side of the translation network.

My question is whether the TN model can be empirically grounded and not only defended on intuitive or rational grounds. This question was forcefully voiced by Lauri Carlson at my PhD defence fifteen years ago, and is in fact something funda-

D. Santos (✉)
University of Oslo, Oslo, Norway
e-mail: d.s.m.santos@ilos.uio.no

D. Santos et al. (eds.), *Shall We Play the Festschrift Game?*,
DOI 10.1007/978-3-642-30773-7_5, © Springer-Verlag Berlin Heidelberg 2012

mental to any linguistic argument: can the translation/aspectual network be used by others to talk about Portuguese grammar? Are the categories there something that can be shared and therefore talked about by others discussing Portuguese grammar, or will the categorization always remain a subjective one in my head, no matter how right?

Since finishing my PhD I have been mostly concerned with making data and programs available to other people who wanted to study and work with Portuguese (monolingually or contrastively) through the Linguateca project (Santos 2009); therefore, the amounts of data I will discuss here have been made public to that community. So I will also describe what is available so that readers can check and counter-react about the classes proposed, as such an approach is the ethically and methodologically right way to proceed in arguing about knowledge.

Before proceeding, I should however state clearly that the purpose of the TN is to describe human translation, and to use human translation as semantic data to make sense of the language pair in question. The TN is not a model or a system for machine translation; rather, it arose from my realisation that a lot would have to be learned about human translation before trying to mimic it.

2 The Translation Network in a Nutshell

The translation network was inspired by Moens's aspectual network (Moens 1987; Moens and Steedman 1988), which I appropriated (and changed) as the best computational model of aspect in language, because it has the following characteristics:

- It uses linguistically motivated categories.
- It makes possible dynamic change in the interpretation process, through coercion.[1]
- It allows unmarkedness (vagueness) to be described—with arrows/transitions which do not have an overt (linguistic) marking.

Then I added another layer, in the sense that two aspectual networks, one for each language, are connected by the translation process itself. It is this juxtaposition, or alignment, of the two texts and the two languages that I attempted to describe with the TN model (see Fig. 1).

This model, thus, presupposes a particular linguistic description of each language, and it encodes their differences and their contact points, and how translators use them, or are misled by them, in their work.

The TN is ultimately motivated and informed (or should be) by the translations themselves. Now, and contrary to linguistic markers that can appear or not in the texts and which can be studied and objectively agreed upon when modelling a particular text (see Fig. 2 for an example), translations carry no explicit marks.

[1] Coercion is how the context forces another interpretation.

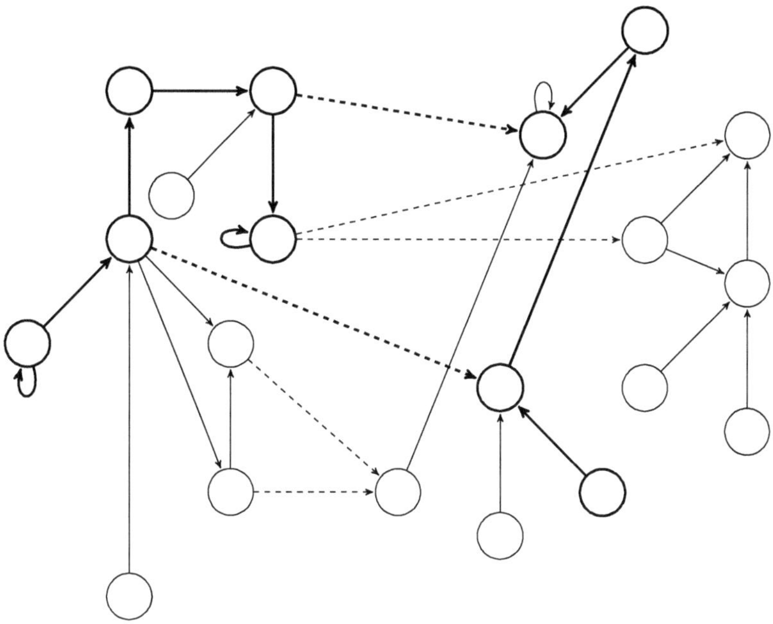

Fig. 1 The translation network model as a model of translation in general, and as a descriptive apparatus to model actual translations

This makes translation arrows harder to empirically ground. The only objective data is quantitative data on the frequency with which similar translations occur, and a more or less intersubjective consensus by translation analysts—even though interpretation can be significantly aided and substantiated by bilingual dictionaries and translation aids (such as the specification of the translation of set phrases).

So, to be able to justify and empirically ground a particular TN model (or two, one in each direction), one has to:

- first, produce some evidence for the monolingual models;
- and then, use the translations to come up with translation arcs which can be argued to have been followed—and which, furthermore, will distort/recreate each language model due to the interference of the translation process.

It has already been beautifully argued by Toury and the Israeli school that the fact of translation changes the target language (Toury 1995; Even-Zohar 1990). The more translations a language includes, the more vitality it shows. And translation contributes to turn foreign, "other", peripheral styles, genres, and even linguistic features, into central ones, especially if they come from a privileged culture or have a mass impact. In other words, it is highly agreed upon nowadays that the translation process changes the literary norms of the target culture, reinforcing features that happen to translate frequent and/or prominent source-language characteristics. So, by allowing the description of source-language influence, the translation network complies with what has long been accepted in translation studies.

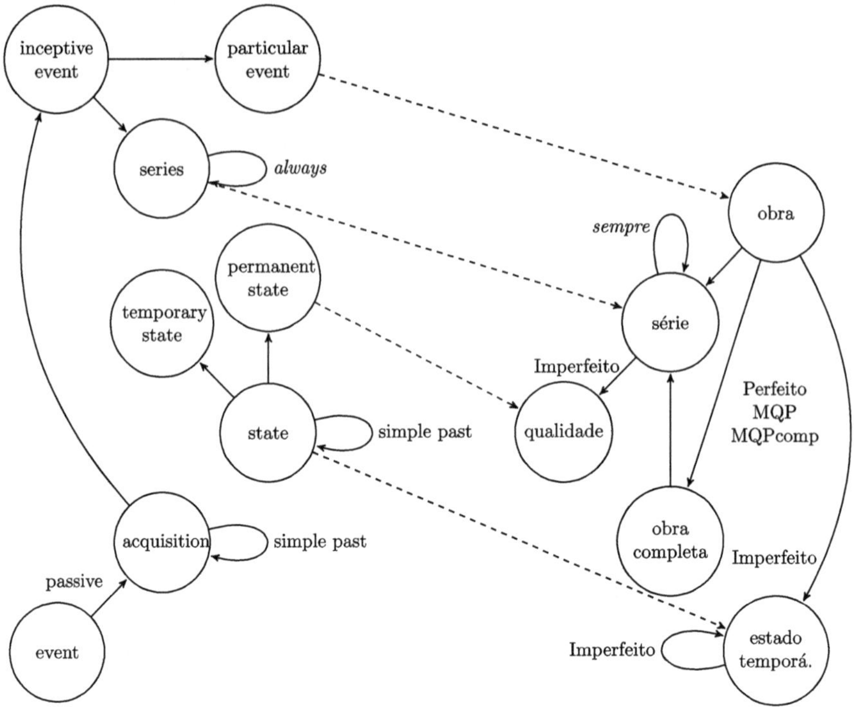

Fig. 2 An example of a TN subset in the English-Portuguese translation direction

Additionally, the translation network model is of interest because it allows a non-objective influence of the source language: the model tries to describe (target-language-native) translators seeing the source language with target eyes. I contend that translators project their linguistic substrate into their interpretation of the source language, seeing things that may not be there and equally often failing to see other things.[2] So, also the *source* language network is affected in the translation network model, no matter how nonsensical this influence may appear at first sight.

The translation network is thus not an objective, contact-independent, description of two languages; rather, it represents one view of both language systems due to their reciprocal influence. Translators may observe or project things that are not there or are not that important, because of the translation task (or context).

[2]Andrew Chesterman pointed out that translators are not necessarily target language native speakers, and this remark of course holds only for them. Still, the opposite phenomenon probably occurs when one is translating from one's mother tongue: one projects into the other language shades and implications which are not necessarily there for a native reader. In any case, and given that my studies so far have concentrated on the first situation, it would be interesting to investigate whether different translation networks are necessary to describe the practices of these two kinds of translators.

This said, I am not at all advocating that grammatical or textual markings in the source text be ignored when doing or analysing translation. One can play them down or misinterpret them, but not ignore them altogether, so, no matter my previous philosophical claims, one must first describe the source language grammar organization in a monolingual context, and only then investigate the distortions, or extensions, that can be observed in the translation into (or from) a particular language.

So, with the ultimate goal of describing human translation, I will therefore begin by studying the broad patterns of a particular language, sketching the method in what follows.

3 Language Categories

One of the building blocks of an aspectual network is the notion of categories, aspectual categories, which I take to be a fundamental part of the language fabric, and not, as Moens argued and conceived, decomposable in a set of language-independent semantic features.[3]

I take this to be one of the most important ways (if not the most important) in which languages diverge and can be described as having a particular "spirit". These categories, and their constant drift and change, explain malleability, language variation, and language evolution. (Language evolution can, by the way, also be brought about by extensive translation into a language.)

Such is my understanding of the value of Vendler's (1967) classification of verbs (or sentences) in accomplishments, achievements, activities or states, and one of the few points about which I disagree with Lauri Carlson and the multitude of scholars who have over the years dissected and further analysed Vendler's categories as general and language-independent (Carlson 1981). In my view, aspectual categories are the basic ingredients a particular natural language is made of, and it is precisely their understanding that allows us to probe the metaphysical and metaphorical properties of each language—and, last but not least, its grammatical properties as well.

I therefore claimed in my thesis that Vendler's categories for English were for English alone. Therefore, for other languages, one should use other categories, discovered using a similar methodology, and not *a priori* expect the same categories in different languages. This last point should be tested through contrastive data, in the form of translations—which I have claimed repeatedly to be the least biased, and thus best, kind of semantic data available (see Santos 1995, 2004, 2012).

Returning to categorization, let me invoke Ellis (1993), who considers it the single most important property of thought and language, and argues that linguistic categories do not differ from other categories in the way they join possibly overlapping (or at least non-exclusive) aspects.

[3]Namely, a nucleus with a preparatory phase, a culmination phase, and a resulting state.

Since grammar data concern lexical and grammatical means, the empirical analysis of these markers and constructions should allow us to identify which distinctions and classes are there. In other words, a language's fabric is defined and characterized by the patterns of co-occurrence and repulsion of different markers, and studying these markers will allow the linguist to discover or confirm linguistic classes.

This study is what I intend to do in the domain of tense and aspect, armed now with an array of parsed data.[4] At the time of my PhD studies, such amounts of data were nowhere to be found, and I had to manually annotate a small corpus, whose size anyway was possibly near the upper limit a single person could analyse in the corresponding time frame. Nevertheless, this corpus allowed me to come up with Portuguese classes based on translation descriptive studies (in my defence, I suspect that Vendler used far less data to arrive at his categories for English).

But now, with much more data, I hope that the study of the distribution of grammatical markers such as tenses and aspectualisers will allow us to find (or confirm) the proposed semantic classes. However, the material is so large that we are actually forced to use statistical methods to handle it.

In any case, such statistical validation of aspectual classes has not, as far as I know, been done for Portuguese, and such an attempt will either show them to be a sound basis for grammatical description, or suggest better replacements.

4 The Data

At Linguateca we have amassed a large number of resources for the computational processing of Portuguese. I will be using the annotated corpora of the AC/DC project, comprising over 275 million running words. For a more detailed description of sources, genres, varieties and dates, see Santos (2011).

Table 1 provides a rough quantitative description of the tenses in the material, and the number of different verbs and clauses at my (and everyone's) disposition at this time. It should, however, be noted that even for such in principle well-known categories as "main verbs" or "tensed auxiliaries", no fool proof definition exists, and after several attempts to correct or change the counts I decided to leave them as the theory underlying PALAVRAS has it, since this is not the place to discuss such matters.[5] But cases where different theories may assign different labels are precisely in verb complexes such as *deixar de comer* ('stop eating'), *desatar a comer* ('start eating'), *deixar comer* ('allow eating') or *conseguir fazer* ('manage to do'), that can be considered as one clause and one main verb, or as two clauses with two main verbs (which is incidentally PALAVRAS's choice for the last three, but not for the first).

[4]Parsed with Eckhard Bick's parser, PALAVRAS (Bick 2000), and made available through Linguateca.

[5]For the record, here are the queries issued: `[pos="V.*"]`, `[func="[IF]MV.*"]`, `[func="FMV.*"]`, `[func="[IF]AUX.*"]`, and `[func="FAUX.*"]`.

Table 1 Quantitative view of the AC/DC corpora, excluding Floresta (on January 2012)

Category	No. of cases
Verbs	35,976,890
Main verbs	29,456,915[a]
Tensed main	18,149,195
Auxiliaries	4,546,453
Tensed auxiliaries	3,644,360

[a]Main verbs plus auxiliaries do not add up to verbs because of the vexingly complex case of past participles used adjectively, which are assigned different labels

I selected, based on the original translation network, a set of linguistic properties relatively easy to ascertain automatically for each verb (and for the set of all verbs), namely:

- how often the verb occurs in the progressive
- how often the verb occurs in a particular tense
- how often the verb occurs in the passive (and more fine-grained, with the *ser*, the *estar*, and the *ficar* passive auxiliaries)
- how often the verb occurs with particular aspectualisers, namely *acabar de*, *deixar de*, *parar de*, *continuar a/GER*,[6] *começar a/GER*, *ficar a/GER*, *passar a/GER*, *voltar a*, *chegar a*, *tornar a*, *andar a/GER*, *acabar por/GER*
- how often the verb occurs with temporal markers, such as *já*, *ainda*, *acabar de*.[7]

Table 2 shows some of the aggregated numbers.

Important to note is that numbers like these must be considered with care: first because they were amassed automatically, and second because there are many fine distinctions that are hardly consensual. For example, concerning the passive, the numbers here encompass a wide definition and include many cases where other interpretations are possible, like past participles working as full adjectives, as *O leite estava estragado* ('the milk was rotten') or *o Paulo ficou zangado* ('Paulo got angry'). They are counted here as passives of *estragar* ('to rot') and *zangar* ('to infuriate'), although some grammatical schools do not even consider them as passives in Portuguese.

On the other hand, reflexive passives have not been counted here as passive, because the task of deciding among the many uses of reflexive pronouns in Portuguese is just too complex to be attempted now.

So, readers are strongly advised to check the data, and the annotation documentation, to ensure they understand what the labels mean, and what their possible uncertainty (or estimated error rate) is.

---

[6]*a/GER* stands for the alternative *a* plus infinitive, usual in Portugal, or gerund, usual in Brazil.

[7]Of course, when the *same* marker is used for two different purposes, it may not be possible to automatically distinguish which is which, as is the case for the auxiliaries *acabar de* with an infinitive construction, or *ir* with a gerund.

Table 2 More detailed quantitative view per tense form, in the indicative and subjunctive moods

Tense	No. of cases	Different lemmas	No. of cases	Different lemmas
Present (simple)	10,981,989	20,304	994,701	8,935
Present Passive	526,191	4,990	56,885	2,514
Present Progressive	212,815	3,391	5,604	980
Present Passive Progressive	31,337	1696	686	317
Perfeito (simple)	6,150,224	13,418	–	–
Perfeito Passive	429,373	4,020	–	–
Perfeito Progressive	6,055	935	–	–
Perfeito Passive Progressive	582	307	–	–
Imperfeito (simple)	1,902,633	7,172	307,107	4,275
Imperfeito Passive	114,680	3,612	24,420	2,055
Imperfeito Progressive	38,743	2,225	2,764	763
Imperfeito Passive Progressive	4,740	916	183	123
PPC	155,008	2,375	46,423	1,841
PPC Passive	16,776	1,407	7,394	1,158
PPC Progressive	1,710	419	28	28
PPC Passive Progressive	368	193	1	1
Future (simple)	1,076,329	3,709	267,570[a]	3,813
Future Passive	146,263	2,835	23,614	1,697
Future Progressive	7,165	1,093	1,495	444
Future Passive Progressive	666	310	132	80
Future with *ir* or *haver*	412,025[b]	3,936	10,728	1,430
Future Perfect	46,807	1,994	2,497	610
MQP	311,047	4,913	29,800	1,685
MQP Passive	36,038	2,062	4,063	934
MQP Progressive	529	241	16	16
MQP Passive Progressive	112	91	2	2
Conditional	490,942	3,519	–	–
Conditional Passive	33,295	2,189	–	–
Conditional Progressive	4,315	881	–	–
Conditional Passive Progressive	466	241	–	–
Conditional Perfect	24,358	1,614	–	–

[a]There is a systematic ambiguity in Portuguese between future subjunctive and personal infinitive, in all regular verbs, which makes this number less reliable than the others in this table

[b]This also includes perfect cases such as *irá ter feito* ('will have done'), future in the past such as *ia fazer* ('was going to do'), and conditional future such as *iria fazer* ('would be going to do')

In any case, Table 2 presents a somewhat distorted view of the actual occurrence in the data in yet another way, since a number of combinations exist that do not

Table 3 Each marker separately

Formal marker	Absolute frequency
passive	1,862,699
present[a]	13,175,779
past	9,391,789
future[b]	1,961,244
progressive	346,406
"perfect" form[c]	454,566
indicative	23,460,718
subjunctive	1,810,167
aspectualizers[d]	439,072
já/ainda[e]	1,005,790
sempre/nunca	281,594

[a]Including in this the cases of future meaning

[b]Including all kinds of futures: morphological, with *ir*, and with *haver de*

[c]Not counting *pretérito perfeito composto (PPC)*

[d]Except for *estar*, which is separately counted under progressive

[e]These are rough counts, so these adverbs do not necessarily modify verbs or clauses

have a "traditional" name. Rather, such combinations represent important temporal-aspectual information, such as the auxiliary *ir* followed by the verb in the infinitive, which conveys (relative) future and can thus be used in all tenses. Examples are *ele irá chegar atrasado* ('he will come late'), and *ele ia cantar na ópera* ('he was going to sing at the opera').

I tried, in any case, to provide a co-occurrence view of, say, passive and progressive, which for some verbs may even correspond to the majority of cases (of these two markers), and in other cases almost totally disjointed situations.

Table 3 offers another (re)presentation of the data, closer to the aspectual network formalism, namely counting each grammatical dimension separately.

Now these cases are organized in the form shown in Fig. 3, and they are ready for exploratory methods to apply, to investigate whether we can obtain meaningful classes from clustering.

In Fig. 4, just to make clear the process, I present the individual occurrences for each verb form in context, from which the numbers of the previous figure are computed. There are almost 34 million of these, as stated in Table 1.

ser	211	10989	248248	342508	739237	282104	3204130	7931
ter	577	782	108217	212567	95165	129164	836159	3152
estar	12	80	38584	152701	44194	43168	767302	1442
fazer	10360	4056	23698	30325	105396	24066	618218	3147
dizer	971	444	12108	21984	158295	6067	421213	628
haver	57	290	25420	68716	42724	25180	375694	451
dar	3908	1280	12129	17299	56372	12394	295507	2015
ver	3149	920	11953	10958	35586	8601	254044	1569
querer	77	466	22394	28820	18644	13533	200592	292

Fig. 3 Figures for passive, progressive, subjunctive, imperfeito, perfeito, future, use as main verb, and future with *ir* for the most frequent Portuguese verbs

```
colocar colocar FMV      FUT_SUBJ         BR    0    0    0    0    0
contendo        conter   IMV      GER     BR    0    0    0    0    0
ficarão ficar   FMV      FUT_IND BR    0    0    0    0    0
presos  prender IMV      FUT_PASSIVA_COMP_IND    BR    0    0    1    0    0
serão   ser     FAUX     FUT_IND BR    0    0    0    0    0
repelidos       repelir  IMV     FUT_PASSIVA_COMP_IND    BR    0    0    1    0    0
atinge  atingir FMV      PR_IND  BR    0    0    0    0    0
exercido        exercer  IMV     PCP      BR    0    0    0    0    0
é       ser     FMV      PR_IND  BR    0    0    0    0    0
devido  dever   N<       PCP     BR    0    0    0    0    0
```

Fig. 4 Information regarding each single occurrence of a verb form, with the information provided by PALAVRAS

5 Experiments

The next step for the translation network, or rather for the Portuguese aspectual network, is to use these data with relevant statistical machinery to identify groups and correlations.

This is a long-term program. This chapter presents only the initial ideas and some preliminary attempts, which come in three forms:

- Blind clustering: what happens if we simply apply different clustering algorithms to all the overt tense and aspect markings identified?
- Hypothesis test: looking specifically at some hypothesised similarities, and seeing whether the data confirms them;
- Classification: to find out, from a small set of pre-classified items, whether a reliable classification procedure can be obtained, and whether the specific tests proposed make linguistic sense.

5.1 Blind Clustering

The task here is to see whether the data can, with minimal guidance, provide any illumination.

Exploratory factor analysis, as given in Fig. 5, succeeds in separating future markers on one side and *perfeito* (closely related to events) on other, as far as the first two factors are concerned.[8]

We input the data illustrated in Fig. 3 into several clustering algorithms, and get the results presented in Figs. 6a to 6c. If we analyse now not the grammatical features, but instead analyse the (60 most frequent) verbs themselves, they are clustered as in Fig. 7, which does not tell us very much, in fact.

The algorithms manage to put *imperfeito* and *perfeito* near, which apparently indicates that these tenses apply to the same verbs in the same way, and also place

---

[8] All results in this chapter were created with R version 2.13.0 (R Development Core Team 2010), using the package `languageR` (Baayen 2011), and libraries `lattice`, `cluster` and `ape`, see Baayen (2008) for details.

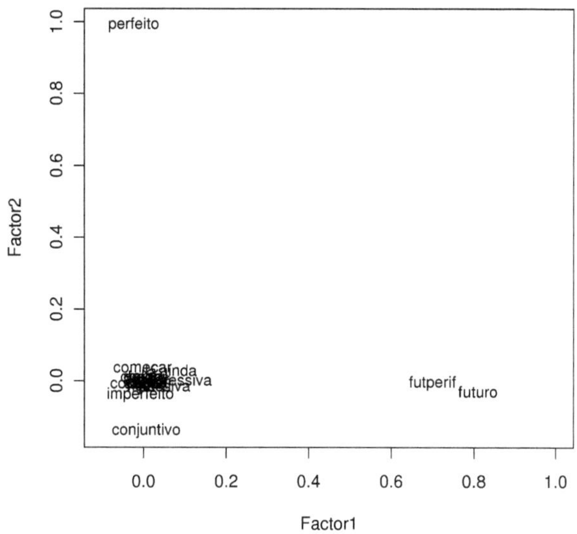

Fig. 5 The results of exploratory factor analysis

similar aspectualisers nearby. *Já* is near the progressive, which is probably the most surprising result, but may simply mean that durative situations are more predictable (and *já* is often connected with prediction in Portuguese).

5.2 Investigating Some Known Issues

In this section, I provide statistical confirmation for existing knowledge.

5.2.1 The *Imperfeito/Perfeito* Distinction in Main Verbs

Is there a clear distinction between cases that attract either *perfeito* or *imperfeito* in Portuguese? Are there verbs that hardly ever appear in one of the tenses, while others are equally at ease, that is, receive meaning from the tenses?

I concentrate on main verbs here, and use the following procedure: all verbs (with a total frequency greater than 100) that occur in the past tense in the AC/DC corpora more than ten times are divided into "perfeito verbs", "imperfeito verbs" and "even", if they respectively occur more than 60 % of the (past) times with *perfeito*, or *imperfeito*, or do not occur more than 60 % of the times with either of these two tenses.

I have thus divided the verbs into three categories, which are illustrated in Table 4, which shows the 15 top verbs in each category. (The verbs are ordered in terms of their frequency with each of the tenses, or—for the "even" ones—by the difference between these two frequencies.)

Be aware that the existence of the "even" verbs gives meaning, or raison d'être, to this grammatical distinction conveyed by tense. Had it been a simple question

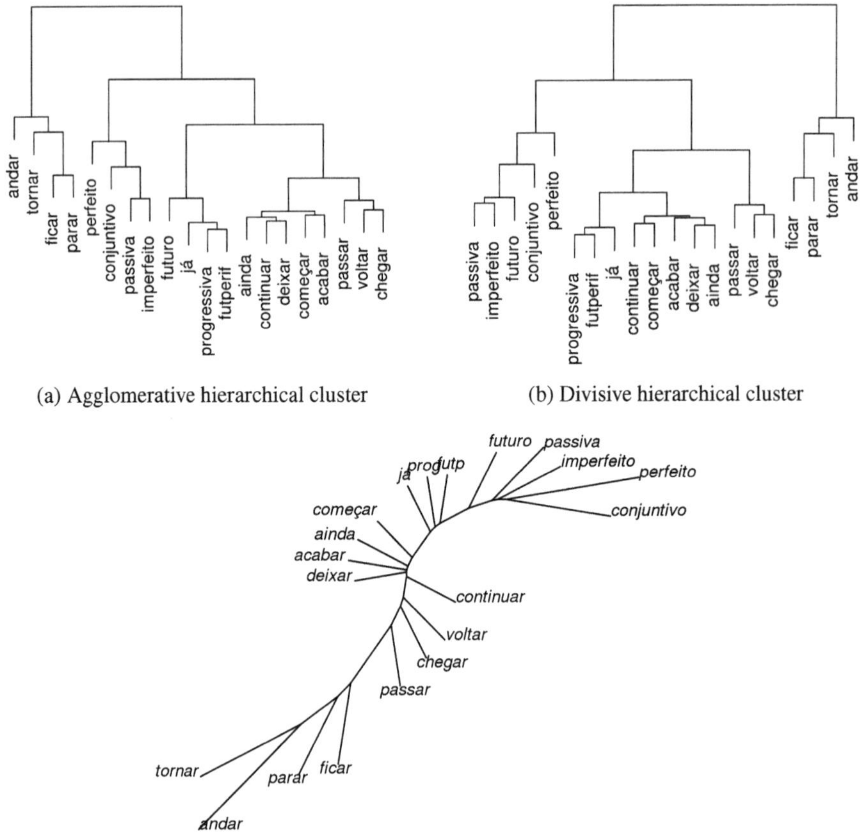

(a) Agglomerative hierarchical cluster

(b) Divisive hierarchical cluster

(c) Neighbour-joining algorithm

Fig. 6 Different clustering results with Spearman correlation

Table 4 *Imperfeito, perfeito* and "even" verbs

Imperfeito	Perfeito	Even
possuir, pressupor, aguardar, esperar, pender, ferver, supor, nutrir assemelhar, odiar, residir, pretender, repousar, prever, figurar	apurar, derrotar, fracassar, vitimar, apreender, decidir, habituar, deliberar, cancelar, lesionar, falecer, aprovar, danificar acabar, notificar	controlar, contemplar perfilar, proteger significar, rir distrair, suprir andar, abrigar armazenar, cobiçar situar, albergar

of lexical choice, and had verbs been used with either one or the other tense, there would be no need for different tenses at all.

In this way, I depart from the view of researchers such as Klavans and Chodorow (1992) who postulate (and compute) a degree of statitivity by measuring the attraction or repulsion of verbs towards some grammatical features (viz. the progressive). They associate to each verb a fuzzy indicator of its occurrence with a grammatical

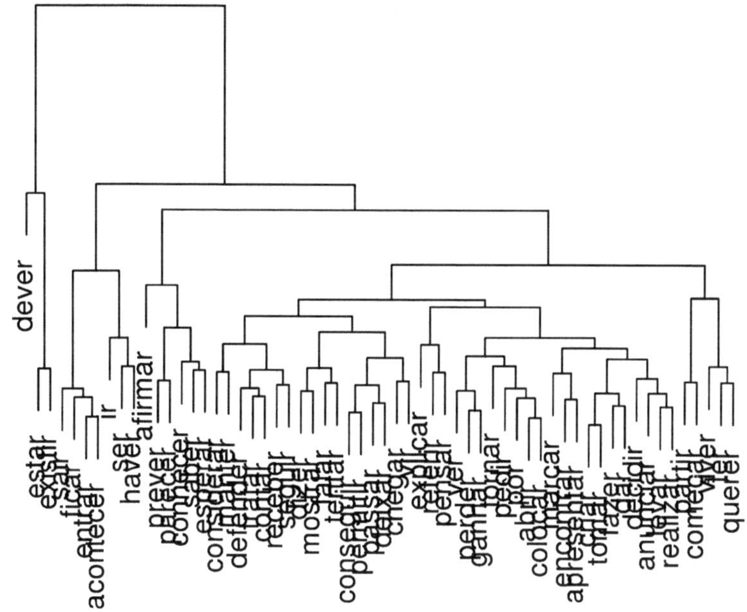

Fig. 7 Clustering the 60 most frequent verbs based on their occurrence with the grammatical features measured

operator, instead of allowing for a binary (or discrete) classification (stative or not) at the lexical level, and acknowledging the existence of several uses of progressivity. On the contrary, with the aspectual network I want to keep separate, and discrete, classes of lexical and grammatical phenomena—and use the quantitative data as (fuzzy) indicators of category status, just as done by Brent (1991).

When turning later to contrastive studies (and the translation network), the pairs involving "even" verbs should thus be selected as the ones useful to investigate when translated. Then one will look at whether translation behaviour—for a specific language pair—consistently separates the two cases (which means that the meaning difference is preserved, or recreated, in the target language), or whether the difference is lost in translation.

5.2.2 The *Presente* in Main Verbs

A similar procedure was done, this time contrasting simple *presente* with the progressive in *presente*, and the results are displayed in Table 5. This procedure is, incidentally, quite similar to that of Brent (1991), who was the first to use a parsed corpus to measure stativity in English by studying co-occurrence with the progressive and rate adverbials.

Since the *presente* form in Portuguese can also indicate future (and does, in many cases), I have attempted to separate the future meaning from the simple present

Table 5 Verbs in the present tense, with a marked preference for the simple tense, and for the progressive tense, and which have future meaning

Simple present	Progressive	Future
arruinar, referendar, pasmar, emigrar, acomodar, discriminar, desfavorecer, assolar, alojar, sobressair, distrair, saborear, batizar, endurecer, tender	investigar, projetar, brigar, planejar, processar, torcer, providenciar, estudar, namorar, preparar, ferver, finalizar, curtir, rolar, mentir	expirar, estrear, terminar, recomeçar, decorrer, pilotar, reabrir, prosseguir, arrancar, prolongar, iniciar, inaugurar, comemorar, antever, defrontar

counts. That is, the cases counted as simple *presente* do not include those with an overt future adverb or adverbial phrase.[9] In any case, since this counting was done automatically, there may be considerable noise in both counts.

Of course, important to note is that progressive versus simple tenses is quite a different kind of opposition than *imperfeito/perfeito*, which is equipollent. Progressive is marked and therefore the numbers are skewed; see, for example, Halliday's (2005) remarks on quantitative distinctions in language.

5.2.3 Is There Any Significant Correlation Between the Two Groups?

First, we can check whether the two groups point in the same direction, that is, we want to assess whether there is any significant correlation between use in the simple *presente* and in the simple *imperfeito*, as I have always assumed (and claimed), when we look at actual language use.

Figure 8 seems to indicate so.

But is this correlation convertible into discrete group assignment (in this case, aspectual classes)? That is, if I create a group label for "verbs that occur mostly in *imperfeito* when in the past tense" and another for "verbs that frequently occur in *presente* (not meaning future)", would these groups contain roughly the same verbs?

Unexpectedly, not at all: From the 1,762 different verbs occurring more than 1,000 times in the material, I selected the 62 for which occurrences in simple present corresponded to 60 % or more, and the 58 where Imperfeito was used in more than 70 % of the past cases. Only eight verbs were in both sets.

This finding raises two issues: First, is this procedure methodologically sound? Baayen argues against "the unfortunate practice in psycholinguistics of dichotomizing continuous variables" (Baayen 2008: 237), "reducing an information-rich continuous variable into an information-poor two-level factor". So this conversion to discrete classes should be rejected by statistical practice.

On the other hand, no evidence exists that *one* grammatical feature should be enough to single out classes. On the contrary, the network shows that it is a set of different properties that allows one to classify a verb as belonging to a special

[9] Such as *amanhã* ('tomorrow'), *no próximo dia 11* ('next 11'), *na próxima semana* ('next week'), *num futuro próximo* ('in the near future'), or *daqui a dois meses* ('in two months' time').

Fig. 8 Correlation between simple *presente* and *imperfeito*

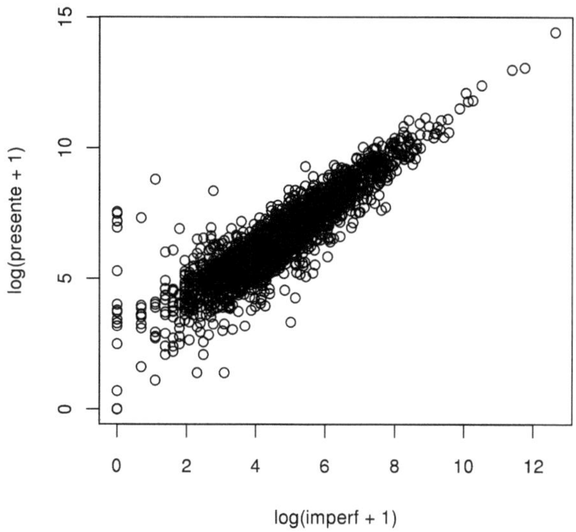

semantic class. So the co-occurrence of two features (in this case, frequency with *imperfeito* and frequency with simple *presente*) is a long way from being able to select elements of a particular class, especially because tenses are obligatory in tensed clauses, and because they have a different import, that of temporal order, as well. If we joined other clues, and instead of intersection we aimed for union, we might be closer to the goal of automatically populating our classes.

I have also tried out the majority cases of *perfeito* and future uses of *presente* as well (both possible indicators of Mudança), but again, of the 201 verbs that had *perfeito* in 95 % of the cases in the past and of the 161 verbs which display more than 20 cases of *presente* meaning future, only 15 verbs were common.

So, this lack of agreement seems to show that trying to find correlations between two single features will not give us very much—also because, given the diverse meanings of the features themselves, we cannot expect them to be indicators of a single class. Also, it is well-established that not only the verb should be classified as to aspectual class; in fact, the verb arguments have a say, as do other elements such as sentential quantifiers. To expect the verb tense alone to illuminate the verb is too big a simplification; in fact, we should be separating the verb occurrences also according to the kind of arguments.

5.3 Can We Get a Reliable Classifier?

A third way to proceed is to investigate the use of the classes I postulated in my dissertation (Santos 1996a) as seeds for a classification process.

Using my own lists and rules to choose a set of relatively clear-cut frequent members of each aspectual class, I classified them, and proceeded to investigate the implementation of a classifier based in the features automatically computed.

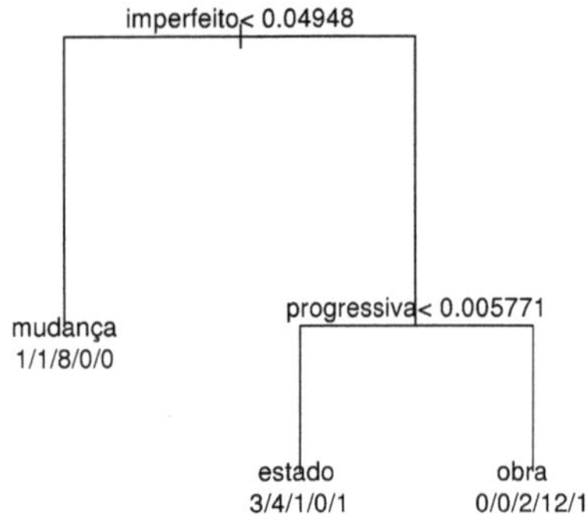

Fig. 9 The classifier obtained using the 36 examples mentioned

Good exemplars of each class—from my perusal of the microcorpus used in my dissertation and from the papers arguing for the classification (Santos 1991, 1993, 1996b)—are presented below:

Obras	pôr a mesa, contar, cumprimentar, trabalhar, aquecer, correr, escrever um livro, rebolar, esconder, cantar o hino nacional, lavar o carro, passar[10]
Mudanças	cair, entrar, ir a Londres, ir ao cinema, chegar, abrir a janela, adormecer, partir, fechar, ficar, crescer, arrefecer[11]
Aquisições	lembrar, chegar a, conhecer, rodear, saber[12]
Propriedades	ser ADJ, ser N, rimar, assemelhar-se, gostar[13]
Estados	estar, ver-se, encontrar-se, ter[14]
Séries	andar

Since this was a purely lexical classification, I had to remove Séries, which were almost always grammatically marked, and also could not take into account the arguments to the verbs, therefore adding some noise. Also, vague classes like Aquisições (vague between states and events) may confuse the issue, but I left them in the input list.

I thus used these cases to produce a classifier to distinguish between them based on the grammatical features available. The solution obtained with the verbs above, with the `rpart` library, was quite boringly predictable, as Fig. 9 shows. (Basically, very few occurrences with *imperfeito* decides on Mudanças, and very few occurrences with *progressiva* decides on Estados; otherwise, we get Obras.)

The resulting classifier makes me conclude that such a small set of verbs is not large enough to create a useful classifier. Going through a larger number of clear

[10]Lay the table, recount/tell/count, greet, work, warm up, run, write a book, go round something, hide something, sing the national anthem, wash the car, go through.

[11]Fall, enter, go to London, go to the movies, arrive, open the window, fall asleep, break, close, become/remain, grow, cool down.

[12]Remember, attain, meet/know, round/circle, know/learn.

[13]Be ADJ, be a N, rhyme, resemble, like.

[14]Be, see one self, find one self, have.

cases (from my subjective knowledge of how the verbs are used in Portuguese), I should probably create a larger set of seeds so that a more complex classifier can be developed, but this task has to left for the future.

In any case, how then can the result of such classifier applied to the huge numbers of non-classified verbs be evaluated? Probably by looking at a sample of instances of the verbs in the corpora, and contrastively, by looking at how they were translated.

6 Concluding Remarks

This chapter obviously describes no more than the very beginning of a path, or program, that will take several years to run, but which was inspired and started by Lauri Carlson's supervision in the realm of tense and aspect, and by his crucial advice to look at authentic data *in translation*. Although all this work should have been done before, I am glad to associate it with Lauri Carlson so that it can be considered a consequence of his linguistic clairvoyance. Also, and given the status of Portuguese computational grammar and corpus studies, it is not too late to foster progress on matters of Portuguese grammar worldwide in this way.

My intention with this chapter was merely to delineate a course of experiments and empirical investigations that I hope will shed light on the organization of the Portuguese language and its inner categories, providing a next step for contrastive studies illuminated by translations of Portuguese into several different languages.

Acknowledgements The writing of this chapter was partially supported by the University of Oslo, and by Linguateca, which over the years has been supported by the Portuguese Government, the European Union, UMIC, FCT, and FCCN. I am most grateful for Janet Pierrehumbert and Andrew Chesterman's comments; both of them helped considerably in shaping the final version of this chapter, but they cannot be considered responsible for the remaining shortcomings. I also acknowledge the support of the Research Computing Services group at the University of Oslo.

References

Baayen, Harald. 2008. *Analyzing linguistic data: A practical introduction to statistics using R*. Cambridge: Cambridge University Press.

Baayen, R.H. 2011. languageR: Data sets and functions with "Analyzing linguistic data: A practical introduction to statistics". R package version 1.2. http://CRAN.R-project.org/package=languageR.

Bick, Eckhard. 2000. The parsing system "Palavras": Automatic grammatical analysis of Portuguese in a Constraint Grammar framework. Doctoral diss. Aarhus University, Aarhus, Denmark.

Brent, Michael R.. 1991. Automatic semantic classification of verbs from their syntactic contexts: An implemented classifier for stativity. In *Proceedings of the 5th conference of the European chapter of the ACL*, 222–226.

Carlson, Lauri. 1981. Aspect and quantification. In *Tense and aspect*, eds. Philip Tedeschi and Annie Zaenen. Vol. 14 of *Syntax and semantics*, 31–64. New York: Academic Press.

Ellis, John M.. 1993. *Language, thought and logic*. Evanston: Northwestern University Press.

Even-Zohar, Itamar. 1990. *Polysystem studies*. Durham: Duke University Press. A special issue (11:1) of *Poetics Today*.

Halliday, M.A.K.. 2005. *Computational and quantitative studies*, ed. Jonathan J. Webster, Vol. 7 of *Collected works of M. A. K. Halliday*. London: Continuum.

Klavans, Judith L., and Martin Chodorow. 1992. Degrees of stativity: The lexical representation of verb aspect. In *Proceedings of COLING'92*, 1126–1131.

Moens, Marc. 1987. Tense, aspect and temporal reference. Doctoral diss., University of Edinburgh.

Moens, Marc, and Mark Steedman. 1988. Temporal ontology and temporal reference. *Computational Linguistics* 14: 15–28.

R Development Core Team. 2010. *R: A language and environment for statistical computing*. Vienna: R Foundation for Statistical Computing. http://www.R-project.org.

Santos, Diana. 1991. Sobre a classificação aspectual dos verbos portugueses. In *Actas do VII Encontro da Associação Portuguesa de Linguística*, 389–401. http://www.linguateca.pt/Diana/download/apl91.ps.

Santos, Diana. 1993. Integrating tense, aspect and genericity. In *Actas do IX Encontro da Associação Portuguesa de Linguística*, 391–405.

Santos, Diana. 1995. On the use of parallel texts in the comparison of languages. In *Actas do XI Encontro Nacional da Associação Portuguesa de Linguística*, 217–239. Lisboa: APL/Colibri.

Santos, Diana Maria de Souza Marques Pinto dos. 1996a. Tense and aspect in English and Portuguese: a contrastive semantical study. Doctoral diss., Instituto Superior Técnico, Universidade Técnica de Lisboa.

Santos, Diana. 1996b. Uma classificação aspectual portuguesa do português. In *Actas do XII Encontro da Associação Portuguesa de Linguística*, 299–315.

Santos, Diana. 2000. The translation network: A model for the fine-grained description of translations. In *Parallel text processing*, ed. Jean Véronis, 169–186. Dordrecht: Kluwer Academic.

Santos, Diana. 2004. *Translation-based corpus studies: Contrasting English and Portuguese tense and aspect systems*. Amsterdam: Rodopi.

Santos, Diana. 2009. Caminhos percorridos no mapa da portuguesificação: A Linguateca em perspectiva. *Linguamática* 1: 25–59. http://www.linguateca.pt/Diana/download/Santos2009Linguamatica.pdf.

Santos, Diana. 2011. Linguateca's infrastructure for Portuguese and how it allows the detailed study of language varieties. *OSLa: Oslo Studies in Language* 3: 113–128. http://www.linguateca.pt/Diana/download/SantosOSLa2010.pdf.

Santos, Diana. 2012. Translation. In *The Oxford handbook of tense and aspect*, ed. Robert Binnick, 335–369. Oxford: Oxford University Press. To appear.

Toury, Gideon. 1995. *Descriptive translation studies and beyond*. Amsterdam: Benjamins.

Vendler, Zeno. 1967. *Linguistics in philosophy*. Ithaca: Cornell University Press.

Core Vocabulary: A Useful But Mystical Concept in Some Kinds of Linguistics

Lars Borin

mys·ti·cal
–adjective
1. mystic; occult.
2. of or pertaining to mystics or mysticism: *mystical writings.*
3. spiritually symbolic.
4. *Rare.* obscure in meaning; mysterious.
(http://dictionary.reference.com, s.v. *mystical*)

Abstract This paper is a theoretical and empirical investigation into the use of the notion "core vocabulary" in some areas of linguistics and related disciplines, originally prompted by the concrete task of compiling core vocabularies in two research projects growing out of two quite different research traditions: (1) lexicostatistics, where "core vocabularies" are used to measure the linguistic distance among languages in order to establish genetic and typological language groupings; and (2) computer-assisted language learning—a long-standing research interest of Lauri Carlson—where the "core vocabulary" is the most central vocabulary, to which language learners should be exposed first. In linguistics we also find a more theoretically motivated notion of "core vocabulary", as so-called "semantic primitives". In the paper, I compare the three kinds of "core vocabulary" and discuss their relationship to the formal knowledge-representation systems called "ontologies" (currently among Lauri Carlson's research interests)—especially "core" ontologies such as SUMO—and the notion of "concept" central to the latter work: What is the relationship—if any—between concepts in such ontologies and lexical items in languages?

L. Borin (✉)
Språkbanken, Department of Swedish, University of Gothenburg, Gothenburg, Sweden
e-mail: lars.borin@svenska.gu.se

D. Santos et al. (eds.), *Shall We Play the Festschrift Game?*,
DOI 10.1007/978-3-642-30773-7_6, © Springer-Verlag Berlin Heidelberg 2012

1 Introduction

This is an investigation into the use of the notion *core vocabulary* in some areas of linguistics and related disciplines. The inspiration for this paper comes from my involvement in two recent research projects where this notion plays a central role.

The KELLY EU project[1] aims at developing vocabularies corresponding to the six language learner proficiency levels of the Council of Europe's Framework of Reference (CEFR). The aim is to have 1,000–2,000 words for each level, further subdivided into thematic areas. The vocabularies are being developed for nine languages—Arabic, Chinese, English, Greek, Italian, Norwegian, Polish, Russian and Swedish—and translated among all language pairs by professional translators. In the KELLY approach, the notion of coreness or centrality corresponds to adjusted frequency in a very large corpus collected from the WWW using the Web-as-Corpus methodology (Baroni and Bernardini 2006). The lists for the lowest CEFR level containing approximately 1,500 vocabulary items are arguably candidates for core vocabularies for these languages. My involvement in this project comes from a long-standing interest in intelligent computer-assisted language learning which I share with Lauri Carlson and on which we have collaborated at one time (Borin et al. 2002).

The goal of the *Digital areal linguistics*—or IDS (Intercontinental Dictionary Series)—project[2] (funded by the Swedish Research Council) is to create a database of comparable lexical items in a number of representative South Asian languages, with a focus on the Himalayan region in India and to use this database for investigating the Himalayas as a linguistic area. The project is a collaboration with the global IDS project (Max Planck Institute for Evolutionary Anthropology, Leipzig),[3] an international initiative for collecting comparable basic vocabulary lists in a large number of languages.

The methodological musings reported in the next section arose from my practical work in the IDS project, where I undertook the task of updating the Swedish word list (approximately 1,500 senses).[4]

In order to put the discussion in Sect. 2 on a surer footing, I made some comparisons of a number of proposed core vocabularies. The results of these comparisons are presented and discussed in Sects. 3 and 4.

2 Afflicted with Ontological Angst: Words—Senses—Concepts

As linguists, we have intuitions about which lexical units are more central in our own language, and which more peripheral. At any rate, there are fairly clear cases, such

[1] http://spraakbanken.gu.se/eng/kelly.

[2] http://spraakbanken.gu.se/eng/research/digital-areal-linguistics.

[3] http://lingweb.eva.mpg.de/ids/.

[4] https://svn.spraakdata.gu.se/sb/fnplusplus/pub/lwt-meanings.html.

as *dog* vs. *cep* 'a mushroom of the species *Boletus edulis*', or *mortal* vs. *fraught*. In other cases it may be more difficult to determine relative centrality. An interesting question in connection with this, which has occupied linguists for centuries is this: If we determine the most central lexical items for a large number of diverse languages, how much overlap will we see in the resulting sets?

The notion of a core vocabulary crops up in more than one linguistic subdiscipline, but with different meanings and based on different theoretical and methodological premises:

- In *lexicology* and *lexicography*, the core vocabulary is equivalent to a defining vocabulary, a set of words using which all definitions in a dictionary must be expressed, directly or indirectly, and which itself will not be defined—only described—in the dictionary. This is in principle a language-specific notion; different languages could have different core vocabularies.
- In *semantics*, as a language-independent extension of the foregoing, the core vocabulary is a set of senses—universal lexical-semantic primitives—in terms of which all vocabulary items in all languages can be expressed. On some construals, however, these primitives need not actually correspond to lexical items in any language.
- In *genetic linguistics*, a core vocabulary—often referred to as a *Swadesh list* (Swadesh 1950, 1955)—is a list of supposedly universal senses together with their lexical realizations in many languages, which are used in an endeavor referred to as *lexicostatistics*, the purpose of which is to investigate genetic and areal relationships among languages. This kind of core vocabulary must be *resistant to replacement* over time in order to work as intended.
- In *lexical typology*, for investigating questions such as the universality of lexical expression, borrowability, etc.
- In *applied linguistics*, corresponding to the notion that vocabulary growth in language learners is not random or spurious, the core vocabulary is the first, most basic set of words that a language learner will need to master in a foreign language in order to fulfill some minimal requirement of competence in the language.

In recent years, the field of *computational linguistics* has arguably been added to the above. Here, core vocabularies enter the stage in the form of *ontologies*, or formally organized concept systems.[5] These systems are not explicitly referred to as consisting of lexical or even linguistic items, but the most reasonable interpretation is in fact that they are a kind of lexical structures. Here I am quite in agreement with the view expressed by Wilks (2009: 4), namely that

> items in ontologies and taxonomies are and remain words in natural languages—the very ones they seem to be, in fact—and that this fact places strong constraints on the degree of formalisation that can ever be achieved by the use of such structures. The word "drink" has many meanings (e.g., the sea) and attempts to restrict it, within structures, and by rules,

[5]Such ontologies and their most salient and high-flying application domain, the so-called *Semantic Web*, are among Lauri Carlson's more recent research interests; see, e.g., the *TermFactory Manual* http://www.helsinki.fi/~lcarlson/CF/TF/doc/TFManual_en.html.

> constraints or the domain used, can only have limited success. [...] Those who continue to maintain that 'universal words' are not the English words they look most like, must at least tell us which of the senses closest to the 'universal word' they intend it to bear under formalisation.

Wilks's remark puts the finger squarely on a practical-methodological difficulty which arises in connection with the comparison of core vocabularies: How do we determine that two vocabulary items are the "same", in one language and—in particular—across languages? In other words: Do we know how to compare vocabulary items?

Actually, it turns out that we do not; there is even some confusion about what a vocabulary item is. If we look for clarification to the field of lexicography—which is where we would expect to find the expert views par excellence on this issue—we will soon learn that there is actually no consensus on what the basic vocabulary unit is.

Lexicographers as a rule do not involve themselves in linguistic discussions about the meaning of the term "word"; this is something that they leave to theoretical linguists. Nevertheless, their actual practices in structuring dictionaries provide ample empirical evidence that there is more than one notion of word involved, if by this we refer to the basic structural unit of a dictionary, the dictionary entry.

Some of the contenders that we encounter in actual dictionaries are:[6]

- the etymological word
- the lemma
- the lempos
- the lemgram
- the sense
- the synset

The *etymological word* is often the basic unit in older dictionaries at least in Scandinavia. Figure 1 shows the three entries with the headword *mál* in an Icelandic–Swedish dictionary first published in the 1940s.[7] Note that there is no difference in inflection among the three entries; they are strong neuter nouns. They are given different entries in the dictionary by dint of each having a different historical origin, i.e., a different etymology.

The *lemma*, in the sense 'citation form', is often used as the basic organizing unit in dictionaries.[8] See Fig. 2, taken from one of the English dictionaries available online at http://dictionary.reference.com. The subdivision into parts of speech is made inside the basic entry.

[6] A reviewer remarked on the absence of *lexeme* from this list. This term is ambiguous, meaning both 'lexical unit'—thus making the lexeme equivalent to any and all of the listed units—and 'lexical morpheme', and is best avoided in our context.

[7] The three entries mean respectively 'language; speech; legal process; cause; opinion', 'measure; time; need; meal', and 'paint'.

[8] Unfortunately, *lemma* is also used in other senses, e.g., roughly equivalent to *lempos* or *lemgram* as explained below.

1. **mál** -*s* ~ *n* mål, talförmåga; språk; tal; mål, process; sak; mening, åsikt; [...]
2. **mál** -*s* ~ *n* mått; tid; behov; mål, måltid; mjölkningstid; *pl* tiden för frukost och aftonmål; [...]
3. **mál** -*s* ~ *n* målarfärg

Fig. 1 Sven BF Jansson: *Isländsk-svensk ordbok*, s.v. *mál*

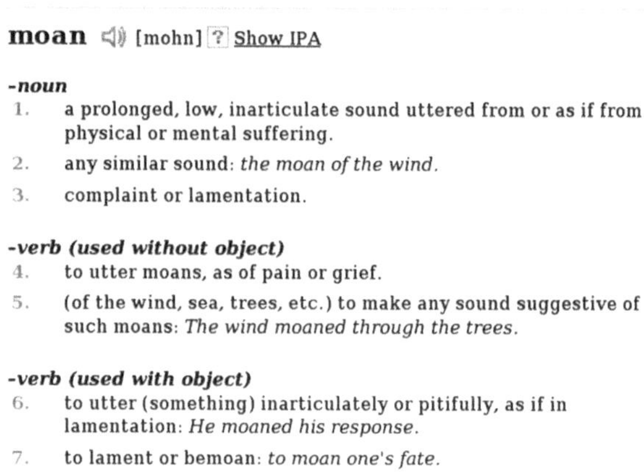

moan [mohn] ? Show IPA

-noun

1. a prolonged, low, inarticulate sound uttered from or as if from physical or mental suffering.
2. any similar sound: *the moan of the wind.*
3. complaint or lamentation.

-verb (used without object)

4. to utter moans, as of pain or grief.
5. (of the wind, sea, trees, etc.) to make any sound suggestive of such moans: *The wind moaned through the trees.*

-verb (used with object)

6. to utter (something) inarticulately or pitifully, as if in lamentation: *He moaned his response.*
7. to lament or bemoan: *to moan one's fate.*

Fig. 2 One of the online English dictionaries at dictionary.reference.com, s.v. *moan*

In our own work on an infrastructure for lexical resources for language technology (Borin et al. 2010, 2012), we have felt the need for a more precise terminology in reference to the various linguistic units appearing in our lexical resources. The terms *lempos* and *lemgram* were coined in this connection, but they reflect already existing ways of organizing dictionaries.

The *lempos* is the combination of lemma and part of speech. Figure 3 shows this with the help of another of the English dictionaries available online at http://dictionary.reference.com. Note that the entry *hang* contains two verbs with different inflectional paradigms—with the past tense forms *hung* and *hanged*—and also verbs with two different syntactic behaviors—transitive and intransitive—although note further that only one of the intransitive usages is explicitly labeled as such (sense 6 in Fig. 3).

The *lemgram* is an extension of the lempos idea. This is a combination of a lemma with a formally definable behavior, such as part of speech, inflectional paradigm, pronunciation, word-formation structure and syntactic behavior. In Fig. 4 we see three entries from the online Swedish dictionary available (to subscribers) at http://www.ne.se. The formal characteristics which determine the subdivision into entries in this dictionary are *part of speech*, *pronunciation* and *inflectional paradigm*. In Fig. 4 there is one noun and two verb lemgrams. The formal distinction between the two Swedish verbs is exactly the same as in the case of English *hang* cited above: We have a verb with strong inflection (past *stack*, supine *stuckit*) meaning 'to stick/prick/stab (tr.); to leave/get lost (itr.; colloquial)' and one with weak inflection (past *stickade*, supine *stickat*), meaning 'to knit'. The two different syntactic behaviors of the strong verb do not play a role in defining lemgrams in this

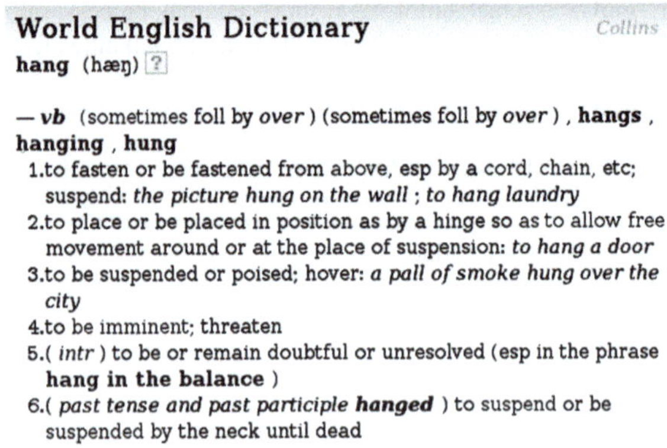
World English Dictionary Collins

hang (hæŋ)

— ***vb*** (sometimes foll by *over*) (sometimes foll by *over*) , **hangs** , **hanging** , **hung**

1.to fasten or be fastened from above, esp by a cord, chain, etc; suspend: *the picture hung on the wall* ; *to hang laundry*
2.to place or be placed in position as by a hinge so as to allow free movement around or at the place of suspension: *to hang a door*
3.to be suspended or poised; hover: *a pall of smoke hung over the city*
4.to be imminent; threaten
5.(*intr*) to be or remain doubtful or unresolved (esp in the phrase **hang in the balance**)
6.(*past tense and past participle* ***hanged***) to suspend or be suspended by the neck until dead

Fig. 3 One of the online English dictionaries at dictionary.reference.com, s.v. *hang*

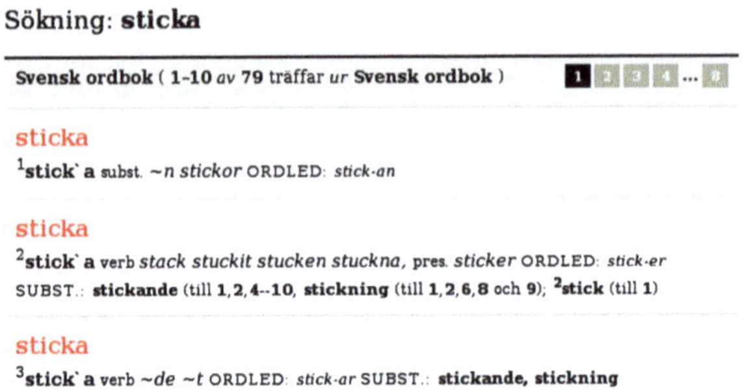
Sökning: **sticka**

Svensk ordbok (**1-10** *av* **79** träffar *ur* **Svensk ordbok**) 1 2 3 4 ... 8

sticka

^{1}**stick`a** subst. ~*n* *stickor* ORDLED: *stick-an*

sticka

^{2}**stick`a** verb *stack stuckit stucken stuckna*, pres. *sticker* ORDLED: *stick-er* SUBST.: **stickande** (till **1**, **2**, **4**--**10**, **stickning** (till **1**, **2**, **6**, **8** och **9**); ^{2}**stick** (till **1**)

sticka

^{3}**stick`a** verb ~*de* ~*t* ORDLED: *stick-ar* SUBST.: **stickande, stickning**

Fig. 4 The online Swedish dictionary at http://www.ne.se s.v. *sticka*

Fig. 5 SALDO, s.v. *sticka*

sticka	hål	sticka (vb)	korpus
sticka^{2}	pinne	sticka (nn)	korpus
sticka^{3}	tillverka + garn	sticka^{2} (vb)	korpus
sticka^{4}	djupgående^{2}	sticka (vb)	korpus
sticka^{5}	sticka^{3}	sticka (nn)	korpus
sticka^{6}	ge_sig_av	sticka^{3} (vb)	korpus
sticka^{7}	stick^{3}	sticka (vb)	korpus

dictionary, even though they arguably influence the inflectional paradigms, since ^{2}*sticka* in the sense 'to leave/get lost (itr.)' does not form a past participle.

The *sense* is of course a dictionary 'atom' with a long and venerable tradition. Our central computational lexical resource for modern Swedish, SALDO (Borin et al. 2008),[9] is organized primarily into word and multi-word senses. Figure 5 shows the senses recognized (at present) in SALDO for the lemma *sticka* (five verbs and two nouns).

One basic lexical unit that cannot be left out of this discussion is the *synset*. The synset is generally defined as consisting of words which are interchangeable in at least one (sentence) context without changing the (truth-conditional) meaning

[9] http://spraakbanken.gu.se/eng/saldo.

Fig. 6 Princeton WordNet: noun synsets s.v. *stick*

Noun

- S: (n) **stick** (an implement consisting of a length of wood) *"he collected dry sticks for a campfire"; "the kid had a candied apple on a stick"*
- S: (n) **stick** (a small thin branch of a tree)
- S: (n) **stick**, control stick, joystick (a lever used by a pilot to control the ailerons and elevators of an airplane)
- S: (n) **stick** (a rectangular quarter pound block of butter or margarine)
- S: (n) pin, peg, **stick** (informal terms for the leg) *"fever left him weak on his sticks"*
- S: (n) **stick** (a long implement (usually made of wood) that is shaped so that hockey or polo players can hit a puck or ball)
- S: (n) **stick** (a long thin implement resembling a length of wood) *"cinnamon sticks"; "a stick of dynamite"*
- S: (n) joint, marijuana cigarette, reefer, **stick**, spliff (marijuana leaves rolled into a cigarette for smoking)
- S: (n) **stick** (threat of a penalty) *"the policy so far is all stick and no carrot"*

of the sentence in question. This is claimed to be the basic lexical unit in Princeton WordNet (PWN; Fellbaum 1998).[10] I say "claimed to be", since a count of the cardinalities of the synsets in PWN 3.0 reveals that 54 % of the synsets are singleton sets, i.e., have only one member. This makes one suspect that senses are logically prior to synsets in PWN, too, as they are in SALDO and many other lexical resources. In Fig. 6 we see the 9 PWN noun synsets for the lemma *stick* (there are also 16 verb synsets for this lemma). Note that six out of these are singleton synsets.

Finally, in the ontologies mentioned earlier, the basic entities are *concepts*. The interesting question—which is mostly consigned to silence in the literature on ontologies—is how concepts in ontologies and lexical units in dictionaries are ontologically, as it were, interconnected. One—perhaps too facile—answer is this (from Pease and Fellbaum 2010):

> The basic unit of WordNet is a set of cognitively equivalent synonyms, or synset. [...] Each synset represents a concept, and each member of a synset encodes the same concept. (p. 25)
> [...]
> [...] the concept-word mappings of any given language are to some extent accidental; existing words do not fully reflect the inventory of concepts that is available. (p. 27)
> [...]
> In a formal ontology, the meaning of the terms only consists of the formal mathematics used to define those terms. The names of the terms could be replaced by arbitrary unique character strings and their meaning would still be the same. This independence from language gives some confidence in SUMO as a starting point for a true interlingua. (p. 30)

As already stated, with Yorick Wilks and others I believe this to be a delusion; either the "concepts" in formal ontologies actually *are* mathematical objects, and have at most a very indirect and incomplete connection to language—the less likely alternative, in my view—or they are simply words in English, in which case they have at most a very tenuous and incomplete connection to mathematics, as well as a largely unexplored connection to a putative set of universal concepts.

It is far from clear exactly what a "concept" is in this literature. One possible interpretation of the quote just given is that the "inventory of concepts that is available" would be the union of those concepts which find lexical expression in some—at least one—language out of the world's approximately 7,000 languages (Lewis

[10] http://wordnet.princeton.edu/.

2009). Another interpretation would be that the inventory of concepts is independent of language, so that there will be concepts that never receive linguistic expression in any language. Logically, this independence must be one-way, however; it seems that everything that gets at least lexical expression—even if this notion is somewhat unclear—in some language, will also necessarily be a concept. The literature on concepts—in linguistics, philosophy and psychology—is actually too vague to be of much use to us in our ontological quandary. It is sometimes proposed in the literature that concepts have compositional structure, a bit like linguistic units. Does this then mean that an utterance like *After work last Tuesday, I took the way by the pub because I felt that I needed some company, but there was nobody there that I knew, so I went to the bookstore and looked for a good book instead* corresponds to a concept? Nobody knows, it seems, or rather, nobody has spent much effort thinking about questions such as where concepts end, as it were, if there is a syntax with composition rules for concepts, etc.[11]

Somewhat in contrast to the quote above, in the introduction to Fellbaum (1998) we read that "[t]he majority of lexicalized concepts are shared among languages" (p. 8). The findings reported in recent work in linguistic typology and language universals clearly run counter to this claim:

> languages do differ almost without limit as to which meanings they choose to lexicalize (von Fintel and Matthewson 2008: 151)
> languages differ enormously in the concepts that they provide ready-coded in grammar and lexicon [... and] many languages make semantic distinctions that we certainly would never think of making (Evans and Levinson 2009: 435)
> There is no sense of "broad" under which "the grammars and lexicons of all languages are broadly similar." (Levinson 2003: 28)
> From even a small sample of languages it is clear that many impressionistically "basic" items of English vocabulary (such as *go*, *water* and *eat*) lack exact equivalents in other languages. (Goddard 2001: 57)

The conclusions of the preceding seem to be that (1) there is a real danger of becoming confused and inconsistent about which kind of lexical unit one is working with, and (2) attempting to keep concepts and lexical senses theoretically distinct is hardly ever worth the effort. However, since even lexicographers working on a single language—arguably the foremost experts in this area—do not seem to come to an agreement about the basic lexical units of a language, (3) until this issue has been resolved, there is absolutely no need to posit language-independent lexical units of any kind, neither the "universal words" of the formal ontology community (see above), nor "comparative concepts" of the kind proposed by Haspelmath (2010).

Tentatively, then—even though, as we have seen, we do not actually know, in a deeper sense, what we are comparing—we may still compare core vocabularies simply using the English glosses and assume that they in the normal case—especially

[11]Although, as we will see below, we do not need to look long in the world's languages in order to find lexical units with 'funny' meanings. Evans and Levinson (2009: 435) provide the example of the Mundari (an Austro-Asiatic language spoken in South Asia) ideophone *rawa-dawa*, which they gloss as 'the sensation of suddenly realizing you can do something reprehensible, and no-one is there to witness it'. This kind of example can be repeated essentially ad infinitum.

for the small vocabularies that we will be concerned with here[12]—reflect the same or at least comparable senses.

3 Comparing Core Vocabularies

To make things more concrete, in Table 1 we show four different 'core' (or 'basic') vocabulary lists (ordered alphabetically):

1. The Automated Similarity Judgement Program (ASJP)[13] 40-item vocabulary for genetic and areal linguistics research (Holman et al. 2008) (referred to as A40 below)
2. The first 40 items of the Leipzig–Jakarta (LJ) vocabulary from the loanword typology project[14] (Haspelmath and Tadmor 2009) (L40)
3. Goddard's 42 universal lexical items (Goddard 2001) (G42)
4. All items common to at least eight of the nine KELLY languages (40 items) (K-8)

The vocabulary that sticks out in Table 1 K-8. For some reason, the translation methodology and selection criteria used in the KELLY project conspire to yield a list conspicuously different from the other core vocabularies. If we instead compare the other five short vocabulary lists with the most basic (A1-level) monolingual English KELLY list (1,119 items), we get on the order of 60–80 % correspondences (percentages in terms of the short 40–100 item lists). This is more like what we would expect from a basic vocabulary list, and comparable to what we find in a comparison of the same five lists with the 800-item Basic English list (Ogden 1930) or the first 2,000 items in the SUBTLEXus word-form frequency list derived from a corpus of subtitles in films.[15] Still, it is noteworthy that at most 80 % of the A40 list and 75 % or less of the A100 list (see below) are found in these longer basic vocabulary lists for English, i.e., a fifth to a quarter of the ASJP items are missing. ASJP sense labels are English words, after all, so somehow one would expect a figure much closer to 100 %.

The K-8 list is thus not comparable to the ASJP or LJ lists, but since it reflects a set of common words that have emerged from a combination of corpus processing and manual translation among all 72 language pairs, a comparison of K-8 with G42 should arguably be meaningful.[16]

---

[12]Since several of the vocabularies ultimately come out of the same research tradition, we may tentatively assume commensurability at least for the items in those lists.

[13]http://email.eva.mpg.de/~wichmann/ASJPHomePage.htm.

[14]http://wold.livingsources.org/; the LJ list has been somewhat edited for the purposes of this presentation, so that, e.g., "1sg pronoun" has been replaced by "I", "arm/hand" by "hand", "who?" by "who", "child (kin term)" by "child", etc., in order to make the word lists mechanically comparable with a computer program.

[15]http://expsy.ugent.be/subtlexus/.

[16]Here the thorny issue of translation equivalence rears its head. The KELLY translators were instructed to provide one translation in the normal case. How this methodological decision has

Table 1 Four different small "core vocabularies"

A40	L40	G42	K-8 (40 items)
blood	arm	above	bomb
bone	big	after	bread
breasts	bitter	all	bridge
come	blood	a long time	channel
die	bone	bad	climate
dog	breast	because	coffee
drink	come	before	dog
ear	do	below	eye
eye	ear	big	father
fire	far	die	forest
fish	fire	do	future
full	fish	good	government
hand	flesh	happen	hospital
hear	fly	hear	kitchen
horn	foot	here	knee
I	go	I	level
knee	hair	if	library
leaf	he/she	inside	logic
liver	hit/beat	know	marriage
louse	horn	like	member
mountain	house	live	minister
name	I	maybe	music
new	louse	much/many	office
night	mouth	not	pocket
nose	name	now	poet
one	neck	one	prison
path	night	people	problem
person	nose	say	queen
see	one	see	revolution
skin	rain	small	sand
star	root	someone	source
stone	say	something/thing	sun
sun	stone	there is	tea
tongue	this	the same	theory
tooth	tongue	think	third
tree	tooth	this	trade
two	water	two	tragedy
water	who	want	university
we	wing	very	water
you	you	when/time	week
		where/place	
		you	

Table 2 The number of shared items in the vocabularies. Three data items are given in each cell (if not empty or 0) on the form *n* (*r*/*c* %): *n* = the number of shared items; *r* = the percentage of shared items in relation to the list named at the beginning of the current row; and *c* = the percentage of shared items in relation to the list named at the top of the current column

	L40	L100	G42	K-9	K-8	K-7
A40	18 (45/45 %)	29 (72/29 %)	7 (17/16 %)	1 (2/20 %)	5 (12/12 %)	11 (27/4 %)
A100	30 (30/75 %)	60 (60/60 %)	15 (15/35 %)	1 (1/20 %)	6 (6/15 %)	23 (23/8 %)
L40			7 (17/16 %)	0	1 (2/2 %)	8 (20/3 %)
L100			12 (12/28 %)	0	5 (5/12 %)	18 (18/6 %)

In Table 2 some detailed comparisons among several vocabulary lists are presented. In addition to the lists shown in Table 1, the following are also given:

- A long (100-item) ASJP list, which is a modified Swadesh list (Swadesh 1950, 1955), where items have been reordered on the basis of empirically measured retention rates in a large lexical material (A100)
- The first 100 items of the LJ list (L100)
- Two additional KELLY lists: KELLY-9 (K-9; 5 items common to all 9 KELLY languages) and KELLY-7 (K-7; 271 items common to at least 7 KELLY languages out of which one is English)

Table 2 lists the number of items shared between the lists and their percentages relative to the sizes of the whole lists.

Further, A40, L40 and G42 have three items in common—*I*, *one* and *you*—and A100 and L100 share 12 items with G42. G42 has no common items with the K-8/K-9 lists, and shares only three items with the longest (271-item) K-7 list: *big*, *time* and *two*.

4 Conclusions

It is perhaps not surprising that there should be so little overlap among different kinds of 'core vocabularies', since they aim at capturing different aspects of 'coreness':

- **Item stability:**
  - The ASJP vocabulary consists of maximally stable form–meaning pairs; it can be seen as a refinement of traditional Swadesh lists, based on a broad range of empirical data.
  - The Leipzig–Jakarta list reflects resistance to borrowing.

influenced this investigation is a very interesting question which we will have to leave for future research.

- **Sense inventory:**
  - Goddard's list contains senses that receive lexical expression in all languages.[17]
  - Basic learner vocabularies contain high-frequency—much-used and consequently highly useful—lexical items.

Still, we would expect the ASJP list to be a subset of the LJ list, instead of showing a not too large overlap with it, but the latter is what we actually find. This is because resistance to borrowing is a special case of resistance to vocabulary item replacement. Another common form of replacement is the substitution of a native vocabulary item for another native word ('semantic change').

There is no logical *need* for universal word-meanings to be highly frequent. In this sense Goddard's criteria and those used in compiling learner vocabulary lists are orthogonal to the criterion of replacement. There is also no logical *reason* for universal word-meanings to be highly frequent, although there may be good pragmatic reasons: Highly technical vocabulary could be expected to behave in a way that could make it universal in Goddard's sense—because such vocabulary items would mean the same wherever they occurred—were it not for the simple fact that this vocabulary will be confined to a small fraction of the world's languages in each individual case. Hence, Goddard's universal word-meanings will by pragmatic necessity belong to everyday language.

High-frequency senses may or may not undergo the linguistic equivalent of an extreme makeover. From experience we know that, e.g., sentence adverbs and indefinite pronouns—arguably central and in part universal vocabulary items—often are non-cognate even in closely related languages.

On the other hand, it is often mentioned in works on historical linguistics that high-frequency items tend to preserve older inflectional patterns as irregularities (seen from the point of view of the present-day inflectional system), which can consequently be used in internal reconstruction for inferring the older system. Intuitively, the older inflectional patterns should be accompanied by the corresponding older lexical items, i.e., this would lead to the conclusion that high-frequency vocabulary should be more stable than the above comparisons with the Basic English and SUBTLEXus lists show.

Why the ASJP and LJ lists do not show the expected inclusion relationship and why high-frequency central vocabulary is less stable than expected are two mysterious aspects of core vocabularies which will need further investigation.

Acknowledgements The work described here has received financial support from the Swedish Research Council (the *Digital areal linguistics* project: VR dnr 429-2009-1448), from the European Commission (the *KELLY* project: Lifelong Learning Programme project no. 505630-LLP-2009-1-SE-KA2-KA2MP), and from the University of Gothenburg through its funding of the Centre for Language Technology. I would also like to thank the reviewers for their illuminating questions and insightful comments.

[17] As we have seen above, this may be true only in an approximate sense.

References

Baroni, Marco, and Silvia Bernardini, eds. 2006. *Wacky! working papers on the Web as Corpus*. Bologna: GEDIT. Online version: http://wackybook.sslmit.unibo.it.

Borin, Lars, Lauri Carlson, and Diana Santos. 2002. Corpus based language technology for computer-assisted learning of Nordic languages: Squirrel. Progress report September 2001. In *Nordisk sprogteknologi. Nordic language technology. Årbog for Nordisk Sprogteknologisk Forskningsprogram 2000–2004. Årbog 2001*, ed. Henrik Holmboe, 257–270. Copenhagen: Museum Tusculanums Forlag, Københavns Universitet.

Borin, Lars, Dana Dannélls, Markus Forsberg, Maria Toporowska Gronostaj, and Dimitrios Kokkinakis. 2010. The past meets the present in Swedish FrameNet++. In *14th EURALEX international congress*, 269–281. Leeuwarden: EURALEX.

Borin, Lars, Markus Forsberg, and Lennart Lönngren. 2008. The hunting of the BLARK—SALDO, a freely available lexical database for Swedish language technology. In *Resourceful language technology. Festschrift in honor of Anna Sågvall Hein*, eds. Joakim Nivre, Mats Dahllöf, and Beata Megyesi. Vol. 7 of *Acta Universitatis Upsaliensis: Studia linguistica Upsaliensia*, 21–32. Uppsala: Uppsala University, Department of Linguistics and Philology.

Borin, Lars, Markus Forsberg, Leif-Jöran Olsson, and Jonatan Uppström. 2012. The open lexical infrastructure of Språkbanken. In *Proceedings of LREC 2012*, 3598–3602. Istanbul: ELRA.

Evans, Nicholas, and Stephen C. Levinson. 2009. The myth of language universals: Language diversity and its importance for cognitive science. *Behavioral and Brain Sciences* 32: 429–492.

Fellbaum, Christiane, ed. 1998. *WordNet: An electronic lexical database*. Cambridge: MIT Press.

Goddard, Cliff. 2001. Lexico-semantic universals: A critical overview. *Linguistic Typology* 5: 1–65.

Haspelmath, Martin. 2010. Comparative concepts and descriptive categories in crosslinguistic studies. *Language* 86: 663–687.

Haspelmath, Martin, and Uri Tadmor, eds. 2009. *Loanwords in the world's languages. A comparative handbook*. Berlin: De Gruyter.

Holman, Eric W., Søren Wichmann, Cecil H. Brown, Viveka Velupillai, André Müller, and Dik Bakker 2008. Explorations in automated language classification. *Folia Linguistica* 42: 331–354.

Levinson, Stephen C. 2003. Language and mind: Let's get the issues straight. In *Language in mind. Advances in the study of language and thought*, eds. Dedre Gentner and Susan Goldin-Meadow, 25–46. Cambridge: MIT Press.

Lewis, M. Paul, ed. 2009. *Ethnologue: Languages of the world*, 16th edn. Dallas: SIL International. Online version: http://www.ethnologue.com/.

Ogden, Charles K. 1930. *Basic English: A general introduction with rules and grammar*. London: Paul Treber.

Pease, Adam, and Christiane Fellbaum. 2010. Formal ontology as interlingua: the SUMO and WordNet linking project and global WordNet. In *Ontology and the lexicon. A natural language processing perspective*, eds. Chu-ren Huang, Nicoletta Calzolari, Aldo Gangemi, Alessandro Lenci, Alessandro Oltramari, and Laurent Prevot, 25–35. Cambridge: Cambridge University Press.

Swadesh, Morris. 1950. Salish internal relationships. *International Journal of American Linguistics* 16: 157–167.

Swadesh, Morris. 1955. Towards greater accuracy in lexicostatistic dating. *International Journal of American Linguistics* 21: 121–137.

von Fintel, Kai, and Lisa Matthewson. 2008. Universals in semantics. *The Linguistic Review* 25: 139–201.

Wilks, Yorick. 2009. Ontotherapy, or how to stop worrying about what there is. In *Recent advances in natural language processing V*, eds. Nicolas Nicolov, Galia Angelova, and Ruslan Mitkov. *Current issues in linguistic theory*, 1–20. Amsterdam: John Benjamins.

Extending and Updating the Finnish Wordnet

Krister Lindén, Jyrki Niemi, and Mirka Hyvärinen

Abstract This paper presents simple methods for adding new words to a wordnet. We use the Finnish wordnet, FinnWordNet, as an example. We pay particular attention to high- and medium-frequency words thus far missing from FinnWordNet, and arrive at an estimate for the number of culture-specific words among them. We also find that the majority of the high- and medium-frequency words are compounds, which makes them relatively easy to add by using the head word of a compound to locate hypernym synset candidates. Another goal of ours is to add new synonyms to the existing synsets of FinnWordNet. We present a method that finds candidates for new synonyms from a bilingual lexical resource by exploiting the direct word sense translation correspondences between FinnWordNet and the Princeton WordNet. We apply the method to the interlanguage links between articles on the same topic in the Finnish and English Wikipedias on the one hand, and to the translations in the Finnish and English Wiktionaries on the other, and compare the results.

1 Introduction

However large a wordnet is, it is never complete but should be open to extending. This article discusses the very concrete problem of adding missing words, but also adds some methodological points to the growing literature on extracting information from freely available multilingual semi-structured resources for (re)use in highly structured language resources for NLP.

Besides adding completely new senses (synsets), new synonyms can be considered for existing synsets. In this paper, we present a simple method for finding new synonym candidates for existing synsets of a wordnet by using a bilingual resource.

K. Lindén (✉) · J. Niemi · M. Hyvärinen
Department of Modern Languages, University of Helsinki, Helsinki, Finland
e-mail: krister.linden@helsinki.fi

J. Niemi
e-mail: jyrki.niemi@helsinki.fi

M. Hyvärinen
e-mail: mirka.hyvarinen@helsinki.fi

D. Santos et al. (eds.), *Shall We Play the Festschrift Game?*,
DOI 10.1007/978-3-642-30773-7_7, © Springer-Verlag Berlin Heidelberg 2012

We wish to extend FinnWordNet, the Finnish wordnet, and we use Wikipedia and Wiktionary as the sources for new synonyms. Part of the results for Wikipedia have been reported in Niemi et al. (2012), but in this article we contrast the results with information from Wiktionary and pay particular attention to adding high- and medium-frequency Finnish words thus far missing from FinnWordNet.

1.1 FinnWordNet as a Translation

FinnWordNet (FiWN)[1] is the Finnish wordnet that was initially created by translating into Finnish all the word senses in Princeton WordNet (PWN, version 3.0). PWN is described in Fellbaum (1998). The first version of FiWN was published in December 2010, and the current version with some corrections is 1.1.2. FiWN has 117,659 synsets, like PWN 3.0. FiWN is freely available under the Creative Commons 3.0 license (CC-BY).

The PWN word senses were translated by professional translators to ensure the quality of the content. The translation process is outlined and discussed by Lindén and Carlson (2010). The direct translation approach was based on the assumption that most synsets in PWN represent language-independent real-world concepts. Thus also the semantic relations between synsets are assumed to be mostly independent of the language, so the structure of PWN can be reused as well. This approach made it possible to create an extensive Finnish wordnet directly aligned with PWN. The direct translation of PWN word senses from English into Finnish also provided us with a translation relation and thus a bilingual wordnet.

A counter-argument to the direct translation approach is that concepts specific to Finland and the Finnish culture and society were left missing from FiWN. Although such concepts certainly exist, our *first hypothesis* is that few of them are common in contemporary Finnish.

1.2 Extending FinnWordNet

A number of common Finnish words are indeed missing from FiWN; see Sects. 5.1 and 6.1. For example, the synset containing the words *cover* and *blanket* lacks the common Finnish word *peitto*, even though the existing translations are valid.

In this study, we wish to estimate the number of missing common words. We also investigate the nature of the missing common words. This is a prerequisite for determining how to add them to the FiWN structure. We found that many of them can be added as synonyms to or hyponyms of existing concepts and that only a small portion of the words actually requires more elaborate conceptual work, discussed

[1] http://www.ling.helsinki.fi/en/lt/research/finnwordnet/.

in Sect. 7.1.1. All in all, we show that FiWN lacks less than 6,000 relevant high- or medium-frequency Finnish words. Adding them would increase the number of words in FiWN by less than 5 %.

Still, adding thousands of new words in their correct places in the semantic hierarchy is a labor-intensive task if done manually. Hence our focus is on such Finnish words that can be automatically placed in the wordnet structure. A general method for finding a location within FiWN for adding new words is described in Pääkkö and Lindén (2012). However, it turns out that as many as half of the relevant missing common words are compounds, and as we look at words of lower frequency, the share of compounds increases. Our *second hypothesis* is that most Finnish compounds have a final part (head) which indicates the hypernym to which they can be added as a hyponym.

1.3 Missing Word Senses in FinnWordNet

In addition to adding Finnish words completely missing from FiWN, we also wish to add missing senses of words in FiWN. For example, the word *aaltoviiva* exists in FiWN at present only as a translation of *swung dash*, but not as a translation of *tilde*, which have different synsets in PWN.

To find new senses of both common and less common words, we use translation pairs extracted from the English and Finnish Wiktionary and Wikipedia. Since the structure of FiWN follows that of PWN, our *third hypothesis* is that the Finnish translation of an English word sense in PWN belongs in the corresponding place in FiWN regardless of whether the Finnish word is new to or existing in FiWN.

1.4 Overview of Methods and Resources

Our first two hypotheses can be verified by simply picking a sample of common words missing from FiWN and evaluating (1) the number of culture-specific words among the relevant missing common words and (2) the number of the relevant missing common words that are compounds with the final part (head) as a hypernym in FiWN. To get an independent estimate, we take a 170-million-word part-of-speech-tagged newspaper corpus of Finnish and extract the most common words missing from FiWN. We also calculate how large a proportion of the missing common words could be covered by Wiktionary and Wikipedia for our third hypothesis.

For the third hypothesis, we follow the method reported in Niemi et al. (2012) for classifying synonym candidates. In this article, we present the method in more detail and also look at some of its assumptions. As the source of synonyms, we use the translation pairs in a bilingual (English–Finnish) resource. The translation pairs are mechanically divided into four different main categories, covered in Sect. 3, and the synonym candidates provided by the pairs are then evaluated manually. The method could be used for any other wordnet with translation links to a wordnet in another language. We test the method by using Wiktionary as the multilingual resource providing new synonym candidates and contrast the results with those on Wikipedia.

Wikipedia[2] is a freely available, collaboratively constructed multilingual Web encyclopedia that contains numerous articles on a broad variety of topics. Wiktionary[3] is a free multilingual Web dictionary, "the lexical companion to Wikipedia".[4] In addition to being available for browsing, they both have been used as resources in various automated tasks; see Sect. 2.

Wikipedia has over 270,000 articles in Finnish, and thus the article titles contain a significant number of words or phrases potentially worth adding to FiWN. Roughly two thirds of the Finnish Wikipedia articles have an interlanguage link to a corresponding article in English. A translation pair is formed by taking the titles of a Finnish article and the corresponding English one.

Wikipedia article titles are nouns or noun phrases, whereas Wiktionary contains words of all parts of speech. The Finnish Wiktionary has about 26,000 entries for Finnish words, with over 10,000 of them having one or more English translations. The English Wiktionary contains over 370,000 English word entries, of which almost 34,000 have at least one Finnish translation. In Wiktionary, we form translation pairs from explicitly marked translations.

The rest of this paper is organized as follows. Section 2 reviews some related work. Section 3 describes the method for finding new synonym candidates for FiWN in bilingual resources. Section 4 presents the notations used in the rest of the paper. Section 5 describes the data we used for evaluating the method, and Sect. 6 presents the results of our evaluation. Section 7 discusses the results and avenues for future work, and Sect. 8 concludes the paper.

2 Related Work

The contents of Wikipedia, Wiktionary and other Wikimedia projects have been exploited in various natural-language processing and information retrieval tasks, among others, and also as sources for lexical information.

An extensive overview on the structure of Wikipedia and the tasks for which it has been used is presented by Medelyan et al. (2009). Also, Zesch et al. (2008) present an overview of both Wikipedia and Wiktionary as lexical semantic resources. Krizhanovsky (2010) describes the structure of Wiktionary and an approach of extracting data from it. Meyer and Gurevych (2010) compare the content of German Wiktionary with GermaNet and OpenThesaurus. Matuschek and Gurevych

[2]http://www.wikipedia.org.

[3]http://www.wiktionary.org.

[4]http://en.wiktionary.org/wiki/Wiktionary:Main_Page.

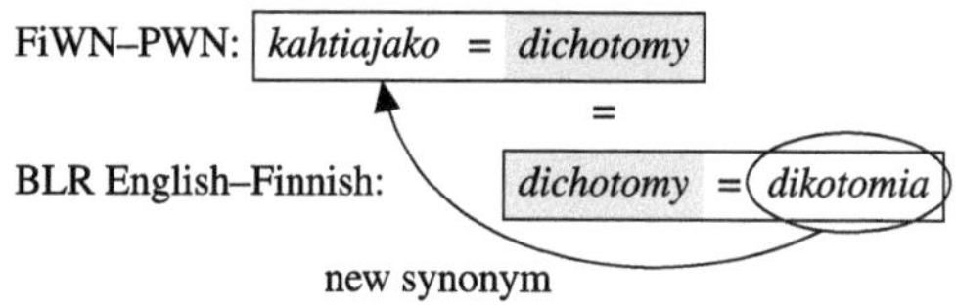

Fig. 1 Finding a new Finnish synonym candidate by joining on the English word: *dikotomia* as a synonym for *kahtiajako*, both being translations of *dichotomy*

(2010) analyze the encoding of synonymy within a single language in such collaboratively constructed lexical resources.

Our approach resembles that of Tyers and Pienaar (2008), who extracted bilingual translation lexicons from the interlanguage links in Wikipedia. The approach of Erdmann et al. (2008, 2009) to extracting domain-specific terminologies is also similar, but since Wikipedia has in general at most one interlanguage link for an article, they also use redirection pages and link texts to obtain synonymous translations. By contrast, we do not construct a dictionary from scratch, since we can use the existing data in FiWN.

Alkhalifa and Rodríguez (2009) use the English–Arabic interlanguage links in Wikipedia to add new named entities to the Arabic WordNet, i.e. synsets corresponding to the ones in PWN. By contrast, in this work, we mainly search the bilingual resources for new synonyms for existing synsets.

3 Method for Finding Synonym Candidates in a Bilingual Resource

Our method, introduced in Niemi et al. (2012), essentially mines new synonyms for a wordnet by using translation pairs in a bilingual resource (BLR) aligned at word (or phrase) level, by joining them on the English word in PWN, and considering the Finnish translations found in the BLR as synonym candidates for FiWN. The principle of joining is illustrated in Fig. 1. Before adding a synonym candidate to FiWN, it must be examined for correctness and semantically disambiguated.

We are able to apply the method to FiWN because it has been created by directly translating the word senses of PWN, so a translation relation between Finnish and English word senses is readily available. The PWN–FiWN translation relation is between individual word senses in synsets instead of between synsets as in many other multilingual wordnets, such as EuroWordNet (Vossen 1998). The translation relation is many-to-many: an English word sense may have several different Finnish translations and vice versa.

When an English word w_{en} is present in both PWN and the BLR, a translation pair with w_{en} in the BLR can be automatically classified in one of the following four categories of occurrence with regard to FiWN:

1. *Exact pair*: FiWN and PWN (the PWN–FiWN translation relation) already have the exact translation pair.
2. *Same synset*: FiWN has the Finnish translation in the same synset as PWN has the English word, but never as a translation pair.

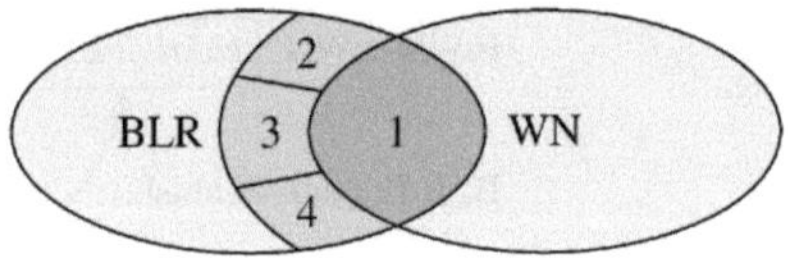

Fig. 2 The categories of translation pairs from two sources. *BLR*: Translation pairs found in BLR. *WN*: Translation pairs found in the bilingual wordnet PWN–FiWN. *1*: Translation pairs found in both BLR and WN. *2*: The Finnish word is the translation of an English word in the same synset, but not as a translation pair. *3*: The Finnish word is in FiWN and the English word is in PWN, but they are in different synsets. *4*: The Finnish word is not found in FiWN. *2, 3 and 4 together*: All the translation pairs in which the English word is found in both BLR and WN but the Finnish word is not its translation in WN

3. *Other synset*: FiWN has the Finnish word and PWN has the English word, but they never occur in the same synset.
4. *No synset*: No synset in FiWN has the Finnish translation.

We use the above categories in the above-mentioned order and mechanically classify each translation pair only in the first matching category.

The diagram in Fig. 2 illustrates the different cases of translation pairs.

Even if a translation pair in the BLR occurs in PWN–FiWN (category 1, *exact pair*), the Finnish word in the pair may also be the translation of some other English word sense in PWN. We estimated that other appropriate word senses for the Finnish word in addition to the one identified in category 1 are rather infrequent: based on a test sample, only around 12 % of them were useful. We therefore disregarded such additional candidates in our current manual analysis.

The Finnish words in the translation pairs in category 2 (*same synset*) could in general be added to FiWN directly, without manual verification, if desired. However, based on a test sample, most of them make the translation relation less crisp, so we decided to omit them. An application can easily cover these cases by accepting translation synonyms as translations if fuzzy translation matching is needed.

The translation pair categories in which we are mainly interested in this paper are 3 (*other synset*) and 4 (*no synset*), since in these categories the found translation *pair* does not occur in the PWN–FiWN synset translation relation. Each of these two categories is further divided into two different groups based on whether the English word occurs in (a) one or (b) more PWN synsets. Our intuition is that a larger part of the synonym candidates in groups (a) are appropriate than in (b), because the words are monosemous (at least in PWN).

A semantic evaluation of categories 3 and 4 can reveal a fifth category, in which a Finnish translation is a representative of a new word sense of an English word in PWN requiring a new synset, but in this study such words are classified among the poor translation candidates since our aim is to find missing word senses for existing synsets.

In general, if a Finnish word in a translation pair in the BLR is found in FiWN but its English translation is not found in PWN, we could use our method to extend PWN by reversing the roles of Finnish and English, but we leave that for future work. If a word sense is new to both FiWN and PWN, we can use the methods described in Pääkkö and Lindén (2012) to find a location for the new word sense within FiWN.

The method for dividing BLR words into categories can be represented more formally as follows. Let *WN* be the PWN–FiWN translation relation where $(w_{en}^W, w_{fi}^W, ss) \in WN$, w_{en}^W is the English word in PWN, w_{fi}^W its Finnish translation in FiWN and $ss \in SS$ a synset identifier (common to PWN and FiWN). Let *BLR* be the translation relation in the BLR, $(w_{en}^B, w_{fi}^B) \in BLR$. We then consider the join J between *BLR* and *WN* on the English word: $J = BLR \underset{w_{en}^B = w_{en}^W}{\bowtie} WN$, where $(w_{en}, w_{fi}^B, w_{fi}^W, ss) \in J$ and $w_{en} = w_{en}^B = w_{en}^W$. A translation pair $tp = (w_{en}, w_{fi}^B)$ is a projection of tuple $(w_{en}, w_{fi}^B, w_{fi}^W, ss) \in J$. The above categories can be defined for *tp* as follows:

1. *Exact pair* For some $(w_{en}, \cdot, w_{fi}^{\prime W}, \cdot) \in J$: $w_{fi}^B = w_{fi}^{\prime W}$.
2. *Same synset* Not *exact pair*, and for some $(w_{en}^{\prime}, w_{fi}^B, w_{fi}^W, ss) \in J$: $w_{en}^{\prime} \neq w_{en}$.
3. *Other synset* Neither *exact pair* nor *same synset*, and for some $(w_{en}^{\prime}, w_{fi}^B, w_{fi}^W, ss^{\prime}) \in J$: $w_{en}^{\prime} \neq w_{en}$ and $ss^{\prime} \neq ss$.
4. *No synset* For all $(\cdot, \cdot, w_{fi}^{\prime W}, \cdot) \in J$: $w_{fi}^{\prime W} \neq w_{fi}^B$.

The subgroups (a) and (b) can be defined as follows:

a. *Monosemous* For all $(w_{en}, \cdot, \cdot, ss^{\prime}) \in J$: $ss^{\prime} = ss$
b. *Polysemous* For some $(w_{en}, \cdot, \cdot, ss^{\prime}) \in J$: $ss^{\prime} \neq ss$

4 Notations

Since this paper refers to (the sizes of) many resources and their subsets and samples, we name most of them to ease tracing the sources of the numbers. Table 1 lists the names and notations used and the table or section in which they are defined or primarily used.

5 Test Data

To test our method outlined above, we used Wiktionary translations as the bilingual resource between Finnish and English. We compare these results with results obtained from the interlanguage (translation) links between the Finnish and English Wikipedia. We begin with presenting the lists of high- and medium-frequency Finnish words, which we in particular wish to add to FiWN.

5.1 Common Finnish Words Missing from FinnWordNet

The list of common (high- and medium-frequency) Finnish words missing from FiWN is combined from two sources. The first one (CW_{Np}) is a word frequency list

Table 1 Notations and names used for referring to resources and their subsets and samples

Notation	Table or section	Description
CW_X	Table 2	A list of (Finnish) common words ($X \in \{Np, F, Fh, Fm\}$)
CW_{fi}	Table 2	The combined list of Finnish common words
$CW_{fi,wnp}$	Table 2	CW_{fi} restricted to the parts of speech in FiWN
$CW_{\overline{WN_{fi}}}$	Sect. 5.1	The words in $CW_{fi,wnp}$ missing from FiWN
$CW_{\overline{W}}$	Sect. 6.1.2	The words in $CW_{\overline{WN_{fi}}}$ not found in Wiktionary ($CW_{\overline{WN_{fi}}} \setminus W_{fi}(TPC^{WT,CW})$)
$cw^{0}_{\overline{W}}$	Table 12	The 200 most frequent words of $CW_{\overline{W}}$
$CW'_{\overline{W}}$	Table 12	$CW_{\overline{W}} \setminus cw^{0}_{\overline{W}}$
$cw'_{\overline{W}}$	Table 12	An even sample of $CW'_{\overline{W}}$
WN_L	Table 3	The wordnet of language L ($L \in \{fi, en\}$)
WP_L	Table 3	The Wikipedia of language L (article titles)
WP_L^{notag}	Table 3	The Wikipedia of language L (article titles excluding those with a disambiguation tag)
WT_L	Table 3	The Wiktionary of language L (words in L)
WN	Table 4	The PWN–FiWN translation relation (bilingual wordnet)
WP	Table 4	Finnish–English translations from the Finnish Wikipedia interwiki links
WT	Table 4	Finnish–English translations from the Finnish and English Wiktionaries
$W(R)$	Table 3	All the different words in resource R
$W_N(R)$	Table 3	All the different nouns in resource R
$W_{wnp}(R)$	Table 3	All the different nouns, verbs, adjectives and adverbs in resource R
$WS(R)$	Table 3	All the different words senses in resource R
$WS_N(R)$	Table 3	All the different nouns senses in resource R
$WS_{wnp}(R)$	Table 3	All the different senses of nouns, verbs, adjectives and adverbs in R
$TP(R)$	Table 4	All the different translation pairs in resource R
$TP_N(R)$	Table 4	All the different noun translation pairs in resource R
$TP_{wnp}(R)$	Table 4	All the different translation pairs of nouns, verbs, adjectives, adverbs in R
$TPS(R)$	Table 4	All the different translation pair senses in resource R
$TPS_N(R)$	Table 4	All the different noun translation pair senses in resource R
$TPS_{wnp}(R)$	Table 4	All the different translation pair senses of nouns, verbs, adjectives and adverbs in resource R
$TPC^{WT,CW}$	Sect. 6.1	The translation pairs in Wiktionary with the Finnish word in $CW_{\overline{W}}$

Table 1 (Continued)

Notation	Table or section	Description
TPC^{R}_{cat}	Table 13	The translation pairs of resource R ($TP_{wnp}(R)$) classified in category *cat*
tpc^{R}_{cat}	Tables 14, 15	A sample of the translation pairs of resource R ($TP_{wnp}(R)$) classified in category *cat*
$Q_{qual}(S)$	Tables 14, 15	The translation pairs in (sample) S evaluated as having the quality *qual*
$Cap(R)$	Table 8	Resource R with the first word of each item capitalized
$\|S\|$	Several	The size of (the set or list) S
$PT(Fn(S))$	Sect. 6.1	The proportion (percentage) $\|Fn(S)\|/\|S\|$
$E_{qual,cat}(R)$	Tables 16, 17	The estimated number of translation pairs of quality *qual* classified in the category *cat* of the resource R
$E^{CW}_{type}(C)$	Table 12	The estimated number of words classified as *type* in the common words list C

for Finnish newspaper language containing the 9,985 most common lemmas from a corpus of almost 44 million words.[5] The list was compiled from texts that had been lemmatized and morphologically analyzed using TextMorfo (Jäppinen et al. 1983; Jäppinen and Ylilammi 1986; Valkonen et al. 1987). The second list (CW_F) is compiled based on the Finnish Text Collection (FTC) 2001, which contains approx. 170 million words of Finnish, consisting of 97 subcollections of Finnish newspaper, magazine and literature texts from the 1990s.[6] The lemmas of the words were obtained by analyzing the corpus with Connexor's Finnish FDG parser.[7]

We considered as high-frequency words (CW_{Fh}) those with a relative frequency of at least the average frequency of the words in FiWN (as computed in FTC), and as medium-frequency words (CW_{Fm}) those with at least one fourth of the average. Based on these criteria, the list CW_{Fh} contains 8,933 high-frequency words and CW_{Fm} a further 17,548 medium-frequency words ($CW_{Fh} \cap CW_{Fm} = \emptyset$). Table 2 shows some statistics on the common words lists. As can be seen, the words on the combined FTC list (CW_F) cover approx. 88 % of all word occurrences in the FTC corpus.

Most of the words, 9,072 out of 9,985, in the newspaper language list CW_{Np} were also present in the larger combined FTC list CW_F, but 913 words were nevertheless

[5] The list was compiled at CSC in 2004, and it is available online at http://www.csc.fi/tutkimus/alat/kielitiede/taajuussanasto-B9996/view.

[6] FTC has been compiled by the Research Institute for the Languages in Finland, the Department of General Linguistics of the University of Helsinki and the Foreign Languages Department of the University of Joensuu. More information is available online at http://www.csc.fi/english/research/software/ftc.

[7] http://www.connexor.eu/technology/machinese/glossary/fdg/index.html.

Table 2 Statistics on the common words lists: the number of words on the list, the absolute and relative frequency of the last word in the list, and how large a part the words on the list cover of all the word occurrences in the corpus

Common words list (m)	No. of words $\|m\|$	Minimum frequency absolute	Minimum frequency relative (%)	% of corpus
Newspaper (CW_{Np})	9,985	436	0.00074	74.7
FTC high-frequency (CW_{Fh})	8,933	1,593	0.00097	80.0
FTC medium-frequency (CW_{Fm})	17,548	399	0.00024	8.2
FTC combined ($CW_F = CW_{Fh} \cup CW_{Fm}$)	26,481	399	0.00024	88.1
All combined ($CW_{fi} = CW_{Np} \cup CW_F$)	27,394	399	0.00024	
CW_{fi} where PoS is N, V, A or Adv ($CW_{fi,wnp}$)	18,957	399	0.00024	

missing, probably largely because different analysis principles had resulted in different lemmas or parts of speech. The large overlap between the two frequency lists is good evidence that the bulk of high-frequency words is relatively stable and therefore adding such missing words to FiWN is all the more important. We combined the two lists to a list of 27,394 words (CW_{fi}).

We filtered out other parts of speech than (common) nouns, verbs, adjectives and adverbs. The filtered list $CW_{fi,wnp}$ contained 18,957 words. Of these, 7,368 words did not occur at all in FiWN (with the given part of speech) ($CW_{\overline{WN_{fi}}} = CW_{fi,wnp} \backslash WN_{fi}$).

5.2 Wikipedia and Wiktionary Data Formats

Various kinds of dumps of the Wiktionary and Wikipedia content are freely available for download.[8] We used the current article contents of the Finnish Wikipedia as of 29 August 2011,[9] the Finnish Wiktionary as of 21 September 2011[10] and the English Wiktionary as of 20 September 2011.[11] The dumps contain the content of each article in the wiki markup embedded in XML, combined with various metadata.

[8]http://dumps.wikimedia.org/.

[9]http://download.wikimedia.org/fiwiki/20110829/fiwiki-20110829-pages-articles.xml.bz2.

[10]http://download.wikimedia.org/fiwiktionary/20110921/fiwiktionary-20110921-pages-articles.xml.bz2.

[11]http://download.wikimedia.org/enwiktionary/20110920/enwiktionary-20110920-pages-articles.xml.bz2.

```
<title>Austronesialainen kielikunta</title>
<text xml:space="preserve">#REDIRECT [[Austronesialaiset kielet]]</text>
<title>Algebrallinen luku</title>
...
[[en:Algebraic number]]
[[es:Número algebraico]]
[[eo:Algebra nombro]]
[[eu:Zenbaki aljebraiko]]
...
<title>Assembly</title>
Täsmennyssivu
[[de:Assembly]]
[[en:Assembly]]
[[es:Assembly]]
[[it:Assembly (disambigua)]]
...
```

Fig. 3 An excerpt of the data extracted from the Wikipedia article dump (an ellipsis indicates omitted text)

5.2.1 Wikipedia

The Wikipedia dump contains the title of an article as a separate XML element and the interlanguage links as wiki links, with the title of the target article prefixed with a language code. We extracted these items with simple regular expressions, without parsing the XML or the wiki markup of the article any further. We also extracted Wikipedia redirection links and wiki markup indicating that a page is a disambiguation page. A short excerpt of the extracted file is shown in Fig. 3.

An analysis of the kinds of translations provided by Wikipedia translation links is presented by Sjöbergh et al. (2008).

5.2.2 Wiktionary

The Wiktionary of a language L contains not only words of L but also words of any other language with definitions in L. However, translations are provided only for words of L.

Similar to Wikipedia, the Wiktionary dump also contains the title of an article (word entry) as a separate XML element. However, extracting the translations is not as simple as in Wikipedia, so we need to process the article text slightly more.

The exact structure of a Wiktionary entry varies from language to language, and it is not fixed even within a language, even though certain structures are strongly recommended. The Wiktionaries of different languages also use different wiki templates for encoding various elements, so a Wiktionary parser or data extractor is necessarily language-specific.

A typical Wiktionary entry contains the language of the entry word at the first heading level, its part of speech at the second level and translations at the third. Translations of polysemous words are further divided by the sense.

Even though the Wiktionary dumps are not as large as the Wikipedia dumps, we first extract from them the relevant parts of the articles: titles and the parts of the articles depicting words in the languages in which we are interested. Figures 4 and 5

```
<title>fork</title>
<text xml:space="preserve">
==English==
...
===Noun===
{{en-noun}}
# A pronged [[tool]] having a long straight handle, used for
    [[dig]]ging, lifting, throwing etc.
...
# A [[utensil]] with [[spike]]s used to put [[solid]] [[food]]
    into the [[mouth]], or to hold food down while cutting.
...
====Translations====
{{trans-top|eating utensil with spikes}}
...
* Finnish: {{t+|fi|haarukka}}
...
{{trans-top|tool with spikes used for digging}}
...
* Finnish: {{t-|fi|talikko}}
...
===Verb===
{{en-verb}}
# {{transitive}} To move with a fork (as hay or food).
...
====Translations====
{{trans-top|use a fork to move food to mouth}}
...
* Finnish: {{t+|fi|haarukoida}}
...
</text>
```

Fig. 4 An excerpt of the data extracted from the entry of *fork* in the English Wiktionary dump, with some Finnish translations

```
<title>haarukka</title>
<text xml:space="preserve">
==Suomi==
[[Kuva:Gabel.jpg|thumb|100px|Haarukka]]
===Substantiivi===
'''haarukka''' ({{taivutustyyppi|14}}-{{taivutustyyppi|A}})
# [[ruokailuväline]], jonka varren päässä on samansuuntaisia
    piikkejä, tavallisesti kaksi, kolme tai neljä piikkiä
...
# arvojoukko jonka tietty arvo voi saada, [[mittaväli]]
...
====Käännökset====
{{ylä|1.|ruokailuväline|}}
...
*{{en}}: [[fork]]
...
{{ylä|arvojoukko}}
*{{en}}: [[range]]

</text>
```

Fig. 5 An excerpt of the data extracted from the entry of *haarukka* in the Finnish Wiktionary dump, with some English translations (*fork*, *range*)

show abridged examples of the English and Finnish Wiktionary data, respectively. From this data, we extract the title word, language, part of speech and the (unprocessed) translations in the other language, including the sense in the translation.

5.3 Preprocessing and Filtering Translations

Although the preprocessing and filtering of the translations are in many ways different for Wikipedia and Wiktionary, some features are in common.

5.3.1 Common Features

The following features are common to preprocessing and filtering both Wikipedia and Wiktionary data. We omit translation pairs with identical words in Finnish and English. They are typically such proper nouns that should not be translated and are not translated in FiWN. By contrast, we include synonym candidates for words untranslated in FiWN, since they might have been left untranslated by accident.

We consider the Finnish Wikipedia title or Wiktionary word to be equal to the FiWN word (and classified in category 1, *exact pair*) even if they differ in (orthographic) case.

In FiWN translations, we disregard the translators' comment tags, which may indicate, for example, that the translation is more general or more specific than the original word (Lindén and Carlson 2010: 129–130). A word is considered as occurring in FiWN even if it occurs only with a translator's comment.

Some entries in FiWN and the Finnish Wikipedia or Wiktionary have the same English translation but differ in the grammatical number of the word: one may be in the singular and the other in the plural. This occurs in particular in the names of taxonomic categories of animals and plants. Since we do not want to add synonyms differing only in grammatical number, we lemmatize the Finnish words in FiWN and the Finnish Wikipedia and Wiktionary and consider the words (or phrases) equal if their lemmas are the same. As the lemmatizer, we use Omorfi, an open morphology tool for Finnish.[12]

5.3.2 Wikipedia

Wikipedia article titles must be unambiguous within a language. To handle subjects that would naturally have the same title, a title may contain in parentheses a *disambiguation tag* distinguishing between the different senses of a word. The disambiguation tag is often a domain or the type of the subject of the article, such as in *Subject (grammar)* or *Subject (album)*. If a title has several different senses with different disambiguation tags, it often has a separate *disambiguation page* with links to the individual articles.

We filter out all article titles with a disambiguation tag and the titles of disambiguation pages, since these words are most likely particularly polysemous and thus the probability of a translation being correct is lower. However, if a title exists both

[12]https://gna.org/projects/omorfi.

with and without a disambiguation tag, the translation pair in question is included. Disambiguation tags could also be used in a different method to assist in choosing the correct sense for a translation, for example, by comparing the tag with the hypernym of a word in a wordnet.

Note, in particular, that we only filter out polysemous data that is explicitly marked as such in the Wikipedia data. This is not done in Wiktionary, which gives us an additional aspect when comparing the results of the tests on the two resources. We are aware that frequency and polysemy are correlated, so excluding polysemous data may in fact filter out some of the most frequent words, which are the ones we actually want to add. To verify the validity and wisdom of ignoring titles with disambiguation tags, we separately evaluated a sample of translation pairs obtained from such titles and found the yield to be low: only about 6 % of the translation pairs would have provided a new synonym to FiWN.

We also filter out Wikipedia redirection links, which typically redirect from an alternative title to the actual article. Although they could provide some additional synonyms, they would also generate noise in the form of alternative spellings.

Because of the encyclopedic nature of Wikipedia, the titles of the articles are in general nouns or noun phrases. We thus include only the nouns in FiWN when considering translation candidates from Wikipedia.

We include Wikipedia article titles with a namespace prefix by simply removing the prefix. The most common namespace is *Category*. Since a word or phrase may occur as a Wikipedia title both as such and as a category, the translation relation obtained from Wikipedia translation links is many-to-many, even though each article has at most one interlanguage link for each language.

A translation link in Wikipedia may point to a section of an article. In such cases, we would have two candidates for translations: the title of the article or the section. Links to sections are uncommon, however, and the synonym candidates that they would provide seem mostly incorrect, so we omit them.

All article titles in Wikipedia have the first letter capitalized regardless of whether the word is a proper noun or not, whereas in PWN and FiWN only proper nouns are capitalized. To overcome the difference, we compare capitalized variants of the PWN words with the unmodified Wikipedia titles. If the Finnish Wikipedia title is to be added to FiWN as a synonym and if it contains only lowercase letters after the capitalized initial, the first letter is lowercased if (at least half of) the existing FiWN synonyms in the target synset are in lowercase. If the title contains other uppercase letters besides the first one, the case is retained as such.

5.3.3 Wiktionary

At the preprocessing phase of the Wiktionary data, we extract the individual translations from the unprocessed (raw) translation strings. The task is made more challenging by the sometimes inconsistent representation conventions, and some translations may still be left out.

Table 3 The number of words and word senses. *WN PoS* = wordnet parts of speech. *N/A* = not applicable: the common words list does not distinguish between the different senses of a word

	Words			Word senses		
Lexical resource (R)	N $\lvert W_N(R)\rvert$	WN PoS $\lvert W_{wnp}(R)\rvert$	All words $\lvert W(R)\rvert$	N $\lvert WS_N(R)\rvert$	WN PoS $\lvert WS_{wnp}(R)\rvert$	All words $\lvert WS(R)\rvert$
PWN (WN_{en})	119,034	156,584	156,584	146,347	206,978	206,978
FiWN (WN_{fi})	101,389	132,696	132,696	131,764	191,797	191,797
Wiktionary En (WT_{en})	235,307	376,577	405,741	247,282	396,336	426,179
Wiktionary Fi (WT_{fi})	17,035	21,653	26,811	17,940	23,231	28,426
Wikipedia En (WP_{en})	5,831,207	5,831,207	5,831,207	6,313,253	6,313,253	6,313,253
Wikipedia En (WP_{en}^{notag})	5,543,618	5,543,618	5,543,618	5,659,294	5,659,294	5,659,294
Wikipedia Fi (WP_{fi})	338,793	338,793	338,793	366,790	366,790	366,790
Wikipedia Fi (WP_{fi}^{notag})	326,546	326,546	326,546	337,567	337,567	337,567
Common words Fi (CW_{fi})	12,030	18,957	27,207	N/A	N/A	N/A

The Finnish–English and English–Finnish translations are then combined into a single list of translations. Since the words in FiWN have been translated from English, we expect that more translations found in the Finnish–English direction have been left missing.

From the Wiktionary word entries, we filter out all parts of speech not occurring in PWN (and FiWN), keeping only nouns, verbs, adjectives and adverbs. We also omit proper nouns, since they are typically left untranslated.

Wiktionary has no equivalent of the Wikipedia disambiguation tags, since a single article (word entry) should describe all the senses of the word.

By contrast with Wikipedia, the article titles in Wiktionary follow the normal orthographic case of a word (only proper nouns are capitalized), so we can compare the words directly with the those in PWN.

5.4 Data Sizes

5.4.1 Overview

Table 3 provides an overview of the sizes of the wordnet, Wikipedia, Wiktionary and Finnish common words data in terms of the number of words and word senses, separately for each language. The table contains separate counts for nouns (or noun phrases); for nouns, adjectives, verbs and adverbs together (the parts of speech in PWN and FiWN); and for all words. Table 4 gives the corresponding figures in the different resources for translation pairs and translation pair senses (each occurrence of a translation pair counted separately).

Table 4 The number of translation pairs and translation pair senses

	Translation pairs			Translation pair senses		
	N	WN PoS	All words	N	WN PoS	All words
Lexical resource (R)	$\|TP_N(R)\|$	$\|TP_{wnp}(R)\|$	$\|TP(R)\|$	$\|TPS_N(R)\|$	$\|TPS_{wnp}(R)\|$	$\|TPS(R)\|$
PWN–FiWN (*WN*)	147,693	211,481	211,481	157,775	230,051	230,051
Wiktionary (*WT*)	42,227	68,508	72,578	51,993	83,650	88,554
Wikipedia (*WP*)	209,438	209,438	209,438	213,796	213,796	213,796

Table 5 The number of Finnish words in the intersections of the resources

$\|W(R_1) \cap W(R_2)\|$	Resource R_2			
	FiWN	Wiktionary Fi	Wikipedia Fi	Common words Fi
Resource R_1	WN_{fi}	WT_{fi}	WP_{fi}	CW_{fi}
FiWN (WN_{fi})	132,696	12,158	22,387	11,589
Wiktionary Fi (WT_{fi})	12,158	26,811	7,869	8,004
Wikipedia Fi (WP_{fi})	22,387	7,869	338,793	5,135
Common words Fi (CW_{fi})	11,589	8,004	5,135	27,207

Table 6 The number of English words in the intersections of the resources

$\|W(R_1) \cap W(R_2)\|$	Resource R_2		
	PWN	Wiktionary En	Wikipedia En
Resource R_1	WN_{en}	WT_{en}	WP_{en}
PWN (WN_{en})	156,584	75,900	52,836
Wiktionary En (WT_{en})	75,900	376,577	70,960
Wikipedia En (WP_{en})	52,836	70,960	5,831,207

Table 7 The number of translation pairs in the intersections of the resources

$\|TP(R_1) \cap TP(R_2)\|$	Resource R_2		
	PWN–FiWN	Wiktionary	Wikipedia
Resource R_1	*WN*	*WT*	*WP*
PWN–FiWN (*WN*)	211,481	25,777	12,643
Wiktionary (*WT*)	25,777	68,508	6,953
Wikipedia (*WP*)	12,643	6,953	209,438

The numbers for Wikipedia in these tables include titles with disambiguation tags, with the tags removed. In Table 3, we also list the numbers for titles without disambiguation tags (WP_L^{notag}).

Tables 5, 6 and 7 show the number of Finnish words, English words and translation pairs, respectively, that the resources have in common, i.e. the sizes of the intersections of the resources.

Table 8 The recall of FiWN and PWN in Wikipedia titles. The columns labeled *No tags* exclude titles with disambiguation tags, whereas ones labeled *With tags* include such titles, with the tags themselves removed

	Finnish ($L = fi$)		English ($L = en$)	
	No tags $WP = WP^{notag}_{fi}$	With tags WP_{fi}	No tags WP^{notag}_{en}	With tags WP_{en}
Unique Wikipedia titles ($W_{WP} = W_N(WP)$)	326,546	338,793	5,543,618	5,831,207
Unique wordnet nouns ($W_{WN} = Cap(W_N(WN_L))$)	100,901	100,901	117,972	117,972
Intersection ($I = W_{WP} \cap W_{WN}$)	19,974	22,387	38,985	52,836
Wikipedia recall of wordnet ($\|I\|/\|W_{WN}\|$)	19.8 %	22.2 %	33.0 %	44.8 %

When calculating the intersection between Wikipedia and another resource, the Wikipedia title was retained as such (capitalized), and the word in the other resource was capitalized.

5.4.2 Wikipedia

The PWN–FiWN translation relation contains 147,693 different English–Finnish noun translation pairs ($TP_N(WN)$), and the interlanguage links from the Finnish to English Wikipedia contains 209,438 pairs ($TP_N(WP)$).

Table 8 shows the number of different Wikipedia article titles in Finnish and English, the number of different nouns (or noun phrases) in FiWN and PWN and how large a part of them are in common.[13] To make the numbers comparable with the number of synonym candidates, we preprocessed and filtered the Wikipedia titles and wordnet nouns as described above in Sect. 5.3 and considered the resulting unique words.[14] The numbers for Wikipedia include the titles of category, template and other meta-pages, in addition to articles proper. For comparison, the table also shows the corresponding figures when including the Wikipedia titles with disambiguation tags.[15]

As can be seen from the table, even though the English Wikipedia has more than 16 times the number of articles in the Finnish Wikipedia, the portion of nouns in

[13]The figures for the English Wikipedia are based on the dump of article contents on 4 August 2011.

[14]The numbers of unique wordnet nouns $|W_{WN}|$ in Table 8 are slightly smaller than the corresponding $|W_N(WN_L)|$ in Table 3 because of capitalizing the first word of all nouns (or noun phrases) and counting only the unique ones.

[15]Even with the titles with disambiguation tags included, the intersection of English Wikipedia titles and PWN nouns is still smaller than the 80,295 reported by Navigli and Ponzetto (2010) because we have omitted the titles of disambiguation and redirection pages.

Table 9 The recall of FiWN and PWN in Wiktionary words

	Finnish ($L = fi$)	English ($L = en$)
Unique Wiktionary word entries ($W_{WT} = W_{wnp}(WT_L)$)	21,653	376,577
Unique wordnet words ($W_{WN} = W_{wnp}(WN_L)$)	132,696	156,584
Intersection ($I = W_{WT} \cap W_{WN}$)	12,158	75,900
Wiktionary recall of wordnet ($\|I\|/\|W_{WN}\|$)	9.2 %	48.5 %

PWN in common with the English Wikipedia is less than twice that of the nouns in FiWN in common with the Finnish Wikipedia.

The Finnish Wikipedia interlanguage links contained 25,062 different translation pairs in which the English word was found in PWN (TPC^{WP}). In preprocessing, we filtered out 8,280 of them, leaving us with 16,782 different translation pairs (TPC^{WP}_{filt}).

5.4.3 Wiktionary

The number of all Finnish–English translation pairs in the FiWN–PWN translation relation is 211,481 ($TP_{wnp}(WN)$), and those in the Wiktionary translations 68,508 ($TP_{wnp}(WT)$), when considering only the parts of speech in the wordnets and when translation pairs with different parts of speech are considered different.

Table 9 shows the number of different Wiktionary article titles in Finnish and English, the number of different words in FiWN and PWN and how large a part of them are in common. The Wiktionary titles and wordnet words were preprocessed and filtered as described above in Sect. 5.3.[16] The same words with different parts of speech are considered different.

Both the Finnish and English Wikipedias are an order of magnitude larger in the number of entries than the respective Wiktionaries. However, the English Wiktionary's recall of all the words in PWN is greater than but relatively close to that of the English Wikipedia. This probably reflects the closer correspondence between the nature of a Wiktionary and a wordnet. By contrast, the Finnish Wiktionary's smaller recall of FiWN compared with that of the Finnish Wikipedia probably only indicates that the Finnish Wiktionary is still rather sparse. Most of the translation pairs were thus provided by the Finnish translations in the English Wiktionary.

The Finnish–English and English–Finnish Wiktionary translations contained 58,110 different translation pairs in which the English word was found in PWN (TPC^{WT}). Even though Wiktionary is a less extensive resource than Wikipedia, it thus provided almost twice the number of translation pair candidates.

[16]However, the wordnet words include proper nouns and abbreviations.

Table 10 The polysemy (in PWN) of the English words in the suggested translation pairs

	Wikipedia	PWN nouns	Wiktionary	PWN all words
Different English words	23,081	119,034	27,610	156,584
Monosemous words	16,390	98,074	15,118	130,207
Polysemous words	6,691	20,960	12,492	26,377
Percentage of polysemous words	29.0 %	17.6 %	45.2 %	16.9 %
Average no. of senses (all words)	1.67	1.33	2.13	1.32
Average no. of senses (polysemous)	3.32	2.85	3.49	2.91

5.4.4 Polysemy

The frequency of a word is reflected in its polysemy: the more frequent a word is, the more senses it typically has. Table 10 compares the Wikipedia and Wiktionary data with regard to the polysemy in PWN of the English words for which the Finnish translations were suggested. The figures for all PWN nouns and all PWN words are shown for contrast.

The words for which translation candidates were found in Wikipedia and Wiktionary were clearly more polysemous than all the words in PWN, which reflects the fact that the former are more frequent on the average. Moreover, a larger part of the words in Wiktionary were polysemous than those in Wikipedia, and they had more senses, which reflects the nature of Wiktionary containing more common and thus more polysemous words than Wikipedia.

6 Results and Evaluation

In this section, we present the results of (1) an evaluation of samples of the common words missing from FiWN, (2) classification of translation pairs found in Wikipedia and Wiktionary in the categories described in Sect. 3, and (3) an evaluation of samples of these categories.

6.1 Common Words

Since one of our main goals in this study was to find common Finnish words missing from FiWN, we separately analyzed both a sample of the common words found with our method for exploiting BLRs and a sample of those common words that were still left missing.

Table 11 The quality of the synonym candidates found in the Wiktionary data with a Finnish word among the common words missing from FiWN

	Data category (C)					
	4a ($tpc_{nsm}^{WT,CW}$)		4b ($tpc_{nsp}^{WT,CW}$)		Total ($tpc_{ns}^{WT,CW}$)	
Synonym candidate quality	$\|C\|$	%	$\|C\|$	%	$\|C\|$	%
(i) Replaces original translation ($Q_r(C)$)	0	(0.0)	2	(1.5)	2	(1.0)
(ii) To be added ($Q_a(C)$)	41	(62.1)	73	(54.5)	114	(57.0)
(a) appropriate as such ($Q_{as}(C)$)	39	(59.1)	70	(52.2)	109	(54.5)
(b) appropriate if edited ($Q_{ae}(C)$)	1	(1.5)	2	(1.5)	3	(1.5)
(c) alternative form ($Q_{aa}(C)$)	1	(1.5)	1	(0.7)	2	(1.0)
(i) + (ii) *Appropriate total* ($Q_{r+a}(C)$)	*41*	*(62.1)*	*75*	*(56.0)*	*116*	*(58.0)*
(iii) Unsure ($Q_u(C)$)	0	(0.0)	0	(0.0)	0	(0.0)
(iv) Poor ($Q_p(C)$)	25	(37.9)	59	(44.0)	84	(42.0)
Total ($\|C\|$)	66	(100.0)	134	(100.0)	200	(100.0)

6.1.1 Found Common Words

As we wanted to pay attention to culturally important words missing from FiWN, the common words that we analyzed were chosen from those missing from FiWN, which by definition fall into translation pair categories 4a and 4b (*no synset*). The Wiktionary data provided a total of 1,279 translation pairs ($TPC^{WT,CW}$) in which the Finnish word was in the list of missing common words, with a total of 980 different Finnish words ($W_{fi}(TPC^{WT,CW})$) out of the 7,368 missing common words ($CW_{\overline{WN_{fi}}}$). The Wikipedia data provided only 140 such Finnish words (nouns), of which 87 were common with the Wiktionary data, so we only analyzed the Wiktionary data.

We analyzed the quality of a sample of 200 translation pairs with a Finnish word in the common words list; the results are shown in Table 11. We determined the number of (i) synonym candidates that should replace an existing translation in FiWN, (ii) ones that should be added to FiWN, and (iii) poor and (iv) unsure ones. The existing translations to be replaced were deemed incorrect with regard to the gloss of the synset. The synonym candidates to be added were further divided into (ii a) appropriate ones as such, (ii b) appropriate ones if edited (e.g. from plural to singular) and (ii c) ones that were an alternative form of the translation in FiWN. In addition to alternative spellings for words, alternative forms included different variants for expressing dates and proper nouns. Poor candidates are poor only with regard to the gloss of the synset. For a further discussion of poor candidates, see Sect. 7.2.3. Unsure candidates included medical terminology and complicated abstract concepts.

As can be seen by comparing with Table 15, the quality of the found translation candidates for common words was somewhat better than for all the synonyms found

Table 12 Samples of common Finnish words missing from FiWN divided by the type of word and the estimated total number of words of each type. The estimated percentage is calculated based on the estimated upper and lower bounds for the number of *relevant* words and the words of the type

	Sample (s)				Estimated in $CW'_{\overline{W}} = C$	
	Most freq. $cw^{0}_{\overline{W}}$		Evenly distrib. $cw'_{\overline{W}}$		Total $E^{CW}_{type}(C)$	Of relevant $E^{CW}_{type}(C)/E^{CW}_{rel}(C)$
Type of word (*type*)	n	%	n	%	n	%
(1) Culture-specific (*cu*)	6	(3.0)	10	(5.0 ± 3.0)	309 ± 187	(6.9 ± 4.5)
(2) Other non-compound (*nc*)	55	(27.5)	44	(22.0 ± 5.7)	1,361 ± 355	(29.5 ± 9.8)
(3) Other compound (*co*)	33	(16.5)	99	(49.5 ± 6.9)	3,063 ± 429	(65.8 ± 14.1)
(1–3) Total relevant (rel)	*94*	*(47.0)*	*153*	*(76.5 ± 5.9)*	*4,734 ± 364*	*(100.0)*
(4) Incorrect or irrelevant (*ic*)	106	(53.0)	47	(23.5 ± 5.9)	1,454 ± 364	N/A
Total ($\|s\|$)	200	(100.0)	200	(100.0)	6,188	

in Wiktionary ($PT(Q_{r+a}(tpc^{WT,CW}_{ns})) = 58.0$ % vs. $PT(Q_{r+a}(tpc^{WT}_{rel})) = 45.0$ %). Still, only 58 % of the sample could really be used in FiWN. Based on that, we estimate that the Wiktionary translation candidate list could provide us with 568 ± 67 common words ($PT(Q_{r+a}(tpc^{WT,CW}_{ns})) \times |W_{fi}(TPC^{WT,CW})|$), which is 7.7±0.9 % of the 7,368 missing common words ($CW_{\overline{WN_{fi}}}$).

6.1.2 Common Words Left Missing

Some of the words in the list of common words missing from FiWN seemed to be analysis errors. To assess the relevance of the words in the list, we considered words that had a part of speech included in FiWN and that were not found as synonym candidates from Wiktionary by our method ($CW_{\overline{W}} = CW_{\overline{WN_{fi}}} \setminus W_{fi}(TPC^{WT,CW})$; $|CW_{\overline{W}}| = 7{,}368 - 980 = 6{,}388$). We analyzed the 200 most frequent words in the list ($cw^{0}_{\overline{W}}$) and 200 words in an evenly distributed sample $cw'_{\overline{W}}$ of the rest of the 6,188 words ($CW'_{\overline{W}} = CW_{\overline{W}} \setminus cw^{0}_{\overline{W}}$).

We classified the words into four categories. (1) Culture-specific words are words that are somehow specific to Finland or the Finnish culture, e.g. words for inhabitants of Finnish towns and provinces. Other relevant words were divided in (2) compound and (3) non-compound words. The group of (4) incorrect or irrelevant words contains probable analysis errors, such as wrong part of speech, proper nouns analyzed as common nouns, abbreviations and non-Finnish words. Table 12 shows the number of words in each category in the two samples and the estimated total number of words in the list $CW'_{\overline{W}}$, based on the evenly distributed sample $cw'_{\overline{W}}$.

The list of the most frequent words contains many more probably incorrect or irrelevant words than the evenly distributed sample. Moreover, of the 55 non-compounds in the most common words, 32 are adverbs, many of which in isolation are of less importance for the typical use of a wordnet, which tends to be various information retrieval and extraction tasks. We thus think that the evenly distributed sample gives a more useful estimate of the distribution of the different types of words in the list of missing common words.

Based on the evenly distributed sample $cw'_{\overline{W}}$, we estimate that $4{,}734 \pm 364$ ($E_{rel}^{CW}(CW'_{\overline{W}})$) of the missing common Finnish words are relevant to FiWN and that 309 ± 187 ($E_{cu}^{CW}(CW'_{\overline{W}})$), or 6.9 ± 4.5 %, of them are specific to Finnish culture. The nature of the missing words is discussed in Sect. 7.1.1.

Compound words could potentially be added as hyponyms to a hypernym found by the final part (head) of the compound. After evaluating the samples, we marked all the compound words in the list of missing common words, and found the list to contain a total of 3,087 compounds (65.2 ± 4.7 % of the relevant words), including both culture-specific and other compounds. To test the validity of the approach of finding hypernyms, we evaluated a sample of 442 compounds in $CW'_{\overline{W}}$, and found a hypernym synset based on the final part of the compound for 345 of the compounds (78.1 ± 3.9 %). We thus estimate that 50.9 ± 2.5 % (65.2 % × (78.1 ± 3.9 %)), i.e. $1{,}571 \pm 77$, of the common words left missing can be added to FiWN based on the final part of the compound. Adding each of them to a new synset of its own would increase the number of synsets in FiWN by about 1.3 % from the current 117,659.

6.2 Classifying Translation Pairs

The translation pairs obtained from the join of the Wikipedia and Wiktionary on the one hand and the wordnets on the other were divided into the categories described in Sect. 3. In addition, we counted untranslated words in the join, which were identical in the Finnish and English Wikipedia or Wiktionary and FiWN and PWN; most of them were proper nouns. The number of translation pairs in each category and their proportion of the total number of translation pairs are listed in Table 13. The table also lists the number of filtered-out translation pairs.

Besides providing more translation pairs than Wikipedia, a much larger part of the pairs from Wiktionary were in the categories 3a–4b, which are relevant for adding new synonyms. In total, Wiktionary provided more than seven times as many relevant translation pairs as Wikipedia.

The data sets 1 to 4 and the evaluated samples of data sets 3a–4b are available for download.[17]

6.3 Evaluating Synonym Candidates

We tested our method on Wikipedia using approximately twenty-percent samples of the translation pairs (tpc_c^{WP}), except for the largest set 4a (*no synset, polysemous*),

[17]http://www.ling.helsinki.fi/en/lt/research/finnwordnet/testdata/lcfs/.

Table 13 The number of translation pairs in each category and their percentage of the total number of candidates

Category (C)	Wikipedia ($R = WP$) $\lvert C \rvert$	%	Wiktionary ($R = WT$) $\lvert C \rvert$	%
Filtered out (TPC^R_{out})	8,280	(33.0)	673	(1.2)
Untranslated (TPC^R_{untr})	3,451	(13.8)	580	(1.0)
1 Exact pair (TPC^R_{ep})	8,478	(33.8)	25,369	(43.7)
2 Same synset (TPC^R_{ss})	1,245	(5.0)	5,579	(9.6)
3a Other synset, monosemous (TPC^R_{osm})	554	(2.2)	4,415	(7.6)
3b Other synset, polysemous (TPC^R_{osp})	224	(0.9)	9,968	(17.2)
4a No synset, monosemous (TPC^R_{nsm})	2,278	(9.1)	5,095	(8.8)
4b No synset, polysemous (TPC^R_{nsp})	552	(2.2)	6,431	(11.1)
Relevant (3a–4b) ($TPC^R_{rel} = TPC^R_{osm} \cup TPC^R_{osp} \cup TPC^R_{nsm} \cup TPC^R_{nsp}$)	*3,608*	*(14.4)*	*25,909*	*(44.6)*
Total (TPC^R)	25,062	(100.0)	58,110	(100.0)

for which we deemed a ten-percent sample to suffice to obtain reliable enough results. On Wiktionary, we used samples of 200 words per category (tpc_c^{WT}). The samples were evenly distributed within each category. As we focus on finding new synonym candidates, we do not analyze category 1 (*exact pair*), which contains only translation pairs already found in FiWN.

The test sample for category 2 (*same synset*) was rather homogeneous, containing entries in which the Finnish word is an appropriate translation for the English one as such, but slightly less precise than the FiWN translation. For instance, *Amur-joki* was suggested as a translation for the word *Amur* in a synset containing the translation pairs *Amur* = *Amur* and *Amur River* = *Amur-joki* (*joki* is Finnish for 'river'). At this point, we decided against using such less precise translations. Adding them would also move the PWN–FiWN translation relation towards one between synsets and lose the finer distinctions between the translations of word senses.

For categories 3 (*other synset*) and 4 (*no synset*), we evaluated the quality of the Finnish synonym candidates provided by the translation pairs in the samples. We used the quality categories described above in Sect. 6.1.1. The number of synonym candidates classified in these quality categories for each data category is shown in Table 14 for Wikipedia and in Table 15 for Wiktionary.

Based on the results from the samples, we estimate the total number of synonyms that could be mined with our method from the Finnish Wikipedia interlanguage links and the translations in the Finnish and English Wiktionaries. We use the percentages obtained from the samples to extrapolate estimates for the whole data set. For each resource $R \in \{WP, WT\}$ and each data category $c \in \{osm, osp, nsm, nsp\}$, the estimated number of synonyms in quality category

Table 14 The quality of the synonym candidates as found in the samples of Wikipedia data categories 3 (*other synset*) and 4 (*no synset*). The numbers in parentheses are percentages

	Data category (C)				
	3a (tpc^{WP}_{osm})	3b (tpc^{WP}_{osp})	4a (tpc^{WP}_{nsm})	4b (tpc^{WP}_{nsp})	Total (tpc^{WP}_{rel})
Synonym candidate quality	$\|C\|$ %	$\|C\|$ %	$\|C\|$ %	$\|C\|$ %	$\|C\|$ %
(i) Replaces orig. ($Q_r(C)$)	4 (3.8)	2 (3.8)	5 (2.2)	2 (1.8)	13 (2.6)
(ii) To be added ($Q_a(C)$)	68 (64.8)	21 (39.6)	198 (86.8)	65 (59.1)	352 (71.0)
(a) as such ($Q_{as}(C)$)	62 (59.0)	18 (33.9)	145 (63.6)	53 (48.2)	278 (56.0)
(b) edited ($Q_{ae}(C)$)	4 (3.8)	3 (5.7)	8 (3.5)	7 (6.4)	22 (4.4)
(c) alternative form ($Q_{aa}(C)$)	2 (1.9)	0 (0.0)	45 (19.7)	5 (4.5)	52 (10.5)
(i) + (ii) *Appropriate total* ($Q_{r+a}(C)$)	*72 (68.6)*	*23 (43.4)*	*203 (89.0)*	*67 (60.9)*	*365 (73.6)*
(iii) Unsure ($Q_u(C)$)	1 (1.0)	1 (1.9)	3 (1.3)	0 (0.0)	5 (1.0)
(iv) Poor ($Q_p(C)$)	32 (30.5)	29 (54.7)	22 (9.6)	43 (39.1)	126 (25.4)
Total ($\|C\|$)	105 (100.0)	53 (100.0)	228 (100.0)	110 (100.0)	496 (100.0)

Table 15 The quality of the synonym candidates as found in the samples of Wiktionary data categories 3 (*other synset*) and 4 (*no synset*). The numbers in parentheses are percentages

	Data category (C)				
	3a (tpc^{WT}_{osm})	3b (tpc^{WT}_{osp})	4a (tpc^{WT}_{nsm})	4b (tpc^{WT}_{nsp})	Total (tpc^{WT}_{rel})
Synonym candidate quality	$\|C\|$ %	$\|C\|$ %	$\|C\|$ %	$\|C\|$ %	$\|C\|$ %
(i) Replaces orig. ($Q_r(C)$)	1 (0.5)	3 (1.5)	3 (1.5)	3 (1.5)	10 (1.3)
(ii) To be added ($Q_a(C)$)	92 (46.0)	62 (31.0)	112 (56.0)	84 (42.0)	350 (43.8)
(a) as such ($Q_{as}(C)$)	90 (45.0)	60 (30.0)	108 (54.0)	70 (35.0)	328 (41.0)
(b) edited ($Q_{ae}(C)$)	1 (0.5)	2 (1.0)	2 (1.0)	0 (0.0)	5 (0.6)
(c) alternative form ($Q_{aa}(C)$)	1 (0.5)	0 (0.0)	2 (1.0)	14 (7.0)	17 (2.1)
(i) + (ii) *Appropriate total* ($Q_{r+a}(C)$)	*93 (46.5)*	*65 (32.5)*	*115 (57.5)*	*87 (43.5)*	*360 (45.0)*
(iii) Unsure ($Q_u(C)$)	7 (3.5)	44 (22.0)	4 (2.0)	48 (24.0)	103 (42.1)
(iv) Poor ($Q_p(C)$)	100 (50.0)	91 (45.5)	81 (40.5)	65 (32.5)	337 (42.1)
Total ($\|C\|$)	200 (100.0)	200 (100.0)	200 (100.0)	200 (100.0)	800 (100.0)

q is $E_{q,c}(R) = |Q_q(tpc^R_c)|/|tpc^R_c| \times |TPC^R_c|$. We separately consider synonyms that should replace the translation in FiWN and synonyms that should be added (all subgroups combined). Tables 16 and 17 show the estimated numbers data by category for Wikipedia and Wiktionary, respectively, with confidence estimates based on the size of the sample of each category. All confidence estimates in this paper are at the 95 % confidence level.

Table 16 Estimated total number of replacement and additional synonyms from the Finnish Wikipedia data. The numbers in parentheses are percentages of the total number of translation pairs in each category

	Data category (c)				
Modification type	3a (*osm*)	3b (*osp*)	4a (*nsm*)	4b (*nsp*)	Total (*rel*)
(i) Replace ($E_{r,c}(WP)$)	21 ± 20	8 ± 11	50 ± 43	10 ± 14	90 ± 51
	(3.8 ± 3.7)	(3.8 ± 5.1)	(2.2 ± 1.9)	(1.8 ± 2.5)	(2.5 ± 1.4)
(ii) Add ($E_{a,c}(WP)$)	359 ± 51	89 ± 30	$1{,}978 \pm 100$	326 ± 51	$2{,}752 \pm 144$
	(64.8 ± 9.1)	(39.6 ± 13.2)	(86.8 ± 4.4)	(59.1 ± 9.2)	(76.3 ± 4.0)
Total ($E_{r+a,c}(WP)$)	380 ± 49	97 ± 30	$2{,}028 \pm 92$	336 ± 50	$2{,}841 \pm 140$
	(68.6 ± 8.9)	(43.4 ± 13.3)	(89.0 ± 4.1)	(60.9 ± 9.1)	(78.8 ± 3.9)

Table 17 Estimated total number of replacement and additional synonyms from the Wiktionary data. The numbers in parentheses are percentages of the total number of translation pairs in each category

	Data category (c)				
Modification type	3a (*osm*)	3b (*osp*)	4a (*nsm*)	4b (*nsp*)	Total (*rel*)
(i) Replace ($E_{r,c}(WT)$)	22 ± 43	150 ± 168	76 ± 86	96 ± 108	344 ± 199
	(0.5 ± 1.0)	(1.5 ± 1.7)	(1.5 ± 1.7)	(1.5 ± 1.7)	(1.3 ± 0.8)
(ii) Add ($E_{a,c}(WT)$)	$2{,}030 \pm 305$	$3{,}090 \pm 639$	$2{,}847 \pm 350$	$2{,}699 \pm 440$	$10{,}666 \pm 890$
	(46.0 ± 6.9)	(31.0 ± 6.4)	(56.0 ± 6.9)	(42.0 ± 6.8)	(41.2 ± 3.4)
Total ($E_{r+a,c}(WT)$)	$2{,}052 \pm 305$	$3{,}240 \pm 647$	$2{,}923 \pm 348$	$2{,}795 \pm 442$	$11{,}010 \pm 882$
	(46.5 ± 6.9)	(32.5 ± 6.5)	(57.5 ± 6.9)	(43.5 ± 6.9)	(42.5 ± 3.4)

An example of a found new synonym is *peitto* for the synset containing the words *cover* and *blanket* in PWN. Although the existing synonyms *peite* and *huopa* are appropriate translations of the English words, *peitto* is the most common Finnish word for a blanket as described in the synset gloss. We also found several official terms and loanwords. For instance, *eristic*, translated as *väittely*, was now offered the additional translation *eristiikka*.

It should be noted that a poor synonym candidate is sometimes an appropriate translation of the English word but in a sense that does not exist in PWN. The different meanings of a polysemous English word tend to be translated as several different words in Finnish.

The differences between the Wikipedia and Wiktionary data are discussed in Sect. 7.1.2.

7 Discussion and Future Work

In this section, we discuss the results obtained with our method from Wikipedia and Wiktionary. We also present some possible enhancements and extensions of the method, and other possible ways of enhancing FiWN in the future.

7.1 Sources

In the following, we discuss the nature of missing common words, contrast Wikipedia and Wiktionary with each other as sources of translation pairs, and discuss options for finding further synonym candidates in Wikimedia and for using other bilingual resources.

7.1.1 The Nature of Missing Common Words

Based on the 200-word sample of the 6,188 common words missing from FiWN and not found in Wiktionary, we estimate that only 6.9 ± 4.5 % of the relevant words are culture-specific (Table 12). The culture-specific words in the sample include words for inhabitants of Finnish towns and provinces, such as *helsinkiläinen* ('inhabitant of Helsinki'), names of or other words related to Finnish institutions, such as *lääninhallitus* (a former governing body of a Finnish province) and names of traditional Finnish dishes, such as *mämmi* (an Easter-time dessert).

Adding the estimated 309 ± 187 ($E_{cu}^{CW}(CW'_{\overline{W}})$) culture-specific missing common words to FiWN would increase the number of words by 0.23 ± 0.14 % from 132,696 ($E_{cu}^{CW}(CW'_{\overline{W}})/W(WN_{fi})$). Rarer words may or may not contain a higher proportion of culture-specific words. The importance of the culture-specific words obviously depends on the use of the resource.

Adding all the estimated $4,734 \pm 364$ relevant missing common words to FiWN would increase the number of words by 3.6 ± 0.3 % ($E_{rel}^{CW}(CW'_{\overline{W}})/W(WN_{fi})$).

7.1.2 Wikipedia vs. Wiktionary as Sources

All in all, we found 25,062 (TPC^{WP}) translation pairs in Wikipedia and 58,110 (TPC^{WT}) in Wiktionary which could be relevant for FiWN (version 1.1.2). Among the relevant words in categories 3 (*other synset*) and 4 (*no synset*), we estimated that the number of those to be added to FiWN as new synonyms or to replace translations in FiWN was $E_{r+a,rel}(WP) = 2,841 \pm 140$ in Wikipedia (11.3 ± 0.6 % of the total of 25,062 translation pairs) and $E_{r+a,rel}(WT) = 11,010 \pm 882$ in Wiktionary (18.9 ± 1.5 % of the total of 58,110). More details can be found in Tables 16 and 17.

The estimated total yield of the relevant categories 3a–4b would be at most $(2,841 \pm 140) + (11,010 \pm 882) = 13,851 \pm 1,022$, which would enlarge FiWN by 7.2 ± 0.5 % in terms of word senses from the current 191,797 ($WS(WN_{fi})$).

The differences between the number and quality of the synonym candidates provided by Wikipedia and Wiktionary reflect the different nature of these two resources. Wikipedia contains encyclopedic information, and the article titles that we used to form translation pairs are nouns or noun phrases. The words in Wikipedia are less common and require more explanations. The translation relation is mostly one-to-one.

By contrast, Wiktionary contains words of all parts of speech and it includes common words. This probably explains the greater proportion of words that are polysemous in PWN (categories 3b and 4b). The translation relation is many-to-many, and the translations may include rather low-frequency word senses, which is perhaps reflected in the smaller proportion of useful synonym candidates.

In addition, the lower number of poor candidates in Wikipedia may also be due to the fact that some of the polysemous words were filtered out during preprocessing based on their multiple category tags. Comparing the two data samples, we can conclude that filtering out some of the polysemous data in advance seems to improve the overall precision of our method while lowering recall. Improving recall is a good reason for why we may also wish to include the polysemous Wikipedia data, and as a topic for future research, we should instead apply more sophisticated methods for detecting incompatible word senses during postprocessing, see Sect. 7.3.1.

7.1.3 Finding Further Synonym Candidates in Wikimedia

In addition to the method presented in this article, other methods could be used to find synonym candidates for FiWN from Wikipedia. We could apply the method of Erdmann et al. (2008) to find synonyms in redirection pages and link texts. Since a link text is often an inflected form of the title of the target article, we should filter out candidates with the same lemma as the article title.

In this study, we have restricted ourselves to the translations in Wiktionary. More synonym candidates could be found by considering the English definitions of Finnish words in the English Wiktionary and the Finnish definitions of English words in the Finnish Wiktionary. However, the processing required by the definitions would differ slightly from that required by the translations. Some Wiktionary entries also contain a synonyms section, which could provide further synonym candidates. We could also apply the methods of Navarro et al. (2009) to extract synonymy networks from Wiktionary.

7.1.4 Using Other Bilingual Resources

The method presented in this article could be applied to other bilingual resources aligned at word or phrase level. Since few such large-scale resources are available, statistical machine translation could be used to find phrase alignment in sentence-aligned corpora. Statistical correspondence estimates could then be used to choose the translations to be searched.

7.2 Methodology

In this subsection, we discuss methodological aspects: the ontological nature of wordnets, the translation quality in FiWN, the nature of poor synonym candidates, and extending FiWN with new senses.

7.2.1 Ontological Nature of Wordnets

With our present method we can find some missing senses of Finnish words existing in FiWN. More specifically, we can find additional translations of senses which exist in PWN. The missing senses of Finnish words can be found in the translation pairs in categories 3a and 3b (*other synset*), which provide synonym candidates that are found in FiWN. For example, the word *aaltoviiva* is found in the sense ‘tilde’ in the category 3a.

This can be seen as evidence for the ontological nature of FiWN and PWN: the sense existed but it had not been given all the Finnish words with this particular meaning.

7.2.2 Translation Quality in FinnWordNet

Of the 25,062 (TPC^{WP}) translation pairs in Wikipedia and 58,110 (TPC^{WT}) in Wiktionary, the estimated number of translations that should replace ones existing in FiWN was $E_{r,rel}(WP) = 90 \pm 51$ (0.4 ± 0.2 % of 25,062) from Wikipedia and $E_{r,rel}(WT) = 344 \pm 199$ (0.6 ± 0.3 % of 58,110) from Wiktionary. More details can be found in Tables 16 and 17. From the small number of words to be replaced, we can conclude that the translation quality of FiWN from PWN is high, i.e. there were few direct errors.

7.2.3 Poor Synonym Candidates

Not all the poor translations provided by the data are absolutely poor, but poor only with reference to the sense for which they are candidates. Some such translations may indicate a culture-specific sense not included in PWN.

Other translations evaluated as poor may indicate a culture-independent sense missing from PWN, which was referred to as the fifth category in Sect. 3. For example, the word *kiertue* is suggested as the translation of *tour*, corresponding to the meaning ‘a journey made by performers or a sports team, in which they perform or play in several different places’ in Oxford Dictionary of English.[18] However, PWN contains no corresponding meaning for *tour*. The closest sense is ‘a journey or route all the way around a particular place or area’, which is *kiertomatka* in Finnish. More generally, Wiktionary seems to contain less common senses or make even finer distinctions of sense than PWN, at least when judged by the glosses in these two resources.

Some of the poor translations are indeed poor and reflect the varying quality of Wiktionary: the data may contain incorrect translations. Some translations may be correct in principle but very rare or non-standard in practice.

A more systematic evaluation of the types of words classified as poor translations is left for future work.

[18] “*tour* noun”, Stevenson (2010). Helsinki University, 18 October 2011, http://www.oxfordreference.com/views/ENTRY.html?subview=Main&entry=t140.e0873630.

7.2.4 Extending FinnWordNet with New Senses

In this study, we have only considered translation pairs in which the English word occurs in PWN. However, Wikipedia and Wiktionary also provide Finnish–English translation pairs in which the English word is missing from PWN. Such pairs could provide English translations for Finnish words added to FiWN, when FiWN is in the future extended beyond being a translation of PWN word senses, for example, by using the method of Pääkkö and Lindén (2012). For example, words that are now deemed to be poor translations because the translation does not match the gloss need to be added as new word senses to FiWN, and they could subsequently be added as new word senses to PWN as well.

7.3 Other Aspects

Here, we present some options for finding the correct target synset for a word and for translating the glosses in FiWN into Finnish.

7.3.1 Finding the Correct Target Synset for a Word

If we knew with reasonable certainty that a Wikipedia article or a Wiktionary entry corresponds to a certain synset, we could improve the precision of especially those synonym candidates which have several possible target synsets. Ruiz-Casado et al. (2005) present a method for linking Wikipedia articles and WordNet synsets based on the similarity between the content of the Wikipedia article and the gloss of the synset. Since the glosses in FiWN are currently copied from PWN untranslated, we should use the correspondences of the English Wikipedia pages via the interlanguage links. Navigli and Ponzetto (2010) use WordNet synonyms, hypernyms, hyponyms and sister words, as well as glosses, in determining correspondences between WordNet synsets and Wikipedia articles. The method of Niemann and Gurevych (2011) allows multiple alignments between synsets and Wikipedia articles, whereas Toral et al. (2009) present several methods for linking Wikipedia *categories* to WordNet synsets. Meyer and Gurevych (2011) present a method for aligning Wiktionary entries with WordNet synsets; their method is monolingual, but we could use it to disambiguate between the senses of polysemous words. Even if imperfect, such methods may speed up the manual verification by often providing good suggestions.

Further methods could be used to test if a synonym candidate found in Wikipedia is likely to belong to a synset in FiWN. For example, we could search for its synonyms, hyponyms, hypernyms or the possible domain in the text of the Wikipedia article, and in particular in the category links classifying the topic of the article. For titles with a disambiguation tag, we could test if the tag matches with the domain or hypernym of the candidate. However, it might require more effort to implement such tests than to select the correct synsets manually, since the number of target synsets for each word is relatively small.

7.3.2 Translating Glosses

At present, the synset glosses in FiWN are left untranslated, directly copied from PWN. To make FiWN a truly Finnish wordnet, it should also have Finnish glosses and examples. We expect that some of them could be added semi-automatically by using various methods.

If we knew the FiWN or PWN synset corresponding to a Wikipedia article or Wiktionary entry, as discussed in Sect. 7.3.1 above, we could extract a gloss and often also examples from the article or entry. Even though Wikipedia and Wiktionary entries are not strictly structured, we expect it to be easier to extract the information from them than from completely free text. The extracted information should obviously be judged by a human.

8 Conclusion

In this paper, we presented a method for adding some common words to FinnWordNet. We estimated that some 4,734 relevant common words, with a frequency on par with the words currently in FiWN, are missing from the version 1.1.2 of FiWN and were not found in Wiktionary as a translation of any English word existing in the Princeton WordNet. We analyzed the nature of the common Finnish words missing from FiWN and estimated that only 6.9 ± 4.5 % of them are culture-specific. The culture-specific words would add less than half a percent of new words to the current 132,696 words in FiWN, which suggests that rather few common culture-specific words are missing from FiWN. It is of course possible that lower-frequency words may contain a larger proportion of culture-specific words. We also found that 3,087 (65.2 ± 4.7 %) of all the relevant missing common words are compound words. We estimated that 78.1 ± 3.9 % of them (half of all the missing common words) could easily be added as hyponyms of existing synsets based on the final part of the compound.

As FinnWordNet has direct word sense translation correspondences with the Princeton WordNet, we presented a method for finding new synonym candidates for synsets that exploits translation relations in bilingual resources having the same languages. We tested the method with the interlanguage links of the Finnish Wikipedia and the translations in the Finnish and English Wiktionaries. With our method, we found both missing words with existing senses in FiWN and missing senses of words existing in FiWN. Based on the samples that we analyzed, we were able to select sets of words in which the proportion of useful word senses, to be added to FiWN in specified locations, was estimated to be 78.8 ± 3.9 % for Wikipedia and 42.5 ± 3.4 % for Wiktionary. The absolute numbers were $2{,}841 \pm 140$ such word senses found in Wikipedia and $11{,}010 \pm 882$ in Wiktionary. The $13{,}851 \pm 1{,}022$ new synonyms would increase the number of word senses in FiWN from the current 191,797 by at most 7.2 ± 0.5 %.

Acknowledgements We are grateful to our two reviewers, Prof Lars Borin and Dr Antti Arppe, for their many insightful comments that helped us clarify many of our claims and statements. All remaining errors are of course our own.

We also wish to acknowledge the FIN-CLARIN and META-NORD funding for making this work possible. The META-NORD project has received funding from the European Union's ICT Policy Support Programme as part of the Competitiveness and Innovation Framework Programme under grant agreement no. 270899.

References

Alkhalifa, Musa, and Horacio Rodríguez. 2009. Automatically extending NE coverage of Arabic WordNet using Wikipedia. In *Proceedings of 3rd international conference on arabic language processing (CITALA'09)*, Rabat, Morocco, 23–30. http://www.emi.ac.ma/citala2009/docs/citala%20papers/%28N%B00%4-Paper%2036%29.pdf.

Erdmann, Maike, Kotaro Nakayama, Takahiro Hara, and Shojiro Nishio. 2008. An approach for extracting bilingual terminology from Wikipedia. In *Database systems for advanced applications*, eds. Jayant Haritsa, Ramamohanarao Kotagiri, and Vikram Pudi. Vol. 4947 of *Lecture notes in computer science*, 380–392. Heidelberg: Springer. doi:10.1007/978-3-540-78568-2_28.

Erdmann, Maike, Kotaro Nakayama, Takahiro Hara, and Shojiro Nishio. 2009. Improving the extraction of bilingual terminology from Wikipedia. *ACM Transactions on Multimedia Computing Communications and Applications* 5: 1–17. doi:10.1145/1596990.1596995.

Fellbaum, Christiane, ed. 1998. *WordNet: An electronic lexical database*. Cambridge: MIT Press.

Jäppinen, Harri, Aarno Lehtola, Eero Nelimarkka, and Matti Ylilammi. 1983. Knowledge engineering approach to morphological analysis. In *First conference of the European chapter of ACL*, Pisa, Italy, 49–51.

Jäppinen, Harri, and Matti Ylilammi. 1986. Associative model of morphological analysis: An empirical inquiry. *Computational Linguistics* 12: 257–272.

Krizhanovsky, Andrew A. 2010. Transformation of Wiktionary entry structure into tables and relations in a relational database schema. *CoRR* 1011.1368. http://dblp.uni-trier.de/db/journals/corr/corr1011.html#abs-1%011-1368, preprint.

Lindén, Krister, and Lauri Carlson. 2010. FinnWordNet—WordNet på finska via översättning. *LexicoNordica* 17: 119–140.

Matuschek, Michael, and Iryna Gurevych. 2010. Beyond the synset: Synonyms in collaboratively constructed semantic resources. In *Workshop on computational approaches to synonymy at the symposium on re-thinking synonymy*, ed. Antti Arppe, 58–59. Helsinki: University of Helsinki.

Medelyan, Olena, David Milne, Catherine Legg, and Ian H. Witten. 2009. Mining meaning from Wikipedia. *International Journal of Human-Computer Studies* 67: 716–754. doi:10.1016/j.ijhcs.2009.05.004, http://dl.acm.org/citation.cfm?id=1618876.1619040.

Meyer, Christian M., and Iryna Gurevych. 2010. Worth its weight in gold or yet another resource—a comparative study of Wiktionary, OpenThesaurus and GermaNet. In *Proceedings of the 11th international conference on intelligent text processing and computational linguistics (CICLing 2010)*, ed. Alexander Gelbukh. Vol. 6008 of *Lecture notes in computer science*, 38–49. Berlin: Springer. http://www.informatik.tu-darmstadt.de/fileadmin/user_upload/G%roup_UKP/publikationen/2010/cicling2010-meyer-lsrcomparison.pdf.

Meyer, Christian M., and Iryna Gurevych. 2011. What psycholinguists know about chemistry: Aligning Wiktionary and WordNet for increased domain coverage. In *Proceedings of the 5th international joint conference on natural language processing (IJCNLP)*, 883–892. http://www.christian-meyer.org/research/publications/ijcnlp20%11/.

Navarro, Emmanuel, Franck Sajous, Gau Bruno, Laurent Prévot, Hsieh ShuKai, Kuo Tzu-Yi, Pierre Magistry, and Huang Chu-Ren. 2009. Wiktionary and NLP: Improving synonymy networks. In *Proceedings of the 2009 workshop on the people's Web meets NLP: Collaboratively constructed semantic resources*, 19–27. Stroudsburg: Association for Computational Linguistics. http://dl.acm.org/citation.cfm?id=1699765.1699768.

Navigli, Roberto, and Simone Paolo Ponzetto. 2010. BabelNet: Building a very large multilingual semantic network. In *Proceedings of the 48th annual meeting of the Association for Computational Linguistics*, Uppsala, Sweden, 216–225.

Niemann, Elisabeth, and Iryna Gurevych. 2011. The people's web meets linguistic knowledge: Automatic sense alignment of Wikipedia and WordNet. In *Proceedings of the 9th international conference on computational semantics*, Oxford, UK, 205–214. http://dl.acm.org/ft_gateway.cfm?id=2002691&type=pdf.

Niemi, Jyrki, Krister Lindén, and Mirka Hyvärinen. 2012. Using a bilingual resource to add synonyms to a wordnet: FinnWordNet and Wikipedia as an example. In *Proceedings of the 6th international global Wordnet conference (GWC 2012)*, 227–231. Matsue: Global WordNet Association. ISBN 978-80-263-0244-5.

Pääkkö, Paula, and Krister Lindén. 2012. Finding a location for a new word in WordNet. In *Proceedings of the 6th international global Wordnet conference (GWC 2012)*, 286–293. Matsue: Global WordNet Association. ISBN 978-80-263-0244-5.

Ruiz-Casado, Maria, Enrique Alfonseca, and Pablo Castells. 2005. Automatic assignment of Wikipedia encyclopedic entries to WordNet synsets. In *Advances in Web intelligence*, eds. Piotr Szczepaniak, Janusz Kacprzyk, and Adam Niewiadomski. Vol. 3528 of *Lecture notes in computer science*, 947–950. Berlin: Springer. doi:10.1007/11495772_59.

Sjöbergh, Jonas, Olof Sjöbergh, and Kenji Araki. 2008. What types of translations hide in Wikipedia. In *Proceedings of the 3rd international conference on large-scale knowledge resources: Construction and application (LKR'08)*, 59–66. Berlin: Springer. http://dl.acm.org/citation.cfm?id=1787800.1787808.

Stevenson, Angus, ed. 2010. *Oxford dictionary of English*. London: Oxford University Press. Oxford Reference Online.

Toral, Antonio, Óscar Ferrández, Eneko Agirre, and Rafael Muñoz. 2009. A study on linking Wikipedia categories to Wordnet synsets using text similarity. In *Proceedings of the international conference RANLP-2009*, 449–454. Borovets: Association for Computational Linguistics. http://www.aclweb.org/anthology/R09-1080.

Tyers, Francis M., and Jacques A. Pienaar. 2008. Extracting bilingual word pairs from Wikipedia. In *Collaboration: interoperability between people in the creation of language resources for less-resourced languages (A SALTMIL workshop)*, 19–22. http://ixa2.si.ehu.es/saltmil/files/EBWPFW.pdf.

Valkonen, Kari, Harri Jäppinen, and Aarno Lehtola. 1987. Blackboard-based dependency parsing. In *Proceedings of IJCAI'87, tenth international joint conference on artificial intelligence*, 700–702.

Vossen, Piek, ed. 1998. *EuroWordNet: A multilingual database with lexical semantic networks*. Dordrecht: Kluwer Academic.

Zesch, Torsten, Christof Müller, and Iryna Gurevych. 2008. Extracting lexical semantic knowledge from Wikipedia and Wiktionary. In *Proceedings of the international conference on language resources and evaluation, LREC 2008*, 1646–1652. Marrakech: European Language Resources Association. http://www.lrec-conf.org/proceedings/lrec2008/summaries/420.html.

Burstiness of Verbs and Derived Nouns

Janet B. Pierrehumbert

Abstract The frequencies of words vary with the discourse context, because any given word is more relevant to some topics of discussion than to others. In the statistical natural language processing literature, the term *burstiness* is used to characterize the tendency of topical words to occur repeatedly in bursts, separated by lulls in which they occur more rarely This article builds on the study of word burstiness by Altmann et al. (PLoS ONE 4:e7678, 2009). The study analyzed the archive of the USENET discussion group talk.origins, developed a novel method for quantifying burstiness, and showed that the burstiness of words is strongly correlated with their semantic type (in the sense of Montague semantics). Using the same dataset, I here explore the burstiness of abstract derived nouns (such as *argument*) in relation to their verb stems (e.g. *argue*) and frequency-matched nonderived nouns (such as *science*). I ask whether the burstiness of the derived form is inherited from the stem along with other stem features, such as the argument structure, or whether it is determined by the deverbal suffix. Overall, derived nouns pattern just like nonderived nouns, indicating that the suffix acts like the morphological head in determining the discourse statistics. This finding is interpreted in the light of Carlson's theory of dialogue games (Carlson in Dialogue games: An approach to discourse analysis. Synthese language library, vol. 17. Reidel, Dordrecht, 1983).

1 Introduction

The frequencies of words vary with the discourse context. People use different words depending on what they are talking about, and what they understand to be their common ground with their interlocutor (Tanenhaus and Brown-Schmidt 2008). Once a topic of discussion is initiated, it is recursively elaborated until the next topic shift (Kintsch 1974; Sharkey and Mitchell 1985). These facts provide the statistical foundation for modern document indexing and retrieval. When people search documents, they have the goal of finding information about some topic, and words

J.B. Pierrehumbert (✉)
Department of Linguistics, and Northwestern Institute on Complex Systems, Northwestern University, Evanston, IL, USA
e-mail: jbp@northwestern.edu

D. Santos et al. (eds.), *Shall We Play the Festschrift Game?*,
DOI 10.1007/978-3-642-30773-7_8, © Springer-Verlag Berlin Heidelberg 2012

that are statistically concentrated in particular documents, in contrast to others, provide good characterizations of the document topics (Bookstein and Swanson 1974; Church and Gale 1995; Katz 1996). If a word characterizes the topic of document, the likelihood that it will occur a second time in the same document is far higher than its average frequency would predict, because people reuse the word as the discussion is elaborated (Sarkar et al. 2005; Church 2000). In the statistical natural language processing literature, the term *burstiness* is used to designate the tendency of topical words to occur repeatedly in bursts, separated by lulls in which they do not occur because different topics are under discussion.

Good keywords for document retrieval are very bursty. But essentially all words are at least somewhat bursty, in that their temporal distributions display significantly more clumping than would be predicted under a baseline model in which words are strung together at random (Altmann et al. 2009). Even common words that everyone knows, such as *she* or *yesterday* are more relevant and useful for some topics of discussion than for others. This essay inquires into the underlying mechanisms by which different burstiness values come about. In particular, I will be interested in the relationship between the meanings of words, and the way that words are used in discourse, which is the central focus of Lauri Carlson's Ph.D. dissertation and 1983 book (Carlson 1983). I will explore this relationship by comparing derived abstract nouns, such as *discussion*, both to the verbs they are derived from (e.g. *discuss*) and to nonderived frequency-matched simple nouns, such as *pool* and *child*. The derived nouns inherit semantic structure from their base verbs. However, they function in discourse like other common nouns.

2 Background

Quantifying the burstiness of words has been the subject of a substantial research literature, because the phenomenon in itself challenges the assumptions of the conventional statistical treatment of words. To estimate the frequency of a word, we normally assume that the frequency is a permanent (e.g. stationary) property of the word, and that a text sample is a frequency-weighted random sample of the words in the lexicon. The statistical estimate of the word frequency is expected to converge to the true word frequency as bigger and bigger text samples are taken. However, the rate of convergence is poor if the word frequency fluctuates. The larger the scale of the fluctuations, as measured in words of text, the worse the convergence to the true frequency becomes. The common theme in proposals for quantifying burstiness is the addition of one or more parameters to the statistical information about each word. The purpose of the additional parameters is to capture local fluctuations in the word frequencies.

The most common approach takes as its point of departure a division of the text corpus into documents, and seeks to characterize the *counting distributions* of words (the distribution of word counts with respect to documents). This approach is the natural one if the division into documents is self-evident, for example if the dataset is a collection of news stories, research articles, or blog posts. It has been successfully applied not only in document retrieval (Church and Gale 1995; Katz 1996) but also in predicting the dynamics of words over time (Altmann et al. 2011) and in psycholinguistic studies of word processing (Heller et al. 2010; Heller and Pierrehumbert 2011). However, the approach casts away all information about the way the word is distributed within single documents, and the results can be very sensitive to the way that the dataset has been partitioned, in cases where the division into documents is not self-evident. The present study builds on the earlier study by Altmann et al. (2009) that adopts a different viewpoint by exploring the distributions of word recurrence times (the times between one use of the word and the next) in a single long stream of text.

The stream of text for Altmann et al. (2009) was obtained by downloading the archive of the Usenet discussion group talk.origins from Google Groups. This dataset contains approximately $N \approx 2 \times 10^8$ words produced by fifty thousand users who debated evolution and creationism over the time period from September 1986 to March 2008. We take it as a model system for the flow of informal dialogue in a social community. Although it is admittedly topically restricted, the same might be said for discourse within any social group, as social groups are often brought together by shared interests and experiences. The dataset consists of threads that in turn consist of posts, where each post is an individual communication by a user. The lengths of their posts range from a single word to over 3,000 words. The text was collated by threads according to the time stamp in the first post of the thread. Unequivocal examples of spam and threads in languages other than English were removed, as well as repetitions of parts of previous posts that were marked as such with >, |, etc. The recurrence time distributions of the 2,128 words that occur at least 10,000 times were modeled; it was shown that the single free parameter of the Weibull (stretched exponential) distribution effectively captures the degree to which the behavior of any particular word deviates from the exponential distribution that would be expected if words were strung together randomly. The model is prefigured by Sarkar et al. (2005), but differs in using only one free parameter to achieve an extremely accurate fit (median $R^2 = 0.993$) for recurrence time distributions. It has been independently validated through a comparison to empirical bootstrapping techniques in the context of setting significance levels of keywords for the British National Corpus and the San Francisco Call Newspaper Corpus (Lijffijt et al. 2011).

What determines the burstiness of any given word? Is the value an idiosyncratic property of the word? Is it predictable from intrinsic properties of the word? Or does it arise indirectly from the interaction of the word with the discourse structure? Altmann et al. (2009) focus on an intrinsic property of the lexical semantics, *logicality*, and on a conjecture by von Fintel that *logicality* is correlated with *permutability*. In von Fintel's words, "logical meanings are invariant under permutations of the universe of discourse [...] The intuition is that logicality means being insensitive to specific facts about the world." (von Fintel 1995). He continues to suggest that high *semantic type*, in the sense of Montague (1973) or Partee (1992) is associated with high logicality, and greater permutability. In order to elucidate this tripartite relationship, I first review the theory of semantic types, and then discuss the operationalization of the concept of permutability.

Formal semantics undertakes to provide a compositional treatment of the semantics of sentences, in which the truth conditions for any sentence can be predicted from the semantic components contributed by its parts. In furtherance of this goal, the formal representation of any word includes the domain and image of the mapping that is implicitly associated with it by virtue of its meaning and the constructions in which it appears. For example, proper names such as *Darwin* are treated as entities (in formal notation, they have type $\langle e \rangle$). At first blush, one might imagine that common nouns such as *monkey* are also type $\langle e \rangle$. Compare:

(1) John likes Sue. John likes that monkey.

This impression is deceptive, however, because *monkey* actually refers to the set of monkeys, that is, the set of things that have the properties characteristic of monkeys. In example (1), the demonstrative *that* functions as an operator to single out an entity from this set. From a semantic point of view, common nouns are thus the same as extensional adjectives, and this fact goes towards explaining why so many words can be used in either syntactic role:

(2) Her dress was blue. Blue looks good on her.

Since common nouns such as *monkey* and *blue* correspond to sets, which are equivalent to properties, they can take entities as arguments and map them to truth values t, as in the sentence *Lake Tahoe is blue*. The sentence is true if Lake Tahoe is a member of the set denoted by *blue*, and false otherwise. In formal notation, this is shown as $\langle e, t \rangle$. Essentially quantificational nouns, such as *everyone*, are characteristic functions of sets of properties of entities (van Benthem 1989; Partee 1992).

A given word can have different types in different contexts, because languages have productive processes of type shifting. *Disney* is originally a proper name for a person, of type $\langle e \rangle$, and retains this type as a proper name for the corporation that created Mickey Mouse and Disney World. However, it can be readily understood as a modifier or predicate in the following attested example:

(3) The reason we don't want to Disney is that we do everything Disney ... (mousepad.mouseplanet.com 11-29-2006)

The listener readily reinterprets the entity *Disney* as the activities and properties that are characteristically associated with that entity.

From the point of view of morphological theory, examples like (3) can be characterized as examples of conversion, or zero-derivation. A proper noun is converted into a predicate without the addition of any phonological material. Its function in the sentence is like that of other predicates, with the result that the apparatus of Montague semantics can integrate the formal representation of *Disney* together with those for the other words in the sentence into a semantic representation of type $\langle t \rangle$ (e.g. the whole sentence is either true or false). This line of analysis is very plausible if part-of-speech conversion is productive and resembles other processes that linguists attribute to the syntax. In languages with rich morphology, however, it can be difficult to draw the line between the compositional syntactic and semantic structures that provide the foundation for Montague semantics, and morphological principles operating within the lexicon. Even for English—whose impoverished

Table 1 The full type hierarchy collapsed to four broad classes

Class	Name	Examples of words
1	Entities	Africa, Bible, Darwin
2	Predicates and Relations	blue, die, in, religion
3	Modifiers and Operators	believe, everyone, forty
4	Higher Level Operators	hence, let, supposedly, the

morphology has allowed computational linguists to go far with a naive orthography-based concept of a word—psycholinguistic evidence now suggests that many or most morphologically complex words have their own entries in the mental lexicon (cf. Baayen et al. 2007) and that there is no clear dividing line between compositional and noncompositional complex words (Hay 2003). While Montague semantics took words as given, and looked to understand how words combine in larger units, such findings raise questions about how semantic properties are combined and inherited within words.

A central assumption in the cognitive theory of the lexicon is that words tend to have a basic or unified representation (Bybee 2001; Blevins and Wedel 2009). Thus, we can ask what a good starting assumption for the basic semantic type of a word is. Montague took the lexical type of a word to be the highest type in which it occurs, leading to the conclusion that all nouns are generalized quantifiers, just like the term *everyone* (Montague 1973). However many recent researchers, including Partee (1992), take the lowest type as basic. Since type raising is far more productive than type lowering, classifying words by their minimal type leads to sharper distinctions amongst the various sets of words. Altmann et al. (2009) follow this scholarly trend. In their data analysis, each word is coded by the lowest type in which it commonly occurs. (Exceptional uses, such as *associated* in the proper name *Associated Press* are disregarded in the interests of statistical clarity.) The end result is a ladder of abstraction, along which words are positioned according to the types of logical relations that they manipulate. In the interests of coding reliability, the full type hierarchy is collapsed to four broad classes, as shown by the examples in Table 1.

Note that the semantic classes are only partially correlated with syntactic parts of speech. Words such as *blue* are treated as predicates or relations no matter whether they appear as nouns or adjectives in a sentence. Any word with an intrinsically quantificational or relational meaning is coded as having a higher type than other words of the same part of speech that lack this meaning component. Notably, adjectives such as *huge*, *former*, *legal* are all coded as Class 3 and not Class 2. The overall coding approach was adopted both for practical and for theoretical reasons. On the practical side, our corpus is much too large to be hand-coded, but automatic part of speech taggers trained on formal prose become less reliable when faced with the short phrases and out-of-vocabulary words of colloquial language. On the theoretical side, the extremely free part of speech conversion in colloquial English can present real challenges to syntactic theory. Further, although correlations of burstiness with part of speech have been reported (Church and Gale 1995; Montemurro and Zanette 2002), no one has put forward a precise proposal about how these correlations might arise. Exploring a semantic point of view is attractive because it offers leverage on the underlying mechanisms for burstiness patterns.

The leverage occurs through the concept of *permutability*. When von Fintel refers to "permutations in the universe of discourse", he appears to have in mind the different ways that a word could be used if one discourse context is substituted for another. A word of high type and high logicality, such as *forty*, has potential relevance to the discourse no matter whether we are discussing onions or some other topic, such as books or houses. This is a paradigmatic view on permutability, in that it deals with the structure of available alternatives in discourse. It can be reinterpreted syntagmatically (e.g. in relation to the sequential structure of discourse) by bringing to bear two assumptions: First, a topic of discussion can be characterized as a probability distribution over sets of words (Blei et al. 2003) and second, as human discourse unfolds in time, it randomly traverses the space of potential topics. Together, these assumptions imply that randomly permuting all the words in a very large text sample is equivalent to randomly reassigning each word from the discourse contexts in which it occurred to other actual or potential discourse contexts. If a given word was very bound to particular contexts, this reassignment would greatly affect its statistical signature. However, there would be little effect on the statistical signature if the word were not bound to particular contexts.

Randomly permuting all the words in a text corresponds to the so-called Bag of Words model in the statistical natural language processing literature (Nigam et al. 2000). This model can be conceptualized by thinking of each word type as a ball with the word written on it. The lexicon is a large bag, in which the number of balls with a particular label corresponds to the frequency of the word. A sequence of words that results from drawing one word after another out of the bag (with replacement) corresponds to a random reordering of a text from which the lexicon was derived. Equally, it exemplifies what the text would look like in the absence of further factors structuring the discourse. This model is trivially false at syntactic time scales, but provides an important comparison at longer, discourse-level time scales.

If words of high logicality are highly permutable, then their temporal statistics should be relatively unaffected by randomizing all the words over a wide-ranging set of discourse topics. If words of low logicality are highly variable under permutation, their temporal statistics should be greatly affected by this operation. Or, to put it differently, we can look for evidence of logicality in the extent to which a word's actual distribution deviates from the hypothetical distribution it would have in the Bag of Words baseline model. In the next section, I will describe a mathematical apparatus for quantifying these deviations.

3 Quantifying Burstiness

Here, I summarize the method used in Altmann et al. (2009) to quantify burstiness in word recurrence distributions while controlling for word frequency. The recurrence

Fig. 1 Occurrences over time of a word with $\langle\tau\rangle = 820$, in a sample outcome of the Bag of Words baseline model. The outcome is shown for text of length $100\langle\tau\rangle = 82{,}000$ words. The black lines (whose thickness is exaggerated for visual clarity) indicate a time point at which the word occurs. Reproduced from Altmann et al. (2009)

Fig. 2 Actual occurrences of *theory*, a word with $\langle\tau\rangle = 820$, in a 82,000-word sample drawn from talk.origins. Reproduced from Altmann et al. (2009)

Fig. 3 Actual occurrences of *also*, a word with $\langle\tau\rangle = 820$, in a 82,000-word sample drawn from talk.origins. Reproduced from Altmann et al. (2009)

time $\tau_j^w = i_{j+1}^w - i_j^w$ is defined by one plus the number of words between two successive uses i_j^w and i_{j+1}^w of word w, where i is an index running from 1 up to the length of corpus. Under the Bag of Words model, the set of observations of any given word is generated by a Poisson process. The average recurrence time $\langle\tau\rangle$ is the reciprocal of the word frequency ν (e.g. $\langle\tau\rangle = 1/\nu$). The recurrence time distribution is predicted to be exponential:

$$f_P(\tau) = \mu e^{-\mu\tau}, \tag{1}$$

where μ is a parameter of the distribution that is equal to the word frequency: $\mu = \nu = 1/\langle\tau\rangle$.

It is important to note that this baseline does not correspond to an even distribution of the word throughout the text. In throwing dice, a number may happen to come up several times in row or happen not to come up over many trials. In the same way, when a given word is randomly selected under the Bag of Words model, it may have a run of good luck in which it appears repeatedly, or a run of bad luck in which it is rarely selected. The ribbon plot in Fig. 1 shows how a hypothetical word is distributed over time in a sample outcome of the Bag of Words model.

We are interested in deviations from the kind of behavior shown in Fig. 1. The ribbon plot in Fig. 2 shows the actual outcome for a fairly bursty word in this dataset. This is the word *theory*, which appears very frequently in talk.origins in connection with arguments about different theories.

This word is more concentrated at some times than the baseline model in general predicts. These concentrations are balanced by long lulls in use of the word. Next, in

Fig. 3 we look at a word of the same frequency and a higher semantic type, namely the word *also*.

Clearly, the word *also* is closer to being exponentially distributed than *theory* is. However, there is still a noticeable difference between Fig. 3 and Fig. 1, which indicate that *also* is somewhat bursty.

The central finding of Altmann et al. (2009) is that the distribution of each of these words—indeed of each of the 2,128 words that occurred at least 10,000 times—can be extremely well captured by fitting the single free parameter β of the stretched exponential distribution

$$f_\beta(\tau) = a\beta\tau^{\beta-1}e^{-a\tau^\beta}, \qquad (2)$$

where $a = a_\beta = [\nu\Gamma(\frac{\beta+1}{\beta})]^\beta$ is obtained by imposing $\langle\tau\rangle = 1/\nu$, Γ is the Gamma function, and $0 < \beta \leq 1$. This formula for the recurrence time distribution can be mathematically derived from the assumption that the probability of a word depends only on the time since its last occurrence, it jumps up whenever the word is used, and decays subsequently by a power-law memory decay function (as proposed in Anderson and Milson 1989, for human memory in general). The stretched exponential (2) is more skewed than the simple exponential distribution (1), which corresponds to the limiting case $\beta = 1$, but less skewed than a power law, which is approached for $\beta \to 0$. This means that the single parameter β effectively captures the burstiness of each individual word. It has low values (close to 0) if the word is extremely bursty, and approaches 1.0 as the word approaches the baseline prediction of the Bag of Words model. Values of $\beta > 1.0$, representing the case in which the word is more evenly distributed than in the baseline prediction, are possible but rarely observed.

Figure 4 shows the interaction of word frequency and word type as predictors of burstiness. At each frequency, the median β values split apart by semantic type. Although there is a visible trend for high-frequency words (low-$\langle\tau\rangle$ words) to be more evenly distributed, the trend associated with semantic class differentiates the β values better.

In summary, word type is a stronger statistical predictor of burstiness than a previously reported factor, word frequency. Words of high type (Class 4) tend to be less bursty than words of low type (Class 1), with the other classes falling accordingly in between. Overall, the analysis provides strong quantitative support for a syntagmatic reinterpretation of von Fintel's conjecture.

4 The Behavior of Deverbal Nouns

In Fig. 4, Class 2 is the most numerous class, and it displays the most diversity in β values. This diversity might have arisen because the coarse-grained semantic coding used in Altmann et al. (2009) ignored important semantic distinctions. But it could also arise from factors at the discourse level. Despite the size and length of talk.origins, it still represents a very particular topic, in comparison to the entire

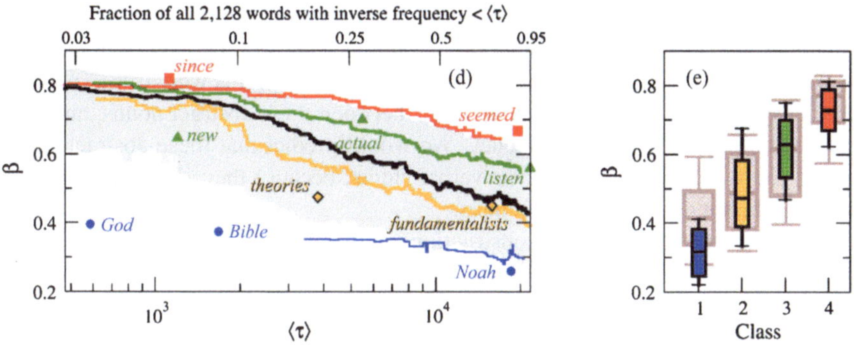

Fig. 4 Relationship of semantic class to β values for words. *Left panel*: Relationship of $\langle\tau\rangle$ to β. The relationship over all the words is displayed through a running median as a *black line*. The running median for each of the semantic classes is displayed with a colored line. Example words for each class shown in the same color code. *Right panel*: *Colored boxplots* display the distribution of β values for each semantic class. *Shadowed boxes* were constructed by first ranking words by their frequency, and then binning them in groups that match the semantic class bins in size. The least frequent words are matched to the low β Class 1 nouns, and more frequent words are matched to higher β, higher class nouns. Reproduced from Altmann et al. (2009)

space of human discussion. In talk.origins, the word *flood* is very bursty ($\beta = 0.28$) in comparison to the word *moment* ($\beta = 0.66$), because of the repeated importance of Noah's flood as an example where biblical and scientific accounts come into conflict. In a physics discussion group, *moment* might be much more bursty, due to its connection with the theory of inertia. Here, I further explore the causes of diversity within the set of common nouns. I consider the behavior of abstract nouns such as *belief*, *argument*, *failure* that are derived from class 3 verbs (*believe*, *argue*, *fail*), in comparison to that of non-derived nouns.

The verb stems of the target nouns have relatively high semantic types because they cannot be defined in terms of sets of properties, but only in terms of functions over predicates or relations. A verb such as *fail* is in this class because of its intensional meaning. It is not possible to determine from direct observation whether someone has failed; for example, falling down is an instance of failing only if the result is contrary to the state of affairs that a person desired. For a clown in a circus, falling down might mean succeeding. A verb such as *evolve* is in this class because it contains an implicit comparison along some scale of time and sets of properties. The nouns derived from these verbs are of interest because they inherit many aspects of the verbal argument structure and semantics. The nouns refer to kinds of activities and events, and full sentences can often be tightly paraphrased as complex noun phrases (Chomsky 1970).

(4) They discussed the theory. Their discussion of the theory.

(5) God created the world. God's creation of the world.

(6) Dawkins asserted that … The assertion by Dawkins that …

The inheritance of the argument structure from the verb stem might suggest that the nouns also inherit intensionality or an implicit scalar comparison from the verb, leading to high logicality, and hence high permutability. If this were true, we would predict systematic differences in burstiness between these abstract nouns, and non-derived nouns of the same frequency. We would predict that these abstract nouns would share the burstiness of their verbal stems, because they share core components of the stems' semantic structures.

However, for the sentential constructions in (4), the subject is obligatory in English. In contrast, for the nominalized form of these constructions, the expression of the agent (through use of the genitive) is optional, and for some words, it is indeed quite unusual. When using the nominalized form, the speaker might effectively step away from the intensional component of the meaning of the verb. These facts cast doubt on the above predictions because they soften the putative distinction between the derived nouns and other nouns. Further, the similarity between sentential and a nominalized formulations of the same general idea begins to break down if we look at the discourse context. By reifying events and actions, nominalization sets the stage for pronominalization with *it*. Compare (7) and (8):

(7) Their discussion$_i$ of the theory was incomprehensible. It$_i$ included ...

(8) They discussed the theory$_i$ incomprehensibly. It$_i$ included ...

In (7), *It* refers to the discussion of the theory. In (8), *It* more readily refers to the theory. This observation can be connected to Carlson's treatment of topic (Carlson 1983), which very innovatively treats topics as questions under discussion. Because nominalized constructions can be used to instantiate *wh* question pronouns, they can be used to answer questions in straightforward way, as in (9). In the same context, the sentential construction is less felicitous; compare (9) and (10).

(9) What was incomprehensible?—Their discussion of the theory.

(10) What was incomprehensible?—# They discussed the theory.

Example (10) is less felicitous than (9) because it involves a bridging inference; the two sentences are related only via the implicit assumption that events can cause mental reactions. Such indirect connections between discourse moves, already prefigured in Carlson (1983), have been subsequently found to place demands on working memory and to vary across individuals (Singer et al. 1992).

4.1 Materials

In the present study, words are defined very superficially as strings of alphabetic characters separated from other strings by white space. Space, tab, and newline, underscore, and punctuation marks *: ; . ! , ?* are treated as white space. In computational linguistics, words with the same stem but different inflectional endings are often collapsed together using a lemmatization algorithm. For example, the singular and plural forms of a noun, or the present and past forms of verbs, are often grouped together with a view to increasing the sample size for the stem. No lemmatization was used in the present study, because the sample sizes are extremely ample, morphologically related words often differ in their contexts of use, and one goal of the study was to understand how they differ.

Specifically, the study looks at the 43 pairs of Class 3 verbs and deverbal nouns for which both members occurred 10,000 times or more in the talk.origins dataset. The nouns were formed with a variety of deverbal suffixes: *-ion*, *-ment*, *-tion*, *-ure*, *-al*, *-er*, *-th* (cf. *evolve/evolution*, *argue/argument*, *fail/failure*, *survive/survival*, *teach/teacher*, *grow/growth*). In order to avoid statistical dependence amongst different word pairs, only one pair of words was used for any given stem, even if several pairs were found in the data. If both the singular and plural form of the noun met the frequency threshold, only the singular form was used. If a verb occurred both in its bare form (corresponding to the 1st and 2nd person present and the infinitive) and in an *-ed* form (corresponding to the past), the bare form was used.

A control set of non-derived nouns was also selected. Because frequency is a known factor in burstiness, these were frequency-matched to the derived nouns. For each derived noun, the noun closest to it in frequency was taken. To match the selection rule for deverbal nouns, plural forms were used only when no nearby singular form was available. Duplication of control items was avoided by taking the second-closest frequency match in the few cases in which the same non-derived word fell closest to two of the derived nouns. Control words included both concrete nouns, such as *book*, *fossil*, *apes*, *child*, *house* and abstract nouns such as *science*, *number*, *context*, *structures*. The argument structures of the nouns played no role in their selection, and many of them can in principle take arguments: cf. *a book about Darwin*; *a dinosaur fossil*; *the House of God*; *the number of species*. . . .

4.2 Results

The control nouns are more bursty than the verb stems. This is evident from their significantly lower β values in the two left boxes of the boxplots in Fig. 5. This result is expected, reproducing within a subset of the data one of the general findings displayed in the previous section. The distribution of β for derived nouns, as shown at the right, essentially matches that of control nouns. In the aggregate, the derived nouns do not inherit the burstiness of Class 3 verbs. The morphological derivation reduces the β value (increasing the burstiness), to such a complete extent that the derived nouns behave like any other noun.

The relative burstiness of the derived nouns in relation to the two comparison sets is displayed in a different way, by the individual word pairs, in Figs. 6 and 7. Figure 6 displays the comparison between control nouns and derived nouns. The points are evenly distributed around the diagonal comparison line, indicating that morphological complexity is not associated with any systematic pattern.

A similar comparison is made in Fig. 7 for the verb stems (e.g. *argue*) in relation to the derived nouns (e.g. *argument*). For all but two word pairs, the verb has a higher β value than the noun.

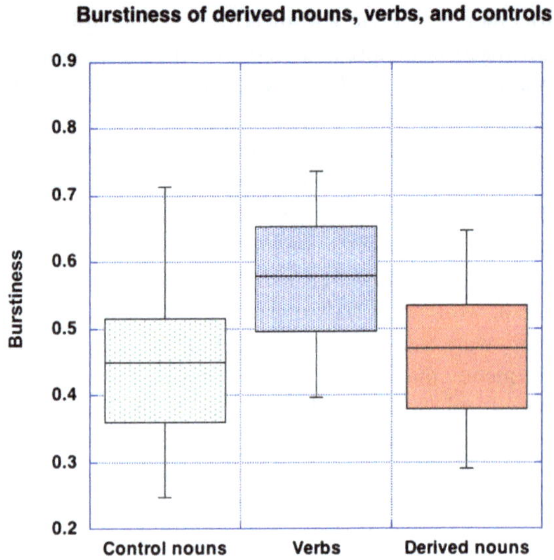

Fig. 5 Distribution of β values for control nouns (such as *science*), verbs (such as *argue*, and derived nouns (such as *argument*). Boxplots defined as the median, quartiles, and octiles of the observed values

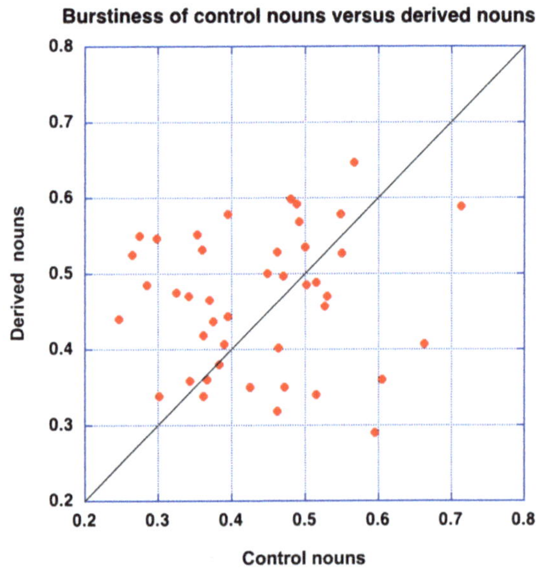

Fig. 6 Burstiness of control nouns versus derived nouns. Each plotting point represents the relationship of the β value for a derived noun (e.g. *argument*) to its frequency-matched control noun (e.g. *science*). The diagonal line $y = x$ shows where the points would fall if these values were equal

These results indicate that the morphological derivation very systematically reduced the β value associated with the verbal concept when converting it into a noun. However, the detail in Fig. 7 also reveals some correlation between the verb burstiness and that of the derived noun, that was not evident from the boxplots. Extremely bursty verbs, such as *evolve*, *predict*, *survive*, *measured*, and *teach*, have even more bursty nouns. Less bursty verbs, such as *argue*, *refer*, and *ignore*, also tend to have less bursty nouns. Overall, the most bursty noun-verb pairs do not seem to differ

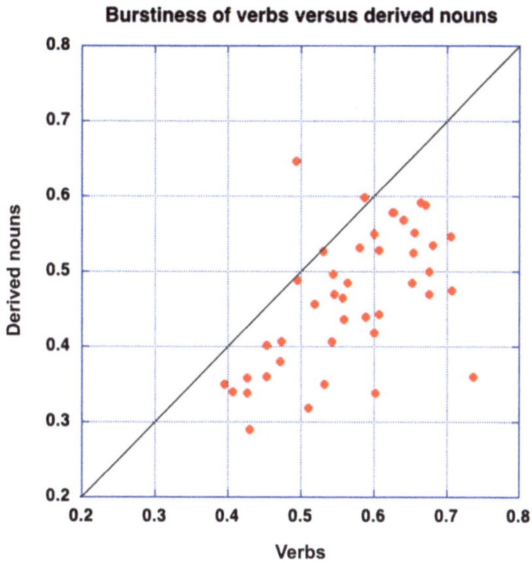

Fig. 7 Burstiness of verbs versus derived nouns. Each plotting point represents the relationship of the β value for a derived noun to its stem verb. The diagonal line $y = x$ shows where the points would fall if these values were equal

from the others in their logical structure. So, we speculate that this correlation arises through more general associative mechanisms. Church (2000) already showed that the occurrence of a topical word in a text increases not just probability of the same word, but also the probabilities of its semantic associates. Morphological relatives are also semantic associates, and therefore should share patterns of distribution in the text. For example, *evolve* and *evolution* are highly topical in this dataset through their connection with Darwinian theory, and should therefore tend to occur in the same bursts. *Teach* and *teacher* may be more associated with the creationist point of view, and so occur in other bursts. *Argument* is widely applicable to different topics and points of view, and *argue* shares this property.

5 Discussion and Conclusion

The tendency of topical words to reoccur in bursts is a mainstay of document indexing and retrieval. However, the relationship of burstiness to the structure of the linguistic system has been little explored. Here, I have reviewed a formal apparatus for elucidating burstiness patterns that was developed in Altmann et al. (2009). Using the single free parameter β of the stretched exponential (Weibull) distribution to parameterize word recurrence distributions, it was possible to establish a connection between burstiness and semantic type. Overall, words of high semantic type prove to have recurrence distributions that are much closer than lower type words to what would be expected under a Bag of Words model, in which the words in a text are simply assembled in random order. This supports the three-way association of semantic type, logicality, and permutability that was advanced in von Fintel's (1995) conjecture.

The same apparatus was also applied in a novel exploration of derivational morphology. A set of nouns derived from intensional verbs by the addition of a suffix was compared both to the corresponding set of verbs, and to a control set of non-derived nouns. The primary empirical findings were:

- The distribution of burstiness values for the derived nouns is systematically lower than for the verb stems.
- The distribution of burstiness values for the derived nouns matches that of the control nouns.
- In a paired comparison, there is a correlation between the burstiness of the verb stem and the burstiness of the corresponding derived noun.

These three observations can be integrated by assuming that the deverbal suffixes exemplified in this study (*-tion*, *-ment*, *-al*, *-ance*, etc.) lower the semantic type of the stem they attach to. However, this formal operation does not affect the associative structure of the lexicon, with the result that noun-verb pairs with shared thematic or social connotations can exhibit correlated burstiness values.

Why aren't the deverbal nouns more permutable? One possibility is that they have lost the semantic type features of their stem verbs. For example, we can compare the usage of *evolve* and *evolution*. *Evolve* requires a specification of a lineage, and the lineage varies from one type of organism to another. Modern birds *evolved* from dinosaurs, whereas modern ferns *evolved* from earlier plants. Supporting von Fintel's intuition, *evolve* is equally a propos in a discussion about birds and a discussion about dinosaurs. The same could be said about the word *evolution*, except that *evolution* has acquired a further sense in which it steps back from questions about how anything in particular evolves, instead referring to the specific theory claiming that all living things evolve. The existence or veracity of this theory can then serve as a topic of discussion in itself. Similar observations can be made about deverbal nouns such as *measurement* and *direction*. These lack the intensional baggage of the stem in many common uses, such as *the wrong direction* or *his wrist measurement*. From a semantic point of view, the deverbal affixes in this study can thus be considered as providing type-lowering. In Altmann et al. (2009), the deadjectival affix *-ly* (as in *frequent*, *frequently*) was similarly found to decrease the burstiness associated with its stem, and by inference to raise the semantic type.

This observation can be connected to the theoretical discussion surrounding the concept of a *head* in syntax and morphology. The head-dependency relations in a complex form (whether a morphologically complex word, or a syntactic phrase) control how properties of the parts contribute to the properties of the whole. The verb stem might be construed as the head in of a nominalization because its lexical semantics (including its overt or implied argument structure) characterizes the sort of event that the nominalization refers to. However, the nominalizing suffix meets the technical and morphosyntactic definitions of *head* presented in Hoeksema (1992); the suffix determines the category of the nominalization and is the locus of inflection. I have here identified a novel correlate of these formal properties, namely statistical signatures at long, discourse-level, timescales. The tendency to drop arguments in nominalizations (compared to the maximal argument structure that could be supported) may be viewed as a further reflex of the dominance of the suffix over the stem.

There is a tension between this suggestion and the idea that semantic type is strongly correlated with logicality and permutability. The term *logicality* was defined as the extent to which the meaning of a word is immune to specific facts about the world. The connection of high type to logicality and permutability follows from the assumption that any relation can be instantiated with a wide variety of entities, and that any function over relations can be instantiated with a wide variety of relations. According to this thinking, relations would inherit all the different contexts of use from the different entities that can instantiate them, and functions over relations would doubly benefit, by inheriting contexts of use from all the different relations. However, intuitively, the claim that *measurement* has lower logicality than *measure* (and hence lower permutability) does not seem right, since anything that can be measured has the corresponding measurement.

This tension reveals an important hidden assumption in the original proposal. The argument would go through if people's conceptualization of reality used a uniform and fixed level of granularity. But it doesn't. A noteworthy cognitive capability of humans is the ability to ramify concepts, that is to elaborate them by taking up more and more questions about them. Though these informational elaborations may involve powerful abstract relations, with a variety of alternative instantiations, they do not necessarily encompass any greater fraction of reality than before. For example, whereas a small child considers *dance* to be an undifferentiated activity associated with music, almost any Finnish adult would differentiate tangos, waltzes, and foxtrots, and other dances. They can build on this variety to acquire the abstract verbal concept *to syncopate*. Although this concept is abstract, and can be instantiated in a variety of different beats, its empirical applicability still does not extend outside of the world of music and dance. Within this world, it has high permutability; but within the world at large, it does not.

In Carlson (1983), discourse is a game in which questions provide the basis for the construction and elaboration of shared knowledge. In this framework, the decision to use a nominalized construction, in preference to a nearly synonymous sentential construction, can be viewed as a game move. Instead of thinking about lowering the semantic type for the stem, we can instead think about raising the point of view of the discussion. Dennett and Haugeland (1987) sketch a theory of *intentionality* in discourse, in which speakers communicative choices reflect their *intentions* of pointing at whatever they are speaking *about*. The choice of a deverbal noun is *intentional* because it reflects the speaker's intention to point at an event or relation. By doing so, the speaker opens the way to further ramification of the information associated with that event or relation. Recalling that the ramification of topics causes the burstiness of topical words, this account provides a mechanism for deverbal nouns to be as bursty as other nouns. Unlike the type-lowering account, the mechanism would apply whether the deverbal noun is bleached of its intensional baggage or not. One can indeed conjecture that type-lowering might be a long term consequence of using a deverbal noun to raise the point of view repeatedly, in a variety of different contexts. This diachronic trajectory would be consistent with other cases in which pragmatic choices eventually become encapsulated in the semantics of a language.

References

Altmann, Eduardo G., Janet B. Pierrehumbert, and Adilson E. Motter. 2009. Beyond word frequency: Bursts, lulls, and scaling in the temporal distributions of words. *PLoS ONE* 4: e7678. doi:10.1371/journal.pone.0007678

Altmann, Eduardo G., Janet B. Pierrehumbert, and Adilson E. Motter. 2011. Niche as a determinant of word fate in online groups. *PLoS ONE* 6: e19009. doi:10.1371/journal.pone.0019009

Anderson, John R., and Robert Milson. 1989. Human memory: An adaptive perspective. *Psychological Review* 96: 703–719.

Baayen, R.H., Lee H. Wurm, and Joanna Aycock. 2007. Lexical dynamics for low-frequency complex words: a regression study across tasks and modalities. *The Mental Lexicon* 2: 419–463. doi:10.1075/ml.2.3.06baa

van Benthem, Johan. 1989. Logical constants across varying types. *Notre Dame Journal of Formal Logic* 30: 315–342.

Blei, David M., Andrew Y. Ng, and Michael I. Jordan. 2003. Latent Dirichlet allocation. *Journal of Machine Learning Research* 3: 993–1022.

Blevins, Juliette, and Andrew Wedel. 2009. Inhibited sound change: An evolutionary approach to lexical competition. *Diachronica* 26: 143–183. doi:10.1075/dia.26.2.01ble

Bookstein, Abraham, and Don R. Swanson. 1974. Probabilistic models for automatic indexing. *Journal of the American Society for Information Science* 25: 312–318. doi:10.1002/asi.4630250505

Bybee, Joan. 2001. *Phonology and language use*. Vol. 94 of *Cambridge studies in linguistics*. Cambridge: Cambridge University Press.

Carlson, Lauri. 1983. *Dialogue games: An approach to discourse analysis*. Vol. 17 of *Synthese language library*. Dordrecht: Reidel.

Chomsky, Noam. 1970. Remarks on nominalizations. In *Readings in English transformational grammar*, eds. Roderick A. Jacobs and Peter S. Rosenbaum, 184–221. Waltham: Ginn.

Church, Kenneth W. 2000. Empirical estimates of adaptation: The chance of two Noriegas is closer to $p/2$ than p^2. In *Proceedings of the 17th conference on computational linguistics (COLING 2000)*, 180–186. Stroudsburg: Association for Computational Linguistics.

Church, Kenneth W., and William A. Gale. 1995. Poisson mixtures. *Natural Language Engineering* 1: 163–190. doi:10.1017/S1351324900000139

Dennett, Daniel C., and John Haugeland. 1987. Intentionality. In *The Oxford companion to the mind*, ed. Richard L. Gregory, 383–386. London: Oxford University Press.

Hay, Jennifer. 2003. *Causes and consequences of word structure*. London: Routledge.

Heller, Jordana, and Janet B. Pierrehumbert. 2011. Word burstiness improves models of word reduction in spontaneous speech. In *Architectures and mechanisms for language processing (AMLaP 2011)*, Paris. http://amlap2011.files.wordpress.com/2011/08/129_pdf.pdf.

Heller, Jordana, Janet B. Pierrehumbert, and David N. Rapp. 2010. Predicting words beyond the syntactic horizon: Word recurrence distributions modulate on-line long-distance lexical predictability. In *Architectures and mechanisms for language processing (AMLaP 2010)*. York: University of York.

Hoeksema, Jack. 1992. The head parameter in morphology and syntax. In *Language and cognition 2: Yearbook 1992 of the research group for linguistic theory and knowledge representation of the University of Groningen*, eds. Dicky Gilbers and Sietze Looyenga, 119–132. Groningen: Universiteitsdrukkerij Groningen.

Katz, Slava M. 1996. Distribution of content words and phrases in text and language modelling. *Natural Language Engineering* 2: 15–59.

Kintsch, Walter. 1974. *The representation of meaning in memory. The experimental psychology series*. Hillsdale: Erlbaum.

Lijffijt, Jefrey, Panagiotis Papapetrou, Kai Puolamäki, and Heikki Mannila. 2011. Analyzing word frequencies in large text corpora using inter-arrival times and bootstrapping. In *Proceedings of European conference on machine learning and knowledge discovery in databases (ECML PKDD 2011). Part II*, eds. Dimitrios Gunopulos, Thomas Hofmann, Donato Malerba, and Michalis Vazirgiannis, Vol. 6912 of *Lecture notes in artificial intelligence*, 341–357. Berlin: Springer.

Montague, Richard. 1973. The proper treatment of quantification in ordinary English. In *Approaches to natural language*, eds. Jaakko Hintikka, Julius Moravscik, and Patrick Suppes, 221–242. Dordrecht: Reidel.

Montemurro, Marcelo A., and Damián H. Zanette. 2002. Entropic analysis of the role of words in literary texts. *Advances in Complex Systems* 5: 7–17.

Nigam, Kamal, Andrew Kachites McCallum, Sebastian Thrun, and Tom Mitchell. 2000. Text classification from labeled and unlabeled documents using EM. *Machine Learning* 39: 103–134. doi:10.1023/A:1007692713085

Partee, Barbara H. 1992. Syntactic categories and semantic type. In *Computational linguistics and formal semantics*, eds. Michael Rosner and Roderick Johnson, *Studies in natural language processing*, 97–126. Cambridge: Cambridge University Press.

Sarkar, Avik, Paul Garthwaite, and Anne de Roeck. 2005. A Bayesian mixture model for term re-occurrence and burstiness. In *Proceedings of the 9th conference on computational natural language learning (CoNLL)*, 48–55.

Sharkey, Noel E., and D.C. Mitchell. 1985. Word recognition in a functional context: The use of scripts in reading. *Journal of Memory and Language* 24: 253–270. doi:10.1016/0749-596X(85)90027-0

Singer, Murray, Peter Andruslak, Paul Reisdorf, and Nancy L. Black. 1992. Individual differences in bridging inference processes. *Memory & Cognition* 20: 539–548. doi:10.3758/BF03199586

Tanenhaus, Michael K., and Sarah Brown-Schmidt. 2008. Language processing in the natural world. *Philosophical Transactions of the Royal Society of London. Series B, Biological Sciences* 363: 1105–1122.

von Fintel, Kai. 1995. The formal semantics of grammaticalization. In *Proceedings of NELS 25*. Vol. 2 of *Papers from the workshops on language acquisition & language change GLSA*, 175–189.

Outsourcing Parsebanking: The FinnTreeBank Project

Atro Voutilainen, Tanja Purtonen, and Kristiina Muhonen

Abstract Morphological and syntactic annotation of large text corpora for use as empirical corpus linguistic research data is typically a work and expertise intensive multi-year process. We outline an ongoing project, FIN-CLARIN FinnTreeBank, that uses outsourcing as a method to enable high-quality annotation according to specification on a large scale (tens of millions of words). We describe the main stages of the project: task specification, subcontractor selection and collaboration with the subcontractor to enable successful delivery evaluation.

1 Introduction

Annotation of text corpora for use as empirical data in corpus linguistic studies is a work and expertise intensive process. For instance, annotating a moderate-sized treebank (a text corpus of some tens of thousands of sentences with morphological and syntactic analysis) is reported to take several years of work from a research team (Abeillé 2003; Hwa et al. 2005), whose actual research interest might be in use rather than annotation of the corpus. Automating the annotation for large corpora (e.g. millions of sentences) requires specialized language technological expertise not usually possessed by a corpus linguist.

Subcontracting the automation is an option for solving this productivity bottleneck. In this paper, we outline a procedure that enables subcontracting most of the annotation: task specification; proposal bidding and subcontractor selection; collaboration with the subcontractor; evaluation and acceptance of the deliverable. We also present our experiences from an ongoing project—the FIN-CLARIN sub-project FinnTreeBank—focused on dependency syntactic analysis of Finnish language corpora.

A. Voutilainen (✉) · T. Purtonen · K. Muhonen
Department of Modern Languages, University of Helsinki, Helsinki, Finland
e-mail: atro.voutilainen@helsinki.fi

T. Purtonen
e-mail: tanja.purtonen@helsinki.fi

K. Muhonen
e-mail: kristiina.muhonen@helsinki.fi

D. Santos et al. (eds.), *Shall We Play the Festschrift Game?*,

DOI 10.1007/978-3-642-30773-7_9,

In Sect. 2, we outline the FinnTreeBank project goals (user needs and proposed solution). Section 3 describes the task specification for outsourcing (specification and manual application of annotation scheme to a systematic collection of example sentences referred to as grammar definition corpus). In Sect. 4, we describe the process of subcontracting (proposal bidding). Section 5 focuses on collaboration with the selected subcontractor during the parsebanking phase and the evaluations of the parsebank deliveries.

2 Project Goals

Sharing of digital resources by and for researchers and other types of users is increasingly common worldwide, for instance there are several ongoing projects to create annotated text corpora and treebanks for various languages (Kromann 2003; Mikulová et al. 2006; Nivre et al. 2006). In Finland, there are language resources for a number of languages at different organizations, but they are generally difficult to locate and take into use by researchers; also their interoperability is restricted. There is an ongoing need for well organized, systematic and readily available language resources and tools. The FIN-CLARIN FinnTreeBank project aims to address this need on the part of syntactically analyzed Finnish language corpora.—In this section, we start with a description of language resources, users and their needs regarding language resources. Then we present an ongoing effort to answer these needs. Then we move on to preparation of syntactically annotated corpora and look at the basic terms "treebank", "parsebank" and "grammar definition corpus".

2.1 Resources, Users and Needs

We use the term "language resource" to refer to a wide range of digital resources: (i) small or large samples of naturally occurring text, speech and multimedia, representing different genres and time periods, and possibly annotated with various levels of linguistic analysis or other metadata, (ii) descriptions of the language (e.g. lexicons, morphologies, syntactic grammars, wordnets, ontologies) for human users, (iii) formal (linguistic or statistical) models of the language for automatic language processing tasks, (iv) tools to facilitate use of language resources, and (v) software and algorithms to enable automatic language processing tasks.

Users of language resources are mainly researchers (e.g. corpus linguists and language technologists); also commercial developers of language and information technological applications and services constitute a potentially large user segment. Language resource users need methods and tools to identify and use interoperable language resources. The less effort the researchers and developers need in determining the existence of the required resource and in negotiating the access and use of the resource, the more time and money can be spent on research and innovation. Here is a partial "wish list" of user needs (Voutilainen and Lindén 2011): (i) researchers need empirical data to facilitate formulation, testing and evaluation of scientific generalizations, (ii) researchers need a way of sharing their empirical data, documentation and tools, (iii) researchers need a facility for persistent storage and sharing of their (annotated) data (i) to help other researchers build on rather than duplicate existing work and (ii) to facilitate evaluation and recognition of an existing contribution, as discussed in Pedersen (2008), (iv) researchers need access to well-documented and modifiable language technological software to enable them to (i) annotate corpora specific to their research need and (ii) provide a "customized" annotation for a better match e.g. with the corpus linguistic research need, (v) language technology companies and system integrators need access to well-documented and modifiable language technological software to help them provide a wider range of solutions and services to answer end-user needs in information discovery, multilingual communication and education.

2.2 *FIN-CLARIN Solution in Outline*

FIN-CLARIN[1] partners with Finnish service providers, research organizations, publishers and archives to set up the following kind of "ecosystem":

- a web service is set up at a service provider where language resources can be deposited, annotated and licensed for research and commercial uses;
- to facilitate resource/service discovery, the web service includes a workflow for metadata creation and use in combination with a search functionality;
- to help start use of the relevant resource, the web service sets up a transparent uniform licensing policy;
- in the long term, the service aims to offer extensive annotated multimodal and multilingual language corpora for researchers;
- the service also aims to provide various types of linguistic descriptions, e.g. morphological lexicons, wordnets, name resources and grammatical descriptions (like valency descriptions);
- the service also aims to offer a variety of software tools and technologies for R&D: user interfaces e.g. for corpus investigations and software libraries for prototype development;
- the initial user base is expected to be mainly Finnish researchers and developers, but in the long run the service aims to operate at European level (along with other CLARIN centers);

[1] http://www.helsinki.fi/fin-clarin.

2.3 *FinnTreeBank—A Dependency Syntactic Treebank for Finnish*

The FinnTreeBank project aims to provide the FIN-CLARIN service with morphologically and syntactically annotated Finnish corpora.

Finnish morphology is largely based on available morphological descriptions (e.g. the morphological lexicon of the Institute for the Languages of Finland[2]) and Helsinki Open Source Morphology tools (Lindén et al. 2009). Regarding syntax, we use a dependency syntactic model largely based on earlier work on surface syntactic dependency parsing (Tapanainen and Järvinen 1997; Voutilainen 1997).

Our work proceeds according to the following process:

1. specify a tentative annotation model and guideline for dependency syntax;
2. manually apply the model to a systematic collection of a large corpus of example sentences extracted from a large descriptive grammar; when necessary, refine the model and annotation guideline. The resulting corpus is a treebank (manually annotated syntactically parsed corpus) and, more specifically, a grammar definition corpus, due to its function as an initial systematic specification of Finnish dependency syntax;
3. evaluate the applicability of the resulting annotation manual and grammar definition corpus on fresh data using the double-blind annotation routine;
4. provide the grammar definition corpus and annotation guideline to an external Language Technology supplier as task specification for construction of automatic syntactic analyzers for automatic corpus annotation (somewhat noisy but operable on a large scale);
5. provide training, consultation and feedback to the selected subcontractor during the project;
6. the resulting automatically parsed corpus ("Parsebank") and parser engine are iteratively evaluated, and provided for FIN-CLARIN use when accepted.

The process is nearing completion, and the first large corpora (some 70 million words) are expected for release during the first half of 2012. In the next section, we look more closely at the specification phase.

3 Task Specification

The treebanking effort of the FinnTreeBank project is split into two phases, the first of which has already been completed. FinnTreeBank 1 is a manually annotated treebank comprising the example sentences gathered from a recent large-scale descriptive grammar of Finnish (Hakulinen et al. 2004a). FinnTreeBank 2 is a parsebank, the building of which has been outsourced to a subcontractor.

[2]http://www.kotus.fi.

Table 1 An example of the CONLL-X format used in FinnTreeBank 1

1	Hän	hän	Pron	Pron | Pers | Sg3 | Nom	_	2	subj	_	_
2	käveli	kävellä	Verb	Verb | Act | Ind | Prt | Sg3	_	0	main	_	_
3	tien	tie	Noun	Noun | Sg | Gen	_	5	attr	_	_
4	vasemmalla	vasen	Adj	Adj | Pos | Sg | Ade	_	5	attr	_	_
5	reunalla	reuna	Noun	Noun | Sg | Ade	_	2	advl	_	_
6	.	.		_	_		_	_	_

The first version of the treebank consists of example sentences or sentence fragments from a large descriptive grammar of Finnish (Hakulinen et al. 2004b). The example sentence corpus has around 19,000 linguistic examples, totaling up to 162,000 word forms including punctuation. The sentences are annotated manually, and the annotation decisions reported in a manual. Basing the annotation of the treebank on a descriptive grammar ensures wide coverage of linguistic phenomena of Finnish. The manually annotated treebank thus functions as an inventory of the phenomena of Finnish grammar as described by Hakulinen et al. (2004b).

The example sentences included in the treebank represent both frequent syntactic structures and rarer text type specific phenomena. Frequency of the phenomena is not taken into account in the treebank. Including also rarer linguistic structures already in the first version of the treebank facilitates the development of a formal language model as well as the documentation of the principles of analyzing the language. Hence, building a grammar definition corpus provides a solid basis for developing and documenting a formal representation of a morphological and syntactical description.

3.1 The Dependency Syntactic Language Model

The VISK sentences are presented in a tabular, CONLL-X standard-conforming format. The CONLL-X standard consists of ten data types (fields), of which seven are utilized for the analysis of the VISK corpus. Table 1 portrays the dependency syntactic representation for the sentence *"Hän käveli tien vasemmalla reunalla."*, glossed in (1) below.

(1) Hän käveli tien vasemmalla reunalla.
(s)he walked road left side
'(S)he walked on the left-hand side of the road.'

All word forms and punctuation marks are placed on a separate line, and each word has a numerical address within the sentence, marked in the left-most column. The next column from the left is the actual word form, followed by its base form in column three. The morphological description is given in both the short, coarse-grained manner (column four), and a fine-grained analysis (column five).

The dependency relations (dependent-regent relations), are marked in column seven by indicating the governing word (regent) using the sentence-internal numerical address of column one. For instance, the word form *hän* ('(s)he') is governed by its regent at position 2, *käveli* ('walked'). The nucleus of the sentence, i.e. the regent of the whole sentence, is usually the main verb of the main clause. Hence, *käveli* ('walked') in Table 1, takes the (non-existent) regent at position 0.

The dependency functions of the word forms are presented in column eight. In (1), *hän* ('(s)he') functions as a subject (subj) to its regent *käveli* ('walked'). Columns six, nine and ten of the CONLL-X standard were not used for the annotation of FinnTreeBank; the unused fields are marked with an underscore (_).

Each word form of a sentence is annotated with a dependency syntactic regent. Words with a certain function are often governed by constituents of a certain type, e.g. a subject usually takes an auxiliary verb as its regent, and is dependent on the main verb only if there are no auxiliaries in the sentence. The principles used in marking dependency relations are described in the annotator's manual. The manual is a key product of FinnTreeBank 1; it contains a detailed description of the syntactic annotation scheme.

3.2 The Annotation Scheme

The grammatical model and annotation schemes are based on dependency syntax (Tesnière 1980). This means that words are linked together with unidirectional two-term relations (dependencies) which are labeled with their dependency functions (subject, object, etc.). The sentence nucleus (usually the main predicate verb) has dependents, and a dependent may have its own internal dependency structure, e.g. a subordinate clause may have its own subject and object etc.

The dependency syntactic analysis in FinnTreeBank 1 is function based and scalable. At the moment, the scheme contains 15 dependency functions. In the future, the palette can be extended to cover more fine-grained distinctions.

The analysis is surface-syntactic: No (empty) word-like categories are postulated, so the analysis is based on word forms that actually exist in the sentence. This means that e.g. no missing verb is postulated in an elliptical clause. Handling elliptical sentences within the dependency syntactic framework is by no means self-evident. For instance, the widely used Stanford typed dependencies representation handles it differently (de Marneffe and Manning 2008): The sentence *Bill went over the river and right through the woods* is transformed into a sentence with VP coordination, and the verb *went* is copied: *Bill went over the river and went right through the woods* (de Marneffe and Manning 2008). FinnTreeBank does not adopt the Stanford copying approach but links the words *woods* and *river* together maintaining the clauses internal structures as such.

The dependency relations used in the language model are non-projective, making it possible for the model to capture many types of long-distance dependencies. This is crucial in languages with free constituent order. In phrase structure grammar framework, modeling non-continuous constituents can be difficult and lead to usually unwanted crossing branches. Example (2) shows how long-distance dependencies caused by object topicalization are handled in FinnTreeBank.

(2) Työhönsä hän oli erityisen tyytyväinen.
work-ILL-SG3 she was especially happy
'She was especially happy about her work.'

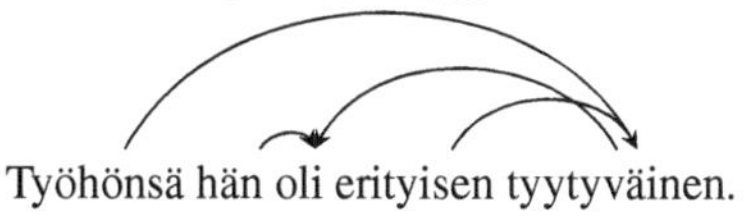

In (2), the first word of the sentence, *työhönsä* ('her work'), is dependent on the last word, *tyytyväinen* ('happy'). In the dependency syntactic framework adopted in FinnTreeBank, the distance between the regent and the dependent plays no role.

All in all, the grammatical model adopted in FinnTreebank is semantically motivated, meaning that semantically heavier words are closer to the sentence nucleus. Words having a grammatical function (e.g. adpositions, conjunctions, auxiliary verbs, quantifiers, expletive pronoun *se*) are modeled as dependents of the semantically heavier words. This semantically motivated principle causes the analysis of FinnTreeBank to sometimes differ from the traditional modeling of Finnish. Also in Hakulinen et al. (2004a), grammatical cases are seen as the criteria for syntactic functions. e.g. the subject cannot be in the elative case, unlike in our scheme:

(3) Osa jäsenmaista äänesti ehdotusta vastaan.
Part member states voted motion against
'Some member states voted against the motion.'

In (3), the NP in the subject position is *osa jäsenmaista* ('some member states'). Since *jäsenmaista* ('member states') is semantically heavier, we mark it as the head of the NP, making it the regent of *osa* ('some'), which in turn is its attribute.

3.3 The Annotation Manual

During the manual annotation process, the annotation manual served as the annotation guidelines for the annotators. After the manual annotation phase, it functions as a user's manual where the annotation decisions are described and the specifics of the scheme illustrated. In addition to the manual being essential in the annotation process, it also plays a crucial role in outsourcing the creation of the parsebank: it functions as the task specification. The end result of the subcontractor needs to conform to the specification in the manual; all that is expected from the subcontractor is listed in it. The manual is thus also what the evaluation of the end result is based on.

The subcontractor delivers a parsebank containing two levels of annotation: morphology and dependency syntax. Since the morphological level was not yet defined during the annotation of the first version of the treebank, and is hence not described in the manual, the only way we evaluate the morphological analysis of the subcontractor is by general knowledge of Finnish grammar; we only correct clear mistakes, and leave the rest as it is. The second version of the treebank and a new version of the manual will contain a morphological specification as well.

Example (4) demonstrates the limitations that underspecified morphological analysis sets on the evaluation of the syntactic analysis. In Finnish, every adjective can be used as a subject, as shown in (4).

(4) Onnelliset elävät pisimpään.
happy live longest
'Happy people live the longest.'

At the time of outsourcing the parsebank creation, we had not decided whether an adjective-like word referring to a physical object e.g. to a person should be analyzed as a noun or an adjective. Hence, we have to accept any analysis provided by the subcontractor: as long as we have not defined the phenomena in the manual, we cannot opt for one analysis over other possible ones during evaluation.

4 Proposal Bidding and Subcontractor Selection

The Finnish HLT research community has a substantial expertise on morphological and syntactic parsing of natural language text (e.g. Nelimarkka et al. 1984; Carlson and Lindén 1987; Koskenniemi et al. 1992; Karlsson et al. 1995; Tapanainen and Järvinen 1997), and several commercial spin-off companies have emerged since the 1980s. Relevant companies were contacted, and those interested were provided with a RFQ (Request for Quotation):

- information was provided on the required products and services, and their use in the FIN-CLARIN service:
  - morphologically and syntactically analyzed versions of the Finnish Europarl and JRC-Acquis corpora available online
  - specification of the analysis task to be performed: the then available version of the Finnish grammar definition corpus (19,000 example sentences with dependency syntactic analysis) and the accompanying documentation (annotation manual)
  - a server license to the parser engine that provides the analysis, for annotation of additional corpora
  - a quality guarantee and maintenance services
  - approximate delivery deadline
  - maximum overall fee (excluding maintenance fees)
- request for the following information:
  - word-level accuracy guarantee for part of speech, lemma, dependency function and dependency relation
  - fee for license and corpus annotation

- pricing for maintenance services
- project plan with description of key personnel
- information on company turnover and balance sheet

Two of the contacted companies sent a quotation, and one of them was selected as the subcontractor.

5 Collaboration with Subcontractor

To ensure the quality of the outsourced treebank and parser, the FinnTreeBank team offered support in choosing the right dependency syntactic annotations of complex structures. The correct annotation is defined with the help of the manual of FinnTreeBank 1, so in the evaluation, deeming an annotation decision to be correct means that the choice is compatible with the manual.

The FinnTreeBank team arranged a two-day training for the subcontractors to get them acquainted with the manual. In the middle of the whole outsourcing process, the team evaluated two intermediate deliveries and composed feedback about the most frequent annotation errors. The first intermediate evaluation was specified in the contract and contained both numeric and verbal feedback. The second additional evaluation concentrated on highlighting the most frequent errors that the parser still made. The team was also available for consultation on the annotation during the whole subcontracting process.

5.1 Finalizing the Annotation Scheme

The first version of the manual did not contain all final definitions of complex structures which are not specified in the descriptive grammar clearly enough, so that they could be easily defined in the dependency syntactic framework. We wanted to investigate these phenomena more carefully and to consult the future users on the most useful annotation before making the final decision on how to annotate them. Among these problematic structures were e.g. the extensions of nominalized verbs, elliptical comparative clauses and superlative adjectives.

Even though the specification was not yet finalized when we outsourced the building of the parsebank, we needed to give some annotation principles to all typical structures. For instance, we defined that the extensions of verb derived nouns should have valency-based functions. By this we mean that a verb-based noun can take e.g. an object or a subject:

(5)	Postimerkkien	keräily	on	kivaa.
	stamps	collecting	is	fun
	OBJ	SUBJ	PRED	SCOMP

‘Collecting stamps is fun.’

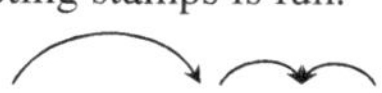

Postimerkkien keräily on kivaa.

FinnTreeBank aims at a semantically informative annotation scheme. Thus, the NP-internal relations in *postimerkkien keräily* ('collecting stamps') should be apparent. The syntactic annotation scheme in (5) is semantically motivated: the word *postimerkkien* ('stamps') is the object of *keräily* ('collecting'), which becomes apparent if the expression is transformed to a finite clause *kerätä postimerkkejä* ('to collect stamps').

In the first manual of FinnTreeBank, the decision to analyze the extensions of verb-based nouns on the ground of valency of the original verb was questioned because of the fuzzy distinction between "original" nouns and verb-based nouns. e.g.:

(6)	Toimin	esittelijän	pyynnön	mukaisesti.
	Acted-SG1	presenter-GEN	request	accordingly

'I acted according to the presenter's request.'

In this sentence, the word *pyyntö* ('request') could be seen as a derivation of a word *pyytää* ('to request'). Hence, in the valency-based annotation of the NP, the word *esittelijä* ('presenter') should be seen as a subject. However, there are two problems in this kind of annotation. First, it is not obvious where to draw the line between regular nouns and nouns that are verbal derivations. Second, based on the treebank user query, the relation between a verb-derived noun and its object is seen more clearly than the relation between the derivation and the subject (Muhonen and Purtonen 2011).

Nonetheless, the subcontractor was asked to annotate cases like (5) using an object reading instead of an attribute reading, thus, to aim at the most informative annotation of the NP's internal relations. However, we cannot discard the results in the questionable borderline cases because of the lack of a clear definition. Only for derivatives with a *-minen* ending did we ask for the consistent valency-based readings because of their clear verbal base; in some theories, *-minen*-ending words are seen as an infinitives.

5.2 Improving the Manual

The whole evaluation process is based on the manual. Incomplete specification of various phenomena in the manual resulted in challenges during the assessment of the subcontractor's annotation. By this we mean that even if there is a consensus within the FinnTreeBank team on the annotation of some structure but it is not specified explicitly in the manual, the subcontractor's differing solution cannot be considered as a wrong one.

The annotation scheme of FinnTreeBank 1 was tested with a double-blind test (Voutilainen and Purtonen 2011). The test revealed that two annotators from the FinnTreeBank team annotated 10 % of the syntactic functions and relations differently when they were asked to mark the function and relation independently. After independent consideration and correction, it was observed that 34 % of the errors were caused by the incomplete specification of the manual. In most of these cases (57 %) the annotators could agree on the correct annotation immediately.

Also the results of the subcontracting can be used as a method to examine the accuracy of the manual. In the evaluation of the subcontractor's annotation, there is no room for negotiation: the annotation solution is either wrong or right. So, if 34 % of the FinnTreeBank annotators' errors were caused by incompleteness of the manual, presumably the rate is even higher, when parsing is conducted by others. This results from the fact that annotators from the same project share a "hidden consensus" on some annotation decisions which are not documented in the manual.

Subcontracting the building of the parser revealed underspecified phenomena that we had annotated similarly without any specifications or that did not occur in the grammar definition corpus or in the double-blind test. Europarl and JRC-Acquis corpora contain for example many sentences with "disconnected additions":

(7)	Asetuksen	muuttaminen	Euroopan	unioniin	liittymisen
	regulation-GEN	amending	European-GEN	Union-ILL	assession
	vuoksi	(äänestys).			
	in-the-course-of	(vote)			

'Amending the regulation in the course of accession to the European Union (vote).'

In (7), the subcontractor offers an adverbial reading for the word *äänestys* ('vote'). The annotators from the FinnTreeBank team expect a post-modifier reading because of the word's nominal head *muuttaminen* ('amending'). At the same time, the word *muuttaminen* ('amending') is seen as the head of the whole sentence and since it is a nominalized verb, the adverbial reading is not problematic. Thus, both readings—post-modifier and adverbial—are equally semantically motivated. However, this kind of structure where the additional word does not function directly as an apposition of some specific word was not clearly specified in the first version of the manual.

Perhaps finding structures described in (7) suggests that we should add an additional tag for additions or at least provide a more specific definition of how to annotate them to guarantee consistent annotation. In addition to other benefits, outsourcing can be used as a measure to improve the existing annotation manual; e.g. the underspecified phenomenon of (7) was revealed by outsourcing the parsing and evaluating the results.

5.3 Subcontractor's Errors in the Annotation

The evaluation was split in two phases. The subcontractor provided an intermediate delivery of the corpus before finalizing the parser so that the FinnTreeBank team could examine the annotation decisions and provide feedback. The purpose of the final evaluation was to ensure that the quality of the result complies with the accuracy guaranteed in the contract. The evaluated extracts contained texts from both

Table 2 Correctness of functions

	Correct/words checked	%
Guaranteed correctness rate	–/–	85 %
Intermediate delivery	1,675/2,060	81%
Final delivery: cross-checking	4,881/5,488	89 %
Final delivery: double-blind test	3,256/3,607	90 %

Table 3 Correctness of relations

	Correct/words checked	%
Guaranteed correctness rate	–/–	87 %
Intermediate delivery	1,732/2,060	84 %
Final delivery: cross-checking	4,813/5,488	88 %
Final delivery: double-blind test	3,213/3,607	89 %

corpora, Europarl and JCR-Acquis. The intermediate evaluation extract contained 2,060 words and the final evaluation extract 9,095 words.

The evaluation of the final delivery was done in two ways. First, the FinnTreeBank team cross-checked the subcontractor's annotations by manually going through 5,488 tokens. The team marked the incorrect functions and relations and provided correct solutions for the erroneous annotations. The team only marked such annotation decisions as errors that contradicted with the annotation manual.

In addition to cross-checking a corpus extract, the FinnTreeBank team also evaluated the syntactic annotation of the final delivery using a double-blind test. Two annotators from the FinnTreeBank team extracted 3,607 tokens from the corpus and assigned the them dependency relations and functions. This extract was compared with the subcontractor's annotation. The differences were classified to the subcontractor's mistakes and underspecified structures. Only specified but incorrectly annotated structures were considered as errors.

The correctness rates of the different deliveries and the subcontractor-provided guaranteed correctness rate can be seen in Tables 2 and 3. Only such errors which can be verified based on the manual are considered. As mentioned earlier, the subcontractors delivery contained some structures that were annotated incorrectly, but that were not explicitly specified in the manual (see Ex. (5)). These are not reported in the tables below.

The FinnTreeBank team also composed feedback based on the most frequent and serious errors. In the feedback, we emphasized errors which complicate the interpretation of the whole sentence e.g. that each sentence should have only one word marked as the head and that one verb can take only one subject.

The correctness rates described in Tables 2 and 3 show that the results improved remarkably between the different rounds. Also the most disturbing errors (e.g. two or more head words in the same sentence) were corrected in the final version based on the feedback.

Table 4 Correctness of lemmas

	Correct/words checked	%
Guaranteed correctness rate	–/–	95 %
Final delivery	3,532/3,607	98 %

Table 5 Correctness of morphological analysis

	Correct/words checked	%
Guaranteed correctness rate	–/–	95 %
Final delivery	3,494/3,607	97 %

To immediately correct the misunderstandings in the interpretation of the manual, we collected the first training annotations from participants in the training session and gave feedback based on them. This enabled comparison of the errors made by human annotators and those of the parser. Certain differences were observed between these two categories of errors; human annotators' errors occurred typically e.g. in different kinds of verb chains and in dependency relations of coordinated words. At the intermediate phase, the errors of the parser occurred mostly in sentences in which the parser had generated more than one subject or object per verb and more than one main word per sentence. There were also some problems with the preprocessing regarding the splitting of sentences; this problem was easily solved by human annotators.

Due to external reasons, the contract with the subcontractor had to be made before the FinnTreeBank team had created the annotation manual for morphology. Because there was no linguistic specification for morphology at the outsourcing phase, we had to evaluate the morphological annotation based only on general knowledge of Finnish and morphology. Therefore, only clear mistakes, e.g. a verb annotated as a noun, are reported in Tables 4 and 5.

In Finnish, there are many borderline cases that can be analyzed in two different ways, e.g. the adjective/participle or the noun/adposition distinctions. Due to the lack of a morphological specification, we had to accept both analysis to these kind of ambiguous structures even if the subcontractor's annotation was not the wanted one. This approach to the morphological evaluation has an impact on the subcontractor's high accuracy rate.

6 Conclusion

We set out to answer the question, how to make corpus annotation more effective to save time and help researchers focus on their core expertise. We hypothesized that with a systematic high-coverage specification, even a highly complex task like automatic syntactic annotation can be externalized to a subcontractor with language technological expertise. We described a process and project based on this hypothesis: specification with Grammar Definition Corpus; competitive subcontracting with annotation quality guarantee; training, consultation and feedback; delivery and evaluation of the selected corpora, parsebanks and parser engine.

Our main experience is that the process described answers the need for time-saving and better focus. However, additional improvement to annotation quality and evaluation objectivity probably would have been accomplished by using some of the most pervasive, domain-specific characteristics of the corpora to be parsed in the specification phase (in addition to the systematic collection of example sentences extracted from a descriptive grammar). The inclusion of such domain-specific data in the specification probably makes for a more objective basis for the delivery and evaluation.

Acknowledgements We gratefully acknowledge the ongoing software and programming support of the Helsinki HFST Team, in particular the help of Tommi Pirinen and Sam Hardwick related to Finnish morphological analysis and various corpus processing tasks. We also thank Nick Ostler and Wanjiku Nganga for constructive comments on an earlier draft. The project has been funded via CLARIN, FIN-CLARIN, FIN-CLARIN-CONTENT and META-NORD by EU, University of Helsinki and the Academy of Finland.

References

Abeillé, Anne, ed. 2003. *Treebanks: Building and using syntactically annoted corpora*. Dordrecht: Kluwer Academic.

Carlson, Lauri, and Krister Lindén. 1987. Unification as a grammatical tool. *Nordic Journal of Linguistics* 10: 111–136.

de Marneffe, Marie-Catherine, and Christopher D. Manning. 2008. The Stanford typed dependencies representation. In *Coling 2008: Proceedings of the workshop on cross-framework and cross-domain parser evaluation, CrossParser '08*, 1–8. Stroudsburg: Association for Computational Linguistics. http://portal.acm.org/citation.cfm?id=1608858.1608859.

Hakulinen, Auli, Maria Vilkuna, Riitta Korhonen, Vesa Koivisto, Tarja Riitta Heinonen, and Irja Alho. 2004a. *Iso suomen kielioppi*. Helsinki: Suomalaisen Kirjallisuuden Seura. ISBN 951-746-557-2.

Hakulinen, Auli, Maria Vilkuna, Riitta Korhonen, Vesa Koivisto, Tarja Riitta Heinonen, and Irja Alho. 2004b. *Ison suomen kieliopin verkkoversio: määritelmät*. Helsinki: Suomalaisen Kirjallisuuden Seura. http://kaino.kotus.fi/cgi-bin/visktermit/visktermit.cgi.

Hwa, Rebecca, Philip Resnik, Amy Weinberg, Clara Cabezas, and Okan Kolak. 2005. Bootstrapping parsers via syntactic projection across parallel texts. *Natural Language Engineering* 11: 311–325. http://dl.acm.org/citation.cfm?id=1088141.1088144.

Karlsson, Fred, Atro Voutilainen, Juha Heikkilä, and Arto Anttila, eds. 1995. *Constraint grammar: A language-independent system for parsing running text*. Vol. 4 of *Natural language processing*. Berlin: Mouton de Gruyter. ISBN 3-11-014179-5.

Koskenniemi, Kimmo, Pasi Tapanainen, and Atro Voutilainen. 1992. Compiling and using finite-state syntactic rules. In *Proceedings of the 15th international conference on computational linguistics (COLING-92)*, Vol. I, 156–162. Nantes: ICCL.

Kromann, Matthias. 2003. The Danish Dependency Treebank and the underlying linguistic theory. In *Proceedings of the second workshop on treebanks and linguistic theories (TLT)*.

Lindén, Krister, Miikka Silfverberg, and Tommi Pirinen. 2009. HFST tools for morphology—an efficient open-source package for construction of morphological analyzers. In *Proceedings of the workshop on systems and frameworks for computational morphology*, Zürich, Switzerland.

Mikulová, Marie, Alevtina Bémová, Jan Hajič, Eva Hajičová, Jiří Havelka, Veronika Kolářová, Lucie Kučová, Markéta Lopatková, Petr Pajas, Jarmila Panevová, Magda Razímová, Petr Sgall, Jan Štěpánek, Zdeňka Urešová, Kateřina Veselá, and Zdeněk Žabokrtský. 2006. Annotation on the tectogrammatical level in the Prague Dependency Treebank. Annotation Manual. Technical Report 30, UFAL MFF UK, Prague, Czech Republic.

Muhonen, Kristiina, and Tanja Purtonen. 2011. Creating a dependency syntactic treebank: Towards intuitive language modeling. In *Proceedings of the international conference on dependency linguistics*, Barcelona, eds. Kim Gerdes, Eva Hajičová, and Leo Wanner, 155–164. ISBN 978-84-615-1834-0.

Nelimarkka, Esa, Harri Jäppinen, and Aarno Lehtola. 1984. Two-way finite automata and dependency grammar: A parsing method for inflectional free word order languages. In *Proceedings 10th international conference on computational linguistics and 22nd annual meeting of the Association for Computational Linguistics*, 389–392. Stroudsburg: ACL.

Nivre, Joakim, Jens Nilsson, and Johan Hall. 2006. Talbanken05: A Swedish treebank with phrase structure and dependency annotation. In *Proceedings of the fifth international conference on language resources and evaluation (LREC 2006)*, 24–26.

Pedersen, Ted. 2008. Last words: Empiricism is not a matter of faith. *Computational Linguistics* 34: 465–470.

Tapanainen, Pasi, and Timo Järvinen. 1997. A non-projective dependency parser. In *Proceedings fifth conference on applied natural language processing, ANLC '97*, 64–71. Stroudsburg: Association for Computational Linguistics. http://dx.doi.org/10.3115/974557.974568.

Tesnière, Lucien. 1980. *Grundzüge der strukturalen Syntax*. 3–12. Stuttgart: Klett-Cotta. ISBN 3-12-911790-3.

Voutilainen, Atro. 1997. Designing a (finite-state) parsing grammar. In *Finite state language processing*, eds. Emmanuel Roche and Yves Schabes, 283–310. Cambridge: The MIT Press. Chap. 9.

Voutilainen, Atro, and Krister Lindén. 2011. Finnish language bank: A framework for depositing and disseminating language resources for R&D. In *Proceedings of the workshop on visibility and availability of LT resources at NODALIDA 2011. NEALT proceedings series.*

Voutilainen, Atro, and Tanja Purtonen. 2011. A double-blind experiment on interannotator agreement: The case of dependency syntax and Finnish. In *NODALIDA 2011 conference proceedings*, 319–322.

On Dependency Analysis via Contractions and Weighted FSTs

Anssi Yli-Jyrä

Abstract Arc contractions in syntactic dependency graphs can be used to decide which graphs are trees. The paper observes that these contractions can be expressed with weighted finite-state transducers (weighted FST) that operate on string-encoded trees. The observation gives rise to a finite-state parsing algorithm that computes the parse forest and extracts the best parses from it. The algorithm is customizable to functional and bilexical dependency parsing, and it can be extended to non-projective parsing via a multi-planar encoding with prior results on high recall. Our experiments support an analysis of projective parsing according to which the worst-case time complexity of the algorithm is *quadratic* to the sentence length, and *linear* to the overlapping arcs and the number of functional categories of the arcs. The results suggest several interesting directions towards efficient and high-precision dependency parsing that takes advantage of the flexibility and the demonstrated ambiguity-packing capacity of such a parser.

1 Introduction

Finite-state transducers (FSTs)—and their underlying string relations—specify elegant but general parsing algorithms. In this contribution, the methodology of weighted FSTs is applied to efficient dependency grammar verification and search for the globally best parse in a dependency-based forest. The solution would not be as practical without memoizing composition and a simple implementation of arc contractions in dependency analyses, which are perhaps the most original aspects of this work.

Dependency grammar (Tesnière 1959) is typically implemented in computational linguistics by parsing algorithms that compromise between efficiency and the linguistic accuracy in different ways:

- Many practical dependency parsers are based on *deterministic parsing algorithms* (Nivre 2008) that can produce all kinds of trees but depend on heuristics that may

A. Yli-Jyrä (✉)
Department of Modern Languages, University of Helsinki, Helsinki, Finland
e-mail: anssi.yli-jyra@helsinki.fi

D. Santos et al. (eds.), *Shall We Play the Festschrift Game?*, 133
DOI 10.1007/978-3-642-30773-7_10, © Springer-Verlag Berlin Heidelberg 2012

not always find the globally optimal parse. This compromises the accuracy or recall of the analysis, but yields practically fast parsers.

- *Projective dependency parsing* gives higher accuracy because the globally optimal parses among all the projective parses can be found. The time complexity of projective parsers is comparable with context-free parsers: for the sentences of length n, it is in $O(n^3)$ in the case of functional and bilexical dependency grammars (Lombardo and Lesmo 1996; Eisner 1997). However, the projectivity condition for the parses restricts the admissible analyses to the subset of dependency trees that do not contain dependencies that cross one other in the drawings of the trees. The condition is fully explained in Yli-Jyrä (2005) and Kuhlmann (2010).
- *Non-projective dependency parsers* relax the projectivity condition by allowing crossing dependencies. The admissible parses thus include all possible dependency trees, some of which are non-projective. Non-projective trees are common in treebanks for major European languages (Kuhlmann 2010). However, unrestricted non-projective parsing is intractable (Neuhaus and Bröker 1997).
- *Parameterized non-projective dependency grammars* (Yli-Jyrä and Nykänen 2004; Nivre 2006; Kuhlmann 2010) have been proposed in order to address the precision, recall and efficiency considerations. For example, well-nested dependency trees with bounded gap-degree can be parsed in polynomial time (Gómez-Rodríguez et al. 2009; Kuhlmann and Satta 2009). The time complexity is in $O(n^7)$—quite much in comparison to deterministic parsing. More research is thus needed in order to make parameterized non-projective parsers practical.

My objective is to describe a practical parsing algorithm (in fact a family of algorithms) that takes advantage of partial projectivity and a performance-motivated parameter, t, for overlapping dependencies. In the case of unrooted projective trees with a fixed bound for t, the current analysis of the worst-case time complexity of the final algorithm (in Sect. 5.4) is based on evidence of $O(n^2)$ space and $O(n^2)$ time complexities that are measured using an efficient finite-state library. I am arguing that the approach is extendible towards non-projective parsing (then the actual complexity bound depends on subtle properties of the grammar, being, in the worst case, exponential to the number of dependencies that overlap but are not nested).

My secondary aim is to demonstrate the relevance of string-based finite-state methods in packing and processing syntactic parse forests. Therefore, I will describe the algorithm using weighted rational relations whose operations can be translated to operations on weighted finite-state transducers. In order to process trees with string automata, the work develops three new techniques:

1. The first new technique is to check the treeness of dependency graphs via *arc contractions*. Under the contractions, the notions of the bottom and the top in the reduction tree are no more based on the dominance or precedence relations

but on the minorization relation.[1] Contractions exhibit also a surprising ability to make the crossing dependencies local.

2. The second technique is the *dependency bracketing* for various kinds of dependency trees. Dependency bracketing with assigned planes is expressive enough for non-projective parsing and it admits finite-state processing of contractions in dependency forests. Dependency bracketing can be customized for functional and bilexical dependency grammars.
3. The third technique is the *memoization* of intermediate results in finite-state cascades. Memoization allows for combining bottom-up and top-down filtering in order to extract only the best parses. Memoization "tabulates" the found arcs via epsilon removal after contractions in finite-state transducers.

The resulting method can be seen as an upgrade to a constraint-based dependency parsing method (Yli-Jyrä 2005) that I developed during my Ph.D. studies.[2] The predecessor was based on a conjunctive decomposition of finite-state constraints that restricted the set of lexicon-generated candidate parses. The new algorithm does not only layerize the constraints (Oflazer 2003; Yli-Jyrä 2004; Yli-Jyrä and Koskenniemi 2004) but it also packs the local ambiguity and shares the subtrees.

2 The Input and Output Representations

In this section, I describe the graph representations manipulated by the parser and give the general principles for validating dependency trees.

2.1 Functional Dependency Tree

In terms of the outcome, the task of the dependency parser is to take a tokenized orthographical string, such as (1a) and annotate it with one or more dependency trees[3] as in (1b).

(1) a. ⟨*time* *flies* *like* *an* *arrow*⟩

b. ⟨*time* *flies* *like* *an* *arrow*⟩

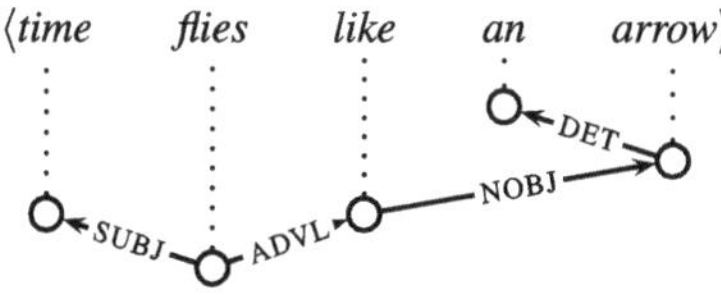

---

[1] It would be interesting to study how the minorization relation compares with the derivation relation of tree adjoining grammars. In both cases, the derived tree is manipulated from inside.

[2] This article is published on the occasion of Professor Lauri Carlson's birthday. As he co-supervised my Ph.D. research together with Kimmo Koskenniemi a decade ago, it is now a great privilege for me to write about these new advances in the research area where we started together.

[3] The tree is drawn with the `xdag.sty` package written by Denys Duchier, Ralph Debusmann and Robert Grabowski. For convenience, the orientation of the tree is flipped in the context of the linguistic example that is typeset with `expex.sty`.

Table 1 The dependency brackets

Left bracket	Right bracket	Head	Corresponding arc	Arc label
<SUBJ	SUBJ\	on the right	functional arc	SUBJ
/OBJ	OBJ>	on the left	functional arc	OBJ
(SUBJ	SUBJ)	(by convention)	undirected functional arc	SUBJ
(OBJ	OBJ)	(by convention)	undirected functional arc	OBJ
time<	\flies	on the right	bilexical arc	–
time/	>flies	on the left	bilexical arc	–
time(	)flies	(not specified)	undirected bilexical arc	–
an(	)arrow	(not specified)	undirected bilexical arc	–

The dependency trees of this work visualize *syntactic* dependency relations, in contrast to deeper, semantic dependencies. A dependency is a link between a *dependent* word (Tesnière 1959: "subordonné") and its *head* (Tesnière 1959: "régissant"). By convention, the arrowhead of each arc in the tree points, in this paper, to the dependent node. The arc has a label that indicates what *syntactic function* is played by the dependent word under the head. For example, the word *an* in (1) is a determiner (DET) for the word *arrow*. Since it is quite common to add several uncoordinated modifier words as dependents, the syntactic functions should not be confused with mathematical functions.

The finite-state parser will encode the actual drawing via special markup that is associated with the input string, as in the example (2).

(2) ⟨*time* *flies* *like* *an* *arrow*⟩
<SUBJ # SUBJ\/ADVL # ADVL> /NOBJ # <DET # DET\NOBJ>

The markup is based on *balanced dependency bracketing* (Table 1) that gives information on the dependency orientation, the syntactic function, and the lexeme. The brackets are viewed as tags that annotate the tokenized string. The order of the tags under each token mirrors the proximity of the connections in order to ensure that nested brackets match neatly, and different kinds of brackets are chosen for different kinds of trees, as demonstrated later in this paper.

In addition to the balanced brackets, the encoding includes a separator, #, that is used to bound the nodes in the encoded dependency graph. The set of brackets and the separator form the grammar alphabet, Γ. In addition, there is a corresponding alphabet, $\overline{\Gamma} = \{\overline{a} \mid a \in \Gamma\}$, that consists of the overlined variants of these symbols.

2.2 Bilexical Dependency Tree

In fully data-driven parsing, the syntactic functions of dependencies are often unknown. Therefore, a bilexical dependency tree (3) focuses on the dependencies between two lexical entries.

(3)

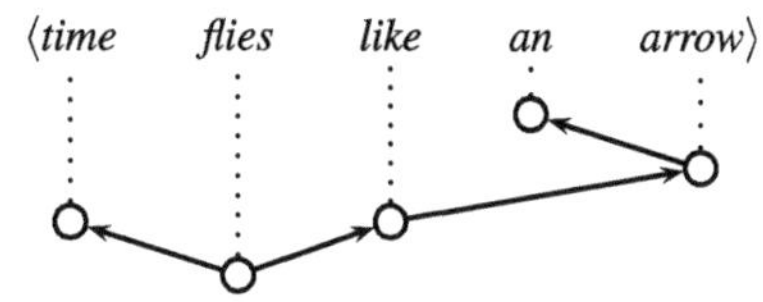

Although the tree in (3) is very elegant without arc labels, the currently described parser needs bracket labels in order to know about the syntactic properties of the linked tokens. Provided that the possible lexical types are fixed, the internal tag alphabet of the parser can be expanded with the brackets that indicate the lexical types (4). The expansion temporarily increases the redundancy in the encoding.

(4) ⟨*time* *flies* *like* *an* *arrow*⟩

time< # \flies flies/ # >like like/ # an< # \arrow >arrow

Although the linguistic aspects of dependency analyses would be an interesting topic for further discussions, the rest of the paper will focus on the computational properties of dependency tree processing.

2.3 The General Properties of Dependency Trees

Syntactic dependency trees have a number of crucial properties that we will need in order to distinguish a valid parse from invalid parses.

- Every syntactic dependency tree is a *labeled directed graph* $G = (V, \Gamma', E)$ where
  - V is the set of *nodes* (vertices) that correspond to the tokens in the sentence;
  - $\Gamma' = \Gamma - \{\#\}$ is the set of *arc labels*, and
  - $E \subseteq V \times \Gamma' \times V$ is the set of *labeled arcs* (aka directed labeled edges).

  In the dependency tree drawings, the arc (d, x, h) is drawn as $d \overset{x}{\leftarrow} h$. The arc indicates that node d depends on node h that is a head for d.
- Every syntactic dependency tree G is a labeled directed graph where every node has at most one head. That is, the set of arcs E can be seen as a partial function $E : V \to (\Gamma' \times V)$. Under this condition, we say that G has the *head property*.
- Every syntactic dependency tree is connected and acyclic. These properties are not local graph properties and, therefore, their definitions require additional machinery. In this paper the machinery consists of *contractions* and *minors*:

Definition 1 Let $G = (V, \Gamma', E)$ be a labeled directed graph with the head property. If there is an arc $(d, x, h) \in E$, then $(d, x, h') \in E$ implies $h = h'$. The *contraction* of arc (d, x, h) produces a new graph $H = (V', \Gamma', E')$ with

$$V' = V - \{d\}, \tag{1}$$

$$E' = \big(V' \times \Gamma' \times V'\big) \cap \big(E \cup \{(d', y, h) \mid (d', y, d) \in E\}\big). \tag{2}$$

The orthographical content corresponding to node h includes now implicitly the content of node d.

Definition 2 In the current sense, a graph H is a *minor* of a directed graph G if a copy of H can be obtained from G via arc contractions.[4]

Now we can test the connectedness and acyclicity as follows:

- A labeled directed graph G with the head property is *connected* if and only if it has a trivial minor $H = (V', \Gamma', \emptyset)$ where $|V'| = 1$.
- A labeled directed graph G with the head property is *acyclic* if and only if it has no minor graph $H = (V', \Gamma', E')$ with a loop $(d, x, d) \in E'$.

• Every syntactic dependency tree is a *rooted tree*. A connected labeled directed graph with the head property is a rooted tree if there is exactly one independent node, called a *root*, and all the arcs point away from the root. In the example (1), the root word is '*flies*'. All the arcs point away from this node.

It can be shown that a labeled directed graph G with the head property is a rooted tree if and only if G is connected and acyclic.

2.4 Validating Syntactic Dependency Trees

The relevant set of dependency trees are now characterized as acyclic and connected labeled directed graphs with the head property. This characterization does not directly involve testing for the existence of a root. Instead, we must (i) check that no word has two heads and (ii) prove the acyclicity and connectedness by contracting non-loop arcs until a trivial graph is reached.

Some contractions can be performed in parallel. For example, (1) can be validated by two layers of contractions:

(5) a. ⟨*time flies like an arrow*⟩

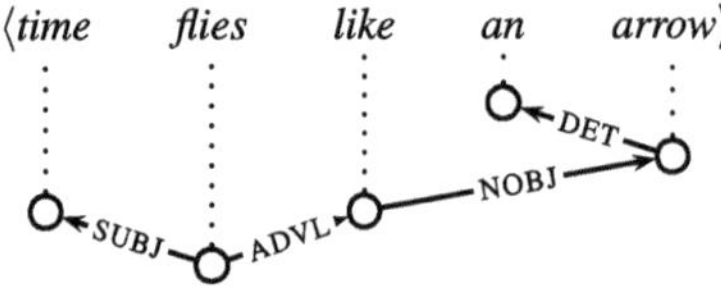

b. ⟨*time flies like an arrow*⟩

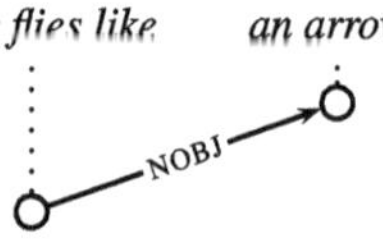

c. ⟨*time flies like an arrow*⟩

[4]This definition excludes arc deletion that is normally included in the definition of graph minors.

An important observation of the current contribution is that the validation can be implemented directly on bracketed dependency trees. In (6), the tags affected by each contraction are indicated with an overline. A contraction of an arc (d, x, h) is an *internal contraction* if h has some other connections and d is a head for some other node. The contraction of the ADVL arc in (6a) is an internal contraction if performed before the SUBJ arc has been contracted.

(6) a. ⟨*time* *flies* *like* *an* *arrow*⟩
$\overline{\text{<SUBJ}}$ $\overline{\#}$ $\overline{\text{SUBJ\textbackslash}}$ $\overline{\text{/ADVL}}$ $\overline{\#}$ $\overline{\text{ADVL>}}$ /NOBJ # $\overline{\text{<DET}}$ $\overline{\#}$ $\overline{\text{DET\textbackslash}}$ NOBJ>

b. ⟨*time flies like* *an arrow*⟩
$\overline{\text{/NOBJ}}$ $\overline{\#}$ $\overline{\text{NOBJ>}}$

c. ⟨*time flies like an arrow*⟩

The validation of bracketed trees is based on three principles:

1. *Decodability*. For each label $\alpha \in \Gamma - \{\#\}$, the left brackets α> and $\alpha\backslash$ are matched with the corresponding right brackets $\alpha\backslash$ and α>, respectively. Each pair of matching brackets corresponds to an arc in the labeled directed graph.
2. *Equicardinality*. There is the same number of arcs and word boundaries. Every boundary between two adjacent words is indicated with a hash symbol (#). A hash symbol is eliminated at the same time as the brackets. This ensures that a loop cannot be eliminated because the left and right brackets are not separated by any hash symbol. Thus, a cyclic dependency graph cannot be fully reduced to a trivial graph. If the graph is not connected, there remains a word boundary that is not eliminated, and the graph does not have a trivial graph as a minor.
3. *Contiguity*. The internal contraction of an arc (d, x, h) is allowed only if node h corresponds to a contiguous string of brackets in the resulting graph. This principle ensures that the resulting minor graph can be encoded with dependency bracketing.

2.4.1 Ensuring Decodability

The bracket labels play a crucial role in non-projective dependency trees and in minors obtained from them.

Any non-projective dependency tree can be bracketed when we adopt a multiplanar decomposition for the arcs and corresponding brackets (Yli-Jyrä 2003). This means that there is no limit for the complexity of non-projective trees, provided that the number of available planes is not fixed. In bracketed encodings of bilexical dependency trees, multiplanarity seems presently to be the only way to encode crossing brackets.

A 2-plane encoding is already enough to achieve very high coverage (Gómez-Rodríguez and Nivre 2010). Syntactic functions could further extend the set of non-projective trees that can be encoded by allocating each function to a plane of its own.

Example (7) shows that the matching brackets of crossing arcs are distinguished using two planes, I and II.

(7) a.

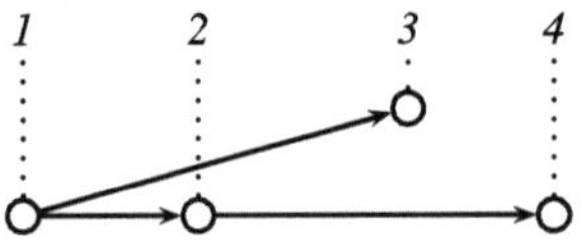

b. *1* 2 3 4

/I /I # I> /II # I> # II>

2.4.2 Ensuring Contiguity

A typical non-projective dependency tree contains a large subgraph that does not contain crossing links. Therefore, it is often possible to reduce many non-crossing arcs before it is necessary to contract any crossing arc.

An interesting observation is that contractions of non-crossing arcs often transform a non-projective tree into a projective tree as demonstrated by Example (8) that is obtained from the non-projective tree in (7).

(8) a.

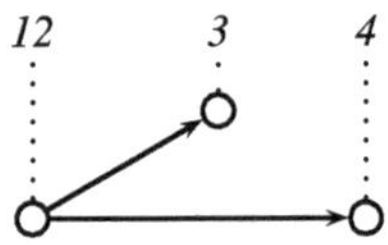

b. *12* 3 4

/I /II # I> # II>

Another interesting observation is that a non-internal contraction does not need to merge adjacent positions in a bracketed tree. This produces a significant extension to simple contractions that can be used to transform a non-projective tree into a projective one. The power of non-internal contractions is illustrated by Example (9) that reduces to (10).

(9) a.

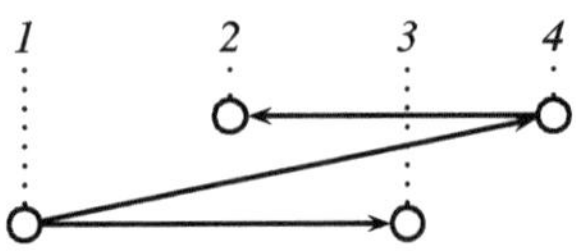

b. *1* 2 3 4

/I $\overline{/I}$ # <II $\overline{\#}$ $\overline{I\rangle}$ # II\I>

(10) a.

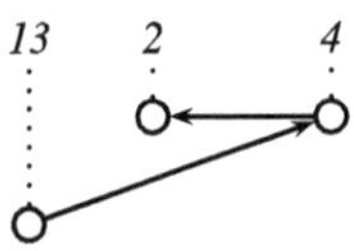

b. *13* 2 4

/I # <II # II\I>

Many of the non-projective trees discussed in Yli-Jyrä (2003) and Kuhlmann (2010) can be reduced to the trivial tree via contractions of non-crossing arcs. The remaining non-projective trees can be reduced with the aid of non-internal contractions, because every nontrivial tree admits at least one such contraction.

3 Computing Weighted Minors

This section describes a mechanical, finite-state implementable deterministic method whose purpose is to perform at least one contraction in any nonempty string. The reader is referred to Mohri (2009) for a detailed exposition of algorithms on weighted transducers.

In this article, the algorithms are specified with weighted rational relations whose operations can be implemented through manipulation of finite-state transducers.

3.1 The Formalism of Weighted Rational Relations

In this paper, weights are nonnegative real numbers ($\mathbb{R}_{\geq 0} \cup \{\infty\}$) with the usual multiplication operation and the *maximum* (max) as the additive operation (i.e., $+$ and $\sum$ denote the max operation). This set of weights gives us an easily understandable starting point and supports Viterbi-decoding of the best parses.

Let Σ be an alphabet. The free monoid generated by Σ is denoted by Σ^*. The neutral element of this monoid is the empty string, ε. The set of rational (i.e., regular) languages includes the finite subsets of Σ^* and is closed, for any two elements L, M, under the rational operations such as concatenation $L \cdot M$, star (L^*), the Boolean operations ($L \cup M$, $L \cap M$, $L - M$, etc.).

The set of (binary) rational relations over Σ^* includes all finite subsets of $\Sigma^* \times \Sigma^*$ and is also closed under concatenation, star and union. It also includes rational relations such as

$$\mathrm{Id}(L) = \big\{(x, x) \bigm| x \in L\big\}, \tag{3}$$

$$L \times M = \big\{(x, y) \bigm| x \in L, y \in M\big\}. \tag{4}$$

Let $R \subseteq \Sigma^* \times \Sigma^*$ be a rational relation. In a pair $(x, y) \in R$, x is called the *input* string and y is called the *output* string. Define the *characteristic weighted rational relations* $\mathbb{1}(R), \mathbb{1}_\varepsilon : (\Sigma^* \times \Sigma^*) \to (\mathbb{R}_{\geq 0} \cup \{\infty\})$ by

$$\mathbb{1}(R)(x, y) = \begin{cases} 1 & (x, y) \in R, \\ 0 & \text{otherwise}, \end{cases} \tag{5}$$

$$\mathbb{1}_\varepsilon = \mathbb{1}\big(\mathrm{Id}(\varepsilon)\big). \tag{6}$$

Simple weighted rational relations can be defined with the comprehension notation, but the notation itself does not guarantee that the defined set is a weighted rational relation. Instead, the set of weighted rational relations over the alphabet Σ^* and the weights $\mathbb{R}_{\geq 0} \cup \{\infty\}$ (with max and multiplication) contains the characteristic weighted rational relations and is closed under certain operations. Let T and U be weighted rational relations $(\Sigma^* \times \Sigma^*) \to (\mathbb{R}_{\geq 0} \cup \{\infty\})$ and let $w \in \mathbb{R}_{\geq 0} \cup \{\infty\}$. Define the *left product*, *union*, *composition*, *concatenation*, *star* and the *projection* operations by

$$w \cdot T = \{((x, y), w \cdot T(x, y)) \mid x, y \in \Sigma^*\}, \tag{7}$$

$$T \cup U = \{((x, y), T(x, y) + U(x, y)) \mid x, y \in \Sigma^*\}, \tag{8}$$

$$T \circ U = \left\{\left((x, z), \sum_{y \in \Sigma^*} T(x, y)U(y, z)\right) \middle| x, z \in \Sigma^*\right\}, \tag{9}$$

$$T \cdot U = \left\{\left((x, y), \sum_{x = x_0 x_1, y = y_0 y_1} T(x_0, y_0)U(x_1, y_1)\right) \middle| x, y \in \Sigma^*\right\}, \tag{10}$$

$$T^* = \left\{\left((x, y), \sum_{\substack{n \in \mathbb{N} \\ x = x_1 \ldots x_n \\ y = y_1 \ldots y_n}} T(x_1, y_1) \cdots T(x_n, y_n)\right) \middle| x, y \in \Sigma^*\right\}, \tag{11}$$

$$\mathrm{Proj}_1(T) = \left\{\left((x_1, x_1), \sum_{x_2 \in \Sigma^*} T(x_1, x_2)\right) \middle| x_1 \in \Sigma^*\right\}, \tag{12}$$

$$\mathrm{Proj}_2(T) = \left\{\left((x_2, x_2), \sum_{x_1 \in \Sigma^*} T(x_1, x_2)\right) \middle| x_2 \in \Sigma^*\right\}. \tag{13}$$

Note that if $T(\varepsilon, \varepsilon) \neq 0$ and $T(x, y) \neq 0$, $T^*(x, y) = \infty$.

For a weighted rational relation T, define its *image* and *support* by

$$\mathrm{Im}(T) = \{T(x, y) \mid x, y \in \Sigma^*\}, \tag{14}$$

$$\mathrm{Supp}(T) = \{(x, y) \mid x, y \in \Sigma^*, T(x, y) \neq 0\}. \tag{15}$$

By convention, T can be viewed as a weighted rational relation $(\Sigma_1^* \times \Sigma_2^*) \to (\mathbb{R}_{\geq 0} \cup \{\infty\})$ where $\Sigma_1, \Sigma_2 \subseteq \Sigma$ if T is a weighted rational relation $(\Sigma^* \times \Sigma^*) \to (\mathbb{R}_{\geq 0} \cup \{\infty\})$ with $\mathrm{Supp}(T) \subseteq \Sigma_1^* \times \Sigma_2^*$, and vice versa.

Let T be a weighted rational relation with a finite support and $p \in \{1, 2\}$. Let w be the maximal value in $\mathrm{Im}(T)$. Let the sequence $\langle x_1, \ldots, x_j \rangle$ contain the elements of the set $\{x \mid x \in \Sigma^*, \mathrm{Proj}_p(T)(x, x) = w\}$ in the lexicographical order. Define the k-bounded *best restriction* of $\mathrm{Proj}_p(T)$ as

$$\mathrm{BestProj}_p(T, k) = \{((x_i, x_i), w) \mid i \in \{1, \ldots, \min\{j, k\}\}\}. \tag{16}$$

3.2 Weighted Contractions

In the parser, the rule component of the grammar defines a weighted rational relation, Contraction: $\mathrm{Id}((\Gamma \cup \overline{\Gamma})^*) \rightarrow (\mathbb{R}_{\geq 0} \cup \{\infty\})$. The support language of this relation is $\mathrm{Id}^{-1}(\mathrm{Supp}(\mathrm{Contraction}))$ and it is a subset of $\Gamma^*\overline{\Gamma}\Gamma^*\overline{\#}\Gamma^*\overline{\Gamma}\Gamma^*$.

A convenient way to specify Contraction is through a finite set of contraction rules $\alpha \mapsto w$ where the expression α gives a rational (i.e., regular) subset of the language $\Gamma^*\overline{\Gamma}\Gamma^*\overline{\#}\Gamma^*\overline{\Gamma}\Gamma^*$ and w is a non-negative real number. The examples of contraction rules include projective functional rules (11a–b), projective bilexical rules (11c–d), and non-projective bilexical rules (11e).

(11) a. $(\ \overline{\text{<SUBJ}}\quad \overline{\#}\quad \overline{\text{SUBJ\textbackslash}}\ ) \mapsto 0.97,$

b. $(\ \overline{\text{/ADVL}}\quad \overline{\#}\quad \overline{\text{ADVL>}}\ ) \mapsto 0.47,$

c. $(\ \overline{\text{like/}}\quad \overline{\#}\quad \overline{\text{>arrow}}\ ) \mapsto 0.00127,$

d. $(\ \overline{\text{an<}}\quad \overline{\#}\quad \overline{\text{\textbackslash arrow}}\ ) \mapsto 0.42,$

e. $(\#\ \overline{\text{<SUBJ}}\quad \overline{\#}\quad (\Gamma - \{\text{<SUBJ}, \text{SUBJ\textbackslash}\})^*\quad \overline{\text{SUBJ\textbackslash}}\ ) \mapsto 0.97,$

When applied by the finite-state implementation, each contraction rule removes a pair of dependency brackets and a respective node separator (#). The overlining of some symbols indicates which three tags in the strings disappear when a contraction is performed. When a rule with weight w is applied, the total weight of the string is multiplied by w. In (11e), there are potentially some symbols that do not disappear.

3.3 Applying Weighted Contractions Deterministically

FreeReduce is a weighted rational relation that reduces bracketed trees by applying a specified set of contractions freely to the strings. It is constructed as follows:

$$\mathrm{Hesitate} = \mathbb{1}\Big(\big(\mathrm{Id}(\Gamma) \cup \{(a, \overline{a}) \mid a \in \Gamma\}\big)^*\Big), \tag{17}$$

$$\mathrm{FreeMark} = \big(\mathbb{1}\,(\mathrm{Id}(\Gamma)) \cup \mathrm{Contraction}\big)^*, \tag{18}$$

$$\mathrm{Perform} = \mathbb{1}\Big(\big(\mathrm{Id}(\Gamma) \cup \{(a, \varepsilon) \mid a \in \overline{\Gamma}\}\big)^*\Big), \tag{19}$$

$$\mathrm{FreeReduce} = \mathrm{Hesitate} \circ \mathrm{FreeMark} \circ \mathrm{Perform}. \tag{20}$$

When an input bracketing is reduced with FreeReduce, each possible place for contractions optionally either undergoes the contraction or is left intact as indicated by the weighted pairs (12a–d) belonging to FreeMark. The optionality generates spurious ambiguity. Spurious ambiguity complicates the extraction of the top k best parses as any optimal parse itself may be reduced in more than k different ways. Furthermore, it restricts the possibilities for generalizing the parsing algorithm and changing the system of weights: if the additive operation over the weights were non-idempotent (*maximum* is idempotent), we would have a danger that spurious ambiguity invalidates the weights of parses.

(12) a. $(\mathrm{Id}(<\textsc{subj}\ \#\ \textsc{subj}\backslash/\textsc{advl}\ \#\ \textsc{advl}>),\ 1)$

b. $(\mathrm{Id}(<\textsc{subj}\ \#\ \textsc{subj}\backslash\overline{/\textsc{advl}}\ \overline{\#}\ \overline{\textsc{advl}>}), 0.47)$

c. $(\mathrm{Id}(\overline{<\textsc{subj}}\ \overline{\#}\ \overline{\textsc{subj}\backslash}/\textsc{advl}\ \#\ \textsc{advl}>), 0.97)$

d. $(\mathrm{Id}(\overline{<\textsc{subj}}\ \overline{\#}\ \overline{\textsc{subj}\backslash}\ \overline{/\textsc{advl}}\ \overline{\#}\ \overline{\textsc{advl}>}, 0.97 \times 0.47)$

The spurious ambiguity can be avoided by restricting the support of (Hesitate ∘ FreeReduce) in such a way that it is a function from inputs to outputs.

In order to make the restriction, the contraction rules are applied deterministically from left to right. This modification can be implemented with a technique (Yli-Jyrä 2008) that is based on earlier ideas of G. van Noord and D. Gerdemann. To apply this technique, define a rational relation Prefer : $(\Gamma \cup \overline{\Gamma})^* \times (\Gamma \cup \overline{\Gamma})^*$ that relates a pair (x, y) of two overline marked copies of the same string if the first copy, x, contains earlier overlines than y. For example, (12b) is preferred over (12a), (12c) is preferred over (12a) and (12b), and (12d) is preferred over (12a–c).

$$\mathrm{Prefer} = \mathrm{Id}\big(\Gamma^*\big) \cdot \big\{(\overline{a}, a) \mid a \in \Gamma\big\} \cdot \big\{(x, y) \mid x, y \in \{a, \overline{a}\}, a \in \Gamma\big\}^*. \tag{21}$$

Now we extract from FreeMark the set of strings, Dispreferred(FreeMark), for which there are preferred alternatives, and construct its complement NotDispreferred(FreeMark).

$$\mathrm{Dispreferred}(S) = \mathrm{Id}^{-1}\big(\mathrm{Supp}\big(\mathrm{Proj}_2\big(S \circ \mathbb{1}(\mathrm{Prefer}) \circ S\big)\big)\big), \tag{22}$$

$$\mathrm{NotDispreferred}(S) = (\Gamma \cup \overline{\Gamma})^* - \mathrm{Dispreferred}(S). \tag{23}$$

By filtering the identity pairs in FreeMark with NotDispreferred(FreeMark), we refine FreeMark and obtain DefiniteMark. We also want to reject all nonempty strings without any overlined symbols ($\Gamma\Gamma^*$). In the end, we obtain a weighted rational relation that "performs" a deterministic, non-empty set of contractions in all non-empty inputs.

$$\mathrm{DefiniteMark} = \mathrm{FreeMark} \circ \mathbb{1}\big(\mathrm{Id}\big(\mathrm{NotDispreferred(FreeMark)} - \Gamma\Gamma^*\big)\big), \tag{24}$$

$$\mathrm{Reduce} = \mathrm{Hesitate} \circ \mathrm{DefiniteMark} \circ \mathrm{Perform}. \tag{25}$$

We have thus defined a weighted rational relation, Reduce, that maps the input strings deterministically to strings that are strictly shorter unless the input is already the empty string.

Reduce can be viewed as a function $\Gamma^* \to (\Gamma^* \times (\mathbb{R}_{\geq 0} \cup \{\infty\}))$. The existence of this alternative structure implies that Reduce can be implemented very efficiently with a deterministic finite-state device. In the following, we will first study the use of the Reduce relation because it is safer, but later, in Sect. 5.4, we observe that the FreeReduce relation gives a more efficient solution whenever applicable.

4 The Structure of the Grammar and the Parser

The purpose of this section is to define the grammar and the respective parser in terms of weighted rational relations.

4.1 The Grammar Relation

In a high level, the grammar can be seen as a composition (26) of four (weighted) rational relations of type $(\Sigma^* \times \Sigma^*) \to (\mathbb{R}_{\geq 0} \cup \{\infty\})$.

$$\text{Grammar} = \text{Lexicon} \circ \text{Abstract} \circ \text{HasMinor}_t \circ \mathbb{1}_\varepsilon. \tag{26}$$

In the composition, Lexicon does tokenization and morphological analysis and then retrieves arguments and functions, Abstract is a relation (27) that deletes all but syntactic symbols in strings, HasMinor_t performs t levels of reductions, being thus a finite composition (28) of t identical Reduce relations, and $\mathbb{1}_\varepsilon$ ensures that we finally obtain a trivial minor graph.

$$\text{Abstract} = \mathbb{1}\big(\big(\text{Id}(\Gamma) \cup \{(x, \varepsilon) \mid x \in \Sigma - \Gamma\}\big)^*\big), \tag{27}$$

$$\text{HasMinor}_t = \underbrace{\text{Reduce} \circ \cdots \circ \text{Reduce}}_{t}. \tag{28}$$

The component relations of the grammar link four representations:

$$\text{Ortho} \xrightarrow{\quad\text{Lexicon}\quad} \text{MorphoSyn} \xrightarrow{\quad\text{Abstract}\quad} \text{Syn} \xrightarrow{\quad\text{HasMinor}_t\quad} \{\varepsilon\}. \tag{29}$$

In this system, Ortho is the set of orthographical strings over the set of orthographical symbols Ω, MorphoSyn is the set of morpho-syntactic strings that consist of morphological symbols M and grammatical symbols Γ, and Syn is the set of syntactic strings over the alphabet Γ.

To be precise, Grammar is a weighted rational relation that maps the pairs $(x, \varepsilon) \in \Omega^* \times \{\varepsilon\}$ to the set of weights. The precise interpretation of the weights remains intentionally open. The Grammar relation also characterizes a string set, Grammatical $\subseteq \Omega^*$, that is defined by

$$\text{Grammatical} = \text{Id}^{-1}\big(\text{Supp}\big(\text{Proj}_1(\text{Grammar})\big)\big). \tag{30}$$

4.2 The Parser Relation

In order to *parse* an orthographical string $x \in$ Ortho, we need to extract the corresponding morpho-syntactic strings $y \in$ MorphoSyn from the internals of the system (29). The extraction process (31) defines a weighted rational relation, Parser : (Ortho $\times$ MorphoSyn) $\to (\mathbb{R}_{\geq 0} \cup \{\infty\})$.

$$\text{Parser} = \text{Lexicon} \circ \text{Proj}_1(\text{Abstract} \circ \text{HasMinor}_t \circ \mathbb{1}_\varepsilon). \tag{31}$$

Let $x \in$ Ortho be an orthographical string. If (x, y) is a pair in Supp(Parser), we say that y is a *parse* for x. The set of all parses for x is denoted by

$$\text{Parses}(x) = \text{Id}^{-1}\big(\text{Supp}\big(\text{Proj}_2\big(\mathbb{1}\big(\text{Id}(x)\big) \circ \text{Parser}\big)\big)\big). \tag{32}$$

Table 2 The growth of HasMinor_t as a function of t and the number of functional bracket pairs

	$c=1$			$c=2$			$c=3$		
t	states	trans.	explanation	states	trans.	explanation	states	trans.	explanation
1	3	3	$2+1$	5	6	$4+1$	7	9	$6+1$
2	7	9	$4+2+1$	21	30	$16+4+1$	43	63	$36+6+1$
3	15	21	$8+\cdots+1$	85	126	$64+\cdots+1$	259	387	$216+\cdots+1$
4	31	45	$16+\cdots+1$	341	510	$256+\cdots+1$	1555	2331	$1296+\cdots+1$
5	63	93	$32+\cdots+1$	1365	2046	$1024+\cdots+1$	9331	13995	$7776+\cdots+1$
6	127	189	$64+\cdots+1$	5461	8190	$4096+\cdots+1$	55987	83979	$46656+\cdots+1$

The weight of each parse $y \in \text{Parses}(x)$ is $\text{Parser}(x, y)$. A k-bounded set of best parses is given by

$$\text{BestParses}(x, k) = \text{Id}^{-1}\big(\text{Supp}\big(\text{BestProj}_2\big(\mathbb{1}\big(\text{Id}(x)\big) \circ \text{Parser}, k\big)\big)\big). \tag{33}$$

4.3 The Grammar Constant

The parameter t limits the number of iterations of Reduce in HasMinor_t. In the dependency trees, the parameter limits the number of overlapping arcs that can be contracted. The parameter can be fixed to a relatively small integer without any observable loss in recall. This makes HasMinor_t a fixed weighted rational relation. The Grammar and Parser relations are thus applicable in linear time, at least according to the asymptotic complexity analysis (as $n \to \infty$).

The asymptotic analysis ignores the fact that the application of the grammar to the input involves a large coefficient, the *grammar constant*, that is bounded from the above by the product of the sizes of the finite-state transducers for Lexicon, Abstract and HasMinor_t. As to their sizes, Lexicon and Abstract are just ordinary kinds of weighted rational relations used in natural-language processing. Their implementation does not require our attention now.

In contrast to Lexicon and Abstract, the finite-state implementation of HasMinor_t is of an impractical size. To see this, assume that $\text{Supp}(\text{Contract}) = \{(i \ \# \ i) \mid i \in \{1, \ldots, c\}\}$ where c is the number of arc types. Table 2 shows experimental results on how the size of HasMinor_t grows as a function of c and t. From these I gather that the number of states in the finite-state implementation of $\text{HasMinor}_t \circ \mathbb{1}_\varepsilon$ is

$$(2c)^t + (2c)^{t-1} + \cdots + 1 = \sum_{k=0}^{t} (2c)^k = \frac{(1-(2c)^{t+1})}{1-(2c)} = O\big((2c)^t\big). \tag{34}$$

4.4 An On-demand Construction

A slight improvement to the precomputation of (28) is obtained by the on-demand computation of $\mathrm{HasMinor}_t$. This idea is used in (36), where Grammar is restricted to the pair of the orthographical string x and the empty string ε.

$$\mathrm{Bot}(x, y) = \mathbb{1}\big(\{(x, y)\}\big) \circ \mathrm{Lexicon}, \tag{35}$$

$$\mathrm{Grammar}_{|\{(x,\varepsilon)\}} = \underbrace{(\ldots(}_{t}(\mathrm{Bot}(x, x) \circ \mathrm{Abstract})\underbrace{\circ\mathrm{Reduce}) \cdots \circ \mathrm{Reduce})}_{t} \circ \mathbb{1}_{\varepsilon}. \tag{36}$$

The worst-case size complexity of the finite-state representation of $\mathrm{Grammar}_{|\{(x,\varepsilon)\}}$ is still exponential to t, but the average-case complexity of (36) can be much smaller than the complexity of the constant grammar (28). This admits practical applicability on similar grounds as some previous parsing approaches that iteratively verify labeled bracketing (Roche 1997; Oflazer 2003).

5 A Non-linear but Efficient Approach

In the above, we have seen that although the parser can be represented as a rational relation that can be applied in linear time to the input string, the hidden grammar constant does not guarantee that the relation could always be restricted efficiently to an orthographical string. There are situations where we need guarantees for the worst-case complexity.

This section describes algorithms that do not fully elaborate the composition (28) of the relations. Instead, the algorithms compute the composition indirectly through intermediate languages. The space complexity of each intermediate representation is not linear to the length of the sentence because their epsilons are removed. Since we never compute the composition as a whole, the algorithms are still more practical than the naive approaches that construct a restriction of $\mathrm{HasMinor}_t$ in one way or another.

5.1 Forgetting Composition

If $\mathrm{Grammar}_{|\{(x,\varepsilon)\}}$ is immediately applied to the pair (x, ε), we may replace, in (37), the input side of the composition with the empty string and still compute the same weight for (x, ε).

$$\mathrm{Grammar}(x, \varepsilon) = \mathrm{Im}\big(\underbrace{(\ldots(}_{t}(\mathrm{Bot}(\varepsilon, x) \circ \mathrm{Abstract})\underbrace{\circ\,\mathrm{Reduce}) \cdots \circ \mathrm{Reduce})}_{t} \circ \mathbb{1}_{\varepsilon}\big). \tag{37}$$

The effect of the modification is significant. It basically makes the composition to forget everything that is contracted. Since the matching pairs of brackets are forgotten, the details of the contracted brackets are not complicating the further processing. The forgetting effect can be implemented also via projections as in (38).

$$\text{Grammar}(x,\varepsilon) = \text{Im}\Big(\underbrace{\big[\cdots\big[}_{t}\big[\text{Bot}(x,x)\circ\text{Abstract}\big]\underbrace{\circ\,\text{Reduce}\cdots\big]\circ\text{Reduce}\big]}_{t}\circ\mathbb{1}_{\varepsilon}\Big),$$

$$\text{where } [X] = \text{Proj}_2(X). \tag{38}$$

The time complexity of this composition-projection method is linear to t and to the worst-case time complexity of the iteration rounds.

5.2 A Preliminary Complexity Analysis

In order to analyze the space complexity of the minimized sizes of the projections, I carried out some experiments. In these experiments, the number of tokens was $n \leq 80$ and the number of iterations $t \leq n-1$, which is sufficient for obtaining all parses. A highly ambiguous lexicon was modeled by replacing $\text{Bot}(x,x)$ either with model (13a), where Γ_{d} contains dependent-side brackets and Γ_{h} contains head-side brackets, or with model (13b), where Γ_{u} consists of brackets that encode undirected arcs.

(13) a. $\mathbb{1}(\text{Id}(\Gamma_{\text{d}}^{*}(\varepsilon\cup\Gamma_{\text{h}})\Gamma_{\text{d}}^{*}(\#\Gamma_{\text{d}}^{*}(\varepsilon\cup\Gamma_{\text{h}})\Gamma_{\text{d}}^{*})^{n-1}))$

b. $\mathbb{1}(\text{Id}(\Gamma_{\text{u}}^{*}(\#\Gamma_{\text{u}}^{*})^{n-1}))$

The first model (13a) gives rise to rooted trees and (13b) to unrooted ones. Bilexical brackets were modeled by adding token numbers to the respective brackets. The contraction rules of the grammar are restricted to those of the shape $\overline{\alpha}\ \overline{\#}\ \overline{\beta} \mapsto 1$, where $\overline{\alpha}, \overline{\beta} \subseteq \overline{\Gamma}$.

In the experiments, I measured the size (number of states and number of transitions) of minimal (unweighted) finite-state transducers that correspond to the first intermediate result, $[[\text{Bot}(x,x)]\circ\text{Reduce}]$, and the subsequent composition-projections in (38). To reduce the number of necessary experiments, I eliminated some dimensions with simple tests. These tests gave the following useful results:

- The sizes of intermediate results grow only by a constant factor when we switch from unrooted trees to rooted trees.
- If the lexical differences were reduced, the size of the largest intermediate result would be become smaller. Thus, the bilexical bracketing presents the maximal complexity.
- If the number of functional categories of the dependencies doubles, the number of transitions will double too, but the number of states does not change.

Table 3 The sizes of the projections of the first, the fifth and the $(n/2-1)^{\mathrm{th}}$ applications

	1st iteration				5th iteration				$(n/2-1)^{\mathrm{th}}$ iteration			
n	states	trans.	exp.	$2n^2$	states	trans.	$6n^2$	secs	$n/2-1$	states	trans.	exp.
20	38	834	1.85	800	90	1974	2400	0.06	9	110	2410	1.66
30	58	1854	1.85	1800	150	4794	5400	0.10	14	240	7665	1.63
40	78	3274	1.86	3200	210	8814	9600	0.19	19	420	17620	1.62
50	98	5094	1.86	5000	270	14034	1500	0.34	24	650	33775	1.61
60	118	7314	1.87	7200	330	20454	21600	0.58	29	930	57630	1.60
70	138	9934	1.87	9800	390	28074	29400	0.94	34	1260	90685	1.60
80	158	12954	1.87	12800	450	36894	38400	1.45	39	1640	134440	1.60

My main experiment focused on unrooted bilexical bracketing without dependency functions. The models of inputs consisting of $n = 20, \ldots, 80$ tokens were compared in order to see how the sizes of the intermediate results in bilexical parsing grow as a function of n. For all sentence lengths, the $(n/2-1)^{\mathrm{th}}$ iteration produced the largest result (Table 3).

In Table 3, the number of transitions in minimized projections is almost quadratic (the exponent is between 1.60 and 1.87) to the number of states. This motivates the observation that the complexity of the algorithm is not linear to n. In each intermediate result, the contractions shorten the strings, which gives, in the finite-state representations, rise to epsilon removal and a quadratic number of transitions. Besides the epsilon removal, the finite-state library automatically performs determinization and minimization of the finite-state representations of the projections.

In Table 3, the number of states in the first intermediate result is $2(n-1)$ and in the largest intermediate result the number of states coincided with the function $(n/2)(n/2+1)$. The number of transitions in the largest intermediate result coincides with the function $n(n/2+1)(n/2+1)-(n/2)$.

Usually, however, t is fixed and much smaller than n. The table indicates that when n doubles from 20 to 40 and 80, the number of transitions in the first intermediate result grows by the factors $2^{1.97}$ and $2^{1.98}$ and the fifth intermediate result by the factors $2^{2.15}$ and $2^{2.07}$. This indicates that the number of transitions in a fixed intermediate result, such as the first and the fifth one, is actually $O(n^s)$ where s is close to 2. The number of iterations does not have any drastic effect on the space complexity, since the 5th intermediate result, for example, has less than $6n^2$ transitions. As the number of compositions is bounded by t, we actually compute only a fixed number of intermediate projections. The transition complexity of each minimized intermediate result seems to be in $O(tn^2)$.

Assuming that the required time would be linear to the size of the results, the total time complexity of computing the value of Grammar(x, ε) would be $O(t^2n^2)$. But Table 3 displays the running times for the fifth iteration round using an unweighted finite-state library (foma, available from http://code.google.com/p/foma/). The measured running time appears to be in $O(n^3)$ since, e.g., $\log_2(1.45/0.19) = 2.93$. The experiment does not allow us, however, to conclude that an implementation with a quadratic time complexity would be impossible. The contributions of the determinization and minimization steps and the actual library implementation have not been analyzed yet.

The current experimental analysis has assumed that the maximally ambiguous sentences and grammars are asymptotically at least as difficult as practical sentences and grammars. I have currently no complete proof for this assumption, but I believe that the complexity of a realistic situation differs only linearly from the current artificial situation. Clearly, the assumption prompts for further study.

The current analysis does not fully apply to the weighted case. Since weighted determinization and minimization (Mohri 2009) can move the weights from the original places, there is a danger that the intermediate results grow more than necessary. The detailed analysis of the weighted case is postponed to further work.

5.3 Memoizing Composition

An efficient decision method for grammatical strings in (38) leads us halfway to obtaining some if not all parses efficiently. This requires reusing the computations done during the decision process. Therefore, the intermediate results are memoized inductively to variables $\mathrm{Up}_0, \ldots, \mathrm{Up}_t$ by setting

$$\mathrm{Up}_0 = \big[\mathrm{Bot}(x, x) \circ \mathrm{Abstract}\big], \tag{39}$$

$$\mathrm{Up}_i = \underbrace{[\ldots[}_{i}\,\mathrm{Up}_0 \underbrace{\circ\, \mathrm{Reduce} \ldots] \circ \mathrm{Reduce}]}_{i} = [\mathrm{Up}_{i-1} \circ \mathrm{Reduce}]. \tag{40}$$

In the end, $\mathrm{Up}_t(\varepsilon, \varepsilon)$ tells the weight of the best parse.

Now we could compute k-bounded best restrictions iteratively in order to obtain (at most k) best parses. This is achieved by processing the intermediate levels i from the top level, t, back to the lowermost level 0 and by filtering the lower level with the information on the partial parses of the best parses.[5]

If x is a grammatical string, the support of the first downward level, Dn_t, contains the encoded trivial graph, ε, whose top-down weight is 1:

$$\mathrm{Dn}_t = \mathbb{1}\big(\mathrm{Supp}(\mathrm{Up}_t \circ \mathbb{1}_\varepsilon)\big). \tag{41}$$

For each level $i \in \{t-1, \ldots, 2, 1\}$, we first compute $\mathrm{DnSupport}_i$ that contains partial parses of the best parses. The best parses are selected on the basis of their total weight, whose factors come from the Up_i, Reduce and Dn_{i+1} components. After this, we compute Dn_i, which contains the same strings with the top-down weights only.

$$\mathrm{DnSupport}_i = \mathrm{Supp}\big(\mathrm{BestProj}_1(\mathrm{Up}_i \circ \mathrm{Reduce} \circ \mathrm{Dn}_{i+1}, k)\big), \tag{42}$$

[5]These minorization and "majorization" phases could be compared to the forward and backward procedures used in trellis algorithms for Hidden Markov Models.

$$\mathrm{Dn}_i = \mathrm{Proj}_1\big(\mathbb{1}(\mathrm{DnSupport}_i) \circ \mathrm{Reduce} \circ \mathrm{Dn}_{i+1}\big). \tag{43}$$

The last level, Dn_0, is computed differently:

$$\mathrm{Dn}_0 = \mathrm{BestProj}_1\big(\mathrm{Proj}_2(\mathrm{Bot}(x,x)) \circ \mathrm{Abstract} \circ \mathrm{Dn}_1, k\big). \tag{44}$$

In the end, the support and the image of Dn_0 contains up to k parses and the best weight, respectively. We can now define the selection of k best parses by

$$\mathrm{BestParses}'(x,k) = \mathrm{Id}^{-1}\big(\mathrm{Supp}(\mathrm{Dn}_0)\big). \tag{45}$$

The previously defined set $\mathrm{BestParses}(x,k)$ in (33) does not necessarily coincide with $\mathrm{BestParses}'(x,k)$ in (45), because the different methods may pick a different selection from the best parses.

The total time complexity of this best-parse algorithm is dominated by the bottom-up phase, because extracting the best k parses from the memoized cascade $\mathrm{Up}_0, \ldots, \mathrm{Up}_{t-1}$ takes only linear time to the size of the memoized finite-state transducers. This result makes use of the linear time complexity of the shortest-distance algorithm for acyclic weighted automata (Mohri 2009).

The same parser algorithm is applicable with non-projective contraction rules. However, the time complexity of the resulting non-projective parser depends on the specifics of the rule component and remains open for the time being.

5.4 *Allowing Spurious Ambiguity*

Since we use *maximum* as the additive operation for the weights, the spurious ambiguity does not actually affect the weights of the parses. This observation allows us to avoid Reduce and use FreeReduce instead. That is, the grammar semantics will be retained even if we replace $\mathrm{HasMinor}_t$ with $\mathrm{HasMinor}'_t$, defined by

$$\mathrm{HasMinor}'_t = \underbrace{\mathrm{FreeReduce} \circ \cdots \circ \mathrm{FreeReduce}}_{t}. \tag{46}$$

Similarly, the use of Reduce could be replaced with FreeReduce in the forgetting composition. In memoizing composition, the change applies too, provided that we then extract only the best parse ($k = 1$).

In practice, FreeReduce is much easier to construct than Reduce. It also induces smaller projections (Table 4) and provides much faster application to long sentences. This is explained by the fact that the states in the composition with FreeReduce do not keep track of the number of applied contractions. On the contrary, the obligatory contractions in Reduce expand the state space of the compositions and the projections, which also complicates the subsequent epsilon removal, determinization and minimization steps.

I experimented with forgetting composition that uses FreeReduce. By comparing the lines for $n = 40$ and $n = 80$ in Table 4, the total time complexity of the projective

Table 4 The sizes of the projections after applying FreeReduce, and of Parses(x) (now avoided)

	1st iteration		5th iteration				t iterations with $t=n-1$		Parses(x)
n	states	trans.	states	trans.	(n^2+2n-1)	tot.secs	tot.secs	parses	states in fsa
10	10	119	10	119	119	0.04	0.04	246675	2036
20	20	439	20	439	439	0.05	0.10	16332922290300	2097130
40	40	1679	40	1679	1679	0.08	0.34	2.1×10^{29}	2.2×10^{12}
60	60	3719	60	3719	3719	0.14	1.80	4.5×10^{45}	2.3×10^{18}
80	80	6559	80	6559	6659	0.27	4.50	1.1×10^{62}	2.4×10^{24}

parser (unrooted trees, $t = n - 1$) appears to be in $O(n^{3.73})$ since $\log_2(4.5/0.34) = 3.73$. However, if we fix $t = 5$, the total time complexity appears to be quadratic to n since $\log_2(0.27/0.08) = 1.75 \approx 2$. Since this is linear to the transitions in each projection, it appears that the worst-case complexity is in $O(tn^2)$ in general.

Table 4 shows also the total number of unrooted trees (i.e., parses) for sentences of different lengths. In the worst case, the growth in the number of trees is really fast. The resulting sequence coincides with the sequence A001764 in Sloane's On-Line Encyclopedia of Integer Sequences (OEIS, oeis.org).

If all the strings that encode the parses for a 20-word sentence would be stored into one minimal deterministic finite-state automaton (fsa), this would require, in the worst case, more than 2 million states (the last column in Table 4). In general, the sequence of the worst-case state counts, $2^{n+1} - n - 2$, for the single-fsa representations coincides with the Eulerian numbers $\langle {1 \atop 1} \rangle, \langle {2 \atop 1} \rangle, \ldots$ (the sequence A000295 in OEIS). This demonstrates that the memoized cascade is much more efficient representation for the parse forest than a single automaton.

A drawback in using FreeReduce is that only one optimal parse can be extracted directly from the memoized cascade, because extracting k parses can actually result in extracting the same parse in k different ways. In order to obtain the next optimal parse, we can "remove" the best parse from Bot(x, x) and rerun the parser on the remainder set. This may be inefficient in practice.

6 Comparison to the Prior Work

The body of research on dependency parsing is already large and it is impossible to recall all approaches. The most relevant prior work combines dependency parsing and string-based finite-state methods, or at least suggests such a combination.

- *Constraint Grammar (CG)* parsers perform morphological and surface-syntactic disambiguation and dependency linking.
  - The core CG parsers refine the ambiguity classes of words iteratively, according to the contextual conditions and rule application ordering.

  - Mature CG variants (Tapanainen 1999; Didriksen 2010) provide actions for inserting dependency links between two words and for producing a single dependency analysis for each sentence.
  - Finite-state automata are used in some CG implementations (Hulden 2011; Yli-Jyrä 2011).
- *Finite-state intersection grammar (FSIG)* has been used to parse dependency structures of varying specificity and complexity.
  - Koskenniemi et al. (1992) denote the syntactic functions of words with tags that additionally specify the direction of the possible governors, leaving possible attachment ambiguity unresolved.
  - Yli-Jyrä (2005) encodes every dependency link with a pair of brackets between the nodes. With such encoding, every projective dependency grammar is representable with an intersection of a strictly locally testable regular language and a language that balances labeled brackets. The representation has efficient implementations, but the grammar semantics is based on inviolable properties of the parses.
- *Constraint network parsers* combine consistency-enforcing methods with backtracking search in order to resolve ambiguity and to produce parses as search results.
  - Maruyama (1990) presents a constraint network parser that can produce non-projective dependency graphs.
  - Debusmann et al. (2004) implemented a dependency parser whose constraint network can be extended with word order and dominance constraints.
- *Finite-state cascades* are used in deterministic parsing approaches:
  - Joshi (1996) describes retrospectively a parser (from 1959) that used finite-state cascades. Each level in the cascade corresponded to a deterministic finite-state transducer that read the input either left to right or right to left and marked syntactic units with various kinds of brackets.
  - Abney (1996) also applies finite-state cascades to phrase structure analysis.
- *Iterated finite-state transducers* control the rule applications with mutable markup. The parsing terminates if a fixed point is reached.
  - Roche (1997) iterates finite-state transducers in order to parse context-free grammars, transformation grammars and tree adjoining grammars. The approach does not include hierarchical ambiguity packing, but it demonstrates the computational power of iteration.
  - Elworthy (2000) uses iterated deterministic finite-state transducers that are augmented with instructions that insert links to the read string. Elworthy's deterministic finite-state parser includes an ambiguity-packing mechanism that adds multiple heads to phrases to avoid the attachment ambiguity. Thanks to the deterministic parsing that does not elaborate all ambiguity, the parsing time is $O(n^2)$ for an input of n words.
  - Oflazer (2003) uses an iterated finite-state transducer that implements projective dependency parsing. The approach is robust but does not include hierarchical ambiguity packing.
- *Bilexical dependency parsers* can carry out projective dependency analysis without lexical functions (Eisner 1997).

- *Restarting automata* perform a sequence of monotonic rewrite steps that reduce the length or weight of the input tape. Plátek et al. (2003) motivate restarting automata as a tool for dependency analysis.

6.1 The Distinctive Characteristics of the Current Approach

While being partially similar to the prior approaches, the currently presented algorithm has clear distinctive characteristics that make it new as for now.

In comparison with most dependency parsers, the current system differs by assuming a *parametric bound for the number of overlapping arcs*. The time complexity is similar to Elworthy's parser, but the method computes implicitly all *parameterized parses*.

The iterated application of Reduce reminds us of the fixpoint method (Roche 1997) and of finite-state cascades (Abney 1996). A striking difference from them is that the current (bottom-up) cascade produces nothing as its output.

Some of the cascading parsers resolve the ambiguity on the basis of deterministic heuristics and underspecification, while the current system *resolves the ambiguity on the basis of the lexical categories (functional tags or bilexical pairs), the performance constraints, and the weights*.

The analysis-by-elimination approach of the current system reminds of one-level intersection grammars that assume a set of candidate parses as their input. In contrast to the early practice in FSIG (Voutilainen 1994), the dependency bracketing of the current system specifies a *full syntactic tree*.

The author has used a similar encoding for trees in an earlier regular approximation method for dependency grammars (Yli-Jyrä 2005). However, the current work operates on *weighted rational relations* rather than parallel constraints.

The use of rewrites rather than constraints as a means for validating the arcs is familiar from Oflazer's dependency parser (Oflazer 2003). However, the new parser *contracts the validated brackets* and *memoizes the intermediate results* of the cascade, which improves efficiency.

Parsing by contractions is a familiar approach from restarting automata and contextual grammars. It is not yet known if the currently presented *memoization technique* is completely new in the context of restarting automata, but it may prove useful in practice. The current contractions operate *directly* on the encoded dependency trees and there is a performance *limit for overlapping rule applications*.

Deterministic contractions and functional rational relations are also a natural approach to Constraint Grammar parsing. However, the current approach *manages sentence-level ambiguity* and *combines deterministic contractions with full parsing*.

7 Conclusions

The paper has described a new approach to dependency parsing. The presented finite-state approach uses three new techniques: dependency bracketing, bracketed arc contraction and cascade memoization. The paper has presented the final parsing algorithm of Sect. 5.4 via an abstract calculus of weighted rational relations and motivated its efficiency through a series of experiments and design choices. In addition, we provided new interpretations for the integer sequences A001764 and A000295, which might be of interest in applied mathematics.

7.1 Practical Benefits

In the case of projective parsing, the proposed memoizing parsing algorithm produces optimal parses and is efficient: its time complexity appears to be in $O(tn^2)$ according to the analysis of the method that uses FreeReduce and $O(t^2n^3)$ according to the preliminary analysis of the method that uses Reduce.

The proposed parser can be tailored for functional and bilexical dependency parsing. Under the performance-motivated parameter t for the overlapping arcs, the parse forest contains all plausible parses of the projective grammar. The parse forest is extendible to non-projective trees that contain crossing arcs.

The method has a rational design and it is easy to implement with finite-state methods. The packed weighted parse forest is computed through composition and projection, two commonly used high-level finite-state operations, and the memoization of the internals of the cascade allows for efficient retrieval of the parses.

7.2 Further Work

There are several directions for further study. (i) The weight structure could be generalized to arbitrary semirings in order to enable the generality of "semiring parsing". (ii) A statistical parser will have to explicate how the weights in Grammar are set and whether they behave like probabilities or indicate some other kinds of weights. Furthermore, the actual implementation of the current illustrative system would replace the semiring of the nonnegative real numbers with the tropical semiring of their negative logarithms (Mohri 2009) in order to improve the numerical stability of the algorithm. (iii) The use of non-projective contractions should be studied further. There are certainly some strategies to reduce the number of non-projective parses while maintaining high recall. (iv) More insight into the packed forest and the growth of the intermediate results is needed. The current experiments were based on unweighted bilexical grammars where all dependencies were possible. In practice, the possible argument structures are more specific, which makes the average case more interesting than the limited experimental results provided so far. (v) The current method throws away all partial parses. For text parsing purposes, the parser can be modified to allow dependency graphs that consist of unconnected trees.

The possible extensions of the presented method include the intriguing option of combining statistics and linguistic knowledge into the same system. Adding handwritten linguistic constraints to Grammar is technically possible and would allow human interventions to complement statistically estimated parameters and would help us finish the precision and recall of the practical implementation of the approach.

Acknowledgements The research has been made possible by the Academy of Finland grant number 128536 "Open and Language Independent Automata-Based Resource Production Methods for Common Language Research Infrastructure", and, more recently, by the FIN-CLARIN project steered by Krister Lindén. Kimmo Koskenniemi, Pasi Tapanainen, Atro Voutilainen and Lauri Carlson supported my first investigations into contractions in finite-state intersection parsing since 1995. More recently, my thinking has benefited from several related discussions with Carlos Gómez-Rodríguez, Jason Eisner, Joakim Nivre, Marco Kuhlmann, and John Hale. During the multi-year creative process, I felt several times need for heavenly empowerment. I look gratefully back to every inspired moment.

I am indebted to the prior anonymous reviewers of the CIAA 2011 and FSMNLP 2011 meetings, as well as Aarne Ranta, Wanjiku Nganga, Jussi Piitulainen, and Miikka Silfverberg for their valuable comments pointing out many areas for further study. The remaining imperfections in the text are mine, of course.

References

Abney, Steven. 1996. Partial parsing via finite state cascades. In *Proceedings of the ESSLLI'96 robust parsing workshop*, Prague, Czech Republic.

Debusmann, Ralph, Denys Duchier, and Geert-Jan M. Kruijff. 2004. Extensible dependency grammar: A new methodology. In *Proceedings of the COLING 2004 workshop of recent advances in dependency grammar*, Geneva, Switzerland, eds. Geert-Jan M. Kruijff and Denys Duchier, 78–84.

Didriksen, Tino. 2010. Constraint grammar manual: 3rd version of the CG formalism variant. GrammarSoft ApS, Denmark. http://beta.visl.sdu.dk/cg3/vislcg3.pdf.

Eisner, Jason. 1997. Bilexical grammars and a cubic-time probabilistic parser. In *Proceedings of the 4th international workshop on parsing technologies*, 54–65. Cambridge: MIT.

Elworthy, David. 2000. A finite state parser with dependency structure output. In *Proceedings of sixth international workshop on parsing technologies (IWPT 2000)*. Trento: Institute for Scientific and Technological Research.

Gómez-Rodríguez, Carlos, and Joakim Nivre. 2010. A transition-based parser for 2-planar dependency structures. In *Proceedings of the 48th annual meeting of the Association for Computational Linguistics (ACL 2010)*, Uppsala, Sweden, 1492–1501.

Gómez-Rodríguez, Carlos, David Weir, and John Carroll. 2009. Parsing mildly non-projective dependency structures. In *Proceedings of the 12th conference of the European chapter of the Association for Computational Linguistics (EACL 2009)*, 291–299.

Hulden, Mans. 2011. Constraint Grammar parsing with left and right sequential finite transducers. In *Proceedings of the 9th international workshop on finite state methods and natural language processing (FSMNLP 2011)*, 39–47. Blois: Association for Computational Linguistics. http://www.aclweb.org/anthology/W11-4406.

Joshi, Aravind K. 1996. A parser from antiquity: an early application of finite state transducers to natural language parsing. In *Proceedings of the ECAI'96 workshop on extended finite state models of language*, ed. András Kornai. *Studies in natural language processing*, 33–34. Cambridge: Cambridge University Press.

Koskenniemi, Kimmo, Pasi Tapanainen, and Atro Voutilainen. 1992. Compiling and using finite-state syntactic rules. In *Proceedings of the 14th COLING 1992 conference*, Nantes, France. Vol. 1, 156–162.

Kuhlmann, Marco. 2010. In *Dependency structures and lexicalized grammars. An algebraic approach*, Vol. 6270 of *Lecture notes in artificial intelligence, FoLLI publications on logic, language and information*. Springer: Berlin.

Kuhlmann, Marco, and Giorgio Satta. 2009. Treebank grammar techniques for non-projective dependency parsing. In *Proceedings of the 12th conference of the European chapter of the Association for Computational Linguistics (EACL'09)*, 478–486.

Lombardo, Vincenzo, and Leonardo Lesmo. 1996. An Earley-type recognizer for dependency grammar. In *Proceedings of the 16th COLING conference*, Copenhagen, Denmark, Vol. 2, 723–728.

Maruyama, Hiroshi. 1990. Structural disambiguation with constraint propagation. In *Proceedings of the 28th ACL 1989 conference*, Pittsburgh, Pennsylvania, 31–38.

Mohri, Mehryar. 2009. Weighted automata algorithms. In *Handbook of weighted automata*, eds. Manfred Droste, Werner Kuich, and Heiko Vogler, 213–254. Berlin: Springer.

Neuhaus, Peter, and Norbert Bröker. 1997. The complexity of recognition of linguistically adequate dependency grammars. In *Proceedings of the 35th annual meeting of the Association for Computational Linguistics and the 8th conf. of the European chapter of the Association for Computational Linguistics*, Madrid, Spain, 337–343.

Nivre, Joakim. 2006. Constraints on non-projective dependency parsing. In *Proceedings of the 11th conference of the European chapter of the Association for Computational Linguistics (EACL 2006)*, 73–80.

Nivre, Joakim. 2008. Algorithms for deterministic incremental dependency parsing. *Computational Linguistics* 34: 513–553.

Oflazer, Kemal. 2003. Dependency parsing with an extended finite-state approach. *Computational Linguistics* 29: 515–544.

Plátek, Martin, Markéta Lopatková, and Karel Oliva. 2003. Restarting automata: motivations and applications. In *Workshop 'Petrinetze' and 13. Theorietag 'Formale Sprachen und Automaten'*, ed. M. Holzer, 90–96. Institut für Informatik, Technische Universität München.

Roche, Emmanuel. 1997. Parsing with finite-state transducers. In *Finite-state language processing*, eds. Emmanuel Roche and Yves Schabes, 241–281. Cambridge: MIT Press. Chap. 8.

Tapanainen, Pasi. 1999. Parsing in two frameworks: finite-state and functional dependency grammar. Doctoral diss., University of Helsinki, Finland.

Tesnière, Lucien. 1959. *Éléments de syntaxe structurale*. Paris: Éditions Klincksieck.

Voutilainen, Atro. 1994. *Designing a parsing grammar*, Vol. 22 of *Publications of the Department of General Linguistics, University of Helsinki*. Helsinki: Yliopistopaino.

Yli-Jyrä, Anssi Mikael. 2003. Multiplanarity—a model for dependency structures in treebanks. In *TLT 2003. Proceedings of the second workshop on treebanks and linguistic theories*, eds. Joakim Nivre and Erhard Hinrichs, Vol. 9 of *Mathematical modelling in physics, engineering and cognitive sciences*, 189–200. Växjö: Växjö University Press.

Yli-Jyrä, Anssi. 2004. Axiomatization of restricted non-projective dependency trees through finite-state constraints that analyse crossing bracketings. In *Proceedings of the COLING 2004 workshop of recent advances in dependency grammar*, Geneva, Switzerland, 33–40.

Yli-Jyrä, Anssi. 2005. Approximating dependency grammars through intersection of star-free regular languages. *International Journal of Foundations of Computer Science* 16: 565–579.

Yli Jyrä, Anssi. 2008. Transducers from parallel replace rules and modes with generalized lenient composition. In *6th international workshop, finite-state methods and natural language processing, FSMNLP-2007. Revised papers*, 197–212. Potsdam: Potsdam University Press.

Yli-Jyrä, Anssi. 2011. An efficient constraint grammar parser based on inward deterministic automata. In *Proceedings of the NODALIDA 2011 workshop constraint grammar applications*, eds. Eckhard Bick, Kristin Hagen, Kaili Müürisep, and Trond Trosterud, Vol. 14 of *NEALT proceedings series*, 50–60.

Yli-Jyrä, Anssi, and Kimmo Koskenniemi. 2004. Compiling contextual restrictions on strings into finite-state automata. In *Proceedings of the Eindhoven FASTAR days 2004*, eds. Loek Cleophas and Bruce W. Watson, Vol. 04-40 of *Computer science reports*. Eindhoven: Technische Universiteit Eindhoven.

Yli-Jyrä, Anssi, and Matti Nykänen. 2004. A hierarchy of mildly context sensitive dependency grammars. In *Proceedings of the 9th conference on formal grammar (FGNancy 2004)*, eds. Gerald Penn, Gerhard Jäger, Paola Monachesi, and Shuly Wintner, 151–165.

Fictive Motion Down Under: The Locative-Allative Case Alternation in Some Australian Indigenous Languages

Patrick McConvell and Jane Simpson

Abstract This paper describes the predication of location of participants in Indigenous languages of northern Central Australia. Two main strategies are discussed: the use of double case-marking, and the co-opting of particular local cases to express scope of predication as well as location. The coopting case in question involves the Allative Nominal Construction (AN). This is the use of an allative case instead of a locative case in the meaning of 'static location' in a secondary predication where the subject of that predication has the same reference as an object or oblique in the main predication.

1 Predicating Location of Events and Participants

Location with respect to a place can be predicated of the event itself (*In Helsinki people work on machine translation*), or of a participant in the event (*I found food in the cupboard*), i.e. the spatial position of a particular participant or entity relative to other entities, in the clause. Some languages are able to distinguish these two types of predication within a clause, differentiating the location of the subject from that of the object.

In English, the distinction between predication over a whole event and over a participant can be expressed by word order, information structure (including prosody), and by using knowledge of the world. In (1a) and (1b), the *Food* (semantic role Theme) is in the *kitchen*, and *John* (semantic role Agent) is most likely to be in the *kitchen* (unless he is looking in through a window, or the referent of *kitchen* is a kitchen in an image that John is looking at). In (1c) the whole event takes place in the kitchen. In (2a) and (2b) the Food (semantic role Theme) is in the *cupboard*, and John (semantic role Agent) is probably not in the cupboard. (2c) gives rise to the strange interpretation that John and the food are in the cupboard.

(1) a. John found the food (*in the kitchen*).
 b. The food was found (*in the kitchen*) (by John).
 c. (*In the kitchen*) the food was found (by John).

P. McConvell (✉) · J. Simpson
School of Language Studies, Australian National University, Canberra, Australia

D. Santos et al. (eds.), *Shall We Play the Festschrift Game?*,
DOI 10.1007/978-3-642-30773-7_11,

(2) a. John found the food *in the cupboard.*
b. The food was found *in the cupboard* (by John).
c. ? *In the cupboard* the food was found (by John).

Both locations can be expressed in a single clause, as in (3a) and (3b), where the whole event takes place in the kitchen, and the food is in the cupboard. (3c) where the location of the Theme, food, is put initially, and the location of the whole event is put finally, is hard to construe in isolation (unless there is a kitchen inside the cupboard).

(3) a. **In the kitchen**, she found the food *in the cupboard.*
b. **In the kitchen**, the food was found *in the cupboard.*
c. ?? *In the cupboard*, she found the food **in the kitchen**.

When the location predicate follows the verb, the order 'Theme-location Event-location' is normal. Prosody distinguishes the embedded PP within a PP structure from the appositional sequence of two PPs. Prosody also marks the reverse order, with a type of appositional reading, zooming in from a larger location to a smaller location within that larger location.

(4) a. She found it *in the cupboard* **in the kitchen**.
b. She found it **in the kitchen** *in the cupboard.* [Specifying larger → smaller]

Thus, word order is helpful in English for determining what the location is predicated of: location predicated of the whole event may appear initially or finally, while the unmarked position for location predicated of the Theme is after the verb.[1]

PP	**NP**	**V**	**PP**	**PP**
Event			**Theme**	**Event**
			[but these two PPs can be reversed]	

The Agent may be at one location (that predicated of the event), but not the other (that predicated of the Theme). If the location of the Agent is to be highlighted in English, this is done by incorporating the location into the NP expressing the Agent (5a), or by using a motion preposition *from* metaphorically (5b), a form of 'fictive motion' whereby the gaze is construed as something which goes from the subject to the object of perception (Gruber 1967). This last method allows the location of the subject (perceiver), object (of perception) and the event to be expressed separately (5c).

[1] Location of the object can appear initially in some contexts, such as the following in which the object's location is part of the location introduced in the previous clause. The 'wall' is a part of the house and acts as a link between the action of the first clause, and the action of the second clause which introduces new information, the object:

He went into the house, and **on the wall** saw a portrait of the Princess of Wales and the Queen. (David Lloyd-George (Member for Carnarvon Boroughs), Hansard, House of Commons. Deb 18 February 1901 vol 89 cc369–434.)

(5) a. The man *on the bridge* saw me.
b. From the bridge the captain saw whales in the current.
c. **In the Pacific Ocean,** the captain saw *a sail on the horizon* from the bridge.

The presence of more than one location in one clause presents a problem for the hypothesis of the uniqueness of semantic roles. Attempts to preserve this hypothesis have resulted in suggestions such as positing two semantic roles, inner locatives and outer locatives (Cook 1989), and considering the use of the 'from' preposition in (5b, 5c) as expressing a separate semantic role of source. A traditional syntactic solution has been to say that the location predicated of the Theme is inside the VP, and the location predicated of the event is either at a higher level in the VP or is a daughter of IP or CP.

These syntactic solutions do not apply in the many Australian languages, in which word order is used for information structure purposes, rather than for expressing grammatical functions, or for the difference between adjuncts and arguments (Hale 1992; Simpson 2007). Other means are therefore needed for construing what a locational expression is predicated of. For grammatical relations, case-marking and verb or auxiliary cross-reference are used extensively, but case-marking is usually not as elaborated as in the Finnic languages: the languages are generally Ergative-Absolutive in case-marking, and there are commonly just three distinct case-forms for expressing location: 'Locative' (static location), 'Allative' (motion towards) and 'Ablative' (motion from). Within a clause, nominals with the same case-marking are usually construed as part of the same grammatical function (so-called 'discontinuous constituents').

This raises the question of whether the location of the Theme can be expressed independently of that of the Agent in one clause. Barry Blake[2] notes that a periphrastic relative clause construction is used to do this in Kalkatungu, a language of western Queensland:[3]

> A locative phrase refers to a whole predication ('outer locatives') or to actants in Si [intransitive subject, JS & PM] or P [object, JS & PM] function ('inner locatives'). Where the location of an actant in the A function is to be expressed, a participial phrase qualifying the ergative must be used, the locative referring to the Si of the embedded phrase.

[2]We thank Barry Blake for drawing our attention to this.

[3]Abbreviations used in this paper: 1, 2, 3: first, second, third person; 111: first person exclusive plural; 333: third person plural; A: transitive subject; ABL: ablative; ACC: accusative; Afs, Afv: Yolngu verb suffixes (Schebeck 1976); ALL: allative; AN: allative-marked nominal location; AS: allative subordination; CAT: catalyst; CPL: completive; DAT: dative; ERG: ergative; EU: euphony; FALL: far allative; FOC: focus; FUT: future; GER: gerund; GO: going (verb stem formative); HN: Kenneth Hale Warlpiri field-notes 1966; ILL: illative; IO: indirect object; IRR: irrealis; LOC: Locative; LS: Locative subordination; M: masculine; MANN: manner; NALL: near allative; NFIN: nonfinite (covers forms glossed by grammarians as infinitive, nominalisation and gerund); NOM: nominative; NM: non-masculine; NPST: nonpast; O: object; part: participle; PL: plural; PCON: past continuous; PER: perlative; PRS: present; REFL: reflexive; S: subject/intransitive subject; SG: singular; TOP: topic; UNM: unmarked inflection; USIT: usitative.

(3.46)	*wakaṛi*	*ŋa-t̪u*	*paa*	*ṇaɲa*	*ku-ŋka*	*ini-ɲin-tu*
	fish	I-ERG	there	saw	water-LOC	be:present-part-ERG

'I saw a fish when I was at the water'.

(Blake 1979: 43–44)

Apart from such periphrastic constructions, we have discovered two main ways of distinguishing location of entities from location of events: using double case-marking, and co-opting another case-marker, primarily Allative case, to predicate location of grammatical objects. A third possibility, of having specialised markers for this function,[4] is also found in some Australian languages, but is part of a larger switch reference system on participles. In this paper, we outline the first two strategies. In the last part of this paper we briefly consider how the grammaticalisation of Allative might have evolved historically in the part of Australia under examination. Control of a non-finite subordinate clause by an object can also be expressed by Allative marking in some languages but space does not permit discussion of this.

2 Types of Locational Case Marking in Central Australia

2.1 Terminology Used

Since the semantics of case do not line up with the form of case-marking, as with 'Allative' case being used in a 'Locative' meaning, we shall refer to a set of 'locational' meanings which include 'locative', which refers to the static location of an entity, and 'allative', which refers to movement to a goal entity; where necessary we refer to these as 'locative semantic function', 'allative semantic function' etc. On the other hand, there are local case affixes which we shall refer to by capitalised abbreviations, e.g. LOC for Locative case, ALL for Allative case. So in the situation referred to as AN, (the use of Allative case to express location of an object), 'locative semantic function' can be expressed by LOC or ALL case, depending on what the location is predicated of.

2.2 Local Cases in Australian Languages

In this paper, we focus on a region in central Australia with languages from the largest Australian language family, Pama-Nyungan (Bowern and Koch 2004), and some neighbouring non-Pama-Nyungan languages. Pama-Nyungan languages have systems varying from three to about eight cases marked on nominals, generally as

[4]Endings which are specialized for predications of particular participants are described by Valenzuela (2005) for Shibipo, a Panoan language of South America.

suffixes. Apart from ergative/instrumental and dative/benefactive, the prime functions of these local case suffixes are semantic, expressing ideas that in many languages would be expressed by adpositions, but which are also grammaticalised in various ways in some languages. Most of the languages have nominal local case suffixes, usually LOC (Locative: *at*, *in* etc.), ALL (Allative: *to*, *towards*) and ABL (Ablative: *from)* with some additional ones in some languages. At least two of these suffixes can be relatively confidently reconstructed to proto-Pama-Nyungan: LOC **-ngka*, **-la* (allomorphs determined by whether the stem is bimoraic or polymoraic, respectively); ABL **-ngu(ru)* (Alpher 2004); ALL is too variable across the family to be confidently reconstructed at this stage.

We turn now to the two means for predicating location of participants in a clause: double case-marking, and co-opting another case.

2.3 Double Case-Marking

Double case marking or *Suffixaufnahme* (Plank 1995) refers mainly to addition of a genitive marker following another case marker, but it is extended to include addition of the case of a controlling NP to other NPs with local case marking. In some Australian languages, this kind of double case-marking (Dench and Evans 1988; Simpson 1991) is used to specify more precisely what a location is predicated of. For example, if an Object has Dative or Accusative case, adding DAT or ACC case to a local-case-marked phrase indicates that the phrase expresses the spatial position of the object rather than the event. An example follows from Ngarluma, a Pama-Nyungan language spoken on the coast of Western Australia[5] which, unusually, has a Nominative-Accusative case-marking system. (6) shows the ACC *-ku* on a locational modifier of an Accusative-marked Object (Kenneth Hale's fieldnotes; Hale 1960; Simpson 1981).

(6) a. **Wanji-la-ku** nyinta marrparnta-nha?
where-LOC-ACC you[NOM] find-PST
'Where did you find (it)?'

b. Ngayi marrparnta-nha **yanthan-ta-ku** **thurnu-ngka-ku**.
I[NOM] find-PST swag-LOC-ACC under-LOC-ACC
'I found (it) under the swag.'

The double-case-marked phrase here expresses the location of the object. This can be treated as a secondary predication with the understood subject of the secondary predication being 'it'. Similar examples are found in other Pilbara languages with Nominative-Accusative systems such as Panyjima (Dench and Evans 1988: 8; Austin 1995).

---

[5]Unlike most Pama-Nyungan languages, which are absolutive-ergative, Ngarluma is a nominative-accusative language. The accusative case marker is cognate with the dative marker in many other languages.

Double case marking for predicating location of participants is also found in some Ergative-Absolutive languages. It is common in southern and western languages of the Ngumpin-Yapa language sub-group of Pama-Nyungan spoken in Western and Central Australia, such as Walmajarri (Hudson 1978: 35), and Ngardi (Cataldi 2011/2004). The most comprehensively described of these languages is Warlpiri, spoken in Central Australia (Hale 1982). (7) and (8) show location predicated of an event and expressed by the LOC case-suffix.

(7) **Minapardu-rla** **wita-ngka** ka=lu nyina jajina wita-wita.
nest-LOC small-LOC PRES=333S sit.NPST mulgara small-small
'The baby mulgaras live in a little nest.' (*Warlpiri Dictionary* in prep.: *jajina* entry)

(8) Karnta-wana-wana kapu=ju=lu pi-nyi **yinya-rla** **nguru-kari-rla**.
woman-because FUT=1O=333S hit-NPST there-LOC place-other-LOC
'Because of a woman they are going to give me a hiding over there in that other place.' (Swartz 1991: 116:G11)

Double-case-marking can be used to show location predicated of a participant rather than an event. Hale (1982) gives the following examples:

(9) Ngarrka-ngku ka yankirri luwa-rni **ngapa-ngka-rlu.**
man-ERG PRS emu shoot-NPST water-LOC-ERG
'The man is shooting the emu at the waterhole.' (Hale 1982: 268, ex. 87a)

(10) Ngarrka-ngku ka=rla-jinta yankirri-ki luwa-rni **ngapa-ngka-ku**.
man-ERG PRS-DAT-DAT emu-DAT shoot-NPST water-LOC-DAT
'The man is shooting at the emu at the waterhole.' (Hale 1982: 268, ex. 87b)

Of these Hale writes:

> In (87a [our 9]) the man is necessarily at the water hole. If the locative case expression were unmarked, the sentence would not stipulate that the man is at the water hole; it would be neutral in this regard. In (87b [our 10]) the locative is marked dative in agreement with the dative object; while this stipulates that the emu is at the water hole, the man may or may not be. (Hale 1982: 268)

Absence of extra case-marking on the LOC is often used for location of objects without explicit case-marking (i.e. Absolutive case), like 'water' in the following example:

(11) Manu kala=lu=nyanu karnta-ngku=ju ngapa=ju ka-nyi
and USIT=333S=REFL woman-ERG=EU water=EU carry-NPST
kartaku-rla jalangujalangu-rlu=ju.
bucket-LOC today-ERG=EU
'And nowadays women carry water for themselves in buckets.' [*Nyurruwiyi kuja kalalu malikikirlirli*, Warlpiri school program written text collection]

While the use of double case-marking in principle allows two predications of different locations in a clause, in fact these are rare. On the other hand, there is no absolute bar against two nominals with the same case ending, and different functions in the same clause: two nominals marked with the plain LOC can occur in the same clause when one of them marks an argument of the verb, rather than predicating location of some entity or event (12), but this is rare, since, as Hale notes, very few verbs select a LOC argument.

(12) Ngarrka-patu ka=lu **karti-ngka** manyu-karri-mi **karru-ngka**.
man-PL PRS=333S card-LOC play-stand-NPST creek-LOC
'The men are playing cards in the creekbed.' (Hale 1982: 272, ex. 94)

2.4 Co-opting Another Case

Another way of expressing location of a participant is to co-opt another case-ending. In the central Australian region, the three cases that we have observed being co-opted are Allative (ALL), Dative (DAT) and Ablative (ABL). Of these, ABL is the most doubtful. Yanyuwa (arguably a Ngarna language; Breen 2004, 2011a) appears sometimes to use an ending glossed as ABL for predicating location of objects. Kirton and Charlie (1996: 113–115) give a few examples of three verbs that they treat as selecting ABL-marked arguments ('bury', 'leave' and 'put'). The ABL is also used for verbs of cooking (cooking crabs **fire-ABL** = 'cooking crabs in the fire'; p. 177), but the interaction with affixes expressing location and direction is very complex. We will not discuss it further, but turn to more commonly co-opted cases.

2.4.1 Allative Expressing Location

Gurindji (a neighbour of Warlpiri) and other north-eastern Ngumpin-Yapa languages do not have double case marking as in the south-western languages of the subgroup discussed in Sect. 2.3. In Gurindji, the ALL case suffix, otherwise used for motion towards a goal, is also found for location of the object. We call the use of allative to denote location the 'AN construction.' For instance in Gurindji,[6] one can say (13) with formal ALL marking on the object instead of LOC case.[7]

(13) Ngu-rna karrap nya-nya jurlak **karnti-kurra**.
CAT-1S see see-PST bird tree-ALL
'I saw a bird on a tree.'

The AN construction is used with the full range of transitive verbs, not just those of perception:

[6]Gurindji data is from Patrick McConvell's fieldwork.

[7]CAT is what is known as a 'catalyst' in Australian linguistics: an element in a small closed set which hosts pronominal enclitics of which one like Gurindji *ngu* has no other meaning or function; in Warlpiri similar elements do have meanings, and are generally called AUX(iliaries).

(14) Ngaja-ngku **ngurra-ngkurra-warla** pa-rru.
LEST-2O camp-ALL-FOC hit-FUT
'He might beat you up at home.'

Use of ALL case is optional, but preferred: LOC case may alternatively be used. In the following example both are used even though the ALL and LOC marked nouns 'ear' and 'head' have the same referent—'your mind'.

(15) **Langa-ngkurra** ngu-n **ngarlaka-la** karrwa-wu kilkilp yunpa-rnu-wu
ear-ALL CAT-2S head-LOC keep-FUT click sing-GER-DAT
'You must keep in your ear, in your head, the clicking of the boomerangs for singing.'

There is some evidence that the AN construction is preferred where the locational predication is only over the object and not the whole event (i.e. including the agent/subject) but this requires more investigation.

A similar use is found in Ngaliwurru and Jaminjung, non-Pama-Nyungan languages to the north-west of Gurindji.

(16) Nindu-ngunyi=malang mung gani-ngayi-m buliki **ngarlu-bina**.
horse-ABL=GIVEN look.at 3S:3O-see-PRS cow shade-ALL
'The horse is looking at the cow, towards the shade.' = 'The horse is looking at the cow in the shade.' (Schultze-Berndt 2000: 59, ex. 2-33)

Schultze-Berndt describes this in terms of the 'prospect path' type of fictive motion of Talmy (1996). Again, the endpoint is not the object of perception, but the place where one sees it, where one's gaze ends. From her description it does appear that the AN construction in Ngaliwurru and Jaminjung is focused on verbs of perception.

In Warlpiri, location of an object is often done by the plain LOC, but the ALL case, otherwise used for motion towards a goal, can also be found for location of the object, whether for perception (17), or for verbs such as cooking (18) when the object (a lizard) is on the fire.

(17) Kula=lpa=rna=ngku purda.nya-ngkarla **wurnturu-kurra=ju**.
not=PST=1S=2O hear-IRR far-ALL=EU
'I can't hear you when you're far away.' (*Warlpiri Dictionary* in prep.: langa entry: jng source)

(18) **Warlu-kurra=ji** wita-kurra=yijala ka=rnalu purra wardapi-piya=yijala.
fire-ALL=EU small-ALL=also PRS=1ES cook NPST sand.monitor-LIKE=also
'We cook it on a small fire as we do with the sand monitor as well.' (HN:1681–2)

The ALL is most common as the way of expressing location of the object of perception verbs, and of the object of verbs like 'cooking' which could potentially be viewed as actions of putting something into, or onto, an endpoint. It is apparently more common in eastern varieties of Warlpiri (Mary Laughren, p.c. 11 March 2011). But what exactly conditions the choice between LOC and ALL in Warlpiri, or whether it just reflects dialect variation, remains to be investigated.

This AN construction is found among some of the eastern neighbours of Gurindji, and occurs in an area of Central Australia where, as Austin (1981) notes, suffixes homophonous with the ALL are used for switch reference (control by grammatical function other than the subject, most often the object).

2.4.2 Languages in Which the Ergative/Locative Morphological Distinction Has Collapsed

In several languages east of Warlpiri and Gurindji, the Ergative/Locative/Instrumental inflections have coalesced, leaving one suffix to carry out both functions. So, in a transitive clause, potentially the same suffix could be used for the agent/subject, the instrument, the location of the event and the location of participants. This makes the use of an alternative suffix for expressing location even more convenient. We discuss Wakaya, Warumungu and two Arandic languages in turn.

Wakaya (Ngarna, Possibly Pama-Nyungan) Wakaya is a language of the Barkly Tablelands (Breen 1974, 2004, 2011b).[8] It had been classified as Pama-Nyungan, but Breen (2011a) proposes that it belongs to a separate family, Ngarna. Reportedly it is no longer spoken since the death in 1975 of Breen's teacher, Avon Willy (Clegg). In Wakaya the Ergative, Instrumental and Locative[9] suffixes have collapsed.

(19) a. **Wurinhathu-rl** kukumu kurrkum-rniy
young.brother-ERG fish catch-PST
'My young brother caught a fish.' (Breen 2011b: Chap. 6, ex. 58)

b. **Wurinhathi-k** kuw-rniy
young.sister.ERG cook.PST
'My young sister cooked it.' (Breen 2011b: Chap. 6, ex. 59)

(20) a. Yuwerr-rl=arn **yimiik-ang** **ngetha-rr-k** **bedi-rr-k,** ba
sit-FUT=1S here.NM.LOC-? 1.GEN-NM-LOC country-NM-LOC and
kurr-rl=arn **yimiik-ang** **ngetharrek** **bedii-k.**
die-FUT=1S here.NM.LOC-? 1.GEN-NM-LOC country-LOC
'I'm going to stay here in my country and I'm going to die here.' (Breen 2011b: Chap. 6, ex. 22)

b. Yuwerr-rdiy yimb **ngetha-rl** **menkad-ij** **marraju-rl.**
sit-PRS you 1.GEN-LOC skin-LOC kangaroo-LOC
'You're sitting on my kangaroo skin.' (Eastern Wakaya, Breen 2011b: Chap. 7, ex. 38)

[8] Breen (1974) was substantially revised as Breen (2011b) with a change of orthography to b/d/k, but the data here is unaffected (Gavan Breen, p.c. 1 February 2012).

[9] The collapse is rendered more complex by having different forms for each gender: /-k/ with non-masculine nouns, /-rl/ with masculine nouns and /-ij/ with plural nouns and a few other nouns mostly ending with an apical consonant (Breen 2011b: Sect. 6.5.4).

So, in a transitive clause, the same suffix form could be used on two separate nominals, one denoting location of the event, and the other denoting agent/subject. Instead, in transitive clauses, two Allative suffixes, one denoting near distance (NALL) and one denoting far distance (FALL) are used. Breen (2011b: Chap. 6) writes:

> The allative suffixes are used to mark the location of the object of a transitive verb. In many cases this is simply the goal of the motion of the object caused by the action of the transitive verb.

In (21) and (22), the subject agent and the object are in the same location and physically interacting but only the object ends up in the specific location, 'ground' and 'water'.

(21) Kurrerniy bulu, ngindewerni **mingkird**
die.PST that, bury.PST ground.NALL
'He died (and they) buried (him) in the ground.' (Eastern Wakaya, Breen 2011b: word-list: *ngindew* entry)[10]

(22) Yinkabu-rl wura ngurrungund-a **yukwa-rr-rd**.
kangaroo-ERG dog drown-GER water-NM-NALL
'The kangaroo drowned the dog in the water.' (Breen 2011b: Chap. 6, ex. 107)

The use of NALL or FALL to mark location of the object when spatially separated from the subject contrasts with the use of the LOC for events seen as wholes. In both examples, NALL and FALL could be construed as representing a goal (putting into the ground/water), rather than static location, as Breen notes. But perception verbs also use an Allative case for location of the object.

(23) Ying-rndiy=ath-ab wuriiki **yukwa-rr-rd**.
see-PRS=1S-REFL shadow water-NM-NALL
'I can see myself in the water.' (Breen 2011b: Chap. 6, ex. 111)

Subject and object can occur in the same location, regardless of whether NALL or FALL is used, as in (24) in which the same shooting event is expressed in a larger location (Alexandria station) with the NALL case, and then in a smaller location (Fish Hole) with the FALL case. Whether the criterion for selection of LOC is lack of physical separation between subject or object, or location of the whole event rather than of the object, needs further investigation.

(24) Wukuthu wurdiki mard-j-anb-a wayibala-rd.
father mother together-LOC-GO-GER white.man-NALL
'My parents went to the white man.'

Wirirdekurl **Alikijandar-rd** la-nth wirirdekurl **Yilawerri-rd**
all.around Alexandria-NALL hit.(with missile)-CPL all.around Alexandria-NALL
'(They) were shooting all round Alexandria',

[10]Breen does not provide morpheme breaks in his transcription.

kirrirr	ngarru	wirirdekurl	la-nth	**yimi-rriy**	**bedii-rriy**
woman:O	man:O	all.around	hit.(with missile)-CPL	here-FALL	place-FALL

Baringkarra
Fish Hole
'men and women, shooting them all around here—at Fish Hole'. (Breen 2011b: Chap. 12, text 7. Reprisal killing)

Warumungu (Isolate Pama-Nyungan) Warumungu is located between Warlpiri and Wakaya. As in Wakaya, Ergative, Instrumental and Locative have collapsed, due to complete vowel assimilation to the preceding vowel. In traditional Warumungu, this form is used for predicating location in intransitive clauses.

(25)

Karnanti	nyi-nta	**warlukun-jju**.
mother	sit-PRS	fire-LOC/ERG

'Mother sits by the fire.' (Simpson 2002: 101)

The ALL suffix *-kina/-kuna/-kana* is used for endpoint of motion, and for location of the object, as in (26) (cooking) and (27) (perception).

(26)

Ngulya-kana	ajjul	kupu-nta	kuyu	maraji.
hole-ALL	333S	cook-PRS	meat	euro

'They (more than two) cook euro in holes in the ground.' (Simpson 2002: 102)

(27)

Warra	arni	karirr.mu-nta	**watta-kana**=ngini.
not	I	know-PRS	far-ALL=TOP

'I can't recognise someone a long way off.' (Simpson field-notes, ref: RNT:T96.2)

But the Warumungu construction differs from the AN construction seen in Warlpiri, since it is not restricted to the location of the object, as in (28) where both the subject and the object are at the location.

(28)

Kartti-ngki	**ngurraji-kina**	kayin	karta-nta.
man-ERG	camp-ALL	boomerang	trim-PRS

'The man is trimming a boomerang at home.' (Simpson 2002: 102)

Indeed, in young people's Warumungu, the use of the ERG/LOC for predicating location has almost disappeared, and the ALL has taken its place as a general suffix denoting location.

Arandic Languages (Pama-Nyungan) Two closely related southern neighbours of Warumungu, the Arandic languages Alyawarr (Yallop 1977) and Kaytetye (Turpin 2000), also have a collapse of Locative, Ergative and Instrumental cases.[11] In Kaytetye this ending is common in sentences with stance verbs (29a). In Alyawarr, this ending is used for both intransitive and transitive clauses (29b).

[11] In Kaytetye, the allomorphs *-le*, *-nge* are used for INST, ERG and LOC (due to neutralisation of an original difference in vowels in Arandic).

(29) a. KAY Awerre **elyenge** anteyane.
boy shade.LOC sitting
'The boy is sitting in the shade.' (Turpin 2000: 78)

b. ALY Amulya akngirra **plain-ila** atuna.
lizard many[NOM] plain-LOC kill-PCON
'(We) killed a lot of lizards on the plain.' (Yallop 1977: 77)

In Kaytetye, "to say where the object or receiver of the action is" (Turpin 2000: 78), either ALL (30a) or the Dative case suffix (30b) is used. But both Subject and Object can be co-located with an ALL suffix, as in (30c), or with a LOC suffix (30d), without an obvious meaning difference.

(30) a. Artnwenge ngkeyenge atye arenhe ampere**warle**.
child your I.ERG saw camp.ALL
'I saw your child at the camp.' (Turpin 2000: 78)

b. Twepe-twepe re rntwenke arwele alkenhe**we**.
around s/he picks tree big.DAT
'She picks (them) off a big bush.' (Turpin 2000: 50)

c. Ahakeye (re) elye**warle** kwenke.
bush.plum s/he shade.ALL swallows
'He eats bush plums in the shade.' (Turpin 2000: 50)

d. **Elyenge=pe** atanthe=pe pweyayne-ee.
shade.LOC=FOC they=FOC cook.used.to-CONTINUE
'They would cook (the meat) in the shade for a long time.' (Turpin 2000: 83)

While Alyawarr does have an ALL case ending, location of the object is expressed by a form which is otherwise used to denote Dative case as in (31a) (perception verb) and (31b) (leaving). This connection is probably due to the frequent overlap in function between DAT and ALL case-markers in many languages: DAT used for destinations and ALL used for purpose etc.[12]

(31) a. Antimirna arrpmila arika, **atnkirrika**.
sugarbag[NOM] again see.PST coolibah.DAT
'(I) saw a sugarbag again, in a coolibah tree.' (Yallop 1977: 74)

b. Aylinapa line-irnima **kwatjika**ntiya iwulalpika.
we (du nom 1).but line[NOM]=SOME water.DAT.still leave.PST
'But we left the lines by the water.' (Yallop 1977: 75)

In Alyawarr DAT can be used as an alternative to LOC when the whole event takes place at a location.

(32) Artula arrpiyla ayliyla **apmirika**.
man.ERG carve.PRS boomerang[NOM] camp.DAT
'The man is making a boomerang in the camp.' (Yallop 1977: 74)

[12] For example, Aet Lees (p.c. October 2011) notes a historical parallel in Finnic languages, where the Livonian Dative case corresponds to the Allative (or sometimes Adessive) case in most of the other Finnic languages.

It is not clear why DAT is chosen over LOC in (32) in Alyawarr, or why ALL and LOC are used in (30c, 30d) in Kaytetye. We may be dealing with a degree of pure optionality here, as is sometimes the case in the choice between ALL and LOC in languages where AN occurs.

2.4.3 Languages to the North

To the north-east of Gurindji, and to the north of Warumungu and Wakaya are non-Pama-Nyungan languages, Wambaya (Nordlinger 1998), Jingulu (Pensalfini 2003), and Wardaman (Merlan 1994). These all lack constructions such as the AN construction or double case-marking to predicate location of participants specifically. Another non-Pama-Nyungan language in the area, Jaminjung, does have the AN construction, as noted above, perhaps borrowed from Pama-Nyungan neighbours. Thus the AN construction appears to be an areal phenomenon, restricted to some Ngumpin-Yapa languages, their neighbours to the east, and one neighbouring non-Pama-Nyungan group to the north-west. But there is an exception.

The Yolngu group of languages are Pama-Nyungan languages which are geographically separated from other Pama-Nyungan languages by blocks of non-Pama-Nyungan languages. The AN pattern is also found in the Yolngu languages. An alternation between ALL and LOC occurs, described by Schebeck (1976: 365) as follows:

> [...] a LOC. appears in a transitive sentence only if the agent and the object 'are in, at, on' a place [...] However, when only the object 'is in, at, on' the place, the LOC. of the underlying intransitive sentence must be transformed into the DIR. ([= ALL]; when only the agent 'is in, at, on' the place, the underlying LOC. must be transformed into the EX. [= ABL]

Thus in (33) agent and object are co-located, and the location is expressed with LOC. In (34) only the object, the bird, is in the tree, and the location is expressed with ALL.

(33)	Yūl=ngu-thu	taykka-nha	puu-ya-n	**palà-nga**.
	man-ERG	woman-ACC	hit-Afs.-Afv.	house-LOC

'Man hit woman in house.' (Schebeck 1976: ex. 14)[13]

(34)	Yūl=ngu-thu	warakkàn-nha	nhā-ngal	**thaṛppa-li.**
	man-ERG	bird-ACC	see-Afv	tree-ALL

'Man saw bird on tree.' (Schebeck 1976: ex. 88)

Morphy (1983: 100), writing of the Djapu dialect of Yolngu characterises the difference in use as follows:

[13]The orthography used by Schebeck and Morphy has been modified here: *ng* is a velar nasal, *nha* a lamino-dental nasal and *th* is a lamino-dental oral stop. Schebeck inserts the character = in *yūl=ngu* to indicate a hypothetical morpheme analysis.

Locational function is clause-wide in scope: a location function case marker (LOC or zero) may only be used if all the participants enumerated in the clause are in the same place. Therefore a sentence like:

[149]	*ngarra*	*nhä-ma*	*d̲arramu-n*	***wänga-ngur***
	1.NOM	see-UNM	man-ACC	camp-LOC
	'I saw the man in the camp'			

can only mean that he was there and I was there too.
If the subject is in one place and the object is in another, the local NP is always marked from the perspective of the subject. Thus [150] would be appropriate if the man was in the shade and I was outside looking in:

[150]	*ngarra*	*nhä-ma*	*d̲arramu-n*	***ngurrnggitj-lil***
	1.NOM	see-UNM	man-ACC	shade-ALL
	'I saw the man in the shade'			

Returning to our initial remarks about event versus participant domain predication, this pattern in Yolngu can be interpreted as a pragmatic inference drawn from the fact that LOC is an event (clausal) domain marker and ALL a participant (grammatical object) domain marker. Since all examples of the AN construction we have found involve perception verbs, it is not clear if this is a necessary condition for its occurrence; neither Schebeck nor Morphy state that this is the case.

The non-Pama-Nyungan southern neighbours of the Yolngu do not appear to use ALL to predicate location of an object, in part because many have quite limited case endings, or because the load is split between a LOC prefix and a LOC suffix as in Bininj Gun-wok (Evans 2003). Interestingly, some of the languages do occasionally use ALL for the actual case of the object, the thing affected by the action. Heath (1978) describes a 'pseudo-Accusative' construction for Ngandi in which the object of perception or hitting or sending is expressed with an ALL case-ending.

(35)	**ṇ-ñara-ŋ-gič**	ŋanu-	ṇ-ni.
	MSG-father-my-ALL	I saw	him
	'I saw my father.' (Heath 1978: 46)		

Heath observes that the ALL is used "because the concept of seeing can be thought of as an action directed toward the perceived entity" (p. 46), that is, fictive motion where the object itself is the endpoint of the path. A similar use of the ALL/DAT affix on direct objects is found in Nunggubuyu (Heath 1984: 204), but the situation is more complicated because the path metaphor is made more explicit by having the Agent in Ablative case.

3 History and Explanations of the Constructions

In sum, two strategies are used to differentiate the location of the theme from the location of the agent in clauses where both are present. The first is the use of double case-marking, found in both Nominative-Accusative languages and Ergative-Absolutive Pama-Nyungan languages. The second is the co-opting of another case to express location of the object in some Ergative-Absolutive Pama-Nyungan languages.

So far, most examples found have been ALL or DAT, cases otherwise associated with Goals, although the source case ABL is occasionally found. Examples with verbs used in this way are primarily perception verbs and finding, which can be plausibly construed as fictive motion (metaphor of gaze as motion), and verbs of leaving or forgetting, cooking or burying, which can be construed as kinds of putting into a place (and so also as motion). However, some languages appear not to have such semantic restrictions on type of verb affected by AN, and to have grammaticalised the distinction as two cases expressing static location.

The distribution of the types surveyed is given in Table 1.

3.1 Origins of the AN Construction

One of the striking things about AN is that it is found in Pama-Nyungan languages in three discontinuous groups: (a) in the west of the Ngumpin-Yapa subgroup in the Victoria River District and Tanami Desert (b) in Warumungu and Wakaya in the Barkly Tablelands; and (c) in the Yolngu group far to the north, with as far as we know, no occurrence in between. This could suggest inheritance of this pattern from fairly deep within the Pama-Nyungan family. However the feature is also absent in the western Ngumpin-Yapa languages and is not present in any Non-Pama-Nyungan languages apart from Jaminjung, which may have adopted it by diffusion from Ngumpin-Yapa. This suggests that this is perhaps an areal feature, whose origin may be in Tablelands-Gulf Pama-Nyungan, perhaps Ngarna.[14] The areal spread of the feature must have developed at a time when Yolngu was still in touch with this area: this scenario avoids the unlikely hypothesis of independent invention in two areas. This construction is absent in other western and central Pama-Nyungan languages but there are other constructions which may have played a role in its development, such as the use of DAT in Alyawarr described in Sect. 2.4.2.

Apart from AN's distribution we need to look at how it may have evolved. As noted, this is a rare type of grammaticalisation of a semantic category meaning 'motion towards'. One conjecture could be that initially this began in contexts which combined motion and transitive objecthood. Perhaps the bridging context is verbs of putting. Many of the languages use an ALL case-marker on the locative goal of

[14] McConvell and Laughren (2004) suggest that a number of elements diffused from Warluwarric (Breen's Ngarna) into Ngumpin-Yapa before these two groups became separated and it is possible that similarly some features like those under discussion in this paper only entered the eastern languages of Ngumpin-Yapa. However another possibility is that AN was present in proto- Ngumpin-Yapa but was lost in the West. An alternative, but less likely hypothesis is that Ngumpin-Yapa and Warluwarric/Ngarna jointly form (part of) a higher level grouping within Pama-Nyungan. There is some lexical evidence that Yolngu could be added to such a putative linguo-genetic grouping. This could account for the sharing of the AN feature.

Table 1 Distribution of types

Patterns	Allative (AN)	Notes
A. Ngumpin-Yapa		
1 Gurindji	yes	Upper Victoria River AN optional? where S & O not co-located
2 Jaru, Walmajarri[a]	no	These languages are on the extreme west of the Ngumpin-Yapa family
3 Warlpiri	yes, alternative exists	some complications
B. Other Pama-Nyungan to the east of Gurindji (with LOC/ERG neutralised)		
4 Warumungu	yes	AN applies whether or not S & O co-located
5 Kaytetye	yes: Dative and Allative used	AN can apply whether or not S & O co-located, but LOC is also possible for co-location
6 Alyawarr	yes: Dative used instead of Allative	Dative can apply whether or not S & O co-located, but Locative is also possible for co-location of S & O
B.i Possibly Pama-Nyungan		
7 Wakaya	yes	S & O co-location for AN not confirmed
C. Yolngu (Pama-Nyungan, to the north)		
8 Yolngu	yes	AN where S & O not co-located
D. Non-Pama-Nyungan		
9 Jaminjung	yes (verbs of perception only?)	North-west of Victoria River Downs
10 Wambaya, Jingulu, Wardaman	no	
11 Ngandi	no	Allative on some objects
12 Nunggubuyu	no	Allative on some objects, Ablative on some subjects

[a] Jaru data comes from Tsunoda (1981) and Walmajarri from Hudson (1978)

verbs of 'putting'. For Alyawarr, Yallop (1977: 80) has some interesting examples where he interpolates an "and put".

I got it (and put it) into a pannikin
We dug yams (and put them) into a piece of bark
We were cutting bush bananas (and putting them) into a baby carrier

In some languages perception verbs seem to be another prototypical locus of AN, and, in the history of the construction, may have been associated with a kind of 'fictive motion' where perception is conceptualised as a kind of path from subject to object location.

A second feature which is found in a number of languages with AN, either categorically or as a tendency, is the requirement that the subject and object be in different locations to trigger a change to AN marking. Alternatively LOC can be seen as marking scope of location as being over the whole clause/event, while ALL functions to mark restricted scope of the location to the object NP. This may well have been important in the semantic matrix leading to the grammaticalisation, even though it is less clear-cut or even absent in some contemporary languages. The action by the agent on the patient may be conceptualised as motion-like since they are in two locations.

Finally, a fuller account needs to relate the appearance in the same languages of AN, (Allative case on nominals for location of objects) with Allative subordination (AS), the use on nominalised verbs of a complementiser suffix homophonous with the Allative case suffix to express control by an object, or non-subject switch reference (Austin 1981; Hale 1982; Simpson 1991). This in turn needs to be related to the use of other cases, especially Locative, as a complementiser suffix indicating control by other grammatical functions (what we call Locative subordination, LS).

3.2 Parallels with Finnish

The AN phenomenon has parallels with a phenomenon in Finnish involving directional locatives (e.g. Fong 2003) and 'fictive motion' (Huumo 2006, 2007, 2010) where the metaphorical motion this time is the separation or coming together of the locations of the subject and object. In some cases the Allative case (or the corresponding 'interior' case Illative) is used for the static location of objects, as in Ngandi and Nunggubuyu, but not the directional path, as with the AN construction in Australia. For instance, consider the (i) interpretation of (36) in Finnish (Fong 2003: 227): in this case Illative is used.

(36)	Metsästäjä	ampu-i	karhu-n	**metsä-än**.
	hunter.NOM	shoot-PST.3s	bear-ACC	forest-ILL

(i) 'A/the hunter shot a/the bear in (lit. 'into') a/the forest.'

(ii) 'A/the hunter shot a/the bear into a/the forest' (i.e. the bear was ejected/propelled into the forest).

Actual motion of the object into the location can be involved in the meaning of such examples (as in interpretation (ii) of (36)) but commonly there is no real motion. The common element seems to be that the object remains in the location in the ultimate phase of the event. ALL and ILL are commonly used for the location of objects with verbs of 'leaving' in Finnish, where the subject is separated from or moves away from the object entity (Huumo 2006: 48, 2007: 85).

Fong (2003) attributes this unusual usage in Finnish to the diphasic nature of the event structure involved, and the fact that Finnish directional cases can represent one phase—in this case the ultimate location—rather than inherently Path. She relates the phenomenon in Finnish, not to grammatical object control but to the semantics of the verbs involved. This seems to be borne out by the occurrence of ALL and ILL for location in intransitives, e.g. (37).[15]

(37) Karhu kuol-i **metsä-än**.
bear.NOM die-PST.3s forest-ILL
'A/the bear died in (lit. 'into') a/the forest.'

We have not found Australian parallels to (37). AN parallels to (36) exist in Australian languages, since the key point is that the ultimate location of the object is the ALL-marked NP, as in the Wakaya sentence (22) repeated here as (38) for convenience.

(38) Yinkabu-rl wura ngurrungund-a **yukwa-rr-rd**.
kangaroo-ERG dog drown-GER water-NM-NALL
'The kangaroo drowned the dog in the water.' (Breen 2011b: Chap. 6, ex. 107)

As we have seen, in some Australian languages verbs of perception frequently take the AN construction. In Finnish (Huumo 2007) a case representing goal/end-point can rarely express the location of the object of perception parallel to English 'I can see [all the way] to the sea'. Underlying both the Finnish and Australian examples may be the metaphor of perception as involving a path where the perceiver and the object of perception are at either end.

Also in Finnish is the construction where the location of the object is marked with Ablative case (or Elative, the 'interior' equivalent). This is found with transitive verbs of buying and finding. The subject is understood as outside the location, and some property of the object fictively 'moves' to the subject's dominion of possession or consciousness (Huumo 2010). Thus 'finding' something (Ablative/Elative-marked location) contrasts with 'losing' something (Allative/Illative).[16] This is not a kind of 'fictive motion' found in Australia; the restricted use of Ablative-case-marked objects of some verbs in Yanyuwa, and Ablative subjects in Nunggubuyu, seems to have a different semantic basis, and different grammatical properties.

4 Conclusions

We have shown two ways of differentiating the location of the object from the location of the subject in north-central Australian languages, through double case-marking and through co-opting cases that express Goal semantic roles, ALL and less commonly, DAT, the AN construction. This second way of marking secondary predications on object NPs is typologically rare as a grammaticalisation of local case-marking. In some of the languages in which this occurs it has the special function of singling out the object NP alone as being in the location, rather than the

[15]Huumo (2006: 61) also gives examples of intransitive process verbs taking allatives for the ultimate location of the subject entity.

[16]A similar contrast is found in Estonian (Aet Lees, p.c. October 2011).

whole event and all the participants.[17] Thus in a certain sense the action or perception 'moves' from the agent to a patient literally, as they are in different spatial positions and it may be a form of this Path metaphor which is encoded in the AN construction. With verbs of seeing, a likely explanation seems to be Gruber's (1967) analogy between seeing and going; the speaker's gaze goes to the object, and thus to the place where the object is. With verbs such as leaving, burying, cooking, a likely explanation appears to be that the object is imagined as moving to the place where it is left/buried/cooked etc. Thus fictive motion may have different underlying metaphors.

An apparently similar phenomenon is found in 'directional locatives' in Finnish. While some of the verbs found in the Finnish examples are semantically similar ('leave', 'see'), the metaphors underlying these directional locatives seems different from those underlying AN in the Australian languages we have been discussing. There is no implication in the Finnish example (36) that the hunter (subject) is outside the forest (where the object 'bear' is) for instance, which would be the case in the most clear-cut cases of semantic differentiation between AN and Locative marking, e.g. in Yolngu. However, the common element between AN and the directional locative/fictive motion constructions may be that there is physical separation of the subject and the location of the object at some phase of the event.

It is possible that the original form of AN in the area formed by Wakaya and its relatives, and Yolngu at least did embody the use of an ALL form for secondary predication indicating locations of grammatical objects which are perceived as being in a separate location from the subject of the clause. If this results from a diphasic event structure, then this event structure is different from what it is generally thought to be for verbs like 'see'. A process which may have resulted in AN of this type is analogical extension of the pattern of verbs which do involve a kind of diphasic event structure—motion of the object as with 'put'—to other transitive verbs.

While clearly the Australian and Finnish phenomena differ in some parameters, they both reflect ways in which a locational case system can be adapted to a particular metaphorical or 'fictive' extension of notions of space and co-location in relation to syntactic arguments. It seems likely that when the AN phenomenon in Australia arose in certain Pama-Nyungan languages, it did express this kind of differentiation of co-location and separation of subject and object. These notions are closely linked to the distinction in predicate domain between event and participant, and at an even more grammatical level between clause and object noun phrase. As the grammaticalisation of this phenomenon expanded to expressing types of control, it also began to lose some of its original semantic character.

[17] Tomioka (2008) calls the predication of a locative to a whole clause 'the Davidsonian event interpretation', and claims that this is the only reading possible of Japanese locative adpositions, unlike in English for instance. In the relevant Australian cases LOC has the whole-event reading and ALL (in the locative sense) does not include the transitive subject (except in Warumungu). Whether the verb together with the object and excluding the subject agent can be interpreted as a 'sub-event' rather than a matter of syntactic scope is not clear.

Acknowledgements It is a pleasure to offer this paper in honour of Lauri Carlson, whose paper on Finnish case (Carlson 1978) remains a classic. Earlier versions of this paper were presented at the PIONIER Workshop on Locative Case, 25–26 August 2008, Radboud University, Nijmegen, the Netherlands, the Research Centre for Linguistic Typology, La Trobe University, 9 February 2011, the Aboriginal Languages Workshop, Stradbroke Island, 11–13 March 2011, and as a seminar in the Department of Linguistics, University of Helsinki (31 October 2011). Thanks to the organisers and participants for comments, and to Barry Blake, Gavan Breen, Lauri Carlson, Diana Forker, Mary Laughren, David Nash, Rachel Nordlinger, Nicholas Ostler, Anne Tamm, and David Wilkins for sharing data and comments. We thank referees, and special thanks to Aet Lees for enlightening discussion of Estonian and Finnish.

References

Alpher, Barry. 2004. Pama-Nyungan: phonological reconstruction and status as a phylogenetic group. In *Australian languages: Classification and the comparative method*, eds. Claire Bowern and Harold Koch. Vol. 249 of *Current issues in linguistic theory*, 93–126. Philadelphia: John Benjamins.

Austin, Peter. 1981. Switch-reference in Australia. *Language* 57: 309–334.

Austin, Peter. 1995. Double case marking in Kanyara and Mantharta languages, Western Australia. In *Double case: Agreement by Suffixaufnahme*, ed. Frans Plank, 363–379. Oxford: Oxford University Press.

Blake, Barry J. 1979. *A Kalkatungu grammar*. Vol. 57 of *Series B*. Canberra: Pacific Linguistics.

Bowern, Claire, and Harold Koch, eds. 2004. *Australian languages: Classification and the comparative method*. Vol. 249 of *Current issues in linguistic theory*. Philadelphia: John Benjamins.

Breen, J. Gavan. 1974. Wakaya grammar: informant: Willy Clegg. Manuscript copy at Australian Institute of Aboriginal and Torres Strait Islander Studies.

Breen, Gavan. 2004. Evolution of the verb conjugations in the Ngarna languages. In *Australian languages: Classification and the comparative method*, eds. Claire Bowern and Harold Koch. Vol. 249 of *Current issues in linguistic theory*, 223–240. Philadelphia: John Benjamins.

Breen, Gavan. 2011a. A new approach to Australian lexicostatistics. *Australian Journal of Linguistics* 31: 233–268.

Breen, J. Gavan. 2011b. *Wakaya grammar*. Alice Springs. Manuscript.

Carlson, Lauri. 1978. *Central problems in Finnish syntax, parts I–II*. Massachusetts Institute of Technology, Cambridge MA. Manuscript.

Cataldi, Lee. 2011/2004. *A dictionary of Ngardi*. Halls Creek: Balgo School.

Cook, Walter Anthony. 1989. *Case grammar theory*. Georgetown: Georgetown University Press.

Dench, Alan, and Nicholas Evans. 1988. Multiple case-marking in Australian languages. *Australian Journal of Linguistics* 8: 1–47.

Evans, Nicholas. 2003. *Bininj Gun-Wok: A pan-dialectal grammar of Mayali, Kunwinjku and Kune*. Canberra: Pacific Linguistics.

Fong, Vivienne. 2003. Resultatives and depictives in Finnish. In *Generative approaches to Finnic and Saami linguistics*, eds. Diane Nelson and Satu Manninen, 201–233. Stanford: CSLI.

Gruber, Jeffrey. 1967. 'Look' and 'see'. *Language* 43: 937–947.

Hale, Kenneth. 1960. Ngarluma field notes. Informant: Bob Churnside (50–60) Roebourne.

Hale, Kenneth. 1982. Some essential features of Warlpiri main clauses. In *Papers in Warlpiri grammar: In memory of Lothar Jagst*, ed. Stephen Swartz. *Work-papers of SIL-AAB, series A*, 217–315. Berrimah: Summer Institute of Linguistics.

Hale, Kenneth. 1992. Basic word order in two 'free word order' languages. In *Pragmatics of word order flexibility*, ed. Doris Payne. Vol. 22 of *Typological studies in language*, 63–82. Amsterdam: John Benjamins.

Heath, Jeffrey. 1978. *Ngandi grammar, texts and dictionary*. Canberra: Australian Institute of Aboriginal Studies.
Heath, Jeffrey. 1984. *Functional grammar of Nunggubuyu*. Canberra: Australian Institute of Aboriginal Studies.
Hudson, Joyce. 1978. *The core of Walmatjari grammar*. Canberra/New Jersey: Australian Institute of Aboriginal Studies/Humanities Press.
Huumo, Tuomas. 2006. 'I woke up from the sofa': Subjective directionality in Finnish expressions of a spatio-cognitive transfer. In *Grammar from the human perspective: Case, space and person in Finnish*, eds. Marja-Liisa Helasvuo and Lyle Campbell, 41–65. Amsterdam: John Benjamins.
Huumo, Tuomas. 2007. Force dynamics, fictive dynamicity, and the Finnish verbs of 'remaining'. *Folia Linguistica* 41: 73–98.
Huumo, Tuomas. 2010. Is perception a directional relationship? On directionality and its motivation in Finnish expressions of sensory perception. *Linguistics* 48: 49–97.
Kirton, Jean F., and Bella Charlie. 1996. *Further aspects of the grammar of Yanyuwa, Northern Australia*. Vol. C-131 of *Pacific linguistics series*. Canberra: Research School of Pacific and Asian Studies, Australian National University.
McConvell, Patrick, and Mary Laughren. 2004. The Ngumpin-Yapa subgroup. In *Australian languages: Classification and the comparative method*, eds. Claire Bowern and Harold Koch. Vol. 249 of *Current issues in linguistic theory*, 151–177. Philadelphia: John Benjamins.
Merlan, Francesca. 1994. *A grammar of Wardaman: a language of the Northern Territory of Australia*. Vol. 11 of *Mouton grammar library*. Berlin: Mouton de Gruyter.
Morphy, Frances. 1983. Djapu, a Yolngu dialect. In *Handbook of Australian languages*, eds. Robert M.W. Dixon and Barry J. Blake, 1–188. Canberra: The Australian National University Press.
Nordlinger, Rachel. 1998. *A grammar of Wambaya, Northern Territory (Australia)*. Vol. C-140. Canberra: Pacific Linguistics, Research School of Pacific and Asian Studies, Australian National University.
Pensalfini, Robert. 2003. *A grammar of Jingulu, an Aboriginal language of the Northern Territory*. Vol. 536 of *Pacific linguistics*. Canberra: Pacific Linguistics.
Plank, Frans, ed. 1995. *Double case: Agreement by Suffixaufnahme*. Oxford: Oxford University Press.
Schebeck, Bernhard. 1976. Yuulngu. In *Grammatical categories in Australian languages*, ed. Robert M.W. Dixon, 352–382. Canberra: Australian Institute of Aboriginal Studies.
Schultze-Berndt, Eva. 2000. Simple and complex verbs in Jaminjung: a study of event categorisation in an Australian languages. Doctoral diss., Katholieke Universiteit Nijmegen, Nijmegen.
Simpson, Jane. 1981. *Ngarluma as a W* language*. Massachusetts Institute of Technology. http://hdl.handle.net/2123/4025, Manuscript 100 p.
Simpson, Jane. 1991. *Warlpiri morphosyntax: a lexicalist approach. Studies in natural language and linguistic theory*. Dordrecht: Kluwer.
Simpson, Jane. 2002. *A learner's guide to Warumungu: Mirlamirlajinjjiki Warumunguku apparrka*. Alice Springs: IAD Press.
Simpson, Jane. 2007. Expressing pragmatic constraints on word order in Warlpiri. In *Architectures, rules, and preferences: Variations on themes by Joan W. Bresnan*, eds. Annie Zaenen, Jane Simpson, Tracy Holloway King, Jane Grimshaw, Joan Maling, and Christopher Manning, 403–427. Stanford: CSLI.
Swartz, Stephen M. 1991. Constraints on zero anaphora and word order in Warlpiri narrative text. SIL-AAIB Occasional Papers 1, Summer Institute of Linguistics, Darwin, Northern Territory.
Talmy, Leonard. 1996. Fictive motion in language and 'ception'. In *Language and space*, ed. Paul Bloom, 211–276. Cambridge: MIT Press.
Tomioka, Naoko. 2008. The distribution and interpretation of adjunct locative PPs. In *Syntax and semantics of spatial P*, eds. Anna Asbury, Jakub Dotlačil, Berit Gehrke, and Rick Nouwen, 253–272. Vol. 120 of *Linguistik Aktuell/Linguistics today*. Amsterdam: John Benjamins.
Tsunoda, Tasaku. 1981. *The Djaru language of Kimberley, Western Australia. Pacific linguistics series B*. Canberra: Pacific Linguistics.

Turpin, Myfany. 2000. *A learner's guide to Kaytetye*. Alice Springs: IAD Press.
Valenzuela, Pilar M. 2005. Participant agreement in Panoan. In *Secondary predication and adverbial modification. The typology of depictives*, eds. Nikolaus P. Himmelmann and Eva Schultze-Berndt, 259–298. Oxford: Oxford University Press.
Yallop, Colin. 1977. *Alyawarra, an Aboriginal language of Central Australia*. Canberra: Australian Institute of Aboriginal Studies.

Necessive Expressions in Finnic Bible Translations

Aet Lees

Abstract A corpus study has been carried out concerning necessive expressions in the Finnic languages Estonian, Finnish, Karelian (Olonets), Livonian and Veps, using the Gospel of St. Matthew in the New Testament in these five languages. The aim of the study is to compare the necessive expressions and their frequency in the various languages synchronically and diachronically. Although Livonian is now virtually a dead language, the New Testament (1942) has been used. In the modern section of the corpus Estonian and Karelian use mainly the verbs *pidama* and *piteä* respectively. In Finnish the construction '*on -(t)tAvA*' is slightly more frequent than *pitää*. Veps has *tarbiž* almost exclusively and Livonian uses a possessive construction with the partitive case of the fourth infinitive '*on V-mõst*'. Diachronic studies show an excessive use of *pidama/pitää* in the older Estonian (southern and northern dialects) and Finnish texts, attributed mainly to German influence. Older translations of the Gospel of St. Matthew in Karelian and Livonian contain some necessive constructions, which are no longer found in the most recent translations.

Abbreviations

ABL	ablative
ACC	accusative
ADE	adessive
AFF	affirmative
ALL	allative
COND	conditional
CONNEG	connegative
DAT	dative
E	Estonian
ELA	elative
EMP	emphatic
ESS	essive
F	Finnish
GEN	genitive

A. Lees (✉)
Department of Linguistics, University of Sydney, Sydney, Australia
e-mail: aet.lees@iinet.net.au

D. Santos et al. (eds.), *Shall We Play the Festschrift Game?*,
DOI 10.1007/978-3-642-30773-7_12,

ILL	illative
IMP	imperative
INE	inessive
INF	infinitive
K	Karelian
L	Livonian
LE	Eastern Livonian
LW	Western Livonian
NEG	negative
NOM	nominative
NP	noun phrase
PAR	partitive
PASS	passive
PL	plural
POT	potential
PPP	passive past participle
PRES	present
PST	past
PTCP	participle
PX	possessive suffix
Q	interrogative particle
SE	Southern Estonian
SG	singular
TRA	translative
V	Veps

1 Introduction

It is a pleasure to contribute to the Festschrift in honour of Lauri Carlson. I first heard about Lauri when Jane Simpson gave me his manuscript "Grammatical case in Finnish" to read. This stimulated me to think about how Estonian is similar and different, and started me on the path of comparing the two languages, a study which later became extended to other Finnic languages, as more material came to hand. When Lauri visited Australia in 2002, I enjoyed his lectures, and had an opportunity to ask him about some points of Finnish grammar that particularly puzzled me. Subsequently I had an opportunity to visit his department in Helsinki, and again found him very helpful. It is really due to Lauri that I am involved in linguistics research.

All languages have ways of expressing obligation and need. Especially in Finnish there are a number of different expressions, which are well known and explained in Finnish grammar books, such as ISK (Hakulinen et al. 2004). In Estonian also these are well known (Viitso 2007: 106). It is more difficult to find information about necessive constructions in other Finnic languages. The aim of this paper is to compare the type and frequency of necessive constructions in five Finnic languages using

Bible translations as a comparable set of data. This paper does not pretend to provide a comprehensive review of all necessive constructions in these languages. The corpus consists of the Gospel of St. Matthew in the New Testament in the Finnic languages Estonian, Finnish, Karelian (Olonets), Livonian and Veps, both modern and old, as detailed in Sect. 5. Diachronic studies have been carried out with the same text in southern and northern (later standard) Estonian and Finnish, to show the changes in each language, especially concerning the main construction with *pidama/pitää* and comparing those with each other, especially with reference to the frequency of these constructions and the choice of the infinitive complement and the case of the person obliged to do something. A limited number of 19th century translations of the Gospel of St. Matthew in Karelian and Livonian have also been examined and compared with the most recent ones to show the changes in those languages. There is no early translation available in Veps. A summary of the study of the contemporary texts is found in Sect. 2.6. A comparison of Estonian and Finnish diachronic studies concerning *pidama/pitää* is given in Sect. 3.3.1, and a final summary in Sect. 4. The study has been carried out manually.

2 Modern Bible Texts

There are several cognate expressions found in these languages, but the constructions vary. Example set (1) gives an illustration of this variability.[1]

(1) a. E mis head ma peaksin tegema
what.NOM good.PAR 1SG.**NOM** must.**1SG**.COND do.***ma*INF**

b. F mitä hyvää minun pitää tehdä
what.PAR good.PAR 1SG.**GEN** must.**3SG** do.***ta*INF**

c. K midä hyviä minul pidäü luadie
what.PAR good.PAR 1SG.**ADE** must.**3SG** do.***ta*INF**

d. L mis jõvvõ um minnõn tiemõst
what good.PAR be.**3SG** 1SG.**DAT** do.**4INF**

e. V midä hüväd minei tarbiž tehta
what.PAR good.PAR 1SG.**ALL** necessary do.***ta*INF**

'what good must I do (to inherit eternal life)'
(Matt. 19: 16)

In most of the languages the expression used in example (1) is the most common in the modern text in the corpus, but Finnish has slightly more instances of the *on -(t)tAva* construction, discussed in Sect. 2.4.

[1]The letter after the number of the example indicates the language.

Table 1 Comparison of the number and type of constructions with *pitää/pidama* and cognates in Finnic languages in the modern section of the corpus

	Estonian	Finnish	Karelian	Livonian	Veps
total (AFF)	27	10	34	1	5
total (NEG)	0	3	3	0	1
subject	nominative	genitive	adessive	nominative	allative
verb	agreement	3SG	3SG	?	3SG
complement	*-ma*INF.ILL	*-ta*INF	*-ta*INF	*-ma*INF.ILL	*-ta*INF

2.1 Pitää and Its Cognates

The verb *pidama* (Estonian), *pitää* (Finnish), and cognate forms in the other languages have several different meanings. They are used as personal verbs with meanings such as 'keep/hold/consider/like', which will not be discussed here. Table 1 shows the frequency of the use of this verb as a modal in a necessive function, and some of the differences in the constructions in the various languages in the Gospel of St. Matthew (see Corpus: Estonian 1989, Finnish 1992, Karelian 2003, Livonian 1942, Veps 2006).

Used as a necessive verb *pidama* 'must' is personal in Estonian, inflecting for person and number, agreeing with the nominative subject, but it can also be used without a subject to mean 'it is necessary', when it is in the 3rd person singular form, but an infinitival complement is still necessary. The complement of 'must' is the *-ma* infinitive in the illative case (also called supine in Estonian grammar). If the infinitive is transitive, the object can be either partitive, or if total, in the genitive case for singular and nominative for plural nouns. However, in the corpus, there are very few transitive complements of *pidama*. In negative clauses in Estonian *pidama* is not used for obligation, but means 'need not'. An Estonian obligative example is shown in (2).

(2) E mida peate rääkima
what.PAR must.**2PL** talk.***ma*INF**
'what you must say'
(Matt. 10: 19)

In the other languages the use of *pitää* differs considerably. The subject is non-nominative, the verb is always in the 3rd singular form, although it can vary in tense, and the infinitival complement is the *-ta* infinitive. Livonian only has one example, so it is difficult to evaluate, but the complement is a *-ma* infinitive.

In Finnish the subject is in the genitive case (sometimes referred to as the dative-genitive). The object of the infinitive can be partitive or total, the latter being in the nominative form for singular as well as plural nouns. An example is shown in (3).

(3) F **minun**-han pitäisi saada sinulta **kaste**
1SG.**GEN**-EMP must.3SG.COND get.***ta*INF** 2SG.ABL baptism.**NOM**

'I should be baptized by you'
(Matt. 3: 14)

Karelian also uses *piteä* for necessive constructions. Like Finnish there is no nominative subject, but instead of the genitive, the adessive is used. The verb is in the 3rd person singular form *pidääu*. The complement is the *-ta* infinitive. An example is shown in (4).

(4)	K	pidäü	**meil**	vie	vuottua	tostu?
		must.3SG	1PL.ADE	still	wait.***ta*INF**	another.PAR

'do we still have to wait for someone else?'
(Matt. 11: 3)

Karelian differs in that *piteä* is used also to mean 'need' in affirmative as well as negative clauses, and in that meaning it can take either a direct noun object or a *-ta* infinitive. It differs in that usage in that the subject is allative instead of adessive. The verb is again 3rd person singular (5). The instances of *piteä* 'need' with an allative subject, of which there are five affirmative clauses and one negative, are not included in the numbers in Table 1, as they form a distinct group.

(5)	K	tädä	kaikkie	**teile**	pidäü
		that.PAR	all.PAR	2PL.**ALL**	need.3SG

'you need all that'
(Matt. 6: 32)

In Veps there are only a few examples, also with the 3rd person singular verb *pidab*. The subject is allative. The verbal complement is the *-ta* infinitive. An example in the past tense is shown in (6).

(6)	V	**hänele**	pidi	mända	veneheze
		3SG.**ALL**	must.3SG.PST	go.***ta*INF**	boat.ILL

'he had to go into the boat'
(Matt. 13: 2)

In modern Estonian *pidama/pitää* is not used for the negative 'must not', but means 'need not'. In the other languages, it is used for negative obligation. In Finnish, Karelian and Veps there is an example in a syntactically negative, but semantically affirmative clause with an obligative meaning (7a–7c).

(7)	a.	F	eikö	**sinun**-kin	olisi	pitänyt
			NEG.**3SG**.Q	2SG.**GEN**-also	be.CONNEG.COND	must.PST.PTCP
			armahtaa	työtovcriasi?		
			have.pity.***ta*INF**	fellow.worker.SG.PAR.2SG.PX		
	b.	K	eigo	**sinul**-gi	pidänüs	ziälöijä
			NEG.**3SG**	2SG.**ADE**-also	must.3SG.PST.COND	have.pity.***ta*INF**
			omua	dovariššua		
			own.SG.PAR	companion.SG.PAR		

c. V

ei-ik	**sinei**-ki	pidanuiži	armahtada
NEG.**3SG**-Q	2SG.**ALL**-also	must.CONNEG.COND	have.pity.***ta*****INF**

radvelled?
fellow.worker.SG.PAR

[as I had pity on you] 'shouldn't you also have had pity on your fellow worker?'
(Matt. 18: 33)

Another Finnish negative example with the meaning 'must not' is shown in (8).

(8) F

sen,	joka	on	katolla,	ei	pidä
that.**SG.GEN**	who.SG.NOM	be.**3SG**	street.ADE	**NEG.3SG**	must.CONNEG

mennä	hakemaan	mitään	tavaroita	talostaan
go.***ta*****INF**	get.*ma*INF.ILL	nothing.PAR	possession.PL.PAR	house.ELA.3PX

'he, who is in the street, must not go to get any possessions from his house'
(Matt. 24: 17)

In the modern Estonian corpus there are no negative examples like (8), and in the corresponding verse the prohibition is rendered by the jussive 'let him not go'.

A Karelian example of the negative use of *piteä* for 'must not' is shown in (9).

(9) K

nenga	ei	pie	olla	teijän	keskes
so	NEG.**3SG**	must.CONNEG	be.***ta*****INF**	2PL.GEN	among

'it must not be so among you'
(Matt. 20: 26)

For 'must not' Estonian uses the verb *tohtima* 'be allowed', which inflects for person and number in the affirmative, but in the negative, the Estonian non-inflected negative particle *ei* is used with the connegative *tohi*, which also does not inflect for person or number (10). This verb takes the *-ta* infinitive.

(10) E

sa	ei	tohi	tappa
2SG.NOM	NEG	be.allowed.CONNEG	kill.*ta*INF

'you must not kill'
(Matt. 19: 18)

There is a cognate *tohtia* in Finnish, but it is not used in the same sense. Used negatively, it means 'does not dare'.

Livonian differs from the other languages in that the cognate verb *piddõ* is barely used at all for obligation in the corpus. The one example has a nominative subject and an unexpected verb form of *piddõ* as shown in (11).

(11) L

kus	Kristus	**pid'im**	**syndõm**
where	Christ.**NOM**	must.**PST**	be.born.***ma*****INF.ILL**

'where Christ had to be born'
(Matt. 2: 4)

The name Kristus has the same form in the genitive, but that case is unlikely here. The verb *pidim* appears to be first person plural past tense, which does not make sense. I would have expected *pidiz*, which is the third person past tense form used elsewhere in a non-necessive context. The use of *piddõ* itself here is unusual, so possibly it is a borrowing from Estonian. In a quick perusal of some of the rest of the 1942 Livonian New Testament, I have not found any other examples, although a small number are found in older translations (see Sect. 3.5). The word itself exists in the language as a personal verb, meaning 'hold/keep' as in the other languages. For the commonly used necessive expression in Livonian, see Sect. 2.5.

2.2 *Tulee and Its Cognates; täytyy, on määra and on pakko*

In both Finnish and Estonian the 3rd person singular form of the verb *tulla* 'come' is used to indicate obligation. In Finnish the construction is similar to that with *pitää*, with a genitive agent and *-ta* infinitive complement. In Estonian, it differs from *pidama* in both the agent and the complement. The subject is adessive and the complement the *-ta* infinitive. It can be used without a subject, in the sense of 'something must be done'. EKG (Erelt et al. 1993: 19) regards the *-ta* infinitive as the subject of the clause. Some examples are shown below.

(12)	E	siis	tuleb	**meil**	karta	rahvahulki
		then	must.**3SG**	1SG.PL.**ADE**	fear.***ta*INF**	crowd.PL.PAR
		'then we have to fear the crowds'				
		(Matt. 21: 26)				

A Finnish example is shown in (13).

(13)	F	Herraa	**sinun**	tulee	kunnioittaa
		lord.PAR	2SG.**GEN**	must.3SG	revere.***ta*INF**
		'the Lord you must revere'			
		(Matt. 4: 10)			

In the corpus, *tulee* was much less common than *pitää*, with four instances each in Finnish and Estonian, which did not correspond in the two languages. Any objects of the infinitive are partitive or nominative.

In a large Estonian study consisting of material from different genres, Penjam (2006: 176) found a larger number of examples, especially in the media during the height of the Soviet occupation in 1950. She quotes Saukkonen (1965: 150–155), saying that cognate constructions occur also in other Finnic languages. However, there were no cognate expressions in the other languages in the corpus.

The constructions with *täytyy* and *on määrä* found in Finnish are similar to those with *tulee*. These expressions also have a genitive subject and the *-ta* infinitive, with or without a nominative or partitive object. There were three examples of *täytyy* and four of *on määrä*. There were no instances of *on pakko*. All of these expressions are used to indicate obligation in Finnish. There are no cognates of these in Estonian, and I have not come across any in the other languages in the corpus.

2.3 *Tarvis* and Its Cognates

With the construction using *tarvis* the meanings 'must' and 'need' overlap, the negative always meaning 'need not'. In Estonian the compound verb *on tarvis* 'is necessary/need' is in common usage, but in the corpus there is only one negative example. It can be used with or without a subject in the adessive case, and with either a partitive direct object or a *-ta* infinitive. The objects of the infinitive can be partitive or nominative, the latter in affirmative clauses only.

In Veps the word *tarbiž* 'necessary/need' is the most common necessive construction, used without the verb 'be' in the present tense. In the corpus there are a total of 34 instances in affirmative clauses, of those 29 with a *-ta* infinitive, and five with an object of *tarbiž*. As in Karelian, there is an overlap of 'must' and 'need', but in contradistinction to Karelian, if a subject is present, it is always in the allative case (14) and (15). The object of the infinitive is nominative or partitive.

(14)	V	hänele	tarbiž	antta	akale	erigoituzbumag
		3SG.**ALL**	necessary	give.***ta*INF**	wife.ALL	divorce.book.NOM

'he must give his wife a book of divorce'
(Matt. 5: 31)

(15)	V	kaiked	necidä	teile	tarbiž
		all.PAR	that.PAR	2PL.**ALL**	necessary

'you need all that'
(Matt. 6: 32)

This construction can also be used without an expressed subject, as in (16).

(16)	V	händäst	tarbiž	surmita
		3SG.PAR	necessary	kill.***ta*INF**

'he must be put to death'
(Matt. 15: 4)

For negation (meaning 'need not') the negative auxiliary in the 3rd person singular (*ei*) is used together with *tarbiž*. There are four examples such negative clauses. For 'must not' a plain negative imperative is used (17).

(17)	V	ala	riko
		NEG.2SG.IMP	kill.CONNEG

'don't kill'
(Matt. 19: 18)

2.4 Finnish Construction on *-(t)tAvA*

In Finnish the passive present participle with the suffix *-(t)tAvA* is used together with the verb 'be' to indicate obligation. This construction can also mean 'can be done/will be done/is done' (Karlsson 1999: 196), but here it is used mostly with its necessive meaning. This is a common way of expressing obligation and in the 1992 Bible there are 14 examples. If an agent is expressed it is in the genitive case both in the singular (18) and plural (19). Example (18) corresponds to (14) in Veps.

(18)	F	hänen	on	annettava	tälle	erokirja
		3SG.GEN	be.**3SG**	give.**PASS.PRES.PTCP**	that.ALL	book.of.divorce.**SG.NOM**

'he must give her (lit. that person) a book of divorce'
(Matt. 19: 7)

(19)	F	silloin	on	kaikkien	Judeassa	asuvien
		then	be.**3SG**	all.**PL.GEN**	Judea.INE	inhabitant.**PL.GEN**
		paettava	vuorille			
		flee.**PASS.PRES.PTCP**	mountain.PL.ALL			

'then all those living in Judea must flee to the mountains'
(Matt. 24: 16)

In Estonian the cognate construction has no sense of obligation and only means 'can be done'. I have not found this construction in other than the Finnish corpus.

2.5 Livonian Construction *um -mõst*

In Livonian obligation is expressed by means of a possessive construction. For a more detailed discussion of Livonian possessive constructions, see Lees (2008: 12). The agent (like the possessor) is dative, the verb 'be' is 3rd person singular and the action is in the form of the action nominalization *-mi* in the partitive case *-mõst*. There is another partitive form *-mist*, which is used in other situations. For that reason I prefer to call the *-mõst* form the fourth infinitive, as it functions in a somewhat similar way to the fourth infinitive in Finnish (Karlsson 1999: 192), which has now disappeared from the latest grammar book ISK (Hakulinen et al. 2004). Kettunen (1938: 67) also calls this form the fourth infinitive and compares the Livonian construction with the Finnish one. Moseley (2002: 51) calls the *-mõst* form the 'infinitive of obligation' and suggests that the Livonian construction has been borrowed from Latvian. However, the Latvian construction consists of a verb with the prefix *jā-* attached to the 3rd person singular of the main verb. The verb 'be' is not involved. The subject is in the dative case in both Livonian and Latvian, but there the similarity ends. Latvian does not use an action nominalization similar to the Livonian fourth infinitive to indicate obligation. In both of the older translations of the Gospel of St. Matthew the *-mist* form is used instead of *-mõst* (see Sect. 3.5). Kettunen (1938: 67) gives both forms as partitive variants. An example is shown in (1d), comparing it with the same clause in all the other languages, and a negative one is shown in (20). The negative is also used for 'need not'.

(20)	L	sinnõn	äb	ūo	Izandt	entš	Jumalt	kērtamõst
		2SG.DAT	NEG.3SG	be.CONNEG	lord.PAR	self.GEN	god.PAR	tempt.4INF

'you must not tempt the Lord your God'
(Matt. 4: 7)

In the corpus there are 38 affirmative instances of this construction, 20 with an object of the infinitive, 15 of which are partitive, one which is definitely genitive, and one noninflected *mis* 'what'. Three were ambiguous, either nominative or genitive. Those cases are homonymous for many singular nouns and all plural ones in Livonian. In other languages any objects of action nominalizations are genitive, and function in a similar way to possessive genitive noun modifiers. There are three negative examples, one of which means 'need not'.

2.6 Summary of Synchronic Studies

Various necessive constructions are in use in the different Finnic languages. In the corpus the most common construction in Estonian and Karelian is with *pidama/piteä*. For the latter it is the only construction found in the modern section of the corpus and doubles for both 'must' and 'need', but with a different case of the subject for the two meanings. In Estonian *pidama* in negative clauses means 'need not' and is not used for 'must not'. Finnish has a number of different constructions, of which *on –(t)tAvA* is the most common, with *pitää* not far behind. Livonian uses a possessive construction, with the possessum being the partitive form of the action nominalization, also called the fourth infinitive. In Veps *tarbiž* is used without a finite verb in the present tense, for both 'must' and 'need'. Estonian is the only one (with some doubt about the one Livonian example) where *pidama* in its necessive use is a personal verb, with a nominative subject and verb agreement. The subject is in a different case in each language, as indicated in Table 1.

The Finnish constructions with *täytyy, määrä* and *pakko* are not found in any of the other languages in the corpus. In written standard Finnish the subject is genitive and the complement the *-ta* infinitive. In Kven (a Finnish dialect which is now accepted as an independent minority language in Norway) *täytyy* has become a personal verb, with a nominative subject and verb agreement (Rosnes 2009: 30). This is probably due to Norwegian influence. Also, deSmit (2006: 117) quotes the findings of Laitinen (1992: 42, 50) that in some Finnish dialects necessive verbs show agreement with a nominative subject, and in others a nominative subject occurs with a unipersonal verb. Laitinen suggests that this has developed due to Swedish influence.

The infinitive complement is the *-ta* infinitive for all constructions, except for the *-ma* infinitive with *pidama* in Estonian and the one example in Livonian.

3 Diachronic Studies

3.1 Southern Estonian

The first Estonian translation of the entire New Testament (*Wastne Testament*) appeared in the southern Estonian dialect in 1686. At that time most of southern Estonia, including Tartu, had varieties of this dialect. Later the university town of Tartu came to use the standard language, but the southern part of the province of Tartu as well as Võro and the surrounding districts still retained the southern dialect. Another edition of *Wastne Testament* from 1857 is similar to the first one, with some modifications. The 1886 edition is also fairly similar. One observation in all of these is the frequent use of *pidama* where obligation does not always appear to be involved, and the construction is used to translate the future in the original Greek (The New Testament in the Original Greek 1926) and *werden* in German (Martin Luther's translation of the New Testament, 1940 edition). Also obvious up to and including 1886 is the often by modern Estonian standards inappropriate use of the partitive case for most objects. This may be due to the fact that in southern Estonian the genitive singular and the nominative plural were written in an identical manner, as the *-t* suffix of the plural had been replaced by a glottal stop, which has only in recent times come to be marked by *-q*. The partitive form was distinct and its use would serve to distinguish singular and plural objects. This predominant use of the partitive case is reflected also in the objects of the infinitive complement of *pidama*. By 1905, which is the last edition of the *Wastne Testament*, there were significant changes in object case. However, *pidama* continued to be used frequently up to and including 1905. The reason for the large number of instances of this construction is discussed in Sect. 3.3.1, as it applies to both dialects of Estonian and also Finnish. A translation of the Gospel of St. Matthew into the southern Seto dialect, which has not been included in the corpus, was published in 1926. In this translation *pidama* is used much less frequently, with only 16 affirmative instances and no negative ones. Without more data it is difficult to know whether this difference is due to the difference in the dialect or the time factor. I suspect the latter.

3.1.1 *Pidama*

In the early texts the semantics of the modal *pidama* covers both obligation and the future tense, which in German is expressed by the use of the auxiliary *werden*. As in modern Estonian, the subject of *pidama* is nominative and the verb agrees with it in person and number. The infinitival complement is the *-ma* infinitive in the illative case, both in active and passive forms. This infinitive takes objects, which are almost all in the partitive case, except for the relative pronoun *mes*∼*mea* 'which', always in the nominative form. This has been omitted from the tables. There are some nouns, whose case could not be determined, which are listed as ambiguous, but which are probably also partitive. One genitive object appears in 1905, at which time there were many more genitive objects generally in the gospel.

Infinitive Complement in the Active Voice Table 2 shows the number of occurrences of the construction with *pidama* with the active *-ma* infinitive.

Apart from *mes* there are no other nominative objects of the infinitive. All the objects in the negative clauses are partitive or ambiguous. The following set of examples (21) illustrates the use of *pidama* throughout this time. In the Greek this clause is obligative, and in German the strongest necessive *müssen* is used.

Table 2 Constructions with *pidama* with an active *-ma* infinitive in southern Estonian

	1686	1857	1886	1905
Total affirmative	43	47	42	42
partitive objects of infinitive	20	21	17	15
genitive objects of infinitive	0	0	0	1
ambiguous objects	2	3	3	3
Total negative	26	25	22	22
intransitive infinitives	11	11	12	15

(21)	a.	SE1686	pahandus	peäb	jo	tullema
	b.	SE1857	pahhandus	peap	jo	tullema
			trouble.**SG.NOM**	must.**3SG**	indeed	come.***ma*INF**
	c.	SE1886	pahhanduse	peawa	jo	tullema
	d.	SE1905	pahanduse	peäwä	jo	tulema
			trouble.**PL.NOM**	must.**3PL**	indeed	come.***ma*INF**

'trouble(s) indeed must come'
(Matt. 18: 7)

Negative clauses with *pidama* in the southern Estonian corpus generally have the meaning 'must not', rather than 'need not' as in modern standard Estonian. An example from 1686 is shown in (22). The following editions are essentially the same with only orthographic changes.

(22)	SE1686	sinnä	ei	peä	mitte	tapma
		2SG.**NOM**	NEG	must.CONNEG	NEG	kill.***ma*INF**

'you must not kill'
(Matt. 5: 21)

Infinitive Complement in the Passive Voice In addition to the usual *-ma* infinitive in the active voice, there is also a form in the passive voice (*-tama*), also illative, which occurs as the complement of *pidama*. In discussing the passive, I am referring to the logical object (patient) of the infinitive as the undergoer, because in different passive constructions it can be either an object or a subject. For a more detailed discussion of this question, see Lees (2006: 3).

The verb *pidama* is in the 3rd person singular form and does not agree with the undergoer in the impersonal passive clauses (23c and 23d). The passive voice is expressed by the infinitive.

The compound passives are constructed with either *saama* 'become' or *olema* 'be', which become the infinitive complements of *pidama*, and the passive past participle, which is in the translative case with *saama* and the nominative case with *olema*. In the personal passive (which can also be thought of as a copula clause) the undergoer of the participle is the subject and the verb agrees (23a and 23b). If the undergoer of a compound passive form is partitive, the construction is a compound tense impersonal clause, and not a personal passive (Lees 2006: 10). Table 3

Table 3 Passive *-ma* infinitive constructions in affirmative clauses in southern Estonian

Passive infinitive	1686	1857	1886	1905
Total (excluding compound forms)	3	3	7	7
undergoer partitive	2	2	5	5
undergoer nominative	0	0	1	1
undergoer ambiguous	1	1	1	1
Compound passive with *saama* + **PPP** trans	2	3	1	1
Compound passive with *olema* + **PPP** nom	4	4	0	0

shows the number of constructions with the passive infinitive found in the southern Estonian corpus.

The case of the undergoer in passive clauses is mainly partitive, but some nominative ones occur. A set of examples follows, which shows the same clause with *saama* as the infinitive complement of *pidama* in (23a and 23b) and the passive infinitive in (23c and 23d).

(23) a. SE1686 nemmä peäwa sahma röhmustetus
b. SE1857 nemma peawa sama römustetus
3PL.NOM must.**3PL** become.***ma*INF** gladden.**PPP.TRA**
'they must become gladdened'

c. SE1886 neid peap rõmustetama
d. SE1905 neid peäb rõõmustetama
3PL.PAR must.**3SG** gladden.**PASS.*ma*INF**
'they must be gladdened'
(Matt. 5: 4)

In the above examples the first two have a nominative undergoer with agreement of the verb, so here the undergoer behaves as a subject. Hence these clauses fit into the personal passive category. The last two clauses have a partitive undergoer with no agreement of the verb and are truly impersonal.

All undergoers of the compound passive forms in the corpus are nominative. In the more recent editions, the compound forms are becoming uncommon, but overall there have only been minor changes over the period studied. There were no negative examples.

3.1.2 Other Expressions

The negative of *tohtima*, which in modern standard Estonian means 'must not/is not allowed', is used once in all four editions with the meaning 'dare not'. For 'must not' only *pidama* is used, which is contrary to modern standard Estonian.

3.2 Northern (Later Standard) Estonian

The first New Testament in northern Estonian was published in 1715, and the complete Bible in 1739, which differ somewhat from each other. The Bible published in 1862 is essentially the same as the 1739 edition, and has not been included in the corpus. The 1903 Bible was published in the southern Estonian town of Tartu in what by then was accepted as the standard language, albeit with some southern influence. In this edition, although much of the language is still old, considerable changes have been made, but not as far as necessive constructions are concerned. There was a further edition in 1914, which differs only slightly from the 1903 one, so it has not been included in the corpus. The New Testament, which was published in exile in 1947, had been revised as part of a plan to issue a revised Bible translation for the 200th anniversary of the first publication of the full Bible in Estonian. World War II and subsequent Soviet occupation put a stop to this plan. There were a couple of Bible editions published in exile, where the New Testament is similar to the 1947 one, so they have been omitted from the study. The first completely new translation of the New Testament, published in 1989 is used for the comparative study here and in Sect. 2.

As in the southern Estonian *Wastne Testament* the most prevalent necessive construction in the older texts involves the use of *pidama*.

3.2.1 *Pidama*

Infinitive Complement in the Active Voice The construction with *pidama* is even more frequent in the northern dialect than in the southern. As in southern Estonian, its semantic scope covers both necessity and future, often with overlap of these meanings. Throughout all this period *pidama* is a personal verb, agreeing in person and number with a nominative subject, which is mostly an agent. However, there are a number of existential or copula clauses, and clauses with an intransitive infinitive, where the subject is non-agentive. Such a clause has been shown in example set (21) in southern Estonian. The corresponding clauses in northern Estonian are similar. Those clauses mostly refer to something which must or will certainly occur in the future. The complement of *pidama* is again the illative case of the *-ma* infinitive. The infinitive may have an object, the case of which varies across the years. Table 4 shows the frequency of occurrence throughout a series of editions.

In addition to the objects listed there were some which were ambiguous for case, non-inflected, or clausal, and have not been listed in the table. Partitive objects predominate. The nominative objects were all plural from 1739 onwards, with the genitive ones being singular. In the 1715 translation there were two singular nominative objects, one of which is shown below.

(24)	E1715	sinna	pead	temmale	Nimmi	pannema	Jesus
		2SG.NOM	must.**2SG**	3SG.ALL	name.**SG.NOM**	put.***ma*INF**	**J.NOM**
		'you must give him the name of Jesus'					
		(Matt. 1: 21)					

Table 4 Constructions with *pidama* with an active *-ma* infinitive in northern Estonian

	1715	1739	1903	1947	1989
Total affirmative	142	147	140	24	27
intransitive infinitive	77	80	78	18	21
partitive object of infinitive	41	36	25	4	4
genitive object of infinitive	6	7	13	0	0
nominative object of infinitive	6	4	4	1	0
Total negative	33	34	36	0	0
intransitive infinitive	20	20	19	–	–

The use of *pidama* has declined sharply by 1947. In some of the expressions *pidama* has been replaced by *saama*, denoting future action, without obligation. In other cases a plain present tense is used, implied future being evident from the context. Some examples showing the shift away from *pidama* are shown in (25) and (26), the first to a simple present tense, which also covers the future, and the second to an imperative. These are the most common changes that took place between 1903 and 1947, shown in the corpus. In other literature these changes occurred even earlier.

(25) a. E1903 seesama peab teid ristima
the.same.**NOM** **must.3SG** 2PL.PAR baptize.***ma*INF**
'he (lit. the same person) must baptize you'

b. E1947 tema ristib teid
3SG.**NOM** baptize.**3SG.PRES** 2PL.PAR
'he will baptize you (with the Holy Spirit and fire)'
(Matt. 3: 11)

The above clause is in the future tense both in German and Greek.

(26) a. E1903 sina pead oma ligimest armastama
2SG.NOM **must.2SG** own.GEN neighbour.SG.PAR love.***ma*INF**
'you must love your neighbour'

b. E1947 armasta oma ligimest
love.2SG.**IMP** own.GEN neighbour.SG.PAR
'love your neighbour'
(Matt. 5: 43)

This clause also has the future in Greek, while in German *sollen* 'should' is used.

There are a number of negative clauses with *pidama* shown in Table 4 above. Many of these have a future implication rather than a necessive one, but there are also quite a number of necessive ones. In old Estonian the negative *pidama* is used for 'must not' (27).

Table 5 *pidama* with a passive infinitival complement in affirmative clauses in the northern (standard) Estonian corpus

	1715	1739	1903	1947	1989
Total (excluding compound forms)	37	44	42	4	1
partitive undergoer	21	30	26	2	0
nominative undergoer	8	3	6	1	1
ambiguous undergoer	2	3	2	1	0
null undergoer	6	8	8	0	0
Compound passive + *saama* + PPP	3	1	1	0	0
Compound passive + *olema* + PPP	4	4	4	0	0

(27) E1739

se	ei	pea	ommast	palgast	mitte
that.SG.**NOM**	NEG	must.CONNEG	own.ELA	wage.SG.ELA	NEG.

ilma	jäma
without	remain.***ma*INF**

'he (lit. 'that person') will not remain without his wage' (Matt. 10: 42)

Here the event is in the future, as the use of the *werden* in the corresponding German indicates, but there is also a sense of inevitability, which is also found in many of the affirmative clauses. In the Greek the aorist subjunctive is used, with the meaning 'should not remain'.

Infinitive Complement in the Passive Voice As in southern Estonian, in the older northern Estonian Bible editions, there are a number of clauses with a passive *-ma* infinitive (*-tama*) as the complement of *pidama*. The constructions are the same as for southern Estonian, discussed above. In the 1947 New Testament there are only a few passive infinitives left, most having been replaced by other constructions. If *pidama* is retained, then a null subject 3rd person singular form of *pidama* is combined with an active *-ma* infinitive complement. The construction with the passive infinitive is much more common in the northern Estonian corpus than in the southern one (Table 5).

In northern Estonian the passive past participles are not in the translative case with *saama* as in the southern dialect. A set of examples of the use of the passive *-ma* infinitive follows. In the Greek this clause is expressed by the future indicative passive. In German *sollen* is used, indicating some degree of obligation.

(28)

a.	E1715	tedda	peab	Naatsareuks	kutsutama
		3SG.PAR	must/will.**3SG**	Nazarene.TRA	call.**PASS.*ma*INF**
b.	E1739	tedda	peab	Naatsareusseks	hütama
		3SG.PAR	must/will.**3SG**	Nazarene.TRA	call.**PASS.*ma*INF**
c.	E1947	teda	peab	hüütama	*Naatsaretlaseks*
		3SG.PAR	must.**3SG**	call.**PASS.*ma*INF**	Nazarene.TRA

'he must/will be called a Nazarene'

d. E1989 Teda hüütakse Naatsaretlaseks
3SG.PAR call.**PASS.PRES** Nazarene.TRA
'He will be called a Nazarene'
(Matt. 2: 23)

The change from the passive *-ma* infinitive to the present tense passive (impersonal) without *pidama* is the most common way to avoid the passive infinitive. Here it occurs after 1947, but many have already changed by 1947. The passive infinitive is still occasionally used even today with *peab*, as in one instance in the 1989 New Testament.

In the corpus there were four negative clauses with the passive infinitive in each of the editions up to and including 1903.

3.2.2 Other Expressions

Other necessive expressions are uncommon in the early editions in the corpus. The verb *tulla* as a necessive occurs only once in 1715–1903, and four times in 1947 and 1989. Penjam (2006: 169) in an extensive study of the modal function of *tulema* in a corpus of old written Estonian ranging from 1600 to 1859 found 114 instances. The earliest examples in her corpus were from the last decade of the 17th century.

3.3 Finnish

The first Finnish New Testament, published in 1548, was translated by Mikael Agricola, who was Finnish-born near Helsinki and received his basic education in Viipuri, which was then in Eastern Finland, and his higher education in Germany. He went on to become the bishop of Turku in Western Finland. He was thus exposed to several Finnish dialects and would have been fluent in Swedish also. In 1642 the full Bible was published in Finnish, with a number of differences from Agricola's translation. In both the 1548 and the 1642 translations long vowels are often not clearly indicated, which makes it difficult to be certain of the case, especially of nouns which have a possessive suffix, where even in the modern language the singular and plural nominative as well as the singular genitive are identical. The final vowel of the possessive suffix is often omitted in the oldest texts. Where the partitive should have the suffix *-A*, it is frequently absent, making it homonymous with the nominative. This has also been pointed out by Magoun (1967: 31). The 1880 text is practically the same as that from 1642, but the orthography is more precise and geminate vowels are always shown, so the partitive especially is more easily distinguishable. Although this gives a clue to the case of the earlier texts, it is not always the same, and I have called the earlier ones ambiguous if the case is not clearly evident. The 1548 New Testament does not have the verses numbered. I have assigned them the same numbers as in the other translations.

In the earliest texts the genitive case is often used for the indirect object, which in many languages is in the dative case.[2] Indeed, the genitive subject case is sometimes also called the dative-genitive.

In the second half of the 19th century the Finnish language was standardized. While the 1880 Bible did not yet incorporate these changes, they are evident in the 1906 New Testament, as is shown in the results of the present study. In the corpus until 1906 the *pitää* construction has been used almost exclusively and excessively, as in Estonian. In the 1906 edition there is a variety of necessive expressions, and *pitää* has almost disappeared.

3.3.1 *Pitää*

As in modern Finnish, the person obliged is mostly in the genitive case, but there are also quite a number of nominative subjects. In the earlier texts the *-ma* infinitive occurs in both the active and passive voice. It has a suffix *-mAn*, which is identical with the illative form in the earliest texts in the corpus, but by 1880, where double vowels are shown, it is evident that the case of the infinitive complement of *pitää* is different, with a single vowel, while the illative case of the *-ma* infinitive has the suffix *-mAAn*. Häkkinen (1994: 313) states that the *-mAn* used by Agricola is instructive, and that the illative is *-mAhAn*, although in the 1548 New Testament it is contracted to *-mAn*. After 1880 there are no more examples of *pitää* with a passive *-(t)tAmAn* infinitive. By 1906 the *-ta* infinitive is beginning to take over from the *-ma* infinitive.

Infinitive Complement in the Active Voice The progressive changes in the use of *pitää* in affirmative clauses with the infinitive in the active voice are shown in Table 6.

It can be seen that the total number of clauses including the verb *pitää* with a necessive or related meaning was especially high in the 1548 translation, with a decrease in 1642 and a marked decrease after 1880. Although most of the subjects are in the genitive case, there are also quite a number in the nominative. These fall into several groups. Plural nouns, even when agentive, are nominative, but the verb does not agree, as shown below.

(29)	a.	F1548	että	**Jnhimiset**	pite	teiden	tekemen
			that	people.**PL.NOM**	must.**3SG**	2PL.GEN	do.***ma*INF**
	b.	F1880	että	**ihmiset**	pitää	teille	tekemän
			that	people.**PL.NOM**	must.**3SG**	2PL.ALL	do.***ma*INF**

'(what you want) that people should do to you'
(Matt. 7: 12)

---

[2]Of the Finnic languages only Livonian has a morphologically distinct dative case.

Table 6 Study of *pitää* with an active complement in affirmative clauses in the Finnish corpus

	1548	1642	1880	1906	1992
Total	103	76	77	4	10
genitive subject	77	53	52	3	10
nominative subject	17	15	16	1	0
ambiguous subject	2	2	2	0	0
null subject	7	6	7	0	0
Infinitive complement	*-mAn*	*-mAn*	*-mAn*	*-mAn/-tA*	*-tA*
genitive object	22	14	11	0	0
nominative object	4 (pl)	1 (pl)	1 (pl)	1 (sg)	1 (sg)
partitive object	12	10	11	0	5
ambiguous object	5	1	0	1	1

In (29a) there is an example of the genitive *teiden* used in a dative function in 1548. In contradistinction to plural nouns, plural personal pronouns as subjects of *pitää* ~ *pite* are in the genitive case (30).

(30) F1548 mite **teiden** pite puhuman
what.PAR **2PL.GEN** must.**3SG** say.***ma*INF**
'what you have to say'
(Matt. 10: 19)

The other group in the corpus which has nominative subjects consists of existential and copula clauses, with the infinitive *oleman* (31), as well as others with intransitive infinitive complements.

(31) F1548 sielle pite oleman idku ia hambain
there must.**3SG** be.***ma*INF** crying.**NOM** and tooth.PL.GEN
kiristus
gnashing.**NOM**
'there will be crying and gnashing of teeth'
(Matt. 13: 42)

Laitinen (1993: 154) points out that in necessive constructions only existential clauses in modern written Finnish have a nominative subject. In dialects and in the spoken language nominative subjects are also found in other intransitive situations. However, personal pronoun subjects are always genitive (Laitinen 1993: 161). Laitinen (1997: 117) mentions that in her dialect corpus 95 % of genitive subjects in necessive clauses are human or at least animate, while 75 % of nominative subjects in intransitive clauses are inanimate. The nominative is sometimes used in evidential contexts (Laitinen 1997: 116), and also where the experiencer is not agentive and has no control over the situation (Laitinen 1993: 154), but this does not apply in my example (29), where the subject is both human and in control. There are examples in the present corpus, where an animate subject is non-volitional, but is still in the genitive case (32).

(32)	F1548	cussa	Christusen	syndymen	piti
		where	Christ.**GEN**	be.born.***ma*****INF**	must.**3SG**.PST

'where Christ had to be born'
(Matt. 2: 4)

Here the German New Testament has *sollen* 'should, ought' and the 1992 Finnish Bible uses the construction with *määrä* for this clause, indicating obligation rather than just future. However, the 1906 New Testament has the *on -va* construction, with only a future meaning. The Greek uses the present subjunctive, with no suggestion of obligation.

In Agricola's time (and up to and including 1880 in the present corpus) all accusative personal pronouns, both singular and plural, were in the genitive form, as were singular total noun objects, while total plural noun objects were nominative. In the corpus the same case combination is also seen in the subjects of *pitää*, at least in intransitive clauses. This resemblance to accusative case-marking has also been pointed out by deSmit (2006: 117) in his study of old Finnish legal texts. He discusses the question of the case of the agent and patient and the possible reasons for this similarity.

In the 1906 translation there is a dramatic change, which presumably started in the general language earlier, but was slower to appear in Bible editions. There are now very few expressions with *pitää* and other ways of expressing obligation have become predominant. It is also evident that the construction with *pitää* is changing. One example in 1906 still has the *-mAn* infinitive complement in the instructive case, whereas the other three have the *-ta* infinitive. The example with *-mAn* is shown in (33).

(33)	F1906	jokaisesta turhasta sanasta ...	pitää	heidän	**tekemän**
		of every unnecessary word ...	must.3SG	3PL.GEN	make.***ma*****INF**
		tili	tuomiopäivänä		
		account.**SG.NOM**	judgment.day.ESS		

'they must account for every unnecessary word (which they utter) on the day of judgment'
(Matt. 12: 36)

The object of *tekemän* is nominative, as in modern necessive constructions (VISK 2008: §934), while the genitive is common for singular objects in the earlier editions. This is shown in the abbreviated example (34) from the same clause as (33). The nominative singular object is also found in the very limited data from the 1992 translation.

(34)	F1880	...pitää	heidän	**luwun**	tekemän
		must.3.SG	3PL.GEN	account.**SG.GEN**	make.*ma*INF

'they must give account'
(Matt. 12: 36)

Negative clauses involving *pitää* also have the meaning of obligation (35).

[3]In the 1548 New Testament a macron over a vowel indicates that a nasal consonant needs to be inserted after the vowel. I have inserted the consonant everywhere: *tappamā* > *tappaman*.

Table 7 Negative clauses with *pitää* constructions in the Finnish corpus

	1548	1642	1880	1906	1992
Total	22	19	22	1	3
genitive subject	13	14	20	1	3
nominative subject	7	4	1	0	0
null subject	2	1	1	0	0

(35) F1548 ei sinun pide tappaman[3]
NEG.3SG 2SG.GEN must.CONNEG kill.*ma*INF
'you must not kill'
(Matt. 5: 21)

Table 7 shows the frequency of *pitää* in negative clauses, again markedly greater in the earlier editions.

All the nominative subjects are non-agentive and often inanimate. Those clauses are generally semantically future, with a sense of inevitability. The objects of the infinitives are partitive in negative clauses, as in modern Finnish.

Infinitive Complement in the Passive Voice The passive *-ma* infinitive complement (*-(t)tAmAn*) of *pitää* is also in the instructive case. It is found only in the earlier Bible editions up to 1880, with none evident in 1906 and 1992. Table 8 shows the results from the Finnish corpus in affirmative clauses. Also in the table are included the few instances of the compound passive, with the construction '*pitää oleman* + passive past participle'.

As in Sect. 3.1.1 on Estonian, in discussing the passive, I am referring to the logical object (patient) of the infinitive as the undergoer, because in different passive constructions it is either the object or the subject.

The number of clauses with the passive *-ma* infinitive is greater in 1548 than in the next two editions. Roughly half have no undergoers, but in those that do, nominative undergoers predominate, with the genitive ones being prominent only in 1548. The genitive undergoers are all pronouns, five of them personal pronouns and the others *sen* 'it, this, that'. This may be a result of analogy with the genitive pronoun subjects in clauses with an active infinitive, suggesting that the undergoer is seen as the subject of *pitää*, as the undergoer of a passive verb is otherwise never genitive in Finnish. However, although partitive undergoers are few, they show that there is some case alternation, which is a feature of objects. The genitive undergoers, except for one 2nd personal pronoun, disappear by 1642, with six of the clauses being converted to a simple passive (impersonal) without *pitää*, and one having the genitive undergoer changed to nominative. Thus there is a trend towards the modern argument structure of the unipersonal passive, with the undergoer alternating between nominative and partitive, and being considered an object by most linguists.

Example (36) shows the change from the passive infinitive in 1548 to the simple passive (impersonal) construction without *pitää* in 1906. In this example *werden* is used in German, so the obligatory sense is not there originally. In Greek also the future tense is used, with no sense of obligation.

Table 8 *Pitää* with passive infinitive complement and compound passive in the Finnish corpus

	1548	1642	1880
Total (excluding compound forms)	33	21	16
nominative undergoer	13	12	11
genitive undergoer	7	1	0
partitive undergoer	1	3	2
ambiguous undergoer	6	2	1
null undergoer	6	3	2
Compound passive	*oleman* + PPP	*oleman* + PPP	*oleman* + PPP
nominative undergoer	4	4	2
genitive undergoer	0	0	2

(36) a. F1548 Jumalan waldakunda pite teilde
god.GEN kingdom.**NOM** must.**3SG** 2PL.ABL
pois-otettaman
away-take.**PASS*ma*INF**
'the kingdom of God must/will be taken away from you'

b. F1906 Jumalan valtakunta otetaan teiltä pois
god.GEN kingdom.**NOM** take.**PASS.PRES** 2PL.ABL away
'the kingdom of God will be taken away from you'
(Matt. 21: 43)

Another conversion has been used in (37), which can indicate obligation, although in this example a future tense translation seems more appropriate. Again *werden* is found in German and the passive future in the Greek.

(37) a. F1548 se pite cutzuttaman swrexi
that.**NOM** must.**3SG** call.**PASS.*ma*INF** great.TRA
'he must/will be called great'

b. F1906 hän on sanottava suureksi
3SG.NOM be.3SG say.PASS.PRES.PTCP great.TRA
'he must/will be said to be great (in the kingdom of heaven)'
(Matt. 5: 19)

In many instances the *pitää* construction in older texts is replaced in more recent editions by the *on -va* construction, which indicates the future without any necessive overtones. This is mostly the case with those expressions which in Greek have the future tense without any sense of obligation, although in some instances there is an implication that the event will certainly come to pass.

The few passive compound constructions with *oleman* mostly have a nominative undergoer, except for two instances in 1880, where they are genitive, together with a genitive passive past participle (38). Here *sen* is the undergoer (patient, logical object) of *oleman päästetyn*, and at the same time the subject of *pitää*. The passive past participle agrees with the subject in number and case. The nominative undergoers listed in the compound passive section of Table 8 are either *caicki* ~ *kaikki* 'all' or *ne* 'they (inanimate), those', plural of *se*. There is no agreement of *pitää* with the plural nominative undergoer.

(38) F1880 ja mitä sinä päästät maan päällä,
and what.PAR 2SG.NOM free.2SG earth.GEN on
sen pitää oleman päästetyn taiwaissa
it.**GEN** must.3SG be.***ma*INF** free.**PPP.GEN** heaven.PL.INE
'and what you free on earth, shall be free in heaven'
(Matt. 16: 19)

Negative clauses with a passive *-ma* infinitive are few, with the same two in each edition from 1548 to 1880, and none after that. In the 1548 both have nominative undergoers, while in the other two there is one partitive and one nominative. Semantically both clauses imply the future, but with a sense that these events are predestined to happen.

Comparison of Finnish and Estonian Use of *pidama/pitää* There are some similarities and differences between Estonian and Finnish in their use of *pidama/pitää*. In the early texts in both languages this construction is used extremely frequently. Comparing the Finnic with the original Greek (The New Testament in the Original Greek 1926), negative clauses in Greek usually have the negative imperative, and such are found in the later Finnic texts also. In affirmative clauses in many instances the Greek has the future tense, with or without a suggestion of obligation. As Finnic languages do not have a morphologically distinct future tense, foreign influences come into the picture. Early written Estonian was heavily influenced by German, as it was the common language of education, and many of the Bible translators were clerics of German origin. Martin Luther's translation of the New Testament from 1522 was available to them, and its use of *werden* 'will' to translate the Greek future would have influenced the Estonian translators to use *saama* or *pidama*, the latter especially where *sollen* 'should, ought' was used in the German. Comparing the Estonian New Testament from 1715 with Martin Luther's translation in a 1940 edition, almost every instance of *pidama* in Estonian has *werden* or *sollen* in German. The stronger necessive verb *müssen* 'must' is less frequently used in the German New Testament. Comparing Martin Luther's translation with the original Greek, it is apparent that Luther often uses *sollen*, where the original Greek has the future tense.

Habicht (2001: 170, 172) in a study of modal expressions in the 17th century Estonian texts by Stahl and Müller reports numerous examples of *pidama*, used to translate *werden* and *sollen*. Habicht (2001: 169) mentions the finding of examples, where *pidama* is used to refer to some event which was predestined to happen in the future. Such are plentiful also in the present corpus, such as the Finnish examples (36)–(38).

Agricola, with his German theological education, may also have been influenced by German in his use of *pitää*, and possibly also by the Swedish *skall* 'shall', which has a meaning of obligation. The first complete Swedish New Testament translation was published in 1526, and was presumably available to Agricola.

The frequency of the construction with *pitää* decreases sharply in Finnish by 1906, but *pidama* is still frequent in the 1905 New Testament in southern Estonian and the 1914 Bible in standard Estonian. The decrease there is first evident in the 1947 New Testament. However, the 1926 southern Estonian Seto dialect translation of the Gospel of St. Matthew has few examples of *pidama*, suggesting that its use is declining earlier. The use of the passive *-ma* infinitive has disappeared from Finnish by 1906, and in Estonian there is only one example in the 1989 New Testament. It is still a possible construction in modern Estonian (Viitso 2007: 64), although not common.

The actual constructions with *pitää/pidama* are different in the two languages, as pointed out in Sect 2.1. The Estonian construction has remained essentially the same throughout the time under study, that is personal with a nominative subject and with the illative *-ma* infinitive complement. Müller always uses the *-ma* infinitive, while Stahl has a combination of *-ma* and *-ta* infinitives, which seem to be in free variation (Habicht 2001: 170). Habicht does not mention passive forms of the infinitives. In Finnish the subject has been mainly genitive, but with a number of nominative ones up to and including 1880. In the corpus there are no nominative subjects of *pitää* after that, although they do exist in existential clauses in the modern written language (Laitinen 1993: 154). The infinitive complement changed from the instructive *-man* to *-ta* around 1906.

The singular total objects of the active infinitive complement of *pitää* are genitive in Finnish up to and including 1880, with all the nominative ones being plural. In modern Finnish singular total objects are nominative rather than genitive. In both southern and northern Estonian the earlier editions have mainly partitive objects. In modern Estonian the form of the object is genitive for the singular total object rather than nominative as in Finnish.

Estonian and Finnish both also have passive *-ma* infinitive complements, the Estonian in the illative and the Finnish in the instructive case. In Estonian these are still used, although infrequently, while in Finnish they are no longer found.

Both (Laitinen 1997: 119–120) and deSmit (2006: 128) postulate the Finnish necessive expression with *pitää* developing from a personal construction. In Estonian the personal construction has remained, perhaps due to German influence, although it can be used without a subject.

3.3.2 Other Necessive Expressions in Finnish

Tulee, täytyy, on määrä, on pakko The use of *tulee* as a necessive appears already in the 1548 edition, and the same single clause is repeated in all the others, except 1992, where *pitää* is used. The subject is genitive and the complement is the *-ta* infinitive. In example (39) the object *rahan(i)*[4] has a possessive suffix, so it

[4]The final vowel of the possessive suffix is often omitted in the 1548 New Testament.

could be either nominative or genitive, but according to modern usage, it should be nominative.

(39) F1548

sinun	sijs	olis	tullut	wlgosanda
2SG.GEN	then	be.**3SG**.COND	must.PST.PTCP	out.give.***ta*****INF**

minun	rahan	Cauppalaisten
1SG.GEN	money.NOM/GEN.3PX	trader.PL.GEN

'then you should have handed my money to the traders'
(Matt. 25: 27)

Here *Cauppalaisten* is an example of the genitive of a plural noun used in a dative function.

The verb *täytyy* is first seen in the 1906 edition. Like *tulee* it has a genitive subject, and takes the *-ta* infinitive. There are no examples of *on määrä* in the older editions or of *on pakko* in any part of the corpus.

Passive Present Participle *-(t)tAvA* The passive present participle with the suffix *-(t)tAvA*, together with *on* is one of the most commonly used necessive expressions from 1906 on, but not found at all before that. Although syntactically passive, it is semantically active. The person obliged is in the genitive case. There are 22 instances of this construction in 1906. The undergoer is nominative (14 instances) or partitive (4 instances). In 1992 there are 14 examples, some of which are shown in Sect. 2.4 examples (18) and (19).

Fourth Infinitive The fourth infinitive occurs for the first time in 1906 where there are five examples. One is shown in (40). They all have genitive subjects and four have partitive objects. One is intransitive. In 1992 there are no examples.

(40) F1906

vai	toista-ko	meidän	on	odottaminen?
or	other.PAR-Q	**1PL.GEN**	be.**3SG**	wait.**4INF**

'or do we have to wait for someone else?'
(Matt. 11: 3)

3.4 Karelian

In Karelian there are three translations of the Gospel of St. Matthew from different time periods and different dialects. In 1820 a translation was made into the Tver dialect, based on the Slavonic Bible. The translation was originally written in Cyrillic script, but was transliterated into Latin script by August Ahlqvist and published in 1865. The second translation was into southern Karelian in 1864. The third one is in the New Testament published in 2003 in the Olonets (Livvi) dialect, which some regard as a separate language. The first two are similar in many respects.

3.4.1 *Piteä*

As in the 2003 New Testament *piteä* is one of the necessive constructions in the other translations. The verb *piteä* is in the 3rd person singular form and its complement is the *-ta* infinitive in all three translations. In the older versions the adessive and allative cases have the same suffix *-la*, while in 2003 the two cases differ, the adessive being used for 'must' and the allative for 'need'. The number of instances of the *piteä* meaning 'must' in affirmative clauses is 10 each for the first two and 34 for 2003. There is one obligative negative clause in each of the early texts and three in 2003. The objects of the infinitives are either partitive or nominative in 1820 and 2003, but in 1864 there is a genitive singular object (41), which in the other two translations is nominative.

(41)	K1864	nīn	pidi	šiula	andua	miun
		then	must.**3SG.PST**	2SG.ADE/ALL	give.***ta*INF**	1SG.GEN
		hobien	kaupitšijilä			
		money.**SG.GEN**	merchant.PL.ALL			

'then you should have given my money to the merchants'
(Matt. 25: 27)

The verb *piteä* is also used in the sense of 'need' in all three translations, with a direct object or with a *-ta* infinitive complement. In the earlier texts the allative/adessive case is used throughout for the subject, while in 2003, the adessive is used for 'must' and the allative for 'need', both in affirmative and negative clauses.

3.4.2 *On -ta* Construction

The other construction which occurs in the two earlier translations consists of *on* + *-ta* infinitive. These are very variable in that the only constant is the infinitive, which can occur on its own, with various other components, the structure being (subject) + (*on*) + *-ta*INF + (object). Any or all of the components in brackets can be omitted. The subject is in the allative/adessive case, there is no verb agreement, the object of the infinitive can be nominative or partitive. In 2003 they are all expressed by means of *piteä*. There are 6 such constructions, which are the same in 1820 and 1864. Some examples follow.

(42)	a.	K1864	mi	miula	luadie	Jīsusala?		
			what.NOM	**1SG.ALL**	do.***ta*INF**	Jesus.ALL		

'what should I do to Jesus?'

b.	K2003	midä	sit	minul	**pidäu**	luadie	Iisusale?
		what.PAR	then	**1SG.ADE**	**must.3SG**	do.***ta*INF**	Jesus.ALL

'what then must I do to Jesus?'
(Matt. 27: 22)

(43) K1820 viiko go tirpua teidä?
long Q suffer.*ta*INF 2PL.PAR
'How long must I put up with you?'
(Matt. 17: 17)

It appears as if the necessive verb has just been omitted, as has the verb *on* 'be' in (43). Similar constructions occur also in older Livonian (see Sect. 3.5). Such constructions are found in modern Estonian with a slight sense of obligation, but none are present in the corpus. The construction with the fourth infinitive in old Finnish and Livonian also bears some similarity.

The finding of fewer expressions with *piteä* in the 19th century translations of Karelian than in the Estonian and Finnish from the same time period relates to the fact that the translation was based on the Slavonic translation rather than that of Luther.

3.5 Livonian

In Livonian there are two translations from 1863 of the Gospel of St. Matthew in different dialects, eastern and western, as well as the New Testament from 1942. The earlier translations were mostly the work of one native speaker, or several from one family, with the help of the linguist F. J. Wiedemann. They show considerable Latvian influence, especially in the use of Latvian aspectual verb prefixes. The 1942 translation was from the original Greek by the native speaker Kaarli Stalte with the help of Lauri Kettunen and others. Stalte also used translations in German, Latvian, Estonian and Finnish to guide him.

In both of the 1863 translations there are two kinds of necessive constructions, as well as a couple of examples of *piddõ*. One construction uses the fourth infinitive in the same way as that in the 1942 translation (Sect. 2.5), but this infinitive has the more typical partitive suffix of *-mist* rather than the *-mõst* of 1942. The other main construction consists of the third person singular potential form *līb* of 'be' and the *-ta* infinitive. This is similar to the construction with *tuleb/tulee* in Estonian and Finnish respectively, as *līb* is also used as the future of 'be'. The objects of the infinitive are partitive or accusative (homonymous forms of nominative and genitive). This construction does not occur in the 1942 translation. In both necessive constructions the person obliged is in the dative case. However, in a number of instances with pronouns, the shorter genitive case is used instead. I have not differentiated between those with genitive and dative case, as semantically they seem to be identical. The genitive form is often also used elsewhere, where the function is obviously dative. Example (44) shows two pronouns in the genitive form in different dative functions.

(44) LW1863 **sin** līb **min** kīt
2SG.GEN/DAT be.3SG.POT **1SG.GEN/DAT** say.*ta*INF
'you must tell me'
(Matt. 26: 63)

There are also occasional clauses with *pidi* (past tense of 'must') in different forms, which are difficult to analyze due to the paucity of examples. They do not all entail obligation. The subject varies in case, and the infinitive complement is the *-ma* infinitive. This does not appear to be a regular construction in Livonian, and may have been influenced by other Bible translations. One example is shown in Sect. 2.1 (11). Some other examples follow (45, 46).[5]

(45)	LE1863	seda	tädõn	pidīks	tiemõ
		this.PAR	**2PL.DAT**	must.PST.COND	do.***ma*INF**

'this you should do'
(Matt. 23: 23)

(46)	LW1863	pidīks	se	Dāvid	púoga	vuolm?
		must.PST.COND	this.**NOM**	David.GEN	son.**NOM**	be.***ma*INF**

'could this be David's son?'
(Matt. 12: 23)

The clause in (46) is basically a copula clause with a nominative subject and copula complement. In this clause the subject *se* does not have any volitional control, and the sense of obligation is lacking. This kind of clause is found in the old Estonian and Finnish texts also. In clauses where the person obliged is dative, the copula complement is also in the dative case, showing agreement with the quirky subject (47).

(47)	LW1863	tädõn	līb	tävdnigõdõn	vuolda
		2PL.DAT	be.**3SG**.POT	perfect.**PL.DAT**	be.***ta*INF**

'you must be perfect'
(Matt. 5: 48)

There are a few instances with a compound tense, with the verb 'be' together with the passive past participle as the infinitive complement of *līb* (48). The passive past participle here agrees with the dative subject.

(48)	LE1863	sien	līb	touvõs	ka	sittõdõn	volda
		it.**GEN/DAT**	be.3SG.POT	heaven.INE	also	bind.**PPP.DAT**	be.***ta*INF**

'it will also be bound in heaven'
(Matt. 16: 19)

This clause can be compared with the second half of the old Finnish example (38) in Sect. 3.3.1 This example does not have a strong sense of obligation and in the 1942 translation, it lacks the necessive construction, and is rendered just by the perfect tense with a future implication, as in the Greek. However, the German translation uses *sollen*.

Table 9 shows the numbers of the various constructions in Livonian. The number of negative clauses is shown in brackets.

[5]The orthography has been changed from the original 1863 translations to approximate that used in 1942. In 1863 lengthening of a vowel has been indicated by a macron either above or below the letter. The letters *ö*, *ä* and *ü* in 1863 have the diæresis under the letter, and *õ* is represented by *o* with a third dot beneath the diæresis under the letter.

Table 9 Proportion of various necessive constructions in the Livonian corpus (negative in brackets)

	East 1863		West 1863		1942	
DAT + *līb* + *ta*INF	45	(28)	32	(20)	0	
compound tense	12	(1)	8	(1)	0	
DAT + *um/līb* + 4INF	20	(2)	16	(3)	38	(3)
compound tense	1	(0)	0		4	(0)
pidim/pidiks	2	(0)	2	(0)	1	(0)

In the eastern dialect there are more necessive expressions than in the western dialect, and the latest translation has the fewest. It is possible that the earlier ones were more influenced by German, in that there may have been felt to be a need to translate *sollen*. Most of the Livonian necessive constructions have *sollen* in German rather than *werden*. In the earlier translations negative commands use mainly the necessive construction, whereas in the 1942 translation these are expressed as negative imperatives (49).[6]

(49) a. LE1863 sinnõn äb lī rištīŋt tappõ
2SG.DAT **NEG.3SG** be.POT.CONNEG human.SG.PAR kill.***ta*INF**
'you must not kill a person'
(Matt. 19: 18)

b. LW1863 sin äb lī mā tappõ
2SG.GEN/DAT **NEG.3SG** be.POT.CONNEG down kill.***ta*INF**
'you must not kill'
(Matt 19: 18)

c. L1942 ala tapa!
NEG.IMP.2SG kill.IMP.2SG
'don't kill!'
(Matt. 5: 21)

Occasionally an affirmative clause with a necessive construction in 1863 is given as an affirmative imperative in 1942.

As well as the decrease in the use of necessive expressions the type of construction has changed from the predominant use of the *-ta* infinitive to the use of the fourth infinitive in 1942, as shown in example set (50).

(50) a. LW1863 tädõn nei līb pallõ
2PL.DAT so be.**3SG.POT** pray.***ta*INF**
'you must pray like this'

b. L1942 täddõn um ni nei Jumalt pālamõst
2PL.DAT be.**3SG** now so god.PAR pray.**4INF**

[6] The letter *ŋ* used here is represented in 1863 by *n* with a dot above the letter. In 1942 the velarization of *n* has not been shown at all.

'now you must pray to God like this'
(Matt. 6: 9)

There is one example in the western dialect 1863 of a construction with a *-ma* infinitive, where a *-ta* infinitive might be expected (51).

(51)	LW1863	sin	äb	lī	lōlatõkst	ül'
		2SG.GEN/DAT	NEG.**3SG**	be.POT.CONNEG	marriage.PAR	over
		astām				
		step.*ma*INF				
		'you must not commit adultery'				
		(Matt. 5: 27)				

The construction with the fourth infinitive has been discussed in Sect. 2.5 in connection with the 1942 New Testament.

The construction *līb* + *ta* infinitive is similar to that found in the older Karelian texts, shown in example (42a). Habicht (2001: 181–182) mentions a German construction with the verb *haben* 'have' + infinitive, with a nuance of obligation, which she considers to have influenced a similar construction with *olema* + *ta* infinitive in 17th century Estonian (no such examples were found in the present corpus). It is possible that the Livonian construction has also been influenced by German, but that is not likely for Karelian. With the Livonian translations being done mainly by few individuals, it is difficult to know how representative of the spoken language these texts are. As the dialects differ, it is also difficult to know whether to attribute changes in the 1942 New Testament to the time factor or to dialectal or individual differences. Since the last native speaker of Livonian died in 2010, any further study has to concentrate on the written and transliterated oral material available.

4 Summary

Different necessive constructions are used in the different modern languages, with Livonian (1942) and Veps (2006) showing the greatest differences from the others. Estonian (1989), Finnish (1992) and Karelian (2003) use *pidama* and cognate verbs, but only in Estonian is it a personal verb. In the others the person obliged is in a non-nominative case, genitive for Finnish and adessive in Karelian, and the verb is in the 3rd person singular form. The infinitive complement is the illative case of the *-ma* infinitive in Estonian, and in Finnish and Karelian the *-ta* infinitive. In Veps there is the expression (*om*) *tarbiž* '(is) necessary', with an allative subject and *-ta* infinitive complement. Livonian uses a possessive expression *um V-mõst* 'have doing', involving the partitive case of the action nominalization (fourth infinitive), with a dative subject. Finnish has several other necessive expressions, the most frequent in the corpus being *-on (t)tAvA*. In negative clauses in modern Estonian *pidama* only means 'need not', in Finnish it always means 'must not', while in Karelian there is overlap between the concepts of obligation and need, with both affirmative and negative constructions using *piteä* in both senses, but in modern Karelian with an adessive subject for 'must' and allative for 'need'.

In the older Estonian (1686–1903) and Finnish Bible translations (1548–1880) foreign influence is clearly evident in the excessive use of *pidama/pitää*. In the absence of a morphologically distinct future tense in Finnic languages, many of these instances are used to translate the German future auxiliary *werden* (or Swedish *skall*), which in modern editions/translations have given way to either the present tense to indicate the future, or imperatives to show obligation, with a much smaller number actually using a necessive construction. Apart from early translations of the Bible and other religious texts, *pidama* has not been used to indicate the future in Estonian. There is the sense in the Bible that the events which will occur are predestined to occur, and *pidama* contains a hint of that, whereas *saama* 'become' (the alternative translation of *werden*) does not. In modern Estonian the present tense is generally used to express the future, with the context and adverbials disambiguating the tense where necessary.

Comparing the translation by Martin Luther with the original Greek, it is apparent that necessive constructions are significantly fewer in Greek than in German, where *sollen* is often used for a straight future in Greek. It appears that both the early Estonian and Finnish translations relied more heavily on Martin Luther's translation, at least in this respect, than on the original Greek.

Karelian differs in that there are fewer necessive constructions in the older texts, which were based on the Slavonic translation rather than the German or Swedish. Finnish necessive expressions become diverse by the 1906 New Testament. The older Karelian and Livonian translations have a construction with the verb 'be' + the *-ta* infinitive, with the subject in the adessive/allative and dative cases respectively.

5 Corpus

5.1 Modern Bibles and New Testaments

Estonian

Uus Testament ja Psalmid [New Testament and Psalms]. 1989. Tallinn: EELK Konsistoorium.

Finnish

Pyhä Raamattu [Holy Bible]. 1992. Helsinki: Suomen Pipliaseura.

Karelian

Uuzi Sana [New Testament]. 2003. Helsinki: Bible Translation Institute.

Livonian

Už Testament [New Testament]. 1942. Helsinki: Suomalaisen Kirjallisuuden Seura.

Veps

Uz' Zavet [New Testament]. 2006. Helsinki: Bible Translation Institute.

5.2 Older Bibles, New Testaments and Gospels

Southern Estonian

Wastne Testament [New Testament]. 1686. Riga.

Wastne Testament. 1857. Tartu.

Wastne Testament. 1886. Tartu: British and Foreign Bible Society.

Wastne Testament. 1905. Tartu.

Northern (later standard Estonian)

Uus Testament [New Testament]. 1715. Tallinn.

Jummala Sanna [The Word of God]. 1739. Tallinn.

Piibli raamat [Bible]. 1903. Tartu.

Uus Testament 1947. London: British and Foreign Bible Society.

Finnish

Se Wsi Testamentti [New Testament]. 1548. Stockholm.

Biblia [Bible]. 1642. Stockholm.

Biblia. 1880. Berlin: British and Foreign Bible Society.

Uusi Testamentti [New Testament]. 1906. Porvoo: WSOY.

Livonian

Das Evangelium Matthäi in den westlichen Dialect des Livischen [The Gospel of Matthew in the western Livonian dialect]. 1863. London.

Das Evangelium Matthäi in den östlichen Dialect des Livischen [The Gospel of Matthew in the eastern Livonian dialect]. 1863. London.

Karelian

Herrän miän sündüruohtinan Svätoi Jovangeli Matveista [Our Lord's Holy Gospel of Matthew]. 1820 (Transliterated into Latin script by August Ahlqvist). Suomi 1865 (4): 1–113.

Das Evangelium des Matthäus in süd-karelischen Mundart revidiert von F.J. Wiedemann [The Gospel of Matthew in the southern Karelian dialect revised by F.J. Wiedemann]. 1864. London.

5.3 Bible Texts Consulted, But Not Included in the Corpus

Estonian

Jummala Sanna [The Word of God] 1862. Tartu.

Jumala Sõna [The Word of God] 1914. Tallinn.

Southern Estonian, Seto dialect

Evangeelium Pühä Matteusõ kirotõt [The Gospel written by St. Matthew]. 1926. Akadeemilise Emakeele Seltsi toimetised 14. evangeeliumid.

German

Das Neue Testament unsers Herrn und Heilandes Jesu Christi nach der deutschen Übersetzung D. Martin Luthers [The New Testament of our Lord and Saviour Jesus Christ according to the German translation by Dr. Martin Luther]. 1940. Stuttgart: Privileg. Württemb. Bibelanstalt.

Greek

The New Testament in the original Greek. 1926. London: MacMillan & Co.

Acknowledgements I am very grateful to Maria Vilkuna for her review of my paper and the correction of errors concerning Finnish. Any remaining errors are of course my own. My thanks are also due to Jane Simpson, who looked at my paper from a non-Finnic perspective and made helpful suggestions concerning some sections which were not easy to follow. Jussi Ylikoski was of great help in finding the transliteration of the 1820 Karelian Gospel of St. Matthew, and I really appreciate that. I am also grateful to Toomas Pill for help with the original Greek text and to Baiba Liepins, who helped me to understand the Latvian construction.

References

deSmit, Merlijn. 2006. *Language contact and structural change. An old Finnish case study*. Vol. 9 of *Studia Fennica Stockholmiensia. Doktorsavhandling*. Stockholm: Acta Universitatis Stockholmiensis. http://urn.kb.se/resolve?urn=urn:nbn:se:su:diva-1402, accessed 17 Dec 2011.

Erelt, Mati, Reet Kasik, Helle Metslang, Henno Rajandi, Kristiina Ross, Henn Saari, Kaja Tael, and Silvi Vare. 1993. *Eesti keele grammatika II. Süntaks (EKG)*. Tallinn: Eesti Teaduste Akadeemia Keele ja Kirjanduse Instituut.

Habicht, Külli. 2001. *Eesti vanema kirjakeele leksikaalsest ja morfosüntaktilisest arengust ning Heinrich Stahli keele eripärast selle taustal*. Vol. 10 of *Dissertationes philologiae Estonicae Universitatis Tartuensis*. Tartu: Tartu University Press.

Hakulinen, Auli, Maria Vilkuna, Riitta Korhonen, Vesa Koivisto, Tarja Riitta Heinonen, and Irja Alho. 2004. *Iso suomen kielioppi (ISK)*. Vol. 950 of *Suomalaisen Kirjallisuuden Seuran Toimituksia*. Helsinki: Suomalaisen Kirjallisuuden Seura.

Häkkinen, Kaisa. 1994. *Agricolasta nykykieleen: Suomen kirjakielen historia*. Porvoo: Werner Söderström Osakeyhtiö.

Karlsson, Fred. 1999. *Finnish: an essential grammar*. London: Routledge.

Kettunen, Lauri. 1938. *Livisches Wörterbuch mit grammatischer Einleitung*. Vol. 5 of *Lexica Societatis Fenno-Ugricae*. Helsinki: Suomalais-ugrilainen seura.

Laitinen, Lea. 1992. *Välttämättömyys ja persoona. Suomen murteiden nesessiivisten rakenteiden semantiikka ja kielioppia*. Vol. 569 of *Suomalaisen Kirjallisuuden Toimituksia*. Helsinki: Suomalaisen Kirjallisuuden Toimituksia. Quoted by deSmit (2006: 117).

Laitinen, Lea. 1993. Nesessiivirakenne, kielliopillistuminen ja subjektiivisus. *Virittäjä* 97: 149–170.

Laitinen, Lea. 1997. Norms made easy: case marking with modal verbs in Finnish. In *Taming the vernacular*, eds. Jenny Cheshire and Dieter Stein, 110–124. London: Longman.

Lees, Aet. 2006. The undergoer in passive clauses in Estonian and Finnish. In *Selected papers from the 2005 conference of the Australian Linguistic Society*, ed. Keith Allan. Australian Linguistic Society. http://www.als.asn.au, accessed 14 Feb 2011.

Lees, Aet. 2008. The partitive case in existential and copula clauses in Balto-Finnic. In *Selected papers from the 2007 conference of the Australian Linguistic Society*, ed. Timothy J. Curnow. Australian Linguistic Society. http://www.als.asn.au, accessed 14 Feb 2011.

Magoun, F.P. Jr., ed. 1967. *Mikael Agricola's gospel according to St. Mark, with foreword, an outline of the language, glossary and appendix*. Vol. 286 of *Suomalaisen Kirjallisuuden Seuran Toimituksia*. Helsinki: Suomalaisen Kirjallisuuden Seura.

Moseley, Christopher. 2002. *Livonian*. München: Lincom Europa.

Penjam, Pille. 2006. Development of the modal function of the verb *tulema* 'come' in written Estonian. *Linguistica Uralica* XLII: 167–191.

Rosnes, Elena. 2009. Getting more personal: Kven must clauses. In *FinDiaSyn workshop abstracts*, 30. http://www.kotus.fi/files/1300/Abstracts_FinDiaSyn_Workshop_2009.pdf, accessed 8 Jan 2011 via link from Necessive constructions in Google.

Saukkonen, Pauli. 1965. *Itämerensuomalaisten kielten tulosijainfinitiivirakenteiden historiaa. 1. Johdanto: adverbiaali infinitiivi.* Vol. 137 of *Mémoires de la Société Finno-Ougrienne.* Suomalais-ugrilainen Seura. Quoted by Penjam (2006: 176).

Viitso, Tiit-Rein. 2007. Structure of the Estonian language. In *Estonian language*, ed. Mati Erelt, 9–129. Tallinn: Estonian Academy Publishers.

VISK. 2008. Ison suomen kieliopin verkkoversio (ISK on-line). Web site. http://scripta.kotus.fi/visk/etusivu.php, accessed 23 Nov 2010.

Building Swahili Resource Grammars for the Grammatical Framework

Wanjiku Ng'ang'a

Abstract Grammatical Framework (GF) is a multilingual parsing and generation framework. In this paper, we describe the development of the Swahili Resource Grammar, a first in extending GF's coverage with a Bantu language. The paper details the linguistic detail and considerations that have to be addressed whilst defining the grammars. The paper also describes an end-user application that uses the developed grammars to achieve multilinguality.

1 Introduction

Grammatical Framework[1] (GF) (Ranta 2011) is a grammar formalism based on type theory. Its main feature is the separation of abstract and concrete syntaxes, which makes it very suitable for writing multilingual grammars. The abstract part of a grammar defines a set of abstract syntactic structures, called abstract terms or trees, while the concrete part defines a relation between abstract structures and concrete structures. An abstract syntax in GF deals with language-independent tree structures while the language-dependent concrete syntax specifies how these trees are mapped into different languages. A multilingual GF grammar is therefore realised as a combination of an abstract syntax which can be mapped to a number of language-dependent concrete syntaxes, thereby achieving multilingualism.

To implement multilingualism, GF uses a Resource Grammar (RG) library, which is essentially a set of parallel grammars for different languages. The grammar defines, for each language, a complete set of morphological paradigms and a syntax fragment. Currently, the library covers sixteen[2] languages: Bulgarian, Catalan, Danish, Dutch, English, Finnish, French, German, Italian, Norwegian (bokmål), Polish,

[1] My first encounter with GF was in the WebALT project where I was part of Lauri's team that was responsible for developing multilingual grammars for the automatic generation of mathematical content in six European languages. The WebALT project used GF as the multilingual generation framework.

[2] See http://www.grammaticalframework.org for the current status of the GF resource grammar library.

W. Ng'ang'a (✉)
School of Computing and Informatics, University of Nairobi, Nairobi, Kenya

D. Santos et al. (eds.), *Shall We Play the Festschrift Game?*,
DOI 10.1007/978-3-642-30773-7_13,

Romanian, Russian, Spanish, Swedish and Urdu. Grammars for other languages are under development. In line with the modern software engineering practice of defining libraries that can be reused in varied applications, GF's grammar library has proven to be a useful resource for multilingual application developers. GF has been used to build a wide range of multilingual natural language engineering applications such as an authoring and documentation system for the KeY software specification system (Burke and Johannisson 2005), WebALT's mathematical exercise translator (Caprotti and Seppälä 2006), and the TALK project on spoken dialogue systems (Ljunglöf and Larsson 2008).

This paper describes ongoing work in the development of Swahili Resource Grammars for GF, a first in extending GF with a Bantu language. With this extension to GF, it will be possible to build multilingual end-user applications targeting Swahili speakers. Section 2 gives a brief summary of the linguistic features of the Swahili language, while the definition of the language-dependent modules for Swahili morphology in GF is covered in Sect. 3. Section 4 describes a multilingual end-user application that has been developed to support visually-impaired Swahili-speaking mobile phone users using the GF framework, while a summary of the presented work is given in Sect. 5.

2 Swahili

Swahili is a Bantu language belonging to the Niger-Congo family. It is widely spoken within the East African region and has approximately 120 million speakers. It is a highly inflecting language where both prefixed and suffixed morphemes play an important grammatical role. The functions of prefixes are particularly important in both nominal and verbal morphology. In the case of nouns, as is typical with Bantu languages, each noun belongs to a noun class which is signaled by a pair of prefixes attached to the nominal stem, denoting singular and plural forms e.g. *m-sichana* 'girl' and *wa-sichana* 'girls'. In addition, some nouns take an optional locative suffix. For example, *nyumba-ni*, which means 'in the house', is obtained by adding the *-ni* locational suffix to the root *nyumba*. Verbs have an agglutinating structure where a system of affixes is used to mark various grammatical relations, such as subject, object, tense, aspect, and mood. Following is an example of the verb *ninawaimbia* 'I am singing for them' that is obtained by attaching various affixes to the root *imba* 'to sing':

ni-	*na-*	*wa-*	*imb-*	*i-*	*a*
subj	tense	obj	root	appl	final_vowel

Swahili enforces a system of concordial agreement in which nouns must agree with the main verb of the sentence in class, animacy and number. Adjectives, possessive pronouns and demonstratives also agree in class, animacy and number with the noun they modify.

Swahili has a fairly fixed word order (SVO) at the sentence level, where the subject precedes the verb and the object, while within constituent phrases, modifiers succeed the head. Therefore adjectives, pronouns, determiners etc., follow the nouns they modify while adverbs come after the verb. Concrete grammars defined for Swahili should therefore capture these rich morphological and grammatical features of the language, to ensure generation of grammatically correct Swahili sentences.

3 Building Swahili Resource Grammars

3.1 GF Resource Grammar Library

The GF resource grammar library comprises of two layers: the user Application Program Interface (API) and the core grammar (Ranta 2011). The user API for every language X[3] consists of three modules: *Syntax*, which gives high-level access to the core syntax, *Paradigms*, which gives the inflection paradigms used for building a lexicon and *Extra*, which gives access to extensions of the core syntax. The core grammar consists of various modules: *Structural*, *Adjective*, *Adverb*, *Numeral*, *Sentence*, *Question*, *Relative*, *Conjunction*, *Phrase*, *Text*, *Idiom*, *Noun* and *Verb*. GF also comprises auxiliary modules *Res(ource)* and *Morpho(logy)* that define language-specific parameter types and morphological requirements.

Building RGs for a given language requires the resource grammarian to define the following: Concrete grammars for all the modules within the core grammar, concrete grammars of *Cat(egory)*, *Paradigms* and *Lexicon*, the abstract and concrete grammars of *Extra* and *Irreg* where applicable, and the auxiliary module *Res*.

In this paper, we describe the definition of *Res*, *Morpho* and *Paradigms* for Swahili, as well as the definition of Swahili concrete grammars for *Cat*, *Lexicon*, *Structural*, *Noun*, *Verb*, *Adjective* and *Sentence*.

3.2 Swahili Grammars

3.2.1 ResSwa

Res is a language-specific resource grammar that defines parameter types specific to a given language. These types denote linguistic features that cut across the language. For nouns, the following parameters are defined:

param Gender = g1_2 | g3_4 | g5_6 | g5a_6 | g6 | g7_8 | g9_10 | g11 | g11_6 | g11_10;

[3] X is a three-letter suffix that identifies a language e.g. *ParadigmsSwa* and *ParadigmsEng* refer to the Paradigms definitions for Swahili and English respectively.

param Case = *Nom* | *Loc* ;
param Animacy = *AN* | *IN* ;

The parameter *Gender* defines Swahili's noun classes where *g1_2* refers to noun class *m_wa* where the singular form begins with prefix *m-* and the plural with *wa-* e.g. *m-sichana* and *wa-sichana.* In this work, we adopt the noun classes as defined by early Bantu scholars such as Ashton (1944) and Denny and Creider (1976), but with refinement of classes 5, 6, 10 and 11. This refinement has been done with a view to create classes with more similarity with respect to noun prefixes, making it easier to generate noun paradigms accurately.

The parameter *Case* defines two options—nominative and locative to handle cases where some nouns take an optional locational suffix as explained in Sect. 2. The parameter *Animacy*, with values *animate* and *inanimate*, is defined to ensure correct subject-verb agreement for animate nouns that do not fall in the noun class *m-wa* that is typically associated with animate entities (Moxley 1998), but whose agreement features must match those of animate nouns. Examples of such nouns include names of most animals as well as family relations e.g. *mama* 'mother', *baba* 'father', *dada* 'sister', *ndugu* 'brother'. Another important parameter is *Number* (singular and plural) which is common to other languages and is already pre-defined elsewhere in the library.

For verbs, the following parameters are defined:

param VForm =
VInf |
VImper Number Person |
VPres Number Gender Animacy Person |
VPast Number Gender Animacy Person |
VFut Number Gender Animacy Person ;

The parameter *Vform* defines five different forms that a verb can take. The first form is the Infinitive form. Next, is the Imperative form which is dependent on Number and Person since this form is only applicable to second person singular (2SG) or plural (2PL) e.g. for the verb *cheza* 'to play', the imperative form for 2SG is *chez-a* while that for 2PL is *chez-eni*. The other three forms define Present, Past and Future tense, which depend on Number, Gender, Animacy and Person, to generate the correct subject prefix as shown in the examples in Table 1.

The parameter *AForm* has been defined for Adjectives:

param AForm = *AF Number Gender Animacy* ;

This captures the fact that adjectives agree with the Number, Gender and Animacy of the modified noun, as the examples in Table 2 show.

The last parameter *Spatial* distinguishes the proximal, distal and referential demonstratives e.g. *hii* 'this', *hiyo* 'that' and *ile* 'that' (distal), and has been defined as follows:

param Spatial = *SpHrObj* | *SpHr* | *HrObj* ;

Table 1 Verb prefixes: gender, animacy, number and person interactions

Gender	Animacy	Number	Person	Verb prefix		
				Present	Past	Future
1_2	animate	Sg	1	ni-na-	ni-li-	ni-ta-
1_2	animate	Sg	3	a-na-	a-li-	a-ta-
1_2	animate	Pl	3	wa-na-	wa-li-	wa-ta-
9_10	animate	Sg	3	a-na-	a-li-	a-ta-
9_10	inanimate	Sg	3	i-na-	i-li-	i-ta-

Table 2 Adjective prefixes: gender, animacy and number interactions

Gender	Animacy	Number	Adjective prefix
1_2	animate	Sg	m-
1_2	animate	Pl	wa-
9_10	animate	Sg	m-
9_10	inanimate	Sg	n-
7_8	inanimate	Pl	vi-
7_8	animate	Pl	wa-

3.2.2 CatSwa

The *Cat* grammar defines all the lexical categories (closed, open and phrasal) that are common to all languages. The concrete syntax *CatSwa* currently defines the type specifications for the base categories as they present in Swahili, as shown in Table 3.

3.2.3 ParadigmSwa

ParadigmsSwa defines the top level morphological functions that are used to construct lexical entries in *LexiconSwa*. The functions correspond to the base lexical categories defined in *CatSwa* as shown in Table 3.

Table 3 Lexical category definitions

Category	Example	Definition
N	*msichana* 'girl'	$N = \{s : Number \Rightarrow Str;\ g : Gender;\ a : Animacy\}$
N2	*ndugu ya* 'brother of'	$N2 = \{s : Number \Rightarrow Str;\ g : Gender;\ a : Animacy\} ** \{c2 : Str\}$
Pron	*mimi* 'I'	$Pron = \{s : Str;\ gp : GenPron;\ n : Number;\ p : Person\}$
V	*ninaimba* 'I sing'	$V = \{s : VForm \Rightarrow Str\}$
A	*mzuri* 'good'	$A = \{s : Degree \Rightarrow AForm \Rightarrow Str\}$
Quant	*Hii/Hizi* 'this/these'	$Quant = \{s : Number \Rightarrow Gender \Rightarrow Animacy \Rightarrow Case \Rightarrow Str\}$
Prep	*Ya* 'of'	$Prep = \{s : Str\}$
Num	*Nne* 'four'	$Num = \{s : Gender \Rightarrow Animacy \Rightarrow Str;\ n : Number\}$

Nouns (N, N2) Swahili Nouns are regular in the sense that given a noun root, gender, number and animacy, it is possible to use rules to generate a correct noun form. Hence, the abstract function *regN* is used to define common nouns of type N. In this definition, *Str*[4] represents the noun root which is passed to the *regN* function together with the values for *Gender* and *Animacy*:

$$\mathit{regN} : \mathit{Str} \rightarrow \mathit{Gender} \rightarrow \mathit{Animacy} \rightarrow N\,;$$

The concrete form of *regN* calls the helper function *mkNomReg* that is defined in *MorphoSwa*[5] to generate the final noun form. *mkNomReg* abstracts over the predefined *Number* parameter to generate both singular and plural forms of the noun root, and hence *Number* need not be passed directly to *regN*.

$$\mathit{regN} = \backslash x, g, \mathit{anim} \rightarrow \mathit{mkNomReg}\ x\ g\ \mathit{anim} ** \{\mathit{lock\_N} = <>\}\,;$$

Nouns of type *N2* which take a Noun of type *N* followed by a preposition, are constructed by the following abstract and concrete definitions of *mkN2*:

$$\mathit{mkN2} : N \rightarrow \mathit{Prep} \rightarrow \mathit{N2}\,;$$
$$\mathit{mkN2} : N \rightarrow \mathit{Prep} \rightarrow \mathit{N2} = \backslash n, p \rightarrow n ** \{\mathit{c2} = p.s\,;\ \mathit{lock\_N2} = <>\}\,;$$

Pronouns (Pron) Pronouns are defined by the function *mkPron* which calls the helper function *mkPronoun* which is defined in *MorphoSwa*.

$$\mathit{mkPron} : \mathit{Number} \rightarrow \mathit{Person} \rightarrow \mathit{Pron}\,;$$
$$\mathit{mkPron} = \backslash n, p \rightarrow \mathit{mkPronoun}\ n\ p ** \{\mathit{lock\_Pron} = <>\}\,;$$

Verbs (V) The category Verb (*V*) is a simple form and is defined by the function *regV* whose abstract and concrete definitions are as shown:

$$\mathit{regV} : \mathit{Str} \rightarrow V\,;$$
$$\mathit{regV} = \backslash \mathit{enda} \rightarrow \mathit{mkV}\ \mathit{enda} ** \{\mathit{s1} = [\,]\,;\ \mathit{lock\_V} = <>\}\,;$$

mkV is defined in *MorphoSwa* and uses the *VForm* parameter defined in *ResSwa* to generate the infinitive, imperative, present, past and future tense forms for any regular verb.

Adjectives (A) Adjectives are constructed by the abstract function *regA* whose abstract and concrete definitions are as shown:

$$\mathit{regA} : \mathit{Str} \rightarrow A\,;$$
$$\mathit{regA}\ a = \mathit{compADeg}\ \{s = \backslash\backslash\_ \Rightarrow (\mathit{mkAdjective}\ a).s\,;\ \mathit{lock\_A} = <>\}\,;$$

compAdeg and *mkAdjective* are helper functions defined in *MorphoSwa*.

[4] *Str* is a built-in type in GF that represents a list of tokens.

[5] *Morpho* contains language-specific resource grammar constructs that define exactly how various morphological paradigms are realized. *Morpho* uses the parameters defined in *Res* to realize the categories defined in *Cat*.

Table 4 Constructing quantifiers using function *mkQuant*

Gender	Animacy	Number	Proximal	Distal	Referential
1_2	animate	Sg	huyu	huyo	yule
1_2	animate	Pl	hawa	hao	wale
3_4	inanimate	Sg	huu	huo	ule
3_4	inanimate	Pl	hii	hiyo	ile
7_8	inanimate	Pl	hivi	hivyo	vile
7_8	animate	Pl	hawa	hao	wale

Prepositions (Prep) Prepositions are constructed by the abstract function *mkPrep* whose abstract and concrete definitions are as shown:

$$mkPrep : Str \rightarrow Prep;$$
$$mkPrep\ p = \{s = p;\ lock\_Prep = <>\};$$

Quantifiers (Quant) Quantifiers are constructed via the helper function *mkQuant* defined in *MorphoSwa*:

$$mkQuant : Spatial \rightarrow Number \rightarrow Gender \rightarrow Animacy \rightarrow Case \rightarrow Person \rightarrow Str;$$

mkQuant takes as input the *Spatial* parameter that specifies whether to construct a proximal, distal or referential demonstrative. In addition, the number, gender and animacy values have to be specified since Swahili quantifiers must agree in number and gender with the modified noun, as shown by the examples in Table 4.

3.2.4 LexiconSwa

Lexicon is part of the top-level grammar and gives access to content words that can then be used by the syntax component of the resource grammar library. *LexiconSwa* uses the functions defined in *ParadigmsSwa* to define lexical entries (words) that conform to Swahili morphology. The content words defined here must be of the types defined in *CatSwa*. Currently, *LexiconSwa* contains 83 content words out of a total 300 words defined in the corresponding abstract file, *Lexicon*. Table 5 shows example lexical definitions from *LexiconSwa*. The abstract function is defined in the abstract grammar while *LexiconSwa* defines the corresponding concrete syntax. For example, *country_N* is the abstract function defined in *Lexicon*, while the definition *country_N = regN "nchi" e_e inanimate*; is its corresponding concrete linearization in Swahili. This definition states that to generate the Swahili form for the noun 'country', the function *regN* defined in *ParadigmsSwa* is called by *LexiconSwa* with the Swahili string for country *nchi*, followed by the gender (*e_e* in this case) and animacy value (*inanimate*). The function *regN* then generates the singular and plural forms for *country_N* in Swahili.

Table 5 Constructing quantifiers using function *mkQuant*

Category	Swahili definition in *LexiconSwa*
N	*country_N = regN "nchi" e_e inanimate*
N	*cousin_N = regN "binamu" e_ma animate*
N	*man_N = regN "mwanaume" m_wa animate*
N	*tree_N = regN "mti" m_mi inanimate*
N	*water_N = regN "maji" ma_ma inanimate*
V	*swim_V = regV "ogelea"*
A	*dirty_A = regA "chafu"*
N2	*father_N2 = mkN2 (regN "baba" e_e animate) (mkPrep "ya")*

3.2.5 StructuralSwa

This file is an extension of the lexicon file and allows for specification of structural words belonging to closed classes. Such words include pronouns, prepositions, determiners, predeterminers, quantifiers, subjunctions, conjunctions and adverbials. So far *StructuralSwa* defines pronouns, predeterminers and quantifiers. Example definitions for each of these classes is given below:

For pronouns, only the nominative form is specified directly. The possessive form is dependent on the agreement features of the modified noun and is therefore generated. Inherent features *Number* and *Person* are also specified.

i_Pron = {*s* = "*mimi*"; *n* = *Sg*; *p* = *P1*};
we_Pron = {*s* = "*sisi*"; *n* = *Pl*; *p* = *P1*};

By using the *Spatial* parameter, it is possible to generate the proximal and distal forms of the quantifiers *this* and *that.* In Swahili, quantifiers have to agree with the number, gender and animacy (represented as *n*, *g*, *anim* in the examples below) of the modified noun, and hence these have to be passed from the noun.

this_Quant = {*s* = *n*, *g*, *anim*, *c* ⇒ *mkQuant SpHrObj n g anim Nom P3*};
that_Quant = {*s* = *n*, *g*, *anim*, *c* ⇒ *mkQuant SpHr n g anim Nom P3*};

Given that the referential reading is not a universal feature in all languages, it is specified in the *Extra* module.

Swahili has both *predeterminers* and *postdeterminers* with the latter being the majority. However, GF does not include *postdeterminer* as a category. To circumvent this limitation, both types have been defined as *predeterminers*[6] but with an additional parameter *Pos* which indicates its positioning (pre, mid[7] or post) within the NP. The combined predeterminer category consequently displays a wide range

[6]It may be possible to define the postdeterminer in the language-specific module *ExtraSwa*, and the implications of doing this are being investigated.

[7]*Postdeterminers* can be located either before or after the adjective. *Mid* is used for the former and *Post* for the latter.

of agreement requirements depending on the particular predeterminer. Some predeterminers e.g. *-ote* 'all' and *-o-ote* 'any' must agree with the modifying noun in terms of animacy and gender, while others like *pekee* 'only' and *sio* 'not' remain unchanged regardless of the modifying noun.

$all\_Predet = \{s = \backslash\backslash n, g, anim, p \Rightarrow mkPredet\ All\ Pl\ g\ anim\ p\, ;\ pos = mid\}\, ;$
$not\_Predet = \{s = \backslash\backslash n, g, anim, p \Rightarrow mkPredet\ Not\ Pl\ g\ anim\ p\, ;\ pos = pre\}\, ;$

3.2.6 NounSwa

The *noun* module defines functions for constructing a noun phrase (*NP*) from various constituents. GF defines three main types of noun phrases—common nouns with determiners, proper names and pronouns. For Swahili, constructing *NP*s from proper names and pronouns is relatively straightforward. Constructing *NP*s from common nouns and determiners is more complex due to the intricate agreement and positioning restrictions for the various modifiers. The following example shows the form a Swahili *NP* can take:

gari	*hizi*	*zote*	*zangu*	*mbili*	*nzuri*
cars	these	all	my	two	good

'all these my two good cars'[8]

Given that any of the above modifiers is optional, care must be taken when constructing the *NP* to ensure that the right order is always maintained. Predeterminers can be located variously within the *NP*, as mentioned in Sect. 3.2.5, and as the following examples show:

sio	*gari*	*hizi*	*zote*	*zangu*	*mbili*	*nzuri*
not	cars	these	all	my	two	good

'not all these my two good cars'

gari	*hizi*	*zote*	*zangu*	*mbili*	*pekee*
cars	these	all	my	two	only

'only all these my two cars'

Sio 'not' and *pekee* 'only' come before the noun and after the adjective respectively, unlike *-ote* 'all', *-engi* 'most' and *-ingine* 'other' which come after the noun (and quantifier if any), but before the adjective.

Currently, *NounSwa* defines functions for constructing common nouns (*UseN*, *UseN2* and *ComplN2*), determiners (*DetQuant*, *NumSg*, *NumPl*), common nouns with adjectives (*AdjCN*), common nouns with determiners (*DetCN*), definite and indefinite noun phrases (*IndefArt*, *DefArt*), proper names (*UsePN*), pronouns and their possessive forms (*UsePron*, *PossPron*), noun phrases comprising solely of a determiner (*DetNP*) and noun phrases modified by a predeterminer (*PredetNP*). With these functions defined, it is possible to generate a wide range of Swahili noun phrases.

---

[8]Though this reading may seem odd for say an English speaker, combining the predeterminer *all* and numeral *two* in one NP achieves emphasis, and this is a perfectly good Swahili sentence.

```
Languages: LangEng LangSwa
3328 ms
Lang> parse -cat=Cl -lang=Eng "beautiful women love Paris" | l -lang=Swa
wanawake warembo wanapenda Parisi

236 ms
Lang> parse -cat=Cl -lang=Swa "sisi tunapenda meno haya mazuri" | l -lang=Eng
we love these good teeth

100 ms
Lang> parse -cat=Cl -lang=Swa "sisi tunapenda nchi hizi zuri" | l -lang=Eng
we love these good countries

36 ms
Lang> parse -cat=Cl -lang=Swa
          "msichana huyu mrembo anapenda milango hii mikubwa" | l -lang=Eng
this beautiful girl loves these big doors

212 ms
```

Fig. 1 GF runtime environment showing actual parses and linearizations

3.2.7 Other Modules

Other modules that have been partially defined include *VerbSwa*, *AdjectiveSwa* and *SentenceSwa*. For these modules, only basic constructs have been defined, and work is ongoing to complete the remaining functions as defined in the corresponding abstract grammars. In GF, verb phrases (*VP*) are constructed from verbs by specifying their complements. For Swahili, the following functions have been defined: *UseV* for verbs that do not take any complement, and *SlashV2a* and *ComplSlash* which allow for the definition of a *VP* that takes an *NP* complement. For the latter function, agreement features of the *NP* are enforced in the *VP*. For adjective phrases (*AP*), two functions have been defined. These are *PositA* and *ComparA* which specify how to construct positive and comparative *APs* respectively. For *SentenceSwa*, *PredVP* that takes a *NP* and a *VP* and returns a Clause (*Cl*) has been defined, making it possible to construct simple declarative sentences.

3.2.8 Example Sentences

Though incomplete, it is possible to generate a wide range of Swahili sentences using the currently defined Swahili resource grammars. Figure 1 is a screenshot of GF's runtime environment with the English and Swahili grammars loaded. The examples shown have been generated by parsing a Swahili sentence and linearizing (translating) it in English and vice versa.

4 Assistive Tool for Visually-Impaired Swahili Mobile Phone Users

As mentioned in Sect. 1, GF resource grammars are an excellent resource for application developers wishing to build multilingual applications. Having developed the Swahili RGs to a usable extent as demonstrated by the examples in Sect. 3.2.8, we put the grammars to test by developing an end-user application which uses the English and Swahili RGs. The application is an assistive tool that supports mobile phone users who are not only visually-impaired, but who can only understand spoken Swahili.

The mobile phone is the default communication, business and data device across much of Africa, registering over 500 million mobile phone subscribers (Rao 2011). In East Africa where Swahili is widely spoken, there are approximately 60 million mobile phone users. More and more business and e-government services are being channeled through short message service (SMS) and unstructured supplementary services data (USSD) applications, with most of these being largely in English. For non-literate, visually-impaired, Swahili only speakers, this scenario hinders them from actively participating in communication-centred services delivered via the mobile phone.

To address this limitation, we have designed an assistive tool that takes as input, text messages written in both Swahili and English. We use the GF resource grammars to translate the English messages into Swahili. The Swahili messages are then synthesized into Swahili audio using a phone-based speech synthesis application, allowing the user to 'listen' to their Swahili messages. The application has been piloted with users located at the Kenya School of the Blind and has been well-received.

We are in the process of extending the Swahili audio interface to various mobile phone[9] utilities such as the clock, calculator, address book (contacts) etc., with a view of enabling visually-impaired Swahili speakers to use these important features. Again, for this extension, we are using the GF library (English and Swahili RGs) to translate English utility data into Swahili, and subsequently synthesize the Swahili data into audio.

5 Conclusion

In this paper, we have described the development of Swahili Resource Grammars for the Grammatical Framework. This work represents the first attempt to extend GF with a Bantu language and serves as a new test case on how sufficiently GF's language-independent representation handles a different language family. We have also described a multilingual end-user application that has been developed using the Swahili RGs.

Development work is ongoing to complete the definition of the Swahili grammars with a focus on the Swahili verb, adjectives, adverbs and sentences (questions and imperatives). Further work will entail abstracting a Bantu resource module along the lines of the Romance and Scandinavian resource modules, and consequently adding more Bantu languages to the GF family.

---

[9]This application is specific to Nokia phones which constitute a large majority of the handsets in use.

Acknowledgements We acknowledge the support and contribution of Aarne Ranta, Juliet Mutahi and Kimani Njogu. Particularly worthy of mention is the contribution of Lauri to this work—first, for introducing me to the Grammatical Framework from where my interest in GF started, and secondly, for his interest in tense and aspect of Bantu languages—discussions[10] which have contributed to the shape and form of the Swahili RGs, and will be particularly important as we extend the RGs to cover the Swahili verb (and verb phrase) in all its complexity.

References

Ashton, E. O. 1944. *Swahili grammar*. London: Longmans.

Burke, David, and Kristofer Johannisson. 2005. Translating formal software specifications to natural language. In *Logical aspects of computational linguistics*, eds. Philippe Blache, Edward Stabler, Joan Busquets, and Richard Moot. Vol. 3492 of *Lecture notes in computer science*, 47–82. Berlin: Springer. doi:10.1007/11422532_4.

Caprotti, Olga, and Mika Seppälä. 2006. Multilingual delivery of online tests in mathematics. In *Proceedings of Online Educa Berlin*. Berlin, Germany.

Denny, J. Peter, and Chet A. Creider. 1976. The semantics of noun classes in Proto-Bantu. *Studies in African Linguistics* 7: 1–30.

Ljunglöf, Peter, and Staffan Larsson. 2008. A grammar formalism for specifying ISU-based dialogue systems. In *6th international conference on advances in natural language processing, GoTAL 2008*, eds. Bengt Nordström and Aarne Ranta. Vol. 5221 of *Lecture notes in computer science*, 303–314. Berlin: Springer. doi:10.1007/978-3-540-85287-2_29.

Moxley, Jeri L. 1998. Semantic structure of Swahili noun classes. In *Language history and linguistic description in Africa*, eds. Ian Maddieson and Thomas Hinnebusch. Vol. 2 of *Trends in African linguistics*, 229–238. Trenton: Africa World Press.

Ranta, Aarne. 2011. *Grammatical framework: Programming with multilingual grammars. CSLI studies in computational linguistics*. Stanford: CSLI.

Rao, Madanmohan. 2011. Mobile Africa report 2011: Regional hubs of excellence and innovation. MobileMonday. http://healthunbound.org/content/mobile-africa-report-2011-regional-hubs-excellence-and-innovation-1.

[10]Lauri and I held very interesting discussions on Bantu tense and aspect, particularly on Gĩkũyũ (my mother tongue), as he worked on his book. It is at this time that I developed more interest in developing the Swahili GF grammars and eventually a Bantu module.

On the Syntax and Translation of Finnish Discourse Clitics

Aarne Ranta

> *One criterion is to think of the description as material for machine translation—that is the level of specificity I'd like to achieve. The description of the clitics should support translation between correct uses of clitics and corresponding devices in other languages. (Carlson 1993: 5)*

Abstract Finnish has a set of morphemes called discourse clitics, which attach to words and express things like contrasting and reminding. This paper builds a formal grammar to specify the syntax and morphology of these clitics. The grammar is written in GF, Grammatical Framework, which has a distinction between abstract syntax (tree structures) and concrete syntax (surface structures such as strings). The abstract syntax of clitics defines their contribution to the discourse semantics of sentences, in particular the topic-focus structure. The concrete syntax defines the realization in Finnish. We also show another concrete syntax, for English, which makes it possible to translate between Finnish discourse clitics and corresponding devices in English. The paper shows a complete GF code of a small grammar demonstrating the main ideas and also gives a link to a web demo for translation. Theoretically, the work can be seen as a synthesis of a Montague semantics for clitics as proposed by Karttunen and Karttunen in 1976 and their explanation in terms of dialogue games following Lauri Carlson's model of 1993.

1 Introduction

Finnish has a set of morphemes called *discourse clitics*, attached to words in a way typical of clitics (Zwicky 1977). Some of these clitics attach to the first constituent of a clause, to express things like the formation of questions (*ko*, much like the

A. Ranta (✉)
University of Gothenburg, Gothenburg, Sweden
e-mail: aarne@chalmers.se

D. Santos et al. (eds.), *Shall We Play the Festschrift Game?*,
DOI 10.1007/978-3-642-30773-7_14,

Latin clitic *ne*), contrasting (*pas*), and reminding (*han*).[1] These three functions are illustrated by the following examples:

Jussi juo maitoa (no clitic, neutral): 'John drinks milk'
Jussiko juo maitoa (*ko*, question): 'is it John who drinks milk'
Jussipas juo maitoa (*pas*, contrasting): 'it is John who drinks milk (and not Peter)'
Jussihan juo maitoa (*han*, reminding): 'as we know, John drinks milk'

There is yet another clitic, *kin*, which can often be directly translated by 'also' or 'even'. It attaches to (almost) any element in a clause:

Jussikin juo maitoa nykyään (subject) 'also John drinks milk nowadays (and not only Peter)'
Jussi juokin maitoa nykyään (verb): 'John even drinks milk nowadays (and not only produces it)'
Jussi juo maitoakin nykyään (object): 'John drinks also milk nowadays (and not only beer)'
Jussi juo maitoa nykyäänkin (adverb): 'John drinks milk nowadays too (and not only in the past)'

In this paper, we shall give a set of formal rules for how the discourse clitics may appear in Finnish sentences: their *syntax*. We shall also take a look at the *translation* of discourse clitics to English, in some of their typical uses. To satisfy the motto of this paper, we have built a system that performs the translation automatically, in both directions. An on-line demo and its source code can be found on the web.[2]

There is a considerable literature around Finnish discourse clitics. We have been particularly inspired by Karttunen and Karttunen (1976), Nevis (1986) and Carlson (1993). Karttunen and Karttunen (1976) concentrate their study on the clitic *kin*, giving a detailed account of its syntax and semantics in a Montague-style grammar (Montague 1974). Carlson (1993) addresses all clitics (but less formally), showing how they can be interpreted and translated in a discourse context following the idea of dialogue games (Carlson 1983). Nevis (1986) is a thorough linguistic study placing the Finnish clitics in the context of a general theory of clitics (Zwicky 1977).

This paper can be seen as a further development of the Montague-style grammar of Karttunen and Karttunen (1976): the rule system is extended from *kin* to the other clitics and integrated in a wide-coverage resource grammar of Finnish (Ranta 2009). The grammar is formalized and implemented by using the grammar formalism GF (Grammatical Framework, Ranta 2004, 2011), which is designed for supporting *multilingual grammars*. The translation system we present is by definition *compositional*, in the sense that the Finnish and English sentences have a rule-to-rule correspondence via a common tree structure, an *abstract syntax*.

Of course, we can only scratch the surface of the translation of discourse clitics in this paper. One reason, repeatedly shown in Carlson (1993), is that the clitics have several functions, and they can only be disambiguated in the context of a dialogue. For instance, *kin* can be used to express 'also' (as above and in Karttunen and Karttunen 1976), but it also has the function of expressing surprise. Thus *Jussi juokin*

[1]The full list is *ko*, *pa*, *han*, and *s*. Also the combinations *kos*, *kohan*, *pas*, and *pahan* exist. The ones we study here are chosen because of their high frequency and clearly distinguishable meanings.

[2]http://www.grammaticalframework.org/demos/finnish-clitics/.

maitoa nykyään has another translation, 'John drinks milk nowadays, after all' (following Carlson 1993). Current machine translation methods are just incapable of selecting between these alternatives in an informed way, as they work sentence by sentence.

A quick experiment with standard machine translation systems confirms how far they are from coping with Finnish discourse clitics. Google Translate[3] often returns Finnish words with clitics untranslated—just because many word+clitic combinations have never appeared in the training corpus. The Sunda system[4] tailored for Finnish does a better job in rendering Finnish clitics in English. But when the English sentences are translated back to Finnish, the clitics disappear. Instead, literal translations of the English sentences are returned. For instance, *Jussikin juo maitoa* is correctly translated to *also Jussi drinks milk*, but the back-translation is *myös Jussi juo maitoa*, which is correct but uses the adverb *myös* ('also') instead of the clitic.

This suggests a conjecture that the frequency of discourse clitics can be used for distinguishing native Finnish from "translationese". This may even be a characteristic of foreign speakers' Finnish, even fluent ones'. Discourse clitics (with the exception of the question clitic *ko*) can *always* be avoided by using paraphrases. When a source text, or a foreign speaker's "mentalese", is being rendered into Finnish (or any other language), the translator/speaker performs a search for an adequate rendering of its meaning. This search has a (legitimate) tendency to return the syntactically closest translation variant. Rendering an English dialogue with Finnish discourse clitics requires a translator with the Finnish speaker's intuitions who continuously poses the question, "how would I express this if I was in the same situation". Then the clitics will naturally appear in many cases.

2 The Abstract Syntax of Discourse Clitics

We will focus on two groups of discourse clitics: *han* and *pas* on the one hand, and *kin* on the other. The clitics *han* and *pas* are always attached to the first constituent of a clause (Nevis 1986; Carlson 1993). The clitic *kin* can be attached to *any* constituent. Both groups include some other clitics, too, as mentioned in Sect. 5 below.

One of the facts we need to formalize is that any sentence contains at most one clitic from each group. They appear in positions that we will call the *topic* and the *focus*; these are not always exactly the traditional semantic topic and focus, which also depend on other things such as intonation and further details of word order.[5] Thus for us, the topic is simply the fronted element, and it may carry *han* or *pas*. The focus is simply any element (including the topic itself) that may carry the focus clitic *kin* (sometimes in combination with a topic clitic). For instance, *maitoakinhan*

[3] http://translate.google.com.

[4] http://www.sunda.fi/eng/translator.html.

[5] Also the Finnish reference grammar Hakulinen et al. (2005) calls *kin* a focus particle, whereas the others are called "tonal particles" ("sävypartikkeli").

Jussi juo, ‘as we know, John drinks milk too’, has *maitoa* (‘milk’, partitive case) as both topic and focus.

What are the “elements” of a clause? We will distinguish four elements: the *subject*, the *verb*, the *object*, and the *adverb* (this will be generalized in Sect. 5). Any of these elements can work as both topic and focus in the way described above.[6]

Our grammar has seven syntactic categories, defined as follows in GF:

```
cat
  S ;          -- declarative sentence
  Clause ;     -- clause with focus on some element (or none)
  Elements ; -- clause elements: subject, verb, object, adverb
  Clitic ;     -- discourse clitic: "han", "pas"
  NP ;         -- noun phrase
  V2 ;         -- two-place verb
  Adv ;        -- adverb
```

The keyword `cat` starts a group of *category declarations*. Each declaration above has a comment (started by a double dash) explaining what the category is meant for.

The `cat` declarations belong to the *abstract syntax* of a GF grammar, similar to the level of “analysis trees” in Montague grammar. In addition to the categories, an abstract syntax contains *function declarations* (`fun`), defining how to construct *abstract syntax trees*. The following five `fun` declarations define five ways of building a top-level sentence from a topic clitic and a clause:

```
fun
  NoTop :                        -- Jussi juo maitoa nyt
    Clitic -> Clause -> S ; -- John drinks milk now
  TopSubj :                      -- Jussi maitoa juo nyt
    Clitic -> Clause -> S ; -- it is John who drinks milk now
  TopVerb :                      -- juo Jussi maitoa nyt
    Clitic -> Clause -> S ; -- John actually does drink milk now
  TopObj :                       -- maitoa juo Jussi nyt
    Clitic -> Clause -> S ; -- milk is drunk by John now
  TopAdv :                       -- nyt Jussi juo maitoa
    Clitic -> Clause -> S ; -- now John drinks milk
```

There is thus one rule for topicalizing each of the elements of a clause, plus a “neutral” rule. Since both the neutral rule and the subject topicalization front the subject, we distinguish the latter by moving the verb after the subject; this seems to capture well the idea of topicalizing the subject.[7]

Clauses are formed in two steps. The *predication* step collects the elements together and chooses their proper forms, in terms of agreement. The *focusing* step

---

[6]The verb does not easily get the focus clitic when topicalized: *juokin Jussi maitoa* (‘Jussi actually does even drink milk’) is strange. On the other hand, *taidankin tästä lähteä* (‘I think I leave now’) is correct, maybe because the subject is omitted. *Tulikin talvi* (‘the winter came, after all’) is also correct, maybe because there is an omitted formal subject different from *talvi* (‘the winter’). We will leave room for overgeneration here to keep the rules simple.

[7]Many other permutations are possible, since Finnish has “free word order”. Notice, however, that this does *not* mean free variation, since each word order has its own meaning and may, consequently, have its own translation.

brings one of the parts of a clause into focus. It can also say that there is no focus (i.e. no *kin*).

```
fun
  Pred : NP -> V2 -> NP -> Adv -> Elements ;

  NoFoc :                       -- Jussi juo maitoa nyt
    Elements -> Clause ; -- John drinks milk now
  FocSubj :                     -- Jussikin juo maitoa nyt
    Elements -> Clause ; -- even John drinks milk now
  FocVerb :                     -- Jussi juokin maitoa nyt
    Elements -> Clause ; -- John even drinks milk now
  FocObj :                      -- Jussi juo maitoakin nyt
    Elements -> Clause ; -- John drinks milk too now
  FocAdv :                      -- Jussi juo maitoa nytkin
    Elements -> Clause ; -- John drinks milk now too
```

As we are only using *kin* as the focus clitic, we do not have an argument place for it.[8] But we do need to define the topic clitics, including the absence of one:

```
  noClitic       : Clitic ;  -- (empty)
  remindClitic   : Clitic ;  -- han / as we know
  contrastClitic : Clitic ;  -- pas / no (but)
```

Finally, to test the grammar with actual examples, we define a small lexicon:

```
fun
  Jussi, Marja, Maito, Viini : NP ; -- John, Mary, milk, wine
  Juoda, Rakastaa : V2 ;            -- drink, love
  Nykyaan : Adv ;                   -- nowadays
```

The abstract syntax we have defined allows us to build 2,400 abstract syntax trees (75 sentence forms times 32 combinations of elements). One example is

```
  TopVerb remindClitic (FocSubj (Pred Jussi Juoda Maito Nykyaan))
```

The tree visualization tool of GF can show it in a nicer form, depicted in Fig. 1.

The tree in Fig. 1 corresponds to the Finnish and English sentences

juohan Jussikin maitoa nykyään
as we know, even John does drink milk nowadays

These translations are produced by *concrete syntaxes* of the abstract syntax. A concrete syntax is a compositional, reversible mapping from trees into strings (and other structures) of a language. The abstract and concrete syntaxes together define a relation of *phrase alignment* between the translations. For the example at hand, the visualization tool of GF gives the result shown in Fig. 2. In the picture, "&+" is the *binding operator* that glues the clitic to the foregoing word (see the next Section).

[8]Adding the other clitic of this class, *kaan*, will not change this, since it is in complementary distribution with *kin* depending on the polarity of the sentence; the positive *kin* is 'also', and the negative *kaan* is 'either'. Negative polarity is usually expressed by sentence negation, but can also appear in unnegated questions.

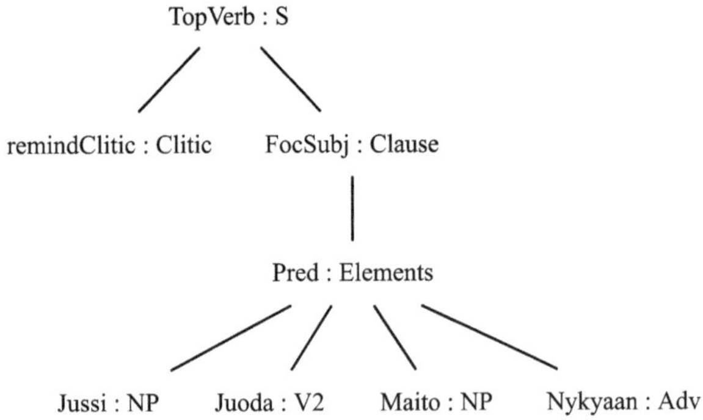

Fig. 1 Tree visualization of the abstract syntax tree `TopVerb remindClitic (FocSubj (Pred Jussi Juoda Maito Nykyaan))`

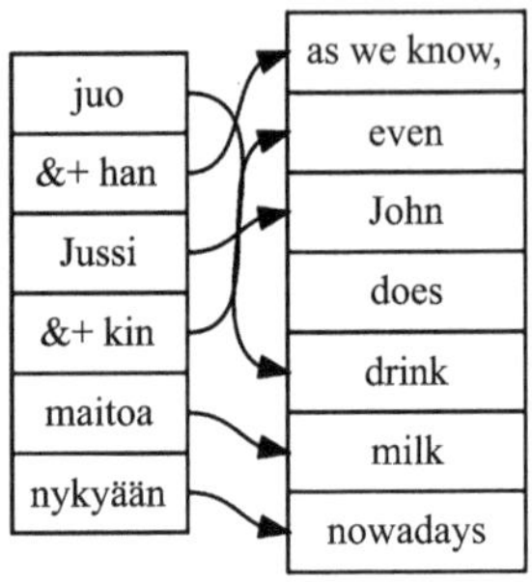

Fig. 2 Phrase alignment between the Finnish and English translations

3 The Finnish Concrete Syntax

A concrete syntax defines, for each language separately, how the trees of an abstract syntax are *linearized*. The output of linearization is often a string, but it can also be a richer data structure. GF has two such structures: *tables* and *records*.

A table is like an *inflection table* in traditional grammar: it gives values to every element in a finite *parameter set*. In the current fragment of Finnish, we use two parameter sets, defined as follows in GF:

```
param
  Case = Nom | Part ;          -- case: nominative or partitive
  Harmony = Back | Front ;     -- vowel harmony: back or front
```

An example of a table is the clitic *han*, which has the form *hän* when attached to a word requiring front vowel harmony. We can define this clitic as a constant whose type is a table type,

```
  han : Harmony => Str = table {Back => "han" ; Front => "hän"}
```

Similarly, noun phrases are tables depending on case,

```
  maito : Case => Str = table {Nom => "maito" ; Part => "maitoa"}
```

So, how do we combine a noun and a clitic? We take the noun in any of the case forms and then attach a clitic, whose form depends on the harmony of the noun: *maitoa+han* (‘milk as we know’) but *viiniä+hän* (‘wine as we know’). A way to implement this in GF is to equip each word in the lexicon with information about its vowel harmony. We do this by means of the record type "string with harmony", defined as

```
oper HStr : Type = {s : Str ; h : Harmony} ;
```

(where `oper` stands for auxiliary operations). When we have a string with a harmony, we can combine it with a harmony-dependent table by using the following operation:

```
oper harmony : HStr -> (Harmony => Str) -> Str =
  \hs,ht -> hs.s ++ ht ! hs.h ;
```

In words: we concatenate (++) the s-field `hs.s` of the harmony-providing string `hs` where we select (`!`) the h-field from the harmony-dependent table `ht`.

To make the harmony explicit for noun phrases, we change their type from `Case => Str` to `Case => HStr`. Thus the harmony of a noun depends also on its case. In practice, it is almost always the same for all cases for a given noun, but there are exceptions such as *meri(+hän)*, *merta(+han)* ('see', nominative and partitive).[9]

The parameter types and data structures are used for defining *linearization types* for each category in the abstract syntax. As the linearization types belong to the concrete syntax, they are language-dependent. Here are the linearization type definitions (`lincat`) in Finnish:

```
lincat
  S = Str ;
  Clause, Elements = {subj,verb,obj,adv : HStr} ;
  Clitic = Harmony => Str ;
  NP  = Case => HStr ;
  V2  = HStr ;
  Adv = HStr ;
```

Thus sentences are linearized to plain strings (`Str`). Clauses are records with separate strings for each of the four components. Clitics are tables depending on vowel

[9]There are two other ways of dealing with the vowel harmony of clitics in GF. One is to introduce the clitics as forms in inflection tables directly. This, however, leads to prohibitively large tables—for instance, every noun then has almost 3,744 forms (26 case-number combinations, 6 possessive suffixes (including none), 3 focus clitics (*kin*, *kaan*, none), and 8 topic clitics (all combinations including none)); the number of distinct forms is a little lower, since some of the combinations of case and possessive suffix produce the same string. The other way is to leave the decision to a separate lexical synthesis procedure (unlexing) after grammar-based linearization. This helps keep the grammar simple, but makes the over-all system more complex. One complication is that the vowel harmony of compound nouns, which are very common in Finnish, is impossible to decide from a string alone, without knowing the compound boundary. The parameter-based all-GF solution used here gives good quality with a reasonable table size. The classic implementation of Finnish morphology by Koskenniemi (1983) treats clitics as lexical forms to preserve accuracy, but avoids the explosion of the lexicon because its run-time representation is a finite-state automaton rather than an explicit table. Our solution similarly results in an automaton at run time, if we add a lexical analysis phase needed for restoring the binding tokens following the ideas of Huet (2005).

harmony. The rest of the categories are strings with harmony, which is needed when combining them with clitics. Noun phrases moreover depend on case.[10]

For each function (`fun`) in the abstract syntax, the concrete syntax gives a *linearization rule* (`lin`). Here are the rules for the sentence-forming functions.

```
lin
  NoTop pa c =
    harmony (c.subj) pa ++ c.verb.s ++ c.obj.s  ++ c.adv.s ;
  TopSubj pa c =
    harmony (c.subj) pa ++ c.obj.s  ++ c.verb.s ++ c.adv.s ;
  TopVerb pa c =
    harmony (c.verb) pa ++ c.subj.s ++ c.obj.s  ++ c.adv.s ;
  TopObj pa c =
    harmony (c.obj)  pa ++ c.verb.s ++ c.subj.s ++ c.adv.s ;
  TopAdv pa c =
    harmony (c.adv)  pa ++ c.subj.s ++ c.verb.s ++ c.obj.s ;
```

Each rule expresses topicalization by fronting one of the elements. This element is combined with the topic clitic by using the `harmony` function to select the proper form of the clitic.

The predication rule selects the proper forms of the constituents; here we only need to select the case of the subject and (partitive) object:

```
lin Pred subj verb obj adv =
  {subj = subj ! Nom ; verb = verb ; obj = obj ! Part ;
   adv = adv} ;
```

The focus rules put the focus clitic *kin* in place if needed. They use the auxiliary operation `kin`, which attaches the *kin* clitic to an `HStr`:

```
oper
  kin : HStr -> HStr = \hs -> {s = hs.s ++ bind "kin" ;
                               h = hs.h} ;
lin
  NoFoc c = c ;
  FocSubj c = {subj = kin c.subj ; verb = c.verb ; obj = c.obj ;
               adv = c.adv} ;
  FocVerb c = {subj = c.subj ; verb = kin c.verb ; obj = c.obj ;
               adv = c.adv} ;
  FocObj c = {subj = c.subj ; verb = c.verb ; obj = kin c.obj ;
              adv = c.adv} ;
  FocAdv c = {subj = c.subj ; verb = c.verb ; obj = c.obj ;
              adv = kin c.adv} ;
```

It remains to linearize the clitics and the test lexicon. For the clitics, we define an auxiliary similar to `mkClause`:

```
oper mkClitic : Str -> Str -> Harmony => Str =
  \ko,koe -> table {Back => ko ; Front => koe} ;
```

Using this, we define

[10] A full Finnish grammar has many more dependencies, in particular for verbs; even nouns have 30 forms in the GF resource grammar.

```
lin
  noClitic         = mkClitic [] [] ;
  remindClitic     = mkClitic (bind "han") (bind "hän") ;
  contrastClitic   = mkClitic (bind "pas") (bind "päs") ;
```

The `bind` operation adds the binding token `&+`,

```
oper bind : Str -> Str = \s -> "&+" ++ s ;
```

The binding token is eliminated by an *unlexer*, a post-processing phase after linearization. It produces

```
Jussi &+ han juo maitoa &+ kin --> Jussihan juo maitoakin
```

As a preprocessing phase before the parser, the *lexer* recognizes possible clitics and introduces binding tokens,

```
Jussikinhan juo maitoa --> Jussi &+ kin &+ han juo maitoa
```

When defining the lexicon, we do not want to give the vowel harmony of each word explicitly, but infer it with a simple heuristics, which inspects a string and determines it as a back vowel string if and only if it includes *a*, *o*, or *u*. This operation is definable in GF by regular-expression pattern matching:

```
oper mkHStr : Str -> HStr = \s -> {
       s = s ;
       h = case s of {
         _ + ("a" | "o" | "u") + _ => Back ;
         _ => Front
         }
       } ;
```

Since verbs and adverbs are plain `HStr`s, just `mkHStr` is needed to define them compactly in the lexicon. For noun phrases, we use a derived operation,

```
oper mkNP : Str -> Str -> Case => HStr =
  \n,p -> table {Nom => mkHStr n ; Part => mkHStr p} ;
```

Now we can define the lexicon compactly:[11]

```
lin
  Jussi     = mkNP "Jussi" "Jussia" ;
  Maito     = mkNP "maito" "maitoa" ;
  Marja     = mkNP "Marja" "Marjaa" ;
  Viini     = mkNP "viini" "viiniä" ;
  Juoda     = mkHStr "juo" ;
  Rakastaa  = mkHStr "rakastaa" ;
  Nykyään   = mkHStr "nykyään" ;
```

[11] The Finnish resource grammar uses regular-expression pattern matching to define a set of much more powerful lexical paradigms, which infer the complete inflection from just the dictionary form for 87 % of nouns and 96 % of verbs (Détrez and Ranta 2012).

4 The English Concrete Syntax

The abstract syntax in Sect. 3 was designed to account for Finnish discourse clitics. Can we map it into English in a compositional way? This turned out to be easy, even though the result is somewhat arbitrary: sure there can be other English translations, some equivalent and some corresponding to different interpretations of the clitics. But the translations chosen here suggest that any other ones could be defined in similar, compositional ways.

Let us assume that the abstract syntax in Sect. 3 encodes a fixed set of meanings—in particular, that the function `remindClitic` is used for reminding and `contrastClitic` for contrasting, and that the focus clitic *kin* means 'too', or 'even'. We will give just one English translation to each construction, aimed to be among the much larger set of semantically faithful and stylistically correct translations. Carlson (1993) uses many more variants to achieve a livelier style.

As English has less inflection than Finnish and no vowel harmony, some linearization types are simpler. But in English we need variation in verb forms. We say *John drinks milk* (third person singular present indicative) in normal cases, *John does drink milk* (infinitive) to topicalize the verb, and *milk is drunk by John* (past participle) to topicalize the object. Since the form can only be selected on the sentence (`S`) level, clauses must use verb inflection tables rather than plain strings.

```
param
  VForm = Inf | Ind | PPt ;
lincat
  S = Str ;
  Clause, Elements = {subj,obj,adv : Str ; verb : VForm => Str} ;
  Clitic = Str ;
  NP  = Str ;
  V2  = VForm => Str ;
  Adv = Str ;
```

As the "corresponding devices" to Finnish topicalization, we will use *it* clefts for the subject, the auxiliary *do* for the verb, passive voice for the object, and plain fronting for the adverb. Reminder is expressed by *as we know* and contrast by a leading *no*. Here are the sentence-forming rules:

```
lin
  NoTop pa c =
    pa ++ c.subj ++ c.verb ! Ind ++ c.obj ++ c.adv ;
  TopSubj pa c =
    pa ++ "it is" ++ c.subj ++ "that" ++ c.verb ! Ind ++ c.obj ++
          c.adv ;
  TopVerb pa c =
    pa ++ c.subj ++ "does" ++ c.verb ! Inf ++ c.obj ++ c.adv ;
  TopObj pa c =
    pa ++ c.obj  ++ "is" ++ c.verb ! PPt ++ "by" ++ c.subj ++
          c.adv ;
  TopAdv pa c =
    pa ++ c.adv  ++ c.subj ++ c.verb ! Ind ++ c.obj ;

  noClitic        = [] ;
```

```
  remindClitic     = "as we know," ;
  contrastClitic   = "no," ;
```

In the clause-forming rules, we use *even* to translate *kin* for the “earlier” elements (subject and verb), and *too* for the “later” ones (object and adverb). This gives a good approximation of what sounds natural.

```
lin
  Pred subj verb obj adv =
    {subj = subj ; verb = verb ; obj = obj ; adv = adv} ;

  NoFoc c = c ;
  FocSubj c = {subj = "even" ++ c.subj ; verb = c.verb ;
               obj = c.obj ; adv = c.adv} ;
  FocVerb c = {subj = c.subj ;
               verb = \\f => "even" ++ c.verb ! f ;
               obj = c.obj ; adv = c.adv} ;
  FocObj  c = {subj = c.subj ; verb = c.verb ;
               obj = c.obj ++ "too" ; adv = c.adv} ;
  FocAdv  c = {subj = c.subj ; verb = c.verb ; obj = c.obj ;
               adv = c.adv ++ "too"} ;
```

The lexicon is simple to define:

```
lin
  Jussi     = "John" ;
  Maito     = "milk" ;
  Marja     = "Mary" ;
  Viini     = "wine" ;
  Juoda     = mkVerb "drink" "drunk" ;
  Rakastaa  = mkVerb "love" "loved" ;
  Nykyaan   = "nowadays" ;
oper
  mkVerb : Str -> Str -> VForm => Str =
    \s,p -> table {Inf => s ; Ind => s + "s" ; PPt => p} ;
```

5 Scaling Up

We have given the complete source code of a toy grammar that translates between Finnish sentences with discourse clitics and English sentences with corresponding devices. Choosing to work on a toy grammar has made it possible to give the complete details, and also to focus on the critical issues.

The main issue we have addressed is the combinatorics of the discourse clitics, dealt with by the use of the clause records `{subj,verb,obj,adv : Str}` in both Finnish and English (with slight variations). The whole account relies on the use of a record data structure, rather than a plain string, as the target of linearization. The elements of the record can then be focalized, topicalized, and otherwise reordered in different ways. This structure is inspired by the *topological structure* of Germanic languages (Diderichsen 1962). The rationale is the same in Finnish as in German and Danish: the use of *discontinuous constituents* exemplified by the topological structure makes it possible to reorder the parts of a clause to express discourse structures.[12]

Another, minor, issue is the treatment of inflection and vowel harmony in Finnish. We have wanted to show how a lexicon can be efficiently built by an underlying morphological machinery and high-level functions that hide it from the user (here, `mkNP` and `mkHStr`). We have also shown that the choice of the correct form of a clitic can be performed accurately by memorizing the vowel harmony of each word.

While being demonstrated in a toy grammar, the approach used here is very much the same as in the full-scale resource grammar for Finnish. The *core resource grammar* (Ranta 2009) is an implementation of an abstract syntax of around 80 categories, 120 combination rules, and 500 lexemes. The core grammar is completed by a GF version of the KOTUS word list of 77,000 lexemes.[13] The core resource grammar implements a set of syntactic structures for 22 languages (in February 2012). Finnish was one of the first languages implemented (starting in 2003), and certainly did have some influence on the design of the abstract syntax. However, the core abstract syntax encodes a kind of "Standard Average European" and does not, in particular, cover the discourse clitics so peculiar to Finnish.[14]

In contrast to the toy grammar, the resource grammar version of clitics aims to cover their syntax completely. Thus it adds, among other things,

- the full set of topic clitics and their combinations (adding *pa*, *pahan*, *ko*, *kos*, *kohan*);
- the focus clitic *kaan* and its complementary distribution with *kin* triggered by negative polarity: *Jussi juo maitoakin* ("John drinks milk too") vs. *Jussi ei juo maitoakaan* ("John does not drink milk either");
- the interplay with negation and tenses, including the fronting of the negation (*eihän Jussi juo maitoakaan* "as we know, John actually does not drink milk either");
- other forms of clauses than just subject–verb–object–clitic;
- larger lexicon, with the generalizations it requires in syntax (e.g. the infamous Finnish object case, which persists in discourse rearrangements).

As an example of what these extensions involve, let us look at the linearization type of clauses:

```
{s : Tense => Polarity => {subj,fin,inf,obj,adv,ext : HStr}}
```

This record generalizes our toy grammar in two ways. First, it has six fields instead of four: the `verb` field is split into a finite and an infinite part (`fin`, `inf`), and an

[12]In a wide perspective, our approach can be seen in relation to the "quantifying in" idea of Montague (1974), which was developed for the clitic *kin* in Karttunen and Karttunen (1976). The common idea is that the clitic does not primarily attach to a word, but to an entire clause, from which a selected word is picked for the final, concrete attachment. Rather than bound variables, we use the idea of "slash categories" of GPSG (Gazdar et al. 1985): categories that have "gaps" in which syntactic constructions can insert new material.

[13]http://kaino.kotus.fi/sanat/nykysuomi/.

[14]Other "non-standard" languages represented in the resource grammar library are Amharic, Arabic, Hindi/Urdu, Maltese, Nepali, Persian, Punjabi, Swahili, and Thai.

`ext` field is added for extensions, such as subordinate clauses and extra adverbs. The extensions are never considered for focus or topic. Thus, when building a clause, there is a choice whether an adverb (or a complement) is placed in the `adv` or the `ext` field. The placement of clitics within constituents can also be controlled at the construction phase, e.g. *tuoretta+kin maitoa* vs. *tuoretta maitoa+kin* (roughly, 'even fresh milk (and not only sour milk)' vs. 'fresh milk too (and not only fresh bread)'). What is needed is simply that the constituents from which clauses are built, such as noun phrases, are themselves discontinuous, and are stored as records rather than strings in the clause.

The second generalization is that tense and polarity may be varied. When full sentences are built from clauses, any of the first five fields can be focalized and topicalized, with some restrictions depending on tense and polarity. For instance, the negation verb *ei* (which works much like *don't* in English), cannot be focalized.[15]

At the time of writing, the resource grammar version of discourse clitics does not yet cover other than declarative sentences, except questions with the standard question clitic *ko*. Some of the sub-clausal discontinuities are not yet covered either. The lexical treatment of vowel harmony is not carried out in all parts of speech; adapting the treatment used here would also help with other clitics, such as the possessive suffix *nsa*/*nsä* ('his', 'her').

The resource grammar of GF is *not* meant to be used as an interlingua for translation, but as a library for implementing concrete syntaxes of more restricted and fine-grained interlinguas. In typical GF applications, an interlingua is specific to a domain, which can range from mathematical proofs to touristic phrases. The interlingua presented in this paper, however, is not domain-specific. When equipped with a large lexicon, it could therefore be able to produce good translations of a large set of sentences whose structures are among the ones treated here.

6 Conclusion

We have discussed the combinatorics of Finnish discourse clitics and shown in full detail a toy grammar formalizing them for a fragment of language. The grammar was given an abstract syntax that permits compositional translation to other languages, which was illustrated by English. The English grammar uses different means (adverbs, fronting, passives, *it* clefts, emphatic *do*) to express the same things as Finnish expresses by discourse clitics. We have also summarized the main issues in the generalization of the toy grammar into a component of a wide-coverage Finnish resource grammar.

[15] Carlson (1993) presents this as a consequence of the general rule that "*-kin*/*-kAAn* cannot modify the polarity alone". Interestingly, this rule seems to be getting less strict, at least for two-syllabic plural forms: Google search finds e.g. the natural-sounding *Maapallo kyllä selviää, vaikka me emmekään selviäisi* ('The globe will certainly survive, even if we did not survive ourselves'; Web version of the newspaper *Keskisuomalainen*, May 2008).

The toy grammar is intended to serve as a prototype of a system able to translate "between correct uses of clitics and corresponding devices in other languages", a goal stated in Carlson (1993). While the resource grammar version of the system already covers a wide range of syntactic combinations, we have not formalized the semantic distinctions between different uses of the clitics. Thus we have not addressed the disambiguation problem, which is a task that seems to need a wider context than the isolated sentence—a dialogue game, as suggested by Carlson.

We do not claim to have solved deep linguistic problems or even taken into account all the theoretical findings that have been made about Finnish discourse clitics. But we have shown one way in which the clitics can be painlessly integrated in formal syntax and lead to running implementations of translation systems. The demo system accompanying this paper seems to be the first one that translates the clitics from Finnish to English without loss, and even produces them when translating from English to Finnish. While it is a system of a minuscule scope, it can be useful for tasks such as language training for learners of Finnish. It can for instance be used in the quiz mode, where the user sees an English sentence and is invited to construct a Finnish translation.[16]

Acknowledgements I am grateful to Janet Pierrehumbert and Atro Voutilainen for useful and encouraging comments on the first version of this paper.

References

Carlson, Lauri. 1983. *Dialogue games: An approach to discourse analysis*. Dordrecht: Reidel.

Carlson, Lauri. 1993. Dialogue games with Finnish clitics. In *Yearbook of the Linguistic Society of Finland*, eds. Maria Vilkuna and Susanna Shore. Helsinki: SKY.

Détrez, Grégoire, and Aarne Ranta. 2012. Smart paradigms and the predictability and complexity of inflectional morphology. In *EACL 2012*.

Diderichsen, Paul. 1962. *Elementær dansk grammatik*. København: Gyldendal.

Gazdar, Gerald, Ewan Klein, Geoffrey K. Pullum, and Ivan A. Sag. 1985. *Generalized phrase structure grammar*. Oxford: Basil Blackwell.

Hakulinen, Auli, Maria Vilkuna, Riitta Korhonen, Vesa Koivisto, Tarja Riitta Heinonen, and Irja Alho. 2005. *Iso suomen kielioppi*. Helsinki: Suomalaisen Kirjallisuuden Seura.

Huet, Gerard. 2005. A functional toolkit for morphological and phonological processing, application to a Sanskrit tagger. *Journal of Functional Programming* 15: 573–614.

Karttunen, Frances, and Lauri Karttunen. 1976. The clitic -kin/-kaan in Finnish. *Texas Linguistic Forum* 5: 89–118.

Koskenniemi, Kimmo. 1983. Two-level morphology: A general computational model for word-form recognition and production. Doctoral diss., University of Helsinki.

Montague, Richard. 1974. *Formal philosophy*. New Haven: Yale University Press. Collected papers edited by Richmond H. Thomason.

Nevis, Joel A.. 1986. Finnish particle clitics and general clitic theory. Doctoral diss., Department of Linguistics, Ohio State University, Columbus.

Ranta, Aarne. 2004. Grammatical Framework: A type-theoretical grammar formalism. *Journal of Functional Programming* 14: 145–189. http://www.cse.chalmers.se/~aarne/articles/gf-jfp.pdf

[16] See http://www.grammaticalframework.org/demos/finnish-clitics/.

Ranta, Aarne. 2009. The GF resource grammar library. *Linguistics in Language Technology* 2. http://elanguage.net/journals/index.php/lilt/article/viewFile/214/158.

Ranta, Aarne. 2011. *Grammatical framework: Programming with multilingual grammars*. Stanford: CSLI.

Zwicky, Arnold. 1977. On clitics. *Indiana University Linguistic Club* 5: 89–118.

MIX
Papier aus verantwortungsvollen Quellen
Paper from responsible sources
FSC® C105338

If you have any concerns about our products,
you can contact us on
ProductSafety@springernature.com

In case Publisher is established outside the EU,
the EU authorized representative is:
Springer Nature Customer Service Center GmbH
Europaplatz 3, 69115 Heidelberg, Germany

Printed by Libri Plureos GmbH
in Hamburg, Germany